Literary Journalism

LITERARY JOURNALISM

A Biographical Dictionary of Writers and Editors

EDD APPLEGATE

GREENWOOD PRESS
Westport, Connecticut • London

Library of Congress Cataloging-in-Publication Data

Applegate, Edd.
    Literary journalism : a biographical dictionary of writers and
editors / Edd Applegate.
       p. cm.
    Includes bibliographical references and index.
    ISBN 0–313–29949–8 (alk. paper)
    1. Journalists—Biography—Dictionaries. 2. Authors—Biography—
Dictionaries. 3. Periodicals editors—Biography—Dictionaries.
I. Title.
PN4820.A66   1996
070'.922—dc20
[B]   96–7142

British Library Cataloguing in Publication Data is available.

Library of Congress Catalog Card Number: 96–7142
ISBN: 0–313–29949–8

First published in 1996

Greenwood Press, 88 Post Road West, Westport, CT 06881
An imprint of Greenwood Publishing Group, Inc.

Printed in the United States of America

The paper used in this book complies with the
Permanent Paper Standard issued by the National
Information Standards Organization (Z39.48–1984).

10 9 8 7 6 5 4 3 2 1

For Eva, Clarice, Judy,
and Carolyn . . . with love.

Contents

Acknowledgments

I wish to thank my editor, George Butler, who was cooperative and supportive throughout the preparation of the manuscript. George provided valuable suggestions. In addition, I wish to thank the other editors and production staff at Greenwood for their efforts.

I wish to thank those scholars who took the time to respond to my letter and tentative list of writers and editors. In addition, I wish to thank those scholars who took the time to make valuable suggestions.

Preface

The so-called new journalism has been described by journalists and scholars as an umbrella term that encompasses several forms of journalism. Among those forms, literary journalism has been discussed perhaps more than any of the others. Literary journalism has been defined as a form of writing that combines the literary devices of fiction with the journalistic techniques of nonfiction. In short, the journalist applies the literary devices of fiction to an actual subject primarily to provide emotional and/or dramatic impact. A more in-depth discussion of new journalism and literary journalism is presented in the Introduction.

Literary journalism is several hundred years old. Indeed, in the 1700s, 1800s, and 1900s some writers were producing what could be considered literary journalism, among them Joseph Addison, Daniel Defoe, Richard Steele, and Edward ''Ned'' Ward in the 1700s; Charles Dickens, William Hazlitt, Lafcadio Hearn, Francis Parkman, Julian Ralph, and Mark Twain in the 1800s; and James Agee, Meyer Berger, Jimmy Breslin, Truman Capote, Michael Herr, John Hersey, Norman Mailer, Joe McGinniss, St. Clair McKelway, George Orwell, Rex Reed, Gay Talese, Hunter S. Thompson, and Tom Wolfe in the 1900s. Other practitioners of this form of journalism are mentioned in the Introduction.

This dictionary presents biographical sketches of the writers mentioned above as well as other writers who practiced literary journalism and editors who encouraged others to write literary journalism during the 1700s, 1800s, and 1900s. Of course, readers may debate why certain writers and editors were included and others were not. Most, if not all, of those profiled in this dictionary have been identified by more than one source as literary journalists or as editors who encouraged literary journalism. Many of these sources are discussed in the Introduction. In addition, lists of writers and editors for potential inclusion were submitted to scholars who have written extensively about the subject, and their responses and additional suggestions were taken into consideration. However, because of space this dictionary does not include every writer who wrote literary journalism, nor does it include every editor who encouraged others to write literary journalism.

The biographical sketches are organized alphabetically. Each includes birth and death dates (if deceased), a chronological narrative of the subject's life, including educational background, professional career, personal interests, and relevant published works or, in the case of editors, magazines published.

Introduction

During the troubled 1960s and 1970s, what has become known as new journalism filled newspapers and magazines. Some journalists became celebrities for what and how they reported, while others became well known for their flamboyant behavior. Tom Wolfe, Gay Talese, Rex Reed, Hunter S. Thompson, and others began to write articles, appear on college and university campuses, and participate in panel discussions, trying to explain new journalism. Its popularity grew as more journalists and novelists discovered the forms; as a result, a furor arose among practicing professionals. Articles critical of new journalism began to appear in numerous journals, some even written by so-called new journalists. As the furor subsided some journalists continued to practice new journalism, while others turned to the novel.

THE EMERGENCE OF NEW JOURNALISM

Why did new journalism become so prevalent in the 1960s and 1970s? John Hellman claimed that reporters were "saddled with rules and formulas that made it impossible for them to deal adequately with their subjects" and consequently revolted against the "inverted pyramid."[1]

In other words, if a reporter used the theory of objectivity to report every story, he would undoubtedly misinform the reader because of the story's controversial subject matter. Michael Schudson explained that the notion of objectivity could be attacked with three kinds of criticism: "*the content of a news story rests on a set of substantive political assumptions . . . ; the form of the news story incorporates its own bias . . .*; and *the process of news gathering itself constructs an image of reality which reinforces official viewpoints.*"[2]

Such criticism prevailed during the 1960s and 1970s—much more so than at any other time in the history of journalism. As a result, certain old journalistic forms, especially literary ones, were inevitably called new. However, new journalism of the 1960s and 1970s was not new. The old literary form was appropriately modified primarily to give emotional impact to the story.

According to Tom Wolfe, such emotional impact was derived from four devices: (1) scene-by-scene construction, (2) the use of dialogue, (3) third-person point of view, and (4) the use of status symbols.[3] John Hollowell listed two additional fictional devices that had been used by certain journalists: interior monologue, or a person's thoughts, and composite characterization, or a person's behavior.[4]

NEW JOURNALISM: A DEFINITION

When new journalism was at the height of its popularity during the late 1960s and early 1970s, professional journalists as well as educators published books on the subject. Many were compilations of articles about new journalists and the forms of expression they used. Few focused on the lives of the journalists themselves. However, several defined new journalism and identified writers who could be classified as literary journalists.

In 1971, Everette E. Dennis noted in *The Magic Writing Machine* that new journalism was used most often to describe a style of nonfiction writing, the new nonfiction or literary journalism. He claimed that newspaper and magazine editors realized that the public relied less and less on their media for entertainment. "As the public demanded something new, the *new nonfiction,* an attempt to enliven with descriptive detail and life-like dialog, emerged."[5]

The same year, Michael L. Johnson claimed that new journalism included the "new journalistic style."[6] In 1974, in *Other Voices: The New Journalism in America,* Everette E. Dennis and William L. Rivers discussed several kinds of new journalism, including literary journalism,[7] and Charles C. Flippen, in *Liberating the Media: The New Journalism,* claimed that new journalism was an umbrella term that included literary journalism.[8]

Nicolaus Mills described new journalism in *The New Journalism: A Historical Anthology* as follows:

As a practical matter, the new journalism may take a hybrid form or utilize neglected possibilities of traditional journalism, but the thrust of the new journalism is in a very different direction from that of the old—toward fiction. The structure, the language, the point of view of the new journalism all go against the grain of the ordered, objective, detached approach of established reporting.[9]

James E. Murphy defined literary journalism as "an artistic, creative, literary reporting form with three basic traits: dramatic literary techniques; intensive reporting; and reporting of generally acknowledged subjectivity."[10]

In 1980, in *American Newspapers in the 1980s,* Ernest C. Hynds claimed that literary journalism involved the application of fiction techniques to reporting news and events: "Much emphasis is placed on the characters involved and the scenes in which they perform."[11]

R. Thomas Berner discussed literary journalism in *Literary Newswriting: The Death of an Oxymoron* (1986). Claiming that the form had been around for four centuries, he described it as "the marriage of depth reporting and literary techniques in newspaper writing."[12] He wrote:

Among those techniques are narration and scene, summary and process, point of view, drama, chronological organization, rhythm, imagery, foreshadowing, metaphor, irony, dialogue, overall organization (beginning, middle and end)—all girded by good reporting.[13]

Thus, writers have used forms of literary journalism for several hundred years to describe their experiences.

LITERARY JOURNALISM: FACT OR FICTION?

If literary journalism uses the techniques described by Tom Wolfe and others, is it journalism or fiction? To answer this question, it is necessary to define and discuss traditional journalism. *The Dictionary of Publishing* defines journalism as

The gathering and publication of news and news-related material, in such publications as newspapers, magazines, newsletters, looseleaf reporters, books, and computerized databases. In popular use, the term is applied to newspaper and some magazine work, but it is applicable to the other forms mentioned as well.[14]

Similar definitions appear in standard dictionaries. Therefore, it is imperative to explain the characteristics of journalism, specifically the theory of objectivity. According to David L. Eason,

objectivity means customary linguistic usage, structuring information in a rigid pattern sometimes referred to as the "inverted pyramid," supplying brief clear answers to the questions Who?, What?, Where?, When?, and Why?, using quotations as evidence, and presenting conflicting points of view.[15]

Reporting methods, especially the theory of objectivity, can be questioned.

John Hellman noted that journalism is a product of the mind and language and consequently cannot "mirror the whole of reality," but has to "select, transform, and interpret it. . . . The problem with conventional journalism is that, while it inevitably shares in these limitations (or opportunities), it nevertheless refuses to acknowledge the creative nature of its news."[16] Such problems have been examined at length by others.

Literary journalism, on the other hand, has yet to be discussed as exhaustively, although it has been criticized extensively in scholarly journals, weekly and monthly periodicals, and newspapers. Nonetheless, because it contains the kernel of traditional journalism—that is, facts—it is without question journalism. In fact, it is one of the oldest forms of journalism.

THE DIFFERENCES BETWEEN LITERARY JOURNALISM AND TRADITIONAL JOURNALISM

Besides the use of fictional devices, how is literary journalism characteristically and analytically different from traditional journalism? According to Hollowell, "The most important difference . . . is the writer's changed relationship to the people and events he depicts."[17] In essence, the reporter becomes involved in what he reports; the writing becomes personalized, subjective. By revealing biases, the "new" journalist strives for a higher kind of "objectivity."[18]

The second major difference concerns style, language, and form.[19]

Obviously, distinct differences exist between traditional and literary forms of journalism. However, because literary journalism uses the techniques of the novelist, problems may inhibit the reporting. Certain factual information, for instance, may be overlooked or changed for dramatic effect by writers.

Most literary journalists research their subjects for days, weeks, and even months. Gay Talese emphasized that literary journalism should be "as reliable as the most reliable reportage."[20] Tom Wolfe, in his autobiographical as well as analytical article on the development of literary journalism, wrote:

The kind of reporting we were doing was more intense, more detailed, and certainly more time-consuming than anything that newspaper or magazine reporters, including investigative reporters, were accustomed to. We developed the habit of staying with the people we were writing about for days at a time, weeks in some cases. We had to gather all the material the conventional journalist was after—and then keep going.[21]

OTHER FORMS OF NEW JOURNALISM

As journalists realized that there was no such thing as objectivity and that there was something to be said for what some new journalists were practicing, several old journalistic traditions surfaced. Schudson labeled these the literary tradition and the muckraking tradition.[22] Others used different labels. For instance, Hollowell divided the subject matter of the new journalism into four categories: (1) celebrities and personalities; (2) the youth subculture and the still-evolving "new" cultural patterns; (3) the "big" event, often violent ones such as criminal cases and antiwar protests; and (4) general social and political reporting.[23] Curtis D. MacDougall used the categories new journalism, activism and advocacy, impressionistic reporting, saturation reporting, humanistic reporting, and investigative reporting (stunts, crusading, muckraking).[24] Flippen identified five categories: literary, advocacy, underground, democracy in the newsroom, and public access. He dismissed precision journalism because it did not contribute to the concerns of the new journalist.[25] Dennis also noted five categories: the new nonfiction (reportage or parajournalism), alternative journalism (modern muckraking), advocacy journalism, underground journalism, and precision journalism.[26] Dennis and Rivers, in addition to the previous list, included certain forms, media, and practices, including journalism reviews and alternative broadcasting—two distinct media. What was formerly labeled underground journalism became known as counterculture journalism.[27]

WHO ARE THE NEW JOURNALISTS?

Numerous writers have been identified as new journalists. For instance, in *The New Journalism,* Tom Wolfe mentioned James Boswell, Truman Capote, Anton Chekhov, Robert Christgau, Stephen Crane, Charles Dickens, Joan Didion, John Gregory Dunne, Joe Eszterhas, Richard Gehman, Richard Goldstein, Barbara L. Goldsmith, Lafcadio Hearn, Ernest Hemingway, Michael Herr, John Hersey, A. J. Liebling, Norman Mailer, Henry Mayhew, Joe McGinniss, James Mills, George Orwell, George Plimpton, Rex Reed, Lillian Ross, John Sack, Adam Smith, Terry Southern, Al Stump, Gay Talese, Hunter S. Thompson, Nicholas Tomalin, Mark Twain, Garry Wills, and Tom Wolfe.[28]

Everette E. Dennis and William L. Rivers, in *Other Voices: The New Journalism in America,* mentioned Joseph Addison, James Agee, Michael J. Arlen, Peter Blake, Stanley Booth, James Boswell, Jimmy Breslin, Truman Capote, Stephen Crane, Daniel Defoe, Edwin Diamond, Joan Didion, David Freeman, Albert Goldman, David Halberstam, Ernest Hemingway, Nat Hentoff, John Hersey, Murray Kempton, Larry L. King, Norman Mailer, Jane O'Reilly, George Orwell, George Plimpton, Fred Powledge, Nicholas Pileggi, Lillian Ross, Damon Runyon, Gail Sheehy, John Steinbeck, Gay Talese, Studs Terkel, Hunter S. Thompson, Calvin Trillin, Mark Twain, Edmund Wilson, and Tom Wolfe.[29]

In *Liberating the Media: The New Journalism* Charles C. Flippen mentioned Truman Capote, Daniel Defoe, William Hazlitt, Ernest Hemingway, Norman Mailer, George Bernard Shaw, Gay Talese, Mark Twain, and Tom Wolfe.[30]

In *Liberating the Media* Jay Jensen mentioned Jimmy Breslin, Truman Capote, Benjamin Franklin, Ortega y Gasset, William Hazlitt, Norman Mailer, Jack Newfield, George Orwell, Dick Schaap, George Bernard Shaw, Gail Sheehy, Gay Talese, Gore Vidal, Dan Wakefield, and Tom Wolfe.[31]

In *The Reporter as Artist: A New Look at the New Journalism Controversy,* Ronald Weber mentioned James Agee, Al Aronowitz, Jim Bishop, Brock Brower, Jimmy Cannon, Robert Daley, Lucinda Franks, Paul Gallico, W. C. Heinz, Nat Hentoff, Murray Kempton, Larry L. King, Seymour Krim, Thomas Morgan, Willie Morris, Jack Newfield, Thomas Powers, Lillian Ross, Gail Sheehy, Harvey Swados, and Gore Vidal.[32]

In *The Reporter as Artist* Harold Hayes mentioned James Agee, James Baldwin, Alva Johnston, Dwight Macdonald, Norman Mailer, Joseph Mitchell, George Orwell, Lillian Ross, Gay Talese, Edmund Wilson, and Tom Wolfe.[33]

In *The Reporter as Artist* Herbert Gold mentioned James Baldwin, Joan Didion, Paul Goodman, Vivian Gornick, Sally Kempton, Norman Mailer, Jack Newfield, Wilfrid Sheed, Gloria Steinem, Gore Vidal, and Tom Wolfe.[34]

John Hollowell, in *Fact and Fiction: The New Journalism and the Nonfiction Novel*, mentioned Joseph Addison, James Agee, James Baldwin, Jimmy Breslin, Claude Brown, Truman Capote, Eldridge Cleaver, Geoffrey Cowan, Paul Cowan, Stephen Crane, Daniel Defoe, Charles Dickens, Joan Didion, John Dos Passos, Theodore Dreiser, John Gregory Dunne, David Halberstam, William Hazlitt, Ernest Hemingway, John Hersey, Henry James, Larry L. King, Oscar Lewis, A. J. Liebling, J. Anthony Lukas, Norman Mailer, St. Clair McKelway, Joseph Mitchell, George Orwell, George Plimpton, Charles Portis, Rex Reed, Lillian Ross, John Sack, Dick Schaap, Gail Sheehy, Upton Sinclair, Susan Sontag, Terry Southern, Richard Steele, Lincoln Steffens, Gloria Steinem, Gay Talese, Ida Tarbell, Hunter S. Thompson, Mark Twain, Dan Wakefield, Garry Wills, and Tom Wolfe.[35]

Ronald Weber, in *The Literature of Fact: Literary Nonfiction in American Writing*, mentioned James Agee, James Baldwin, Jim Bishop, Jimmy Breslin, C.D.B. Bryan, Jimmy Cannon, Truman Capote, Richard Henry Dana, Martin Duberman, Jo Durden-Smith, Joe Eszterhas, Albert Fried, Paul Gallico, John Hersey, Alva Johnston, Edward Keyes, Jane Kramer, Peter Maas, William Manchester, Norman Mailer, Joe McGinniss, John McPhee, Joseph Mitchell, George Orwell, Charles Portis, Lillian Ross, Dick Schaap, Vincent Sheehan, Gay Talese, Thomas Thompson, Mark Twain, Joseph Wambaugh, Tom Wicker, James Willwerth, and Tom Wolfe.[36]

John Hellman, in *Fables of Fact: The New Journalism as New Fiction*, mentioned Jimmy Breslin, Truman Capote, Timothy Crouse, Joan Didion, Michael Herr, John Hersey, Norman Mailer, George Plimpton, Gay Talese, Hunter S. Thompson, and Tom Wolfe.[37]

Norman Sims, in *The Literary Journalists*, mentioned James Agee, Bill Barich, Truman Capote, Sara Davidson, Joan Didion, John Gregory Dunne, John Hersey, Tracy Kidder, Jane Kramer, Mark Kramer, A. J. Liebling, Norman Mailer, John McPhee, Joseph Mitchell, George Orwell, Richard Rhodes, Lillian Ross, Mark Singer, Gay Talese, Hunter S. Thompson, Calvin Trillin, Richard West, and Tom Wolfe.[38]

Shelly Fisher Fishkin, in *From Fact to Fiction: Journalism and Imaginative Writing in America*, mentioned John Dos Passos, Theodore Dreiser, Ernest Hemingway, Mark Twain, and Walt Whitman.[39]

Chris Anderson, in *Literary Nonfiction: Theory, Criticism, Pedagogy*, mentioned Bill Barich, Stephen Crane, Joan Didion, Annie Dillard, John McPhee, George Orwell, Richard Selzer, and E. B. White.[40]

In *Literary Journalism in the Twentieth Century*, Norman Sims mentioned James Agee, Gloria Anzaldua, Abraham Cahan, Stephen Crane, Daniel Defoe,

Joan Didion, W.E.B. DuBois, Norman Hapgood, Ernest Hemingway, A. J. Liebling, Mary McCarthy, John McPhee, H. L. Mencken, Joe Mitchell, Tillie Olsen, George Orwell, Lincoln Steffens, Jonathan Swift, and Tom Wolfe.[41]

In *Literary Journalism in the Twentieth Century,* John J. Pauly mentioned Jimmy Breslin, Truman Capote, Robert Christgau, Joan Didion, John Gregory Dunne, Joe Eszterhas, Frances FitzGerald, Marshall Frady, Barbara Goldsmith, Richard Goldstein, David Halberstam, Pete Hamill, Michael Herr, Larry L. King, J. Anthony Lukas, Norman Mailer, Joe McGinniss, John McPhee, James Mills, Willie Morris, Jack Newfield, George Plimpton, Rex Reed, James Ridgeway, Lillian Ross, John Sack, Dick Schaap, Jonathan Schell, Neil Sheehan, Robert Sherrill, Adam Smith, Terry Southern, Gloria Steinem, Gay Talese, Hunter S. Thompson, Nicholas von Hoffman, Dan Wakefield, Tom Wicker, Garry Wills, and Tom Wolfe.[42]

Barbara Lounsberry, in *The Art of Fact: Contemporary Artists of Nonfiction,* mentioned Sir Thomas Browne, Robert Burton, Truman Capote, Joan Didion, Annie Dillard, Ralph Waldo Emerson, John Hersey, Edward Hoagland, Samuel Johnson, Tracy Kidder, Maxine Hong Kingston, Anne Morrow Lindbergh, Thomas Macaulay, Norman Mailer, John McPhee, Montaigne, Lillian Ross, John Ruskin, Gay Talese, Lewis Thomas, Henry David Thoreau, and Tom Wolfe.[43]

Thomas B. Connery and others, in *A Sourcebook of American Literary Journalism: Representative Writers in an Emerging Genre,* mentioned George Ade, James Agee, Meyer Berger, Jimmy Breslin, C.D.B. Bryan, Abraham Cahan, Truman Capote, Frances X. Clines, Richard Ben Cramer, Stephen Crane, Harry Crews, Sara Davidson, Richard Harding Davis, Dorothy Day, Joan Didion, John Dos Passos, Theodore Dreiser, John Gregory Dunne, Joe Eszterhas, Janet Flanner, Josiah Flynt, Richard Goldstein, Bob Greene, Hutchins Hapgood, William Hard, Lafcadio Hearn, Ben Hecht, Ernest Hemingway, Michael Herr, John Hersey, Tracy Kidder, Jane Kramer, Ring Lardner, A. J. Liebling, Jack London, J. Anthony Lukas, Norman Mailer, Joe McGinniss, John McPhee, Joseph Mitchell, Thomas Morgan, John O'Hara, Ernie Pyle, Julian Ralph, John Reed, Richard Rhodes, Jacob Riis, Lillian Ross, Damon Runyon, John Sack, Mark Singer, Terry Southern, Lincoln Steffens, John Steinbeck, Gay Talese, Hunter S. Thompson, Calvin Trillin, Mark Twain, Joseph Wambaugh, Chilton Williamson, Jr., and Tom Wolfe.[44]

Although many of the journalists and writers mentioned above wrote literary journalism, some wrote other forms of new journalism, such as advocacy and muckraking, which were mentioned earlier.

NOTES

1. John Hellman, *Fables of Fact: The New Journalism as New Fiction* (Urbana: University of Illinois Press, 1981), p. 2.

2. Michael Schudson, *Discovering the News* (New York: Basic Books, 1978), pp. 184–185.

3. Tom Wolfe, *The New Journalism,* with an anthology edited by Tom Wolfe and E. W. Johnson (New York: Harper and Row, 1973), pp. 31–32.

4. John Hollowell, *Fact and Fiction: The New Journalism and the Nonfiction Novel* (Chapel Hill: University of North Carolina Press, 1977), pp. 25–26.

5. Everette E. Dennis, "The New Journalism: How It Came to Be," in *The Magic Writing Machine: Student Probes of the New Journalism,* edited by Dennis (Eugene: University of Oregon School of Journalism Press, 1971), p. 2.

6. Michael L. Johnson, *The New Journalism: The Underground Press, the Artists of Nonfiction, and Changes in the Established Media* (Lawrence: University of Kansas Press, 1971), p. xii.

7. Everette E. Dennis and William L. Rivers, *Other Voices: The New Journalism in America* (San Francisco: Canfield Press, 1974).

8. Charles C. Flippen, "The New Journalism," in *Liberating the Media: The New Journalism,* edited by Flippen (Washington, D.C.: Acropolis Books, 1974), pp. 9–17.

9. Nicolaus Mills, ed., *The New Journalism: A Historical Anthology* (New York: McGraw-Hill, 1974), p. xiii.

10. James E. Murphy, *The New Journalism: A Critical Perspective,* Journalism Monographs 34 (Lexington, Ky.: Association for Education in Journalism, May 1974), p. 16.

11. Ernest C. Hynds, *American Newspapers in the 1980s* (New York: Hastings House, 1980), pp. 173–174.

12. R. Thomas Berner, *Literary Newswriting: The Death of an Oxymoron,* Journalism Monographs 99 (Columbia, S.C.: Association for Education in Journalism and Mass Communication, October 1986), p. 22.

13. Ibid.

14. David M. Brownstone and Irene M. Franck, *The Dictionary of Publishing* (New York: Van Nostrand Reinhold, 1982), p. 156.

15. David L. Eason, "New Journalism, Metaphor and Culture," *Journal of Popular Culture,* Spring 1982, p. 145.

16. Hellman, *Fables of Fact,* p. 4.

17. Hollowell, *Fact and Fiction,* p. 22.

18. Ibid.

19. Ibid., p. 24.

20. Gay Talese, *Fame and Obscurity* (New York: World Publishing, 1970), p. vii.

21. Tom Wolfe, "The Birth of 'The New Journalism'; Eyewitness Report by Tom Wolfe," *New York,* February 14, 1972, pp. 43, 45.

22. Schudson, *Discovering the News.*

23. Hollowell, *Fact and Fiction.*

24. Curtis D. MacDougall, *Interpretative Reporting* (New York: Macmillan, 1977).

25. Flippen, "The New Journalism."

26. Dennis, "The New Journalism."

27. Dennis and Rivers, *Other Voices.*

28. Wolfe, *The New Journalism.*

29. Dennis and Rivers, *Other Voices.*

30. Flippen, "The New Journalism," pp. 9–17.

31. Jay Jensen, "The New Journalism in Historical Perspective," in Flippen, *Liberating the Media,* pp. 18–28.

32. Ronald Weber, "Some Sort of Artistic Excitement," in *The Reporter as Artist: A New Look at the New Journalism Controversy,* edited by Ronald Weber (New York: Hastings House, 1974), pp. 13–26.

33. Harold Hayes, "Editor's Notes on the New Journalism," in Weber, *The Reporter as Artist,* pp. 260–262.

34. Herbert Gold, "On Epidemic First Personism," in Weber, *The Reporter as Artist,* pp. 283–287.

35. Hollowell, *Fact and Fiction.*

36. Ronald Weber, *The Literature of Fact: Literary Nonfiction in American Writing* (Athens: Ohio University Press, 1980).

37. Hellman, *Fables of Fact.*

38. Norman Sims, ed., *The Literary Journalists* (New York: Ballantine Books, 1984).

39. Shelly Fisher Fishkin, *From Fact to Fiction: Journalism and Imaginative Writing in America* (Baltimore: Johns Hopkins University Press, 1985).

40. Chris Anderson, ed., *Literary Nonfiction: Theory, Criticism, Pedagogy* (Carbondale: Southern Illinois University Press, 1989).

41. Norman Sims, ed., preface to *Literary Journalism in the Twentieth Century* (New York: Oxford University Press, 1990), pp. v–x.

42. John J. Pauly, "The Politics of the New Journalism," in Sims, *Literary Journalism in the Twentieth Century,* pp. 110–129.

43. Barbara Lounsberry, *The Art of Fact: Contemporary Artists of Nonfiction* (Westport, Ct.: Greenwood Press, 1990).

44. Thomas B. Connery, ed., *A Sourcebook of American Literary Journalism: Representative Writers in an Emerging Genre* (Westport, Ct.: Greenwood Press, 1992).

Literary Journalism

THE
DICTIONARY

A

Joseph Addison
(1672–1719)

Joseph Addison, who was born in 1672, had written poetry and literary criticism and had traveled to France and Italy before he had composed one article for Richard Steele's *Tatler.* Unlike Steele, Addison came from a refined family, and his social class awareness helped him immensely. When he dedicated a poem to Lord-Chancellor Somers, Somers reciprocated. For instance, on learning that Addison wished to travel and write, Somers helped him obtain a yearly pension of 300 pounds from the Crown. Thus encouraged, Addison left England for the Continent and upon his return wrote *Travels,* which he dedicated to Somers. In 1704 he wrote the heroic poem "The Campaign," which celebrated the battle of Blenheim. The poem was read by the Lord-Treasurer Godolphin, who not only approved of it but bestowed on Addison the vacant position of commissioner of appeals.

In 1706 Addison was appointed undersecretary of state, and in 1708 he was elected to Parliament. During these years he wrote operas, comedies, and poetry. He moved to Ireland in 1709 when he became secretary to the Marquess of Wharton, who had been appointed Lord-Lieutenant of Ireland. Although he contributed to Steele's *Tatler,* readers did not recognize his distinct style of writing until the *Spectator* appeared on March 1, 1711.[1]

The *Spectator* and the *Tatler* were similar in appearance. However, according to G. Gregory Smith, "the *Tatler* stands first in importance, not merely because it came as a kind of prelude to the *Spectator,* but because it was the direct model for the literary plan and details of the later journal."[2]

Thus it could be said that the *Tatler* was the *Spectator* in the rough, or that the *Spectator* was the polished *Tatler*. The same could be said about Steele and Addison. As Austin Dobson wrote:

There is little doubt that in the finely-wrought La Bruyere-like sketches of Tom Folio, Ned Softly, and the Political Upholsterer, in the Rabelaisian "Frozen Voices" and the delightful "Adventures of a Shilling," Addison attained a level higher than anything at which his friend had aimed.[3]

The *Spectator* reflected Addison's philosophy. According to Edward and Lillian Bloom:

A disciple of Sir Andrew and his mercantile code, Addison is also respectful of Sir Roger and the "landed" principle. He is a traditionalist who stands on the side of change when the new contributes to national order and prosperity and to learning and civility. He is a Whig who moves with ease among moderate Tories. He praises the beauty of faith, but his is a belief derived more often than not from earth-bound demonstrations. Arguing for tolerance as a token of good nature, he is a staunch Anglican who extends the hand of Christian fellowship to orthodox dissenters and turns his back on Catholics.[4]

This philosophy was voiced by personae in at least 274 of the 555 issues. Steele's philosophy was voiced by other characters in 236 issues. Eustace Budgell, a clergyman, was responsible for 28 issues, and other contributors were responsible for the remaining 17 issues. Considering the various characters, such as Sir Roger de Coverley (the most famous), a Templar, Will Honeycomb, a Clergyman, Captain Sentry, and Sir Andrew Freeport, Addison undoubtedly was responsible for the first three.

The *Spectator,* which appeared daily until December 6, 1712, published entertaining as well as informative pieces, including essays, stories, and articles of criticism. It was read by the poor as well as the rich, and unlike the *Tatler,* which was read mostly by men in coffee-houses, the *Spectator* was read by women as well as men, in homes and coffee-houses. Together, the two publications molded ideas and developed tastes, and helped establish the magazine as a journalistic as well as a literary product.

Joseph Addison saw numerous imitators of the *Tatler* and the *Spectator* before his death in 1719.

WORK: *Spectator* (1711–1712).

NOTES

1. G. Gregory Smith, ed., *The Spectator, with Introduction by Austin Dobson* (New York: Charles Scribner's Sons, 1897), p. xx.

2. Ibid., p. xii.

3. Ibid., p. xxi.

4. Edward A. Bloom and Lillian D. Bloom, *Joseph Addison's Sociable Animal* (Providence, R.I.: Brown University Press, 1971), pp. 7–8.

George Ade
(1866–1944)

Born in Kentland, Indiana, in 1866, George Ade was the sixth of seven children. Ade's parents, unlike many citizens of Kentland, lived and worked in town, not on a farm. His father, John, had migrated with his family from England, and his mother, Adaline (Bush), had been reared in Ohio. Ade's father worked in a bank; his mother worked at home.

Ade attended the local schools, where he earned excellent grades. When he was in high school he wrote an essay that impressed his teacher; she sent it to the editor of the local paper, who published it.

Although Ade enjoyed reading the works of Mark Twain and Charles Dickens, his parents insisted that he work during the summers. The only work available was farming. Before he graduated from high school, he had grown to dislike the drudgery of sweating in a field.

Ade's father realized that his son would not be content working in Kentland. Thus, when the superintendent of schools informed him of a scholarship to Purdue, he was relieved; George would attend college. In 1883 George, who was 17, went to Lafayette, 50 miles away, and enrolled in college. His father had expected him to pursue agriculture or the mechanical arts, but Ade's grades in these subjects were low. He earned above average grades in literature and composition. At college he joined a literary society and a social fraternity, and edited the monthly literary magazine one semester. He became very popular among his classmates. During his junior year, he met John T. McCutcheon, another student, who was to become not only a lifelong friend and collaborator, but a successful illustrator and cartoonist. During his senior year, Ade met Lillian Howard. They dated and discussed marriage, but they went their separate ways about a year after he graduated from college.

Ade returned to Kentland with his degree, but opportunities were limited, and farming was out of the question. He studied with a law firm in Lafayette for seven weeks, but soon realized that law was not for him. Ade remained in Lafayette and was hired by the *Morning Call,* a Republican newspaper, as a reporter, a job he enjoyed. When the paper folded, he was hired by the *Lafayette Call,* but for an extremely low salary. When the manager of a local patent medicine company offered him a job as a copywriter at a higher salary, he accepted. Writing advertising copy, such as "Cascarets: They work while you sleep," was easy. However, when the company reduced its payroll, Ade's position was one of the first to be eliminated.

John T. McCutcheon, who was working in the art department of the *Chicago Morning News,* urged George to come to Chicago. Ade resisted for several months, fearing that Chicago was too big for him. Out of work and almost out of money, he reconsidered McCutcheon's invitation in June 1890.

Ade was hired as a reporter after an interview with Charles Dennis, the city editor of the *Chicago Morning News.* His assignment was the weather. Unlike most reporters who had been assigned the weather, Ade looked at the subject just as he would any other. He asked stable owners, company presidents, and waiters, among others, about the weather; as a result of his ability to capture accurately accents as well as dialogue, his stories became very popular among readers. Consequently, Dennis moved the stories to the front page. Dennis commented: "From the outset Ade was a brilliant success as a news gatherer. This fact, together with his skill as a writer and his fine sense of humor, brought him rapidly to the front."[1] Dennis assigned him to other stories, including major strikes, politics, and trials; George covered each with the same journalistic style. He was fast but accurate, and he seldom rewrote anything.

In 1893, when the *Morning News* had become the *Chicago Record,* Dennis assigned a small group of reporters to cover the Chicago World's Columbian Exposition several months before it opened. Ade was the "star" writer of the group. His intriguing two-column articles on the exposition appeared on the editorial page under the headline "All Roads Lead to the World's Fair" and were the most widely read pieces in the paper. When the exposition ended, Ade continued the column under the headline "Stories of the Streets and of the Town." McCutcheon provided illustrations. Franklin J. Meine said of this collaboration, "The turn of the phrase and the simple pencil line were expertly woven into a rich tapestry which revealed the mood and the manner of Chicago in the Gay Nineties."[2] As a result, both enjoyed recognition, even though Ade's by-line seldom appeared above a story. Yet it is because of these stories that George Ade is so fondly remembered; according to Meine, they form the matrix of all his work:

Everything that is crucial in the development of Ade as an interpreter of the great American scene is present: the rich, colorful everyday life, the vernacular, the character studies, the fables, the dramatic forms, the jingles—as well as the moods, the sly humor, the turn of the phrase, the quaint artistry of indirection which was so peculiarly his.[3]

The stories appeared in the *Chicago Record* for seven years. During this time the newspaper published eight compilations, each of which was well received. Although the columns originally had appeared without titles, titles were provided when the columns appeared in book form. For instance, the first compilation contained "Her Visit to Chicago," "A Run to a Fire," "About Arrests and Those Arrested," and "A Victim of the Slot Machine Habit," to mention a few.

Critics praised the column for its verbal and visual descriptions of the sights and sounds of Chicago. Mark Twain was impressed by the collaboration. William Dean Howells believed Ade had captured the American spirit with all its foibles.

In 1895 Ade and McCutcheon toured Europe and sent illustrated articles about their travels to the newspaper. The articles, which appeared under the headline

"What a Man Sees Who Goes Away from Home," were collected and published by the newspaper a year later. When Ade and McCutcheon returned, Ade resumed writing his previous column. However, he experimented. In addition to using recurring characters such as Artie Blanchard, he offered the reader verse as well as dialogue in what could be considered short stories or fables. After Artie came Pink Marsh, a stereotypical black who spoke what Ade referred to as the vernacular of the period, not what some critics called slang. Then came Doc' Horne, the crusty, self-educated bumbler who lived in the Alfalfa European Hotel. Doc' Horne was a world traveler who spouted wisdom on almost every subject. As William Hoffa wrote:

While Doc' dispenses both practical and worldly wisdom in the manner of an urban cracker-barrel philosopher, it becomes increasingly apparent to his circle and even more so to the reader that he is more an *alazon* figure than a sly *eiron*. Yet his anecdotes and yarns bring into the lonely lives of his fellow roomers a color and adventure and camaraderie which is otherwise missing from their tired and all urban routines.[4]

Columns in which these characters appeared were later collected and published by Herbert S. Stone and Company of Chicago under the titles *Artie* (1896), *Pink Marsh* (1897), and *Doc' Horne* (1899).

In 1897 Ade introduced readers to his version of the Aesop fable, which was filled with slang and the use of capital letters for emphasis. By 1900 he had written enough fables to fill several books. His first, *Fables in Slang,* published in 1900, was received enthusiastically by critics and readers alike. The same year he negotiated to syndicate his stories to newspapers throughout the country, and subsequently resigned from the *Record.* A second book of fables, *More Fables,* was published in 1901. Other titles followed over the next several years.

In 1902 he wrote the musical *The Sultan of Sulu,* which achieved a certain amount of success. *The County Chairman* followed a year later. In 1904 *The College Widow* was produced; Ade was crowned the "Baron of Broadway" and earned about $2 million in royalties. When his play *U.S. Minister Bedloe* was trashed by critics in 1911, Ade left New York. Broadway had seen the last of him. However, he had become enormously wealthy. He had amassed more than 2,000 acres of Indiana farmland on which he had built a spacious country estate called Hazelden. Although he no longer had to write to earn a living, he continued to contribute essays and other forms of journalism to various newspapers and magazines. Some of these were collected and published under the titles *Single Blessedness and Other Observations* (1922) and *The Old-Time Saloon* (1931). Ade's writing became dated in the late 1920s and 1930s. He died at his estate on May 16, 1944, at the age of 78.

Melvin Maddocks said of his collection *Chicago Stories* (1963):

With the alertness, though not the interesting malice, of a social satirist he roamed [Chicago's] waterfront, its swank hotels, its barberships, its museums, its wardheelers' hangouts. He knew its streetvendors, its socialites, its market-gardeners, its entrepreneurs, its junk-dealers. He caught the adolescent feel of a city, gangling with skyscrapers, whose personality had not yet caught up with its growing physique.[5]

In *Chicago Stories* Ade employed literary devices later discussed by Tom Wolfe. For instance, he vividly described characters, recording dialogue that realistically captured their verbal expressions. In short, he observed and presented a slice of life.

WORKS: *The Chicago Record's "Stories of the Streets and of the Town"* (1894); *Second Series of the Chicago Record's "Stories of the Streets and of the Town"* (1894); *Third Series of the Chicago Record's "Stories of the Streets and of the Town"* (1895); *Fourth Series of the Chicago Record's "Stories of the Streets and of the Town"* (1895); *What a Man Sees Who Goes Away from Home* (1896); *Artie: A Story of the Streets and Town* (1896); *Pink Marsh: A Story of the Streets and Town* (1897); *Fifth Series of the Chicago Record's "Stories of the Streets and of the Town"* (1897); *Sixth Series of the Chicago Record's "Stories of the Streets and of the Town"* (1889); *Seventh Series of the Chicago Record's "Stories of the Streets and of the Town"* (1899); *Doc' Horne: A Story of the Streets and Town* (1899); *Eighth Series. The Chicago Record's Stories of the Streets and of the Town* (1900); *Stories of the Streets and of the Town* (1941); *Chicago Stories,* edited by Franklin J. Meine (1963).

NOTES

1. George Ade, *Chicago Stories,* selected/edited with an introduction by Franklin J. Meine (Chicago: Henry Regnery, 1963), p. xii.

2. Ibid., p. xiii.

3. Ibid., p. xx.

4. William W. Hoffa, "George Ade," *American Humorists, 1800–1950: Part 1: A-L,* edited by Stanley Trachtenberg (Detroit: Gale Research, 1982), p. 8.

5. Melvin Maddocks, "George Ade's Chicago," *Christian Science Monitor,* February 27, 1964, p. C11.

James Agee
(1909–1955)

Born in Knoxville in 1909, James Agee suffered a painful loss at six when his father died in an automobile accident. Agee, whose father had been, and whose mother was, devoutly religious, attended public schools until 1919, when he entered St. Andrews, an Episcopal boarding school. There he met Father James Harold Flye, who became a sincere friend and confidant. Six years later, after having attended Knoxville High School for a year, he enrolled at Phillips Exeter Academy in Exeter, New Hampshire, where he prepared for Harvard. He studied for three years at Harvard and wrote poetry, short stories, and essays, some of which are published in literary magazines. According to Robert E. Burkholder,

Agee was influenced by professor I. A. Richards' theories about using language to embody physical reality:

The most important direct influence Richards' theories had upon Agee's approach to his art involve[s] an increased role for the narrator in Agee's stories. Because he was impressed by Richards' idea that the final effect of any poetic endeavor depends upon the complex relationship between the poem, referent, and reader, Agee decided that it would increase chances for the original poetic experience to be communicated if his first-person narrators not only served as major characters in the chronological narrative, but also as aestheticians who explain the problems of perception involved in their secondary roles as intermediaries between the experience and the audience[1]

This form, which he eventually perfected, appeared often in his writing. Indeed, it is because of this form that his writing is not only considered documentary in part, but considered literary journalism.

When he graduated from Harvard in 1932, *Fortune* magazine opened its doors to him. Agee wrote articles during the day and poetry at night. In 1934 a collection of his poetry was published. Unfortunately, *Permit Me Voyage* appeared during the Great Depression and was all but forgotten soon after publication. Two years later he and Walker Evans, a photographer on loan from the Farm Security Administration, were assigned to do an article on cotton tenancy. According to William Stott, Agee was to write an article about the daily life of an "average" family of white tenant farmers for the series "Life and Circumstances," about poor, lower-middle-class Americans, for *Fortune*.[2]

Fortune found the article unsatisfactory. It was too long, too biased, and too poetic. In 1937 Harper and Brothers contracted for a book from the manuscript, which Agee completed two years later. However, when the editors read the manuscript they requested numerous changes. Agee agreed, then later refused. In 1940 Houghton Mifflin accepted the manuscript with minor changes, but when the book appeared a year later it failed to sell:

Let Us Now Praise Famous Men was an outrage. It was *more* outrageous even than the *Fortune* article, because Agee didn't accept the advice of *Fortune*'s editors. The "errors" they criticized he willfully compounded. They thought the piece too long; . . . Agee vastly enlarged the section on the houses. They thought the report too subjective; Agee made his "individual, anti-authoritative human consciousness" more firmly "the governing instrument" and "one of the centers of the subject." They thought his writing too personal, too self-revealing; Agee told how he used to masturbate in his grandfather's house, complained of his need for a whore, and imagined one of the tenant families having group sex with Evans and him.[3]

The book was nevertheless Agee's masterpiece, for in it he used every form and style to depict the realities of living poor. Through writing that was sometimes poetic, journalistic, autobiographical, and philosophical, he accurately portrayed the South.

Agee, who had left *Fortune* in the late 1930s, wrote book reviews, then movie reviews for *Time* and later the *Nation* until 1948. For the rest of his life he devoted his time to writing screenplays and fiction. He died in 1955.

WORK: *Let Us Now Praise Famous Men* (1941).

NOTES

1. Robert E. Burkholder, "James Rufus Agee," *American Novelists Since World War II,* edited by Jeffrey Helterman and Richard Layman (Detroit: Gale Research, 1978), vol. 2, p. 3.

2. William Stott, *Documentary Expression and Thirties America* (New York: Oxford University Press, 1973), p. 261.

3. Ibid., pp. 264–265.

Jane Amsterdam
(1952?–   )

Jane Amsterdam, the third of four children, was born in the early 1950s. She was raised in Bala-Cynwyd, Pennsylvania. Her father was a dentist as well as a professor at the University of Pennsylvania in Philadelphia. Her mother was a housewife.

Amsterdam attended Montgomery Country Day School, where she worked on the *Lamp,* the school's newspaper. Upon graduation, she enrolled at Cedar Crest College, a small liberal arts women's college in Allentown, Pennsylvania. During her senior year she worked as an intern at *Philadelphia* magazine, which she enjoyed because she was given the opportunity to conduct research and to write offbeat stories.

She was hired as the assistant editor of *Connecticut* magazine after she received her degree. Amsterdam stayed at the magazine three years and was promoted to associate editor, then executive editor. She was happy at the magazine, but she was offered the position of managing editor at the *New Jersey Monthly,* which she accepted. She pursued other editing positions, particularly at *New Times,* which was having financial problems even though Jonathan Larsen, the editor, had assembled an excellent staff of writers.

Amsterdam started hiring writers for Larsen, including Robert Sam Anson. Eventually, Larsen offered her the position of executive editor, which she accepted. Amsterdam worked at *New Times* until the magazine folded in 1978; she had been with the publication for almost a year.

Steven Brill, who launched *The American Lawyer,* offered Amsterdam the position of executive editor. Amsterdam accepted the offer with the stipulation that she would not serve more than six months. When the six months passed, she was hired as executive editor of *New York* magazine, a position she did not enjoy. Indeed, within seven weeks she left the magazine. Shelby Coffey, the editor of the "Style" section of the *Washington Post,* hired Amsterdam as a "Style" editor. Amsterdam, now 28, was cocky, self-confident, and somewhat flirtatious. She became friends with Coffey, Ben Bradlee, the executive editor of the *Post,* and Sally Quinn, Bradlee's wife and one of "Style's" writers. She dated Bob Woodward.

Amsterdam, in addition to her duties with "Style," worked with Woodward and Pat Tyler on a story about Max Hugel of the CIA. The story alleged that Hugel had engaged in insider trading when he headed an export company. Hugel resigned from the CIA the day after the story was published. However, it was Amsterdam's skill as an editor, not her writing or reporting skills, that most of her colleagues admired.

After four years in Washington, Amsterdam yearned to return to New York. In 1983 Herbert Lipson, on the recommendation of Alan Halpern, hired her to edit *Manhattan, inc.,* his new business magazine. The first issue appeared in September 1984. Through Amsterdam's careful guidance, the magazine published entertaining and informative stories that criticized as well as satirized the wealthy. Eight months later, the magazine won a National Magazine Award for General Excellence. Amsterdam had her share of critics. For instance, *Crain's New York Business* ran a story about her problems with executive editors under the headline " 'Manhattan, Inc.' Editor: Good, but Who Can Work with Her?" It seemed that executive editors were hired one week, then fired the next at *Manhattan, inc.*

In 1987, after two and a half years, Amsterdam resigned, accusing Lipson of trying to interfere with the editorial content of the magazine. Within weeks she was hired by the *Wall Street Journal* to work on a new business magazine, but the project was scrapped after Black Monday, the day the stock market plunged some 500 points.

She was subsequently hired as a senior editor at Alfred A. Knopf, but resigned when she was offered the position of executive editor at the *New York Post,* a tabloid newspaper, several months later. Peter Kalikow, the owner, assured Amsterdam that she would have editorial autonomy when she became editor after the current editor, Frank Devine, left to return to Australia. The *New York Post* had been losing subscribers and consequently advertisers for several years. Rupert Murdock, the previous owner, sold the newspaper to Kalikow in March 1988 primarily because of its declining readership.

At the time, Amsterdam was one of only six or seven women in the country running a newspaper with a circulation of over 100,000. Although she had signed a contract for three years, she was dismissed a year later when Kalikow admitted that not enough newspapers were being sold. Indeed, the newspaper's circulation was about the same as it had been before Amsterdam was made editor. Another reason cited for her dismissal was her disagreement with Kalikow over the paper's political coverage.

Although Amsterdam had not succeeded in improving the fortunes of the *New York Post,* she had succeeded as editor at several magazines, including *Manhattan, inc.,* where she developed stories and nurtured writers such as Ron Rosenbaum. She favored eye-opening articles that were unquestionably characteristic of literary journalism and was instrumental in having such pieces written and published. In the early 1990s she was named senior editor of ABC-TV's "Day One" program.

WORKS: *Connecticut* (executive editor); *New Jersey Monthly* (managing editor); *New Times* (executive editor); *The American Lawyer* (executive editor); *New York* (executive editor); *Washington Post* "Style" (editor); *Manhattan, inc.* (editor); *New York Post* (editor).

Michael J. Arlen
(1930–)

Michael J. Arlen was born in London, England, on December 9, 1930, but moved to the United States with his parents, Michael and Atalanta Arlen, when he was 10. He attended Harvard University from 1948 to 1952, then worked as a reporter for *Life* magazine for four years. In 1966 he became a staff writer and television critic for the *New Yorker,* for which he wrote numerous reviews and articles. His criticism, which was not so much about television as it was about American culture or American society, discussed the weaknesses and possible effects of programs, including the evening news. His first book, *Living Room War,* a collection of critical articles, was published in 1969. Arlen explained the title:

I call this book *Living Room War* not because I especially like the piece I first attached the title to, . . . but because quite a number of the pieces *are* about the war and television—because during the period I was writing them the war seemed to be the central fact in American life, seemed to be there, whether one talked about it or not at first, whether one claimed to be bored by it or not, later offended, later outraged, later bored. It was a changing shape beneath everything else in American life in that period, in a way that no other war we'd experienced had been, and most of us knew about it, felt about it, from television.[1]

A year later *Exiles,* a memoir of Arlen's search for his father, was published. Although the book was filled with personal journalism, it was a minor effort.

In 1973 Arlen turned his attention to the Hanrahan trial in *An American Verdict.* Using short, direct sentences, Arlen told of the questionable shootings of two Black Panther party members by Chicago police officers and the subsequent trial of Cook County State's Attorney Edward Hanrahan and the police officers involved in the shootings. Benjamin De Mott found Arlen's method of writing to be impressionistic:

Scenes and snippets of testimony from the trial are interspersed with short takes on the character of Mayor Daley, the birth and history of the Panthers, developments in the culture of street gangs, a cop awards night, the Chicago Irish in fact and fiction, Campaign '72, and a number of other subjects.[2]

Arlen attempted to connect the pieces, even if some did not fit, much as he had in his collection of articles. The latter work, however, contained a logical progression and consequently was better received by the critics.

In *Passage to Ararat,* which was published in 1975, Arlen searched his father's homeland, Armenia, and told of his heritage, including the brutality of Turkey toward the Armenian women and children at the turn of the century. The book, which exhibited, perhaps better than any other, the power of Arlen's writing, earned the National Book Award in contemporary affairs in 1976.

Other collections of his articles appeared as well. *The View from Highway 1,* published in 1976, covered a variety of topics in television news and entertainment. Through the use of such literary techniques and devices as informal style, dialogue, questions and answers, and explanations, Arlen presented his subjects in an arresting fashion. *Thirty Seconds,* published in 1980, examined a six-month effort by advertising agency personnel to produce a 30-second television commercial for AT&T. Arlen observed the process of creating and producing a commercial and he interviewed those involved. The book presented a candid look at another aspect of television. *The Camera Age: Essays on Television* (1981) contained 25 reviews and articles. At least 13 concerned news or other "fact" broadcasting, while 8 discussed dramatic series or films. The book was praised by critics who appreciated the author's literary style as well as his insight.

Arlen's unique style of writing was not limited to criticism for the *New Yorker,* however. His enlightening articles were published in the *Atlantic Monthly, Cosmopolitan, Esquire, Harper's, Holiday,* the *New York Times Magazine, Saturday Review,* and other publications. *Say Goodbye to Sam,* his first novel, was published in 1984, to mixed reviews.

Arlen's articles and collections were examples of literary journalism primarily because they examined in a literary, personal manner the various kinds of programs that were broadcast on a popular medium. More important, his articles and collections examined American society, which had allowed television to dominate life. Several of his collections were published with new introductions in the early 1990s.

WORKS: *Living Room War* (1969); *Exiles* (1970); *An American Verdict* (1973); *Passage to Ararat* (1975); *The View from Highway 1* (1976); *Thirty Seconds* (1980); *The Camera Age: Essays on Television* (1981).
NOTES
1. Michael J. Arlen, *Living Room War* (New York: Viking Press, 1969), p. xi.
2. Benjamin De Mott, "Alone in Cover-up Country," *The Atlantic,* October 1973, pp. 117–118.

Peter (Pete) Axthelm
(1943–1991)

Born in New York City in 1943, Pete Axthelm earned his bachelor's degree from Yale University in 1965. He then returned to his native city and got a job with the *New York Herald Tribune* as a sports writer and columnist. In 1966 he was hired as a staff writer for *Sports Illustrated.* Axthelm enjoyed writing about sports, particularly horse racing.

In 1968 he got a job as sports editor with *Newsweek* and covered the Olympic Games in Mexico City. He remained with the magazine for 20 years. In that time, he contributed a regular sports column, of which he said in an interview: "My *Newsweek* column is probably the best job in sports journalism. . . . I have freedom, I have time. I spend a lot of time reporting, but the bottom line is I'm only writing once a week, and that's a break."[1] Axthelm focused on what regular news stories failed to cover. As he put it, his responsibility was to cut through the "bullshit" and come up with some sort of cogent opinion.

In 1978 he started writing for the *Washington Post,* which also published *Newsweek.* A year later he started writing a column about gambling for *Inside Sports.* When asked why he wrote this column as well as the *Newsweek* column, he replied:

In the gambling column I write for *Inside Sports,* I do a lot of anecdotal stuff that I think is amusing, and the readers seem to agree, but I couldn't always justify doing a *Newsweek* column on anecdotes about gamblers and Runyonesque characters, because its audience is broader and includes a lot of non-sports people.[2]

In 1980 Axthelm was hired as a commentator by the National Broadcasting Company. He commented about football on programs that aired before games; he discussed horse racing on other programs; and he reported on sports on the "Today" show. He also kept writing for the *Washington Post* and producing columns for *Newsweek* and *Inside Sports.*

By 1987 he had moved to ESPN, the sports network, where he provided commentary on football and horse racing on the "NFL GameDay" and "NFL Prime Time" programs.

Although he had attempted to stop drinking alcohol several times, especially when doctors warned him about his health, he could not. In February 1991, he died of complications caused by liver failure at the Presbyterian-University Hospital in Pittsburgh, where he was awaiting a liver transplant.

Although Axthelm was well known as a result of his columns in magazines and commentary on NBC and later ESPN, his books, particularly *The City Game: Basketball in New York from the World Champion Knicks to the World of the Playgrounds* (1970) and *The Kid* (1978), brought him additional recognition. *The City Game,* for example, brought accolades from reviewers for its unusual journalistic approach as well as its subject matter. Murray Kempton said of it:

I suspect that I have never read a better book about New York. Axthelm's subject here becomes the rite of passage in Harlem schoolyard basketball; his heroes are the boys who never escaped that schoolyard and who wasted their lives leaping there—legends with names like The Hawk and The Helicopter, men who stuffed themselves on Wilt Chamberlain and then drifted off into drugs or lonely country colleges and came back only to leap in that schoolyard again.[3]

Rex Lardner summed up Axthelm's point: "You can bask in local fame only so long, then you see the pimps and pushers with their snazzy suits and long cars and derive a new sense of values."[4]

The City Game contained two stories, one about the New York Knicks and their championship season, the other about the amateurs and their asphalt playgrounds. Both stories were insightful, but the second, about Harlem, was undoubtedly Axthelm's favorite.

The Kid, which concerned Steve Cauthen's life in horse racing, was also well received by critics primarily because Axthelm focused on the sport as well as Cauthen, providing the reader with an overview of horse racing as it related to Cauthen's life.

Both books used literary devices found in fiction, including dialogue and extensive description, to involve the reader. Consequently, both books were examples of literary journalism.

WORKS: *The City Game: Basketball in New York from the World Champion Knicks to the World of the Playgrounds* (1970); *The Kid* (1978).

NOTES

1. Peter Benjaminson, "Peter Axthelm: CA Interview," *Contemporary Authors,* edited by Hal May (Detroit: Gale Research, 1983), p. 33.

2. Ibid., pp. 33–34.

3. Murray Kempton, "Jock-Sniffing," *New York Review of Books,* February 11, 1971, p. 38.

4. Rex Lardner, "And They Did It Without a Superstar," *New York Times Book Review,* November 29, 1970, p. 49.

B

James Baldwin
(1924–1987)

Born in Harlem on August 2, 1924, James Baldwin became one of the foremost essayists and novelists of the 1960s. Throughout his writing he explored and deplored the injustices committed against African Americans. His essays, which moved critics and politicians, appealed to the human conscience to look beneath the skin and to think in terms of equality.

Baldwin, whose stepfather was a minister from New Orleans, preached "hell fire and damnation" at Harlem's Fireside Pentecostal Church before he was 15. After three years, however, he resigned because of a growing interest in writing.

After graduating from De Witt Clinton High School in 1942, he worked briefly in Belle Meade, New Jersey; since the country was at war, employment was available to those who wanted jobs. He moved from Belle Meade to Greenwich Village, where he worked during the day and wrote at night. He reviewed books about the black problem for such publications as the *Nation,* the *New Leader,* and *Commentary.* In addition, he wrote two books that earned him fellowships but were not published. Finally, after five years of frustration, he moved to France. Although his life in Paris was free in the sense that he felt little or no discrimination, he often suffered from not earning enough to live on. Nonetheless, he remained in France 10 years.

His first partly autobiographical novel, *Go Tell It on the Mountain,* which concerned a confused Harlem youth named John Grimes and his religious family, was published in 1953. The book was critically acclaimed for its insight into the American race problem. His next book, *Notes of a Native Son,* which appeared in 1955, was a collection of essays previously published in magazines such as *Commentary* and *Partisan Review.* The essays vividly penetrated the social injustices and prejudices of American society. Baldwin immediately was recognized as a humanitarian spokesman for the oppressed. *Notes* was followed by another novel, *Giovanni's Room,* which explored homosexuality. He continued to write novels and to contribute essays to such periodicals as *Harper's,* the *Reporter,* the *New Yorker,* the *Nation, Esquire, Commentary,* and *Partisan Review.*

In 1961 *Another Country* was published. The novel concerned an African-American woman and a white man who discarded the rules imposed on them by a basically white society and subsequently lived for themselves. Baldwin's second volume of essays, *Nobody Knows My Name: More Notes of a Native Son,* was published the same year. In 1963, in *The Fire Next Time,* Baldwin returned to the problems of racial prejudice with relentless power and magnitude. In two essays, both in the form of letters, Baldwin recounted his experience as a preacher in Harlem and examined the movement founded by the Black Muslims. Any white who read the book sensed the degradation that confronted most African Americans.

Baldwin, in addition to writing the novels *Tell Me How Long the Train's Been Gone* (1968), *If Beale Street Could Talk* (1974), and *Just Above My Head* (1979), and the essay collections *No Name in the Streets* (1972) and *The Devil Finds Work* (1976), also explored the black problem in the plays *The Amen Corner* and *Blues for Mister Charlie.* Although the plays were produced and his messages understood, neither had the impact of his essays. Baldwin died of cancer in 1987.

Baldwin's essays were examples of advocacy journalism for several reasons. First, his essays explored racism, a major issue. Second, they presented the topic from a personal perspective; that is, Baldwin showed the reader what it was like being black in America. And, perhaps in the form of a warning, his essays called for reform.

His autobiographical novel *Go Tell It on the Mountain,* and his collection of essays *The Fire Next Time* were examples of literary journalism because of the elements used to depict the respective topics. Some critics consider other works by Baldwin as representative of literary journalism as well.

WORKS: *Go Tell It on the Mountain* (1953); *Notes of a Native Son* (1955); *Nobody Knows My Name: More Notes of a Native Son* (1961); *The Fire Next Time* (1963).

Bill Barich
(1943–)

Bill Barich was born in 1943 to upper-middle-class parents. The oldest of three children, Barich lived with his parents in Westbury, New York. His father was the president of Ace Books, a paperback publishing company in New York.

Barich played on the basketball and baseball teams in high school. When he graduated he attended Colgate University, where he majored in the humanities. During his junior year, he lived in Florence and studied the Italian Renaissance. In Joe Flaherty's words, "he came to know the galleries of the Uffizi by heart, the statuary and cafes, and fell in love with the Humanist philosophers who had formed ranks around the Medici."[1]

Barich graduated from Colgate in 1966, and for the next year served in the Peace Corps in Biafra. Upon his return, he was hired to teach seventh grade at a boarding school in New Jersey. By 1969 Barich had had enough of teaching and moved to San Francisco, where he worked as a stock boy for a book distributor. Although he advanced within the company, his desire to write eventually overtook him in 1972, a year after he met his wife, Diana.

Barich turned out one novel after another. However, all were rejected by publishers. In 1978, after he and his wife had suffered miserably—their mothers had died of cancer; Diana had had two miscarriages and had been misdiagnosed as having a brain tumor; Barich was unemployed and consequently almost out of money; and they were living in a battered rented mobile home about 70 miles north of San Francisco—Barich announced to his wife that he was going to Golden Gate Fields, a horse track, about 60 miles away. He planned to get a room at a motel near the track where he could stay while gathering information about horse racing, a subject that he knew something about. Indeed, says Norman Sims, Barich discovered a favorite pastime of the Florentines, horse racing, while his mother lay dying.[2]

Barich visited Golden Gate Fields, on San Francisco Bay, for at least 10 weeks. What he saw, what he learned about horses and racing from trainers and jockeys, and what he learned about gambling from those who gambled filled page after page in his journal. He wove these notes, together with memories of his mother and of Florence, into a remarkable book entitled *Laughing in the Hills*, which was published in 1980. Barich's book was noticed by Robert Bingham and William Shawn, the editors of the *New Yorker*. Shawn wanted to purchase the first serial rights, so he called Barich and made an offer. Barich agreed, and excerpts from the book appeared in the magazine.

Joe Flaherty commented in his review of *Laughing in the Hills:*

Mr. Barich offers a touching portrait of a young man in trouble. He interrupts his narrative, constantly and audaciously, and segues into the history of the horse and of Albany, Calif., examines the theories of thoroughbred breeding, attempts to cross-pollinate 15th-century philosophy and contemporary life and applies the logic of philosophy to the magic of plunging—Damon Runyon and the Renaissance.[3]

Other reviewers criticized Barich's writing. Roger Sale, for instance, claimed that Barich's prose suffered from defects he associated with the *New Yorker*: "When Barich calls nature 'hydrogen intertwined with embryos and tumors,' I see only showiness; and his description of Sunday afternoons in the East Bay is worse."[4] Sale's review, however, ended on a positive note: "*Laughing in the Hills* can be placed alongside Andrew Beyer's *My $50,000 Year at the Races* and James Guetti's novel, *Action,* as being among the books honorably describing a fascinating subculture."[5] Sale also admitted that Barich's book belonged alongside *Zen and the Art of Motorcycle Maintenance* and *A Fan's Notes.* Its personal style of writing made *Laughing in the Hills* an example of literary journalism.

Over the next year Barich traveled through the Northwest, particularly in Oregon, and contributed articles to the *New Yorker.* Then he and his wife put their furniture in storage, packed their Datsun, and headed east. He wrote in the preface to *Traveling Light,* which was published in 1984: "Over the next year or so, we had three different addresses. We lived on eastern Long Island; in London; and in the Arcetri district, above Florence. There were side trips to upstate New York; to the English countryside; and to Rome, Venice, and Ravenna."[6]

Traveling Light contained most of the articles he contributed to the *New Yorker* on his travels. John Skow said of the book: "Barich is especially good at the travel writer's peculiar con—getting the reader to enjoy his enjoyment—in a couple of pieces he wrote about spending several months in Florence. He is so deft at this that even a long list of pasta types . . . seems to be infused with joy."[7] The book included 10 essays about friends, fishing, horse racing, family, art, and history. His writing was fresh; he captured everyday conversation extremely well.

Barich not only interested the reader by what and how he wrote, but made the reader want more. As Skow put it, "Take more trips . . . for those of us whose luggage has grown too heavy to lug."[8] Using a personal style of reporting, Barich allowed the reader to experience what he had experienced, to see what he had seen, to taste what he had tasted, and to hear what he had heard. *Traveling Light,* like *Laughing in the Hills,* was a work of literary journalism.

In 1987 his collection of seven stories, *Hard to Be Good,* was published to mixed reviews. All but one of the stories had been published in magazines. In 1994 he returned to a subject that he knew: California. *Big Dreams: Into the Heart of California* was a well-written but somewhat disappointing attempt to paint a picture of the state. Barich journeyed from Northern to Southern California and provided historical details as well as descriptions of those he met along the way. He traveled the minor and major highways and visited Indian reservations, San Francisco, the San Joaquin Valley farming communities, Los Angeles, Disneyland, and Venice. He searched the areas that attracted illegal immigrants. Although he tried to explain California's appeal in an impressive style, the size and the complexity of the state made the task overwhelming. Some reviewers found his use of stereotypes to depict actual people a distraction. Nonetheless, the book was an example of literary journalism.

WORKS: *Laughing in the Hills* (1980); *Traveling Light* (1984); *Big Dreams: Into the Heart of California* (1994).

NOTES

1. Joe Flaherty, "Saving Your Soul at the Track," *New York Times Book Review,* June 15, 1980, p. 7.

2. Norman Sims, *The Literary Journalists* (New York: Ballantine Books, 1984), p. 321.

3. Flaherty, "Saving Your Soul," p. 7.

4. Roger Sale, "Golden Gaits," *New York Review of Books,* March 5, 1981, p. 39.

5. Ibid.

6. Bill Barich, *Traveling Light* (New York: Viking Press, 1984), p. x.

7. John Skow, "Voyager," *Time,* February 6, 1984, p. 72.

8. Ibid.

Carleton Beals
(1893–1979)

Carleton Beals, the grandson of Carrie Nation, was born in 1893, in Medicine Lodge, Kansas. His father, Leon Beals, was a lawyer and journalist. When Beals was three his family moved to California, where he attended public schools in Pasadena.

Beals graduated from high school in 1911 and worked at a number of jobs, including foundryman, waiter, grocery clerk, cashier, cowboy, shoe salesman, and tutor, while attending the University of California. Beals won the Bonnheim Essay Prize twice and the Bryce History Essay Prize once. As a result of his outstanding academic achievement, he was awarded a graduate scholarship to Columbia University.

Although he had studied engineering and mining at the undergraduate level, Beals' interests changed at the graduate level. For instance, he wrote a thesis on the self-sufficient state (economics), earned a Teachers College certificate, and wrote a book on economics which unfortunately was destroyed in a fire. He earned his master of arts degree in 1917.

Writing was now a part of his life. He tried writing short stories but could not find a publisher. Finally he found a job with the Standard Oil Company of California. However, punching an adding machine in the export department was boring to him. Beals left the company to see the world. Driving a secondhand Ford, he set out for Mexico. Before he reached Mexico City, his car had stalled; he had ridden on rented burros; he had walked; and he had endured considerable hardship—from nearly starving to almost being ambushed by soldiers.

Although he had some money, he was in desperate need of work. Within a few months, he founded the English Preparatory Institute. In addition, he got a job as a teacher, then principal, at the American High School, and landed another job as an instructor of English to staff members of President Carranza. These jobs took up most of his time; however, he continued to write. By 1920, when a revolution forced President Carranza to flee, ultimately causing Beals to lose two of his three jobs, he had contributed at least four articles to magazines and had completed a book about Mexico.

Beals left for Spain, where he studied at the University of Madrid, traveled, and wrote articles. About a year later, he moved to Italy, where he studied at the University of Rome, watched Mussolini rise to power, and wrote articles and a book about fascism.

He returned to Mexico City, then New York City. He worked on the books about Mexico and fascism, and both were published in 1923. While living in New York City, he wrote *Brimstone and Chili,* about his experiences in Mexico. The book was published in 1927, the year General Augusto Sandino led a revolt against the United States Marines who were occupying Nicaragua; the revolt lasted until 1933, when the United States withdrew its forces.

Beals was sent to Nicaragua by the *Nation* to write a series of articles. As Joan Cook wrote, "Mr. Beals ... made his way from Honduras, partly on horseback, partly on foot, hacking his way through the jungle, accompanied by an escort of Sandinistas."[1] Beals finally reached the general and interviewed him before the marines started their daily bombing mission.

This scoop, which represented the first confrontation of United States forces in combating guerrilla troops under tropical conditions, ended with Mr. Beals's dispatches being printed not only in *The Nation,* but also in *The New York Herald Tribune* and other papers across the country, in Europe, Japan and China.[2]

Beals returned to the United States in 1929, then headed back to Europe. He revisited Spain and became a close friend of Manual Azana. He traveled to North Africa, Spanish and French Morocco, Algiers, and Tunisia. He journeyed on horseback through the Rif country. He studied Italy under Mussolini, then visited Greece and Turkey. Later he traveled into the Soviet Union and part of Germany. Beals continued to contribute articles based on his travels and observations to the *Nation* and the *New Republic,* among others.

He returned to New York City, then set off on a journey through the Oaxaca Mountains. The book based on this journey, *Mexican Maze,* was praised for its anthropological, sociological, and historical interpretation of revolution, war, and peace in this region of the world. No longer was Beals considered just another travel writer.

In 1932 his book *Banana Gold,* based on his experiences in Honduras and Central America, was published. Like *Mexican Maze,* it was unusual in its depiction of patriotism and corruption. Indeed, the first-person point of view was used, giving the reader a personal account of what happened. Beals was more than an observer; he was a participant.

Banana Gold was an example of literary journalism. Beals used a personal style of reporting to describe the characters and milieu. In short, he presented slice-of-life experiences to the reader. Beals' descriptions were realistic and authentic. Only through description could the reader see what Beals witnessed.

The same year Beals traveled to Cuba to investigate the dictator Geraldo Machado. A year later *The Crime of Cuba* was published, in which Beals criticized Machado and the role of the United States. Machado was overthrown, and Beals became a hero to the young people of Cuba.

Beals later covered a general strike in Cuba for the North American Newspaper Alliance, then went to Louisiana to study Huey Long, the controversial governor of that state. In 1936 he served as a correspondent for the *New York Post*; he covered the Scottsboro trial in Alabama. Later, after the trial, he studied living conditions of sharecroppers.

For the remainder of his life, he lived primarily in the United States, although he visited other countries, particularly in Central and South America, as well as numerous islands in the Caribbean. He said in an interview, "I have done most of my writing in Spain, Italy, Mexico and Peru, and in this country, chiefly in New York, later in Guilford, Conn., since 1957 in Killingworth."[3] Beals died on June 26, 1979. He had written more than 45 books.

WORKS: *Brimstone and Chili: A Book of Personal Experiences in the Southwest and in Mexico* (1927); *Mexican Maze* (1931; 1971); *Banana Gold* (1932; 1970).

NOTES

1. Joan Cook, "Carlton Beals Dies; Correspondent, 85," *New York Times,* June 28, 1979, p. B15.

2. Ibid.

3. Ann Evory, ed., "Beals, Carlton 1893–1979," *Contemporary Authors: New Revision Series* (Detroit: Gale Research, 1981), p. 59.

Meyer Berger
(1898–1959)

Born in 1898 to an impoverished Jewish family in New York City, Meyer Berger began learning the newspaper business at an early age. When he was eight he was selling papers on the street. At 12 he was working for the *New York Morning World.* His formal education had ended, but his employment as a messenger boy enabled him to learn the newspaper business well, and before enlisting in the army when the United States entered World War I he had become head office boy.

When he returned to the *World* in 1919 he was promoted to police reporter. Three years later he worked as a rewrite man for the Standard News Association. With each position Berger learned another aspect of newspapering, and in 1928 he moved to the *New York Times.* Berger's ability as a reporter was almost unequalled; indeed, few journalists of his day could match his power of perception. His writing, too, was excellent. Whenever he covered a murder or trial, the *Times*' editors knew they would have a literary edge over their competition. From Chicago Berger filed a series of stories that graphically depicted the trial of Al Capone; the series was filled with description and dialogue, two elements commonly found in literary journalism.

In 1939 he began a column, "About New York," in which he presented compassionate episodes of New York life. The column was filled with sensitive sketches of everyday New Yorkers, from taxi drivers to sales personnel. It realistically captured the people who made up the city.

Three years later he traveled to London as a World War II correspondent and wrote stories on how the war affected Britain. Berger, who learned from interviews the fears and frustrations of Londoners, reported what they told him and what he observed.

When he returned to New York City he continued writing similar stories from Americans' perspectives; these stories were well received. Perhaps his greatest column was written in 1949, about Howard Unruh, a veteran who shot 13 people in Camden, New Jersey. According to Gay Talese, "Berger . . . spent six hours retracing Unruh's footsteps . . . interviewed fifty people who had seen parts of the rampage, and then . . . sat down and reconstructed the whole scene in a 4,000-word article in two and one-half hours."[1]

The scene was vividly presented to the reader through description. Adjectives were used effectively. Readers sensed the intensity. Indeed, readers had to tell themselves that what they were reading was true, not fiction. Elements common in literary journalism were present: abundant description, scene-by-scene construction, and the third-person point of view. The most obvious element, however, was the extensive research. Berger interviewed numerous witnesses to the tragedy before he wrote a word. Then, as if he had seen the massacre, he accurately depicted Unruh's movements.

The article won the Pulitzer Prize in 1950, and Berger gave the prize money to Unruh's mother. He wrote *The Story of the New York Times* and *New York, City on Many Waters* before he died in 1959.

WORK: *New York, City on Many Waters* (1955).

NOTE

1. Gay Talese, *The Kingdom and the Power* (New York: World Publishing, 1969), p. 224.

Carl Bernstein
(1944–)

Carl Bernstein and Bob Woodward uncovered a series of events that first angered President Richard Nixon, then indirectly forced him from office. Bernstein was born in 1944 and reared in Washington, D.C. A year younger than Woodward, he disliked school. When he was 16 he became a copy boy at the *Washington Star,* but his determination to become a reporter encouraged him to write stories about various civic meetings, and he eventually advanced to city desk clerk, then telephone dictationist. In addition to typing stories called in by reporters, he wrote obituaries from information supplied by funeral directors as well as articles based on press releases.

Bernstein was eventually promoted to head dictationist on the day shift, but he covered crimes, meetings, and fires at night. Although he became a member of the *Star*'s reporting staff as a summer replacement, and attended the University of Maryland part-time, he grew frustrated when he was ordered back to the dictation bank. Shortly thereafter he joined the Elizabeth, New Jersey, *Daily Journal,* for which he wrote features and a column. His colorful personal reporting of the Manhattan blackout of 1965 appeared on the *Daily Journal*'s front page and won first prize from the New Jersey Press Association.

After trying unsuccessfully to get a job with one of New York City's dailies, he was hired by the *Washington Post* in 1966. Bernstein was assigned to various beats, including the police department, city hall, the courts, and the Virginia legislature. However, like Woodward, he also began to cover stories he thought were interesting. Indeed, his stories about the various lifestyles in and around Washington were historically sound, for he captured the milieu as no other reporter had done. Through vignettes, he allowed readers to see as well as hear the characters who gave the city its color.

Before Watergate, Bernstein also wrote several investigative stories on such topics as drug traffic, slum landlords, fly-by-night schools, and police corruption.

Although Woodward had been assigned to cover the July 1972 burglary at the Democratic party headquarters in the Watergate building and had written several other stories concerning Watergate, Bernstein realized that Woodward could not cover all the tips or leads alone, and persuaded the editors to let him work with Woodward. Within four months "Woodstein" had traced the money to Attorney General John Mitchell, the campaign director of CREEP (Committee to Re-Elect the President) at the time of the break-in.

In 1974 Woodward and Bernstein's first book, *All the President's Men,* was published. It detailed how the team had investigated the various leads, describing their successes as well as failures in obtaining information for stories. The book, written in the third person for the sake of objectivity, was praised by critics for its realistic depiction of the newspaper business and its authentic record of history.

Two years later the reporters' second book, *The Final Days,* was published. Although they had intended to write of the impeachment and subsequent trial of the president from the perspective of six senators involved in the case, they had to dismiss the idea when they learned that the president would resign. Woodward and Bernstein investigated the last 15 months of the Nixon White House. After interviewing almost 400 persons, they wrote an in-depth account of the last days. The book sold well, but several critics harshly criticized it for its disregard of historical reporting. Other critics termed the book a nonfiction novel because of its literary style and its use of anonymous sources. Most critics, however, considered the book to be an extraordinary piece of contemporary history.

Woodward stayed at the *Post,* but Bernstein resigned from the paper to devote his time to freelance writing. He contributed articles to several periodicals, including *Rolling Stone* and the *New Yorker.* In 1989 his *Loyalties: A Son's Mem-*

oirs was published. An autobiography, it focused on Bernstein's relationship with his father during the McCarthy era.

WORKS: *All the President's Men* (with Bob Woodward, 1974); *The Final Days* (with Bob Woodward, 1976).

Ambrose Bierce
(1842–1914?)

Ambrose Bierce was a journalist who wrote sketches, columns, articles, and short stories, some of which contained elements characteristic of literary journalism. Born in Ohio in 1842, Bierce briefly attended the Kentucky Military Institute prior to the firing on Ft. Sumter. Immediately, he volunteered for service and admirably served the Union. According to Joseph Henry Jackson:

When the Civil War ended, the young man had seen action on a dozen fronts, suffered a severe wound, earned a commission, served on General Hazen's staff where he drew admirably neat military maps; at Missionary Ridge it was Bierce's survey which formed the basis of the strategic plan. He had marched through Georgia with Sherman, discovered what it was to be a prisoner of war for a few brief days in Alabama, and learned about the thrill of escape by engineering his own when the war was nearly at its close.[1]

After his release Bierce worked for the Treasury Department, then for General Hazen, his old commanding officer, who was in charge of an expedition west. For almost a year he accompanied Hazen, surveying the territory. When Hazen sailed for Panama, Bierce remained in San Francisco, where he worked for the U.S. Sub-Treasury during the day. In the evening he wrote articles on politics and Poe-like short stories. His writing appeared in the *News-Letter* and *Alta California.* In 1868 he wrote editorial comments under "The Town Crier," a page filled with invective and consequently enjoyed by the readers. Bierce used "The Town Crier" to present forcefully his scathing remarks. He attacked the ills of society as well as the rogues responsible. Through the *News-Letter* he became a fixture in San Francisco, a position he readily accepted.

He moved to London in 1872, hoping to make his mark abroad, but

the London episode lasted less than four years and was not the triumph of which Bierce had dreamed. Writing for half a dozen magazines, publishing his *Fiend's Delight, Nuggets and Dust,* and *Cobwebs from an Empty Skull,* all under the pseudonym of "Dod Grile," he did gather some small fame.[2]

When he returned to San Francisco, the city had changed; hard times had set in. Dennis Kearney and his Workingmen's Party attributed the high unemployment among whites to the Chinese migrant workers, and unfortunately his prejudiced views were becoming popular. In response, Bierce published and edited the *Argonaut,* where perhaps his most famous column, "Prattle," was born. In this column, Bierce used wit to criticize every form of hypocrisy; consequently, he became a champion of causes in the eyes of San Franciscans. In addition, he wrote short stories, essays, and poetry. When his wife left him he used his pen to belittle women. Men, too, were dissected and analyzed in almost every column; indeed, even simpletons and incompetents were brought before Bierce's scornful eyes and criticized.

In 1880 Bierce sold the *Argonaut* and moved to the Black Hills to manage a gold mine. Before the year ended the company was bankrupt, and Bierce, having been refused a position with the *Argonaut,* was in desperate need of a job. Finally, his old column was accepted by the *Wasp,* a San Francisco weekly. Six years later, Bierce was approached by William Randolph Hearst, who enjoyed Bierce's column as well as his other writing. Hearst offered Bierce a position with the *San Francisco Examiner,* and "Prattle" remained there until the turn of the century. To say the least, the *Examiner* helped popularize Bierce's column as well as his short stories. In 1891, after he had written a number of stories about the Civil War, he published *Tales of Soldiers and Civilians.* Two years later he published *Can Such Things Be?,* a book of stories about the supernatural.

Bierce moved to Washington, D.C., in 1896 to report against an appropriations bill that was before Congress. If passed, the bill would help the Southern Pacific Railroad postpone loan repayments to the U.S. government. As a result of his accurate reports, as well as Hearst's power, the bill was defeated. Although he returned to San Francisco, he eventually talked Hearst into allowing him to move to Washington so that he could write more for the *New York Journal* and less for the *Examiner.* However, the column he produced, "The Passing Show," was nothing compared to "Prattle," and after a few years Hearst put it in *Cosmopolitan.*

In 1912 Bierce published his *Collected Works;* he was 70 years old. He visited California, then journeyed to Tennessee to stand on the battlefields where he had fought and had witnessed numerous deaths. Heading southwest, he visited New Orleans, San Antonio, and El Paso, where he received credentials to enter Mexico. He had grown old and needed another battle to rejuvenate himself. In his last correspondence, he was with troops near Chihuahua. He was never seen again.

Bierce was a champion when it came to writing biting editorials. His battle stories, which were based on fact, used realistic dialogue, scene-by-scene construction, accurate description, the third person point of view, and, occasionally, interior monologue, all elements found in literary journalism.

WORKS: "Prattle" (newspaper column); *Tales of Soldiers and Civilians* (1891); *Can Such Things Be?* (1893); *Collected Works* (1912).

NOTES

1. Joseph Henry Jackson, ed., *Tales of Soldiers and Civilians—Ambrose Bierce* (New York: Heritage Press, 1943), p. xii.

2. Ibid., p. xvi.

Jim Bishop
(1907–1987)

Jim Bishop was born on November 21, 1907, and attended St. Patrick's school in Jersey City, from which he graduated in 1922, and Drake Secretarial College, where he learned shorthand and typing. He began his newspaper career in 1928 as a copy boy for the *New York Daily News.* Two years later he became a reporter for the *New York Daily Mirror,* where he remained for the next 13 years. From 1932 to 1934 he was the assistant to Mark Hellinger, the newspaper's Broadway columnist, who taught Bishop the skills of rewriting and writing features, which enabled Bishop to become part of the rewriting staff as well as one of the newspaper's feature writers in 1934.

He resigned from the *Mirror* in 1943 to serve as associate editor, then war editor, for *Collier's* magazine. In addition, he held five other positions between 1943 and 1955. As executive editor of *Liberty* magazine, director of the literature department of the Music Corporation of America, founding editor of Gold Medal Books, executive editor of *Catholic Digest,* and founding editor of the *Catholic Digest* Book Club, Bishop broadened his experience in writing and editing. In addition to these duties, he wrote six books; one, *The Day Lincoln Was Shot,* became a best-seller. More important, perhaps, the book, a thoroughly researched account depicting hour by hour the events of Lincoln's last day, was also a critical success. Presenting fact in novel form, the book preceded Truman Capote's *In Cold Blood* by 10 years, and established a pattern Bishop used in other "day" books and articles.

During 1956 Bishop candidly explored desegregation in a series of articles that appeared in the *Washington Post and Times Herald.* He also interviewed President Eisenhower for an article titled "A Day with Dwight D. Eisenhower," which appeared in *Cosmopolitan.*

In 1957 he began writing a human interest column for King Features Syndicate, and saw his second "day" book published. *The Day Christ Died,* like the first "day" book, became an instant best-seller. *The Day Christ Was Born: A Reverential Reconstruction* appeared three years later.

Bishop's popularity increased. His columns attracted thousands of readers, and his books were serialized in magazines. Indeed, his "day" books, each of which had taken months of research, appealed to President John F. Kennedy. Bishop wrote:

The last time I saw President Kennedy was at the White House. . . . I was present to research an article for *Good Housekeeping* magazine to be called "A Day in the Life of President Kennedy." He was cordial and helpful, and he seemed anxious for me to write a book rather than a magazine piece.[1]

A Day in the Life of President Kennedy appeared in 1964 and became another best-seller; but three years later, when *A Day in the Life of President Johnson* was published, neither the public nor the critics reacted favorably. In 1968 *The Day Kennedy Was Shot* appeared, much to the dismay of President Kennedy's family. Nonetheless, the book was commercially and critically successful. *The Day Kennedy Was Shot* exemplified Bishop's use of realistic description and actual dialogue, two elements essential to literary journalism.

Although Bishop wrote other books, including *The Golden Ham,* a critical biography of Jackie Gleason, *The Days of Martin Luther King, Jr.,* and *FDR's Last Year,* his "day" books were his most challenging and ambitious journalistic undertakings. Bishop died in 1987; he was 79.

WORKS: *The Day Lincoln Was Shot* (1955); *A Day in the Life of President Kennedy* (1964); *A Day in the Life of President Johnson* (1967); *The Day Kennedy Was Shot* (1968); *The Days of Martin Luther King, Jr.* (1971); *FDR's Last Year* (1974).

NOTE

1. Jim Bishop, *The Day Kennedy Was Shot* (New York: Funk and Wagnalls, 1968), p. xi.

Winifred Black
(1863–1936)

Winifred Sweet, known as "Annie Laurie," was born in Chilton, Wisconsin, in 1863. Perhaps the second most daring young woman after "Nellie Bly" to invent stunts and unusual situations in order to obtain information and write sensational stories during the "yellow" journalism period, Sweet was educated at the Sacred Heart Convent in Chicago, the Lake Forest Seminary in Illinois, and Miss Burnham's Preparatory School at Northampton, Massachusetts.

Interested in the theater, she moved to New York City, where she learned quickly that the only roles she could play were minor ones. Frustrated and disgusted, she left for San Francisco, where she changed careers. In 1889 she obtained a reporting position on the *San Francisco Examiner.* Two years later she married Orlow Black and became Winifred Black, a name she retained even though she divorced Black in 1897 and married Charles Allen Bonfils in 1901.

Like many other reporters of the period, Black had to learn new journalistic techniques. The old impersonal style that had filled newspaper columns for years was passé. Joseph Pulitzer and the staff of his *New York World* were using an informal, lively, and hard-hitting style that attracted readers and mirrored the times. Learning how to write for newspapers took time. Her early stories were stilted and filled with too many adjectives. She was not writing for the average newspaper reader, complained Sam S. Chamberlain, the *Examiner's* managing editor.

Nonetheless, she persevered, learning how to compose personal, vivid prose and how to investigate and obtain information of interest. For one story she "fainted" on a San Francisco street in order to be brought to the receiving hospital. There, like other patients, she was neglected. Her story criticized the handling of patients and as a result forced the city to dismiss several hospital employees and improve patient care.

Her success was due to at least two factors: she knew what would make an interesting story, and she knew that William Randolph Hearst wanted stories with short sentences, short paragraphs, and direct quotes. Therefore, she abandoned mid-Victorian prose, going in for "startling effects—hard jolts in short paragraphs. She used adjectives, but not in such dizzy numbers. Her stories were highly charged with emotion."[1]

Her articles on "Little Jim," a crippled boy born to a prostitute in San Francisco's prison hospital, helped launch a newspaper campaign that ultimately provided a ward for incurables at the city's Children's Hospital.

In 1892 she somehow sneaked aboard President Benjamin Harrison's campaign train and was eventually granted an interview. She was persistent, but she had to be in order to compete with her male counterparts. She interviewed other prominent people of the times, including Governor William S. Taylor, Sarah Bernhardt, Henry Stanley, and Henry Irving.

In 1895 Hearst purchased the *New York Journal* in order to compete against Pulitzer. He brought "Annie Laurie" with him, but within two years she had had enough of New York. She moved back to California, then to Denver, where she obtained an additional position with the *Denver Post.*

As a feature writer for Hearst, she covered America and England. According to Ishbell Ross, "She went to England to write about the suffragettes when they were still horrifying creatures who poured acid into bright red letter boxes and kicked bobbies in the stomach."[2] She wrote about Chicago's juvenile court system. She investigated the Charity Organization Society of New York. She wrote about the so-called last prize fight in America, held in El Paso. She depicted the ugliness of pigeon shooting at Del Monte. The story received international attention, and Black received medals from the humane societies of the United States and Great Britain.

When Galveston was devastated by a tidal wave in 1900, Black, disguised as a boy, was the first female reporter to see the 7,000 bodies. Immediately, the Hearst empire had relief trains sent, and Black received word that she was to have a hospital ready. She directed the relief workers and distributed thousands of dollars, which Hearst and others had donated, to the survivors.

In addition to disasters, including the San Francisco earthquake of 1906, Black covered trials. When Harry Thaw was charged with the murder of architect Stanford White, she was one of four female reporters later termed the "sob sisters" because of their sentimental and charitable treatment of Evelyn Nesbit Thaw.

Black's marriage to Charles Bonfils did not last because of her career. Bonfils, who had been managing editor of the *Kansas City Post,* then a freelance writer in New York City, seldom saw her, for she was constantly traveling and reporting. After 1917 their separation became permanent. Black was in Europe covering the war and later the Versailles peace conference.

Black remained a reporter until her death in 1936. Her later work, except for her coverage of World War I in Europe and the Versailles peace conference, was confined to a regular column for the *San Francisco Examiner.*

NOTES

1. Ishbell Ross, *Ladies of the Press: The Story of Women in Journalism by an Insider* (New York: Harper and Brothers, 1936), p. 62.

2. Ibid., p. 66.

Carol(yn) Bly
(1930–   )

Born April 16, 1930, in Duluth, Minnesota, Carol Bly attended Wellesley College, from which she graduated in 1951. She earned graduate credit at the University of Minnesota in 1954 and 1955, the year she married Robert Bly.

Bly served as manager of several magazines from 1958 to 1971, including *Fifties, Sixties,* and *Seventies,* which were published in Madison, Minnesota. Extremely active in religious and civic organizations and institutions, Bly co-founded the Prairie Arts Center in Madison in 1971 and served as a member of Madison's Chamber of Commerce from 1971 to 1978, the year she became proprietor of Custom Crosswords in Sturgeon Lake, Minnesota.

In the 1980s Bly worked as a consultant for the American Farm Project, which was sponsored by the National Endowment for the Humanities and the National Farmers Union, and for the Land Stewardship Project, in addition to lecturing at numerous college and university writing workshops and programs.

During this time, she contributed essays to *Minnesota Monthly,* published by Minnesota Public Radio, and *Preview;* short stories to the *New Yorker, Twin Cities, Ploughshares,* and *American Review;* and poems to *Poetry Northwest* and *Coastlines.*

Although her short stories and poems reflected her experiences in small towns, it was her essays that were intriguing and unarguably a form of literary journalism. Published under the title *Letters from the Country,* they were praised by reviewers for their insight and candid portrayal of small-town America. As Rosellen Brown wrote:

Few novelists have distilled as accurately and poignantly as Bly the essences of small-town life—its dense configuration of satisfactions and impoverishments, the contradictory pleasures of community and isolation, and, perhaps the most elusive element, the difficulty of coming to a full exercise of individual capacity without seeming an alien, even a threat, to one's neighbor.[1]

Bly's brief essays dealt with problems faced by her characters. To say that she did not care about her characters would be absurd. She seemed to expect more of them than they expected of themselves. She questioned whether they were capable of solving every problem. As she saw it, they were too positive in their thinking or they had been taught not to feel anything:

Americans are always mourning that "the kids everywhere" have no feeling: that's another kind of phenomenon, but what you have to be clear about in Minnesota is that the Scandinavian-American doesn't feel because he doesn't *believe* in feeling. He's against it. It isn't only that he has watched too much television; his timidity and frigidity were there long before he was seduced by "The Edge of Night."[2]

Thus Bly wanted her small-town characters to seek outside help. In Brown's words, "She wants her small-town kids to have the addresses of all the reformers' organizations, of Jungian and yoga conferences, and of Common Cause, as if the accessibility of information were all that mattered."[3] In short, Bly wished that her characters would open up, broaden their minds, and question what they had accepted as a "normal" lifestyle.

In one essay, "Brethren Too Least for Country Life," Bly allowed the reader to experience what she had experienced. She described an individual and in the process an entire subculture. Yet she was not condescending; more important, she was not relying on a stereotypical generalization to describe the individual.

Bly observed the human condition and commented on it in no uncertain terms. She exhibited a sharp eye for detail, like a novelist, and grew involved editorially speaking, like an essayist. Combining the two allowed her to express what she had observed as well as what she had grown to believe.

Backbone, a collection of her short stories, was published in 1985. The stories concerned the stirrings of active individuals who lived in or frequented retirement homes, churches, and the various ethnic organizations of the Minnesota communities. These individuals had remained socially conscious, just like the author.

The Passionate Accurate Story, a book on how to write fiction, was published in 1990. Bly's second collection of short stories, *The Tomcat's Wife: And Other Stories* (1991) contained eight stories about individuals who lived in small communities and had surrendered to mediocrity. The stories were unified by the themes of hypocrisy and cruelty.

WORK: *Letters from the Country* (1981).

NOTES

1. Rosellen Brown, *"Letters from the Country* by Carol Bly," *New Republic,* June 20, 1981, p. 39.

2. Carol Bly, "From the Lost Swede Towns," in *Letters from the Country* (New York: Harper and Row, 1981), p. 2.

3. Brown, *"Letters from the Country,"* p. 40.

Jimmy Breslin
(1930–)

One of the first journalists of the 1960s to write literary journalism was Jimmy Breslin, the heavyweight Irishman born to James and Frances Breslin on October

17, 1930, in Jamaica, New York. Breslin, who attended St. Benedict Joseph Labre Elementary School and John Adams High School, began his newspaper career as a copy boy with the *Long Island Press* in 1948. The same year he entered Long Island University, which he attended until 1950. Within a few years, after having moved from one newspaper to another, he became a sportswriter for the *New York Journal-American* and wrote articles for magazines in his spare time.

In the early 1960s he turned to books. His first, *Sunny Jim: The Life of America's Most Beloved Horseman, James Fitzsimmons,* published in 1962, was a modest success. His second was popular, if only in New York City. Published in 1963, *Can't Anybody Here Play This Game? The Improbable Saga of the New York Mets' First Year* was read by baseball fans, including the *New York Herald Tribune*'s publisher, John Hay Whitney, who apparently enjoyed Breslin's style and wit, for he purchased the serial rights. Later the same year the publisher asked Breslin to write a column for the *Herald-Tribune.* Breslin, who had not been happy working at newspapers, was finally persuaded.

What began as a sports column changed when Breslin left the offices of the *Herald-Tribune* and started hanging out in bars in neighborhoods most journalists never knew existed. His columns, which were vignettes not very different from short stories, concerned New York City characters such as Fat Thomas, the bookmaker; Marvin the Torch, the professional arsonist; Jerry the Booster, the shoplifter; and Bad Eddie, among others. When the *Herald-Tribune* merged with the *World-Telegram and Sun* and the *Journal-American* to become the *World Journal Tribune,* Breslin's column was kept intact until the newspaper's demise in 1967. Clay Felker, who had been with the *Herald Tribune,* managed to purchase the rights to *New York,* the newspaper's magazine, which he had edited, and published his first issue in 1968. Breslin, who was not only a friend of Felker's but one of his financial supporters, contributed lengthy articles to the new venture in addition to writing a column for the *New York Post.* He contributed realistic but poetic coverage of the civil rights march in Selma, Alabama; his personal, emotional Vietnam War copy; and his emotional story "A Death in Emergency Room One," about the efforts of a Dallas surgeon to save President John F. Kennedy. His stories about the Vietnam War contained description, poetic phrases, and realistic dialogue that captured the scene, the characters, and the reality of the times. Many were examples of literary journalism, for they contained the necessary elements.

In 1969 Breslin and Norman Mailer sought public office in New York City. The two proposed to make New York City the fifty-first state, an idea that was severely criticized, and both lost. The same year his column for the *Post* ended. Also in 1969, Breslin, while contributing to *New York* and working as a commentator for WABC-TV, wrote his first novel, *The Gang that Couldn't Shoot Straight,* which hilariously spoofed a Mafia-style gang in Brooklyn. The book sold well and was made into a film.

Two years later, together with several members of the *New York* staff, Breslin disagreed with Felker's editorial policies and subsequently resigned from the magazine. Before he was hired in 1973 as a commentator by WNBC-TV, he spent several months in Ireland doing research for his second novel, *World Without End, Amen.*

In 1975 his book about the fall of the Nixon administration appeared. *How the Good Guys Finally Won: Notes from an Impeachment Summer* was witty and entertaining, and marked a return to nonfiction. Even though he was contributing to such periodicals as the *Saturday Evening Post, Time, Sports Illustrated,* and *Penthouse,* and was producing a book about every two years, he returned to writing a column, joining the *New York Daily News* in 1978.

The same year he and Dick Schaap collaborated on the novel *.44.* Four years later he wrote *Forsaking All Others,* a novel about a poor, young Puerto Rican who became a lawyer and grew to love a spoiled daughter of a Mafioso. The novel depicted the young lovers in an atmosphere of poverty and violence, and was praised by critics for its insight and authenticity.

The World According to Jimmy Breslin, published in 1984, contained columns that had originally appeared in the *New York Daily News.* It was another example of literary journalism.

The novels *Table Money* and *He Got Hungry and Forgot His Manners* were published in 1986 and 1987, respectively. The first concerned blue-collar "sandhogs," the men responsible for building the massive tunnels that bring water to New York City. The second was a farce based partly on the events surrounding the racial attacks that occurred at Howard Beach in 1986. Although *Table Money* received considerable praise from critics, *He Got Hungry and Forgot His Manners* was dismissed.

Breslin remained with the *New York Daily News* until 1988. He also hosted "Jimmy Breslin's People," which was broadcast by ABC-TV for 13 weeks in 1987, in addition to appearing in commercials and television programs. He moved his column to *Newsday* in 1988.

Three years later his critical biography *Damon Runyon* was published, to mixed reviews. It too was an example of literary journalism.

WORKS: *Can't Anybody Here Play This Game? The Improbable Saga of the New York Mets' First Year* (1963); *How the Good Guys Finally Won: Notes from an Impeachment Summer* (1975); *The World According to Jimmy Breslin* (1984); *Damon Runyon* (1991).

Claude Brown
(1937–   )

Born in New York City in 1937, Claude Brown, a member of "the first Northern urban generation of Negroes," termed that generation "a misplaced people in an extremely complex, confused society." In his penetrating autobiography, *Manchild in the Promised Land,* he wrote:

The characters are sons and daughters of former Southern sharecroppers. These were the poorest people of the South, who poured into New York City during the decade following the Great Depression. These migrants were told that unlimited opportunities for prosperity existed in New York and that there was no "color problem" there. They were told that Negroes lived in houses with bathrooms, electricity, running water, and indoor toilets. To them, this was the "promised land" that Mammy had been singing about in the cotton fields for many years.[1]

Brown was reared in Harlem, where he lived on the streets. A tough youth, he learned quickly that in order to survive he had to be as brave as the next person. Fighting and stealing became a way of life for him. By the time he was 10 years old he was a member of a "bebopping gang," the Buccaneers, for which he stole. He seldom attended school and in fact was expelled several times.

Although his family sent him to his grandparents' farm in the South for a year, the work failed to discipline him. When he returned to New York City he immediately got into trouble. The authorities sent him to the Wiltwyck School, a special school for boys, where he grew to respect Dr. Ernest Papanek, the school's psychologist and director. After two years he was released. Unfortunately, two years could not erase or alter what he had experienced during the previous eleven years, and within weeks he was selling marijuana and stealing. In one incident he was wounded in the stomach, and within the year was sent to a reformatory, Warwick School, where he eventually served two additional terms. Brown, who dealt in drugs and con games, never became an addict. As he grew older he realized that his life would never improve unless he left the ghetto. He resumed his education and worked at various jobs. He received his high school diploma in 1957 and, two years later, moved to Washington, D.C., and entered Howard University, where he studied business and government. During Brown's first year there, Dr. Papanek, who had been approached by the editors of *Dissent* to write an article on Harlem, asked Brown to write it instead. The article was eventually published and stirred the emotions of an editor at Macmillan, who offered Brown a contract for a book. In 1963 Brown completed a 1,537-page manuscript. When the book was published two years later critics praised Brown for his ability to capture on paper a pilgrimage from boyhood in an environment society condemned to manhood in an environment of which society approved. The book was both a critical and commercial success, and undeniably brought attention to civil rights issues.

Manchild in the Promised Land illustrated Brown's realistic writing. He captured the environment in dialogue that was undeniably honest, and his candid description of his mother was well written.

Brown graduated from Howard University in 1965, then briefly attended law school at Stanford University and later Rutgers University. His second book, *The Children of Ham,* was published in 1976. It concerned a group of Harlem teenagers who transformed not only abandoned apartments, where they could live free of heroin, but their own lives. The group's efforts to improve themselves prompted others to do the same.

WORKS: *Manchild in the Promised Land* (1965); *The Children of Ham* (1976).

NOTE

1. Claude Brown, *Manchild in the Promised Land* (New York: Macmillan, 1965), p. 7.

C.D.B. Bryan
(1936–)

Born to Katharine and Joseph Bryan III, a writer, on April 22, 1936, in New York City, C.D.B. Bryan graduated from Yale University in 1958, then served in the U.S. Army until 1962. Before his release he had several short stories published in the *New Yorker,* and wrote and edited *Monocle,* a magazine of political satire, which had a relatively brief life in the early 1960s.

His first novel, *P. S. Wilkinson,* contained autobiographical details and was published in 1965. In it a white Anglo-Saxon Protestant youth cheated in school, graduated from Yale, and served in Korea. In short, it was about growing up in the 1950s. It won the Harper Prize Novel award later that year.

Bryan was a writer-in-residence at Colorado State University and a visiting lecturer at the University of Iowa's Writers Workshop before his second novel, *The Great Dethriffe,* was published in 1970. The book's main character, George Dethriffe, was a Gatsby who got more than he desired. The book received mixed reviews primarily because it was not as good as Fitzgerald's *The Great Gatsby,* on which it was modeled.

Bryan was not interested in writing another novel. Like millions of other Americans, he watched news reports about the war in Vietnam. When Vance Bourjaily told him about Peg Mullen, who ran a newspaper advertisement against the war after losing a son in Vietnam, Bryan approached William Shawn, the editor of the *New Yorker,* about writing an article for the magazine. Shawn thought the article would be interesting to readers. When Bryan met the Mullens and listened to their story he realized that he had enough material for a series. The series appeared in the *New Yorker,* then in book form as *Friendly Fire* in 1976. A disturbing book, it depicted the tragic death of Michael Mullen and its effects on his midwestern American parents.

Ronald Weber called it "a book about loss, the loss of life and the loss of faith—faith in neighbors, in country, in the essential decency and honesty of national leaders. At its deepest level it is a book about the greatest casualty of the war—the loss of truth."[1]

Mullen, the son of Peg and Gene Mullen, Iowa farmers, was drafted and sent to Vietnam in 1969, where he was killed by U.S. artillery shelling six months later. The Mullens, who had been given only speculative information about their son's death, became angry when his body was finally returned. Although the information provided by military officials had led them to expect that the body would be in pieces, it was intact.

Bryan, through dramatic and descriptive scenes, graphically depicted the Mullen's actions, especially Peg's. From their refusal to have a military funeral for Michael to their efforts to gather information from his comrades, the reader learned what the country's leaders believed: that such atrocities must be covered up or the public would oppose the war.

The Mullens and others like them eventually demonstrated and did indeed voice their opinions. However, Bryan, who thoroughly investigated how Michael was killed, concluded that the military had not tried to cover up the incident. By questioning officers and enlisted men alike, soldiers who had been with Michael, Bryan presented the apparent truth: Michael had been killed accidentally. The Mullens refused to believe Bryan's findings and indeed, considered him to be part of the conspiracy to hide the truth.

Bryan returned to teaching as a visiting or adjunct professor at several universities over the next few years and contributed articles to the *New York Times Magazine* and the *New York Times Book Review* before publishing his next book. Titled *The National Air and Space Museum,* the book was a photographic history of a museum that is extremely popular with the public.

His interest in the novel resurfaced in 1982, when *Beautiful Women; Ugly Scenes* was published. A novel about relationships, its main character, a filmmaker, acknowledged that he had been at war with women for most of his life. Yet his relationship with a French woman named Odette grew and matured into a meaningful one. Some critics believed that because of the novel's realism it had to be partly autobiographical.

In 1987 Bryan published *The National Geographic Society: 100 Years of Adventure and Discovery.* Like his book about the space museum, it contained photographs as well as a well-written historical essay.

Bryan returned to teaching part time at several universities and contributed articles to *Harper's,* the *Saturday Review,* and *Esquire.* He attended a five-day conference on UFO abductions held at the Massachusetts Institute of Technology, then interviewed various supposed abductees. His book *Close Encounters of the Fourth Kind: Alien Abduction, UFOs, and the Conference at M.I.T.* (1995) was based on the conference and interviews. Abductees explained how they were floated aboard alien spacecraft by gray, four-foot-tall beings with large heads. The book was well written, but Bryan remained undecided as to whether the abductions actually occurred.

WORK: *Friendly Fire* (1976).

NOTE

1. Ronald Weber, "Art-Journalism Revisited," *South Atlantic Quarterly,* Summer 1979, p. 283.

Vincent T. Bugliosi
(1934–   )

Born in Hibbing, Minnesota, on August 18, 1934, Vincent Bugliosi attended the University of Miami, from which he graduated in 1956, and later the University of California, Los Angeles, from which he received a law degree in 1964.

From 1964 until 1972 he worked as a deputy district attorney for the city of Los Angeles. In this capacity, he prosecuted five members of the Manson Family in connection with the 1969 Tate–La Bianca murders, and wrote a disturbing piece of literary journalism entitled *Helter Skelter: The True Story of the Manson Murders,* which traced the murders, the bungled police investigation, and the trial.

According to William Crawford Woods, Charles Manson, the undisputed leader of the Family, was a demon who had been inspired by the Beatles' song "Helter Skelter," which was on the group's "White" album. Woods wrote:

As family members testified at the trial, he had worked out with scholarly precision correlations between his murderous doctrine and virtually every line of every lyric; more than that he had searched beyond his origins in the Beatles to *their* origins in the *Book of Revelations,* where in the ninth chapter he found the "four angels" with "faces as the faces of men" but "hair as the hair of women"; even mention of their electric guitars ("breastplates of fire") and much else besides.[1]

The rationale behind the crimes was to leave clues that would implicate underground black groups; consequently, members of these organizations would be charged and a confrontation between whites and blacks would ensue. Manson believed that the blacks would be victorious and that he would become their leader.

Bugliosi's book was unarguably a very insightful study of criminal behavior as well as a penetrating courtroom drama. To provide realism, Bugliosi included transcripts from the trial. In addition, the book contained vivid description and realistic—if not actual—dialogue, two elements found in fiction and often used by literary journalists. Many critics praised the book for its analysis of one of the worst crimes of the century.

In addition to practicing law, Bugliosi taught courses in criminal law at the Beverly Hills School of Law from 1968 to 1974, the year *Helter Skelter* was published. In 1972, he opened a law office with another attorney in Beverly Hills, where he represented several individuals accused of criminal activity.

In 1978 he published *Till Death Us Do Part: A True Murder Mystery.* Another piece of literary journalism, it concerned two murders committed two years apart, the perpetrators involved, and the ultimate trial. Bugliosi was the assistant district attorney who tried the case. Through dialogue, description, and transcripts of the trial, the reader learned how and why the murders occurred. Sandra Stockton, a married woman, met Alan Palliko, an insurance adjuster who had tried to kill his first wife three times for her insurance policy. Palliko and Stockton had her husband killed in 1966 for his insurance policy. Then Palliko married another woman in 1968; she was murdered soon thereafter. Although the evidence linking the victims with their murderers was weak, Bugliosi prevailed and the jury convicted both.

Bugliosi wrote another piece of literary journalism in 1991, *And the Sea Will Tell.* Like his previous books, it also concerned murder and the ultimate trial.

WORKS: *Helter Skelter: The True Story of the Manson Murders* (1974); *Till Death Us Do Part: A True Murder Mystery* (1978); *And the Sea Will Tell* (1991).
NOTE

1. William Crawford Woods, ''Demon in the Counterculture,'' *New Republic,* January 4, 1975, p. 25.

Paul Bullock
(1924–1986)

Born on November 6, 1924, in Pasadena, California, Paul Bullock served in the U.S. Army from 1943 to 1946. He was educated at Occidental College in Los Angeles, where he earned his bachelor's and master's degrees in 1948 and 1949, respectively. In 1949 he pursued postgraduate study at the University of California, Los Angeles, and started teaching economics at El Camino College.

In 1950 Bullock became an instructor of economics at Occidental College, then was hired as a wage analyst by the Wage Stabilization Board of the Los Angeles Region in 1951. In 1953 he was offered a position as a research economist at the Institute of Industrial Relations, located on the campus of the University of California, Los Angeles. This position lasted until 1985.

Bullock was responsible for several studies of minorities and employment while employed at the institute, including *Standards of Wage Determination* and *Merit Employment,* published in 1960, and *Equal Opportunity in Employment* and *Hard-Core Unemployment and Poverty in Los Angeles,* published in 1965. The latter was written with Fred Schmidt and Robert Singleton. He also edited and/or contributed to other studies published by the institute. Among them were *Full Employment Policy for America,* published in 1974; *Goals for Full Employment,* published in 1976; *Creative Careers: Minorities in the Arts,* published in 1977; *Directory of Organizations in Greater Los Angeles,* published in 1979; *CETA at the Crossroads: Employment Policy and Politics,* published in 1981; and *Building California: The Story of the Carpenter's Union,* published in 1982.

Although the studies noted above were scholarly and often filled with statistics, charts, and graphs, his articles were written for a much larger audience. In them Bullock analyzed the predicament of minorities, especially African Americans. These articles were published in the *New Republic,* the *Journal of Negro Education,* and the *Progressive,* to mention three. Bullock contributed to the book *Poverty: Views from the Left* (1968), edited by Irving Howe and Jeremy Larner. *Watts: The Aftermath, by the People of Watts* prompted some who analyzed new journalism and its practitioners, particularly Nicolaus Mills, to consider Bullock a possible contender. The book was published in 1969, just after the riot occurred. Bullock allowed residents of Watts to explain their version of what happened. His background in educational as well as employment problems of minorities enabled him to acknowledge the tensions between blacks and whites. With very little editorializing, Bullock provided another perspective about African Americans.

Bullock served as a consultant to the McCone Commission in 1965 and to the Kerner Commission in 1967. He also served as chairman of the New Careers Task Force of the Los Angeles County Commission on Delinquency and Crime from 1968 to 1970. Bullock died on February 14, 1986, in Redondo Beach, California.

WORK: *Watts: The Aftermath, by the People of Watts* (1969).

C

Abraham Cahan
(1860–1951)

Abraham Cahan was born in Podberezy, a small village near Vilna, a city with a large Jewish population. Napoleon had called Vilna the "Jerusalem of Lithuania." Although his father, a teacher of Hebrew, had wanted his son to have a secular education, it was too costly. Cahan studied the Talmud as well as the Russian language, and was admitted to the Jewish Teachers' Institute of Vilna when he was 17.

Before he graduated in 1881, he had become a devout socialist, in part because of the unstable conditions in Russia. Revolution was in the air, and when the czar was assassinated in 1881, Cahan was teaching at a school in Velizh, where his involvement in socialist activities became suspect. Cahan, like other revolutionaries, had anticipated a peasant uprising. However, an uprising never occurred. Instead, those who had been involved in the assassination were apprehended, tried, and executed.

Cahan saw friends arrested; realizing that he, too, was in danger, he thought of fleeing to Switzerland, but joined other immigrants seeking asylum in the United States. He reached New York in June 1882.

Considering himself an exiled radical Russian socialist rather than a Jewish immigrant, Cahan nonetheless settled on the Lower East Side of Manhattan, where many other Jewish immigrants lived. He worked at several jobs and grew extremely interested in the socialist union movement. He became a member of the Propaganda Verein, for which he gave speeches. He learned some English in a very short time and began to tutor other immigrants. To learn even more he sat in on classes at the Chrystie Street School. By 1883 he had learned enough

English to have an article about the czarist autocracy accepted by the *New York World.* An evening school hired him to teach English to other immigrants. This allowed him to write and continue working in the labor movement. In 1884, for instance, he helped organize the first Jewish labor union.

In 1886 he edited *Neie Zeit* (New Era), a newspaper published primarily to promote socialist doctrine. Although the paper had a short life, it helped establish Cahan's reputation as an advocate for labor as well as a writer. Four years later he was named editor of *Arbeiter Zeitung,* a Yiddish-language newspaper not unlike *Neie Zeit.* Two years later, he was also editing *Die Zukunft,* a Yiddish periodical published for members of the Socialist Workers party. For the former, Cahan used a number of pseudonyms, sometimes writing an entire issue. He gained acclaim as the folksy "Proletarian Preacher" from Proletarishuk. His lengthy moral fable, "Raphael Naarizoch," appeared in the paper in 1894. Cahan enjoyed writing about the sensational and the sublime, and he realized that he could express himself in fiction. When friction developed in the labor movement as a result of personality clashes, Cahan left his editing positions and devoted his time to writing fiction.

Cahan translated and revised a story that had appeared in *Arbeiter Zeitung,* then submitted it to a literary magazine, which published it in 1895. William Dean Howells saw Cahan's story and helped find a publisher for his first novel, *Yekl: A Tale of the New York Ghetto.* Cahan described immigrant life in America in this and other novels, including his masterpiece, *The Rise of David Levinsky* (1917), based on the four-part series "The Autobiography of an American Jew" which had appeared in *McClure's.*

Although Cahan edited the first issue of the *Jewish Daily Forward,* which appeared on April 22, 1897, he grew disgruntled over employee dissension about the paper's content and subsequently resigned. Cahan also lost his job as an English teacher because of his socialist activities. However, Lincoln Steffens, the city editor of the *New York Commercial Advertiser,* offered him a job as a police reporter. Although hesitant, Cahan accepted the job and contributed tragedies as well as penetrating dramas about the Jewish inhabitants of the Lower East Side. When Steffens moved to *McClure's* in 1901, Cahan soon realized that the paper was not the same. His first collection of short stories, *The Imported Bridegroom and Other Stories of the New York Ghetto,* had appeared in 1898, and he considered writing fiction full time again. In 1902 he returned to the *Forward.* The Jewish paper was not faring well. Indeed, it contained only six pages. Cahan was asked to revitalize it, so he added features about everyday life. Instead of espousing socialist dogma, Cahan wrote stories. Some readers, particularly the intelligentsia, did not like the changes, and even though the paper's circulation increased, Cahan was forced to resign.

In 1903 Jews were massacred in Kishinev, Ukraine. Cahan, like other Jewish immigrants, was shocked. Soon he was asked to return to the *Forward.* He was assured of absolute control. Cahan, much to the dismay of his wife, Anna, whom he had married several years before, accepted the editorship.

For the next four decades, Cahan edited the paper primarily for the common laborer and housewife; as a result, it became the pacesetter of the Yiddish press. Cahan implemented the "Bintel Brief" (Bundle of Letters) section in which readers could discuss whatever they desired. Hundreds of letters on topics important to Jewish immigrants arrived at the newspaper offices each week.

During World War I, Cahan contributed a column on the war even though the paper opposed the war. As a socialist, Cahan found German militarism less objectionable than czarist despotism. The paper argued that the Allies' efforts were necessary—indeed, that the Allies were, in actuality, the lesser of two evils. In 1915 Cahan visited Germany and Austria as a war correspondent; as a result of his coverage, he was charged as a German spy. Two years later, when the United States entered the war, the paper was subject to the Espionage Act and consequently directed to translate war news.

Although the paper's circulation increased, Cahan was harshly criticized when he defended Lenin's communist revolution. In 1923 he recanted his defense when he toured Europe and learned from refugees that Russians had less freedom under the Bolsheviks than under the czars.

Between the world wars, Cahan crossed the Atlantic numerous times. In 1924, for instance, he was present at the opening of Britain's first Labour Parliament. In 1925 he attended the Socialist Congress at Marseilles, then visited Palestine. In 1927 he visited the Soviet Union. In 1929 he returned to Palestine and witnessed Arab rioting there. The paper seemed to move toward the mainstream when it criticized Stalin for his concentration camps and supported Roosevelt's New Deal policies.

However, after World War II the paper's prestige declined. Cahan was growing old, and the Yiddish language was losing its audience. Cahan suffered a stroke in 1946, then died of heart failure in 1951 at age 91.

Cahan's journalism, especially the stories he contributed to the *New York Commercial Advertiser,* contained elements of literary journalism. Moses Rischin pointed out that in Cahan's writings one encountered "a glowing sense of life, sustained in voice, language, nuance, and especially situation—of a tumultuously varied ethnic, religious, and human milieu where people emerging from age-old constraints inhale the alternately liberating and intimidating air of the great American city."[1]

Cahan brought to light the immigrants' plight; however, he did not focus on their poor living conditions or environment just to arouse sympathy. He focused on how they adapted to their new country. In addition to covering what was happening to the United States—specifically, the Spanish-American War—Cahan wrote about incoming immigrants and their initial reactions to America. As Rischin wrote:

Cahan's reports, sketches, and stories abound with the maneuvers of matchmakers, marriage brokers, and matrimonial agents as "thick as huckleberries"; with the stratagems of arranged, proxy, and diploma marriages; with the dilemmas of imported brides, if not the famed Japanese picture brides, and college bridegrooms; with the stresses and strains of unexpected romances, love matches, and intermarriages.[2]

In 1894 Alfred Dreyfus, a French captain of Jewish descent, had been arrested for high treason, then sentenced to Devil's Island, the infamous prison off the coast of French Guiana. In 1899 Dreyfus was granted a second trial after Hubert-Joseph Henry, a colonel, confessed to falsehoods before he committed suicide. Dreyfus was found guilty again and sentenced to 10 years. Within a week, he was pardoned by the president of the Third French Republic. The Dreyfus Affair, like the war with Spain, affected Jews living on the Lower East Side by reinforcing their passion for their new country. It was on their minds as well as their tongues. Cahan wrote about this incident and its effect on inhabitants of the Lower East Side. Through description, he allowed the reader to visualize the characters and their dress. Through dialogue, the reader learned what the characters thought about the affair. And through their choice of words, the reader learned how the characters had adapted to their environment.

WORKS: *New York Commercial Advertiser; Jewish Daily Forward.*

NOTES

1. Moses Rischin, ed., *Grandma Never Lived in America: The New Journalism of Abraham Cahan,* with an introduction by Moses Rischin (Bloomington: Indiana University Press, 1985), p. xxvi.

2. Ibid., p. xxxiv.

Erskine Caldwell
(1903–1987)

Tobacco Road and *God's Little Acre,* which were published in 1932 and 1933 respectively, were read by thousands, criticized and praised by critics, and banned by some. In them Erskine Caldwell portrayed with humor the impoverished conditions of rural living.

Caldwell, whose father was a Presbyterian minister and whose mother was a teacher, was born on December 17, 1903, in Georgia. Before he entered high school, he had lived in numerous towns in several southern states. He entered Erskine College in 1920, but a year later he transferred to the University of Virginia. His desire to write—a desire he had fulfilled by writing for several newspapers while still in high school—led him to return to newspapering in 1925. He wrote obituaries for the *Atlanta Journal* and book reviews for the *Charlotte Observer.* He also wrote fiction, but for years received only rejections from publishers. Then, in 1929, his luck changed; one story was accepted. Within a few months several other stories had been accepted, and Caldwell's career as a writer was secure.

In the 1930s he published more of his work, including novels and volumes of nonfiction. *Some American People* contained several exposés and about two dozen sketches. Some of the sketches were straight reportage, some were fiction, and some were a combination of the two.

The documentary *You Have Seen Their Faces,* which combined Margaret Bourke-White's photography with Caldwell's descriptive editorial accounts of the South, appeared in 1937. One of many documentaries of the 1930s and 1940s, *You Have Seen Their Faces* was a powerful, eye-opening treatise on the poor who tried to make a living from the weak, underdeveloped agricultural system. This documentary was followed by *North of the Danube* (1939), in which he and Bourke-White explored Czechoslovakia. Scott MacDonald said of it:

In what was something of a departure for him, Caldwell used rather highly suggestive language to present what would now be called a nonfiction novel. In eight sketches Caldwell and Bourke-White travel from eastern to western provinces; their journey is both across the countryside and, implicitly, through history, which in 1938 was bringing the end of the Czechoslovakian republic and increasingly heavy Nazi influence.[1]

North of the Danube illustrated Caldwell's ability to use literary devices to depict incidents. For instance, he described a despicable scene in which a German couple insulted and assaulted an Austrian woman aboard a train. The scene was powerful for several reasons. First, through his description of the characters, their manners, and their speech, the reader was able to visualize them. Second, he described the actions and reactions not only of the main characters but of others on the train. Third, he used scene-by-scene construction to present the incidents in the story. Fourth, he effectively used accurate, forceful dialogue to show the Germans' attitude toward Jews, even though the Austrian was not Jewish.

Another collaborative effort, *Russia at War* (1942), was not as effective as his previous volumes. The journey was more emphatically depicted in Caldwell's nonfiction novel, *All-Out on the Road to Smolensk,* which was published the same year.

When Caldwell and Bourke-White's collaborative efforts ceased in the early 1940s, he returned to writing fiction. Most of his short stories and novels were set in the South. He also wrote occasional volumes of nonfiction such as *In Search of Bisco* and *Deep South,* but none were comparable to his earlier work. Caldwell died in 1987.

WORKS: *Some American People* (1935); *You Have Seen Their Faces* (1937); *North of the Danube* (1939); *Russia at War* (1942); *All-Out on the Road to Smolensk* (1942).
NOTE
1. Scott MacDonald, ''Erskine Caldwell,'' *American Novelists, 1910–1945,* edited by James J. Martine (Detroit: Gale Research, 1981), Vol. 9, p. 128.

Jimmy Cannon
(1909–1963)

Jimmy Cannon was born in New York City in 1909 and grew up in Greenwich Village. A tough youth, he attended public schools until he obtained a position as a copy boy with the *New York Daily News.* Eventually he became a reporter and covered murder trials, wars, and big league sports. He moved from the *Daily News* to the *World-Telegram* (a newspaper he returned to more than once), the *PM,* and in 1946 the *New York Post,* for which he wrote a syndicated sports column. His sports writing, like that of his friend Damon Runyon, captured more than the sport itself. Through description and dialogue, Cannon conveyed what occurred during and after the event. Before he died in 1963 he had moved his column to the *Journal-American.* His sports stories were collected and published under the titles *Nobody Asked Me* and *Who Struck John?*

"Lethal Lightning," which appeared in the *New York Post* in 1946, concerned the Louis-Conn championship match. Cannon described the crowd, conversation between the boxers while they exchanged blows, the locker room, and the awful truth about the sport of boxing: "the dark and frightened insides of a boxer who would much rather be doing something else at that particular time."[1] The story was an example of literary journalism, containing scene-by-scene construction, the use of dialogue, and third-person point of view. Another element was also evident: the reporter included himself in the story.

WORKS: *Nobody Asked Me* (1950); *Who Struck John?* (1956).
NOTE
   1. Irving T. Marsh and Edward Ehre, eds., *Best of the Best Sports Stories* (New York: E. P. Dutton, 1964), p. 58.

Truman Capote
(1924–1984)

Truman Capote was born to Julian and Nina Persons of New Orleans on September 30, 1924. When he was four his parents divorced, and he was reared by relatives until he was 11. When his mother married Joseph Garcia Capote, a businessman from the East, Truman attended schools in New York City. Although educated at the Trinity School and St. John's Academy, he did not excel at either. His interest in writing did not become evident to his teachers until he attended Greenwich High School in Connecticut. There his interest grew, and when he completed his education at 17 he returned to New Orleans to write a novel and short stories.

In 1945 *Story* magazine accepted one of his short stories. Capote, whose insecurity had been a burden throughout childhood and adolescence, gained confidence. He returned to New York City and became an errand boy for the *New Yorker.* Later that year *Mademoiselle* purchased his short story "Miriam," which won an O. Henry Memorial Award in 1946. Capote signed a book contract with Random House, left the *New Yorker,* and moved to Alabama to write a novel, *Other Voices, Other Rooms,* which was published three years later. Capote was immediately recognized by critics as a major writer. His writing flourished, and his short stories appeared in the *New Yorker, Harper's,* the *Atlantic,* and other periodicals. In 1949 a collection of his stories, one of which had received a second O. Henry Memorial Award, appeared under the title *A Tree of Night.*

Capote, in addition to writing fiction, experimented with colorful essays on various cities in which he had lived. His talent as an insightful observer was candidly revealed when the essays were eventually collected and published as *Local Color* in 1950.

His second novel, *The Grass Harp* (1951), was rewritten as a play in 1952. Several critics severely questioned Capote's talents as a dramatist. Nonetheless, he persevered and wrote a second play, *House of Flowers,* which appeared on Broadway during the 1954–1955 season. Then he wrote for the screen. *Beat the Devil* (1954), which starred Humphrey Bogart, was unsuccessful. Even John Huston could not save it from the critics.

According to Capote, these years were his experimental cycle. As he wrote in *Music for Chameleons:*

I experimented with almost every aspect of writing, attempting to conquer a variety of techniques, to achieve a technical virtuosity as strong and flexible as a fisherman's net. Of course, I failed in several of the areas I invaded, but it is true that one learns more from a failure than one does from a success. I know I did, and later I was able to apply what I had learned to great advantage.[1]

Capote experimented further. He combined the devices of fiction with actual events when he wrote *The Muses Are Heard.* This exercise ignited the spark for what was to become *In Cold Blood.* He wrote:

For several years I had been increasingly drawn toward journalism as an art form in itself. I had two reasons. First, it didn't seem to me that anything truly innovative had occurred in prose writing, or in writing generally, since the 1920s; second, journalism as art was almost virgin terrain, for the simple reason that very few literary artists ever wrote narrative journalism, and when they did, it took the form of travel essays or autobiography. *The Muses Are Heard* had set me to thinking on different lines altogether: I wanted to produce a journalistic novel, something on a large scale that would have the credibility of fact, the immediacy of film, the depth and freedom of prose, and the precision of poetry.[2]

While perfecting his technique in aural memory, a technique he had used to some degree for *Muses,* Capote continued to contribute short stories to magazines. *Breakfast at Tiffany's,* a collection of several stories and a novella, appeared in 1958 to mixed reviews. In 1959 he went to Kansas to speak to people who had known Herbert Clutter, his wife, son, and daughter, who had been murdered at their farm. When Richard Hickock and Perry Smith were arrested for the murders, Capote talked with them also. Instead of taking notes during their many conversations, however, he used the aural memory technique and recorded the conversations later. He devoted six years to *In Cold Blood,* the nonfiction novel that was destined to catapult him into literary history. In 1965 the first installment appeared in the *New Yorker.* At first, Capote was hailed as a writer of distinction, one who had devised a new literary technique to tell, graphically and truthfully, a story as old as man. However, some claimed that it was not a new art form, while others "questioned the accuracy of the scenes Capote had constructed."[3]

Not all of the criticism was negative. Indeed, *In Cold Blood,* which was published in 1966, was praised for its objectivity, its dialogue, its interior monologue, and its insight into the criminal element. The book was a phenomenal best-seller; several million copies were sold in the United States alone.

In one section of the book, Capote depicted in the murderers' own words a few of the disturbingly frightful events that occurred within the Clutter home. Through dialogue, Capote allowed the characters to explain their actions. Through this technique, the reader learned of the events from one of the accused, and subsequently the reasons for those events. Though Perry essentially confessed to murder, the reader learned that he was nonetheless concerned about each victim. For example, instead of forcing Mr. Clutter to lie down on the cold basement floor, he provided a mattress box. Irony, though seldom found in traditional objective journalism, was used effectively by Capote to provide another perspective on Perry's behavior.

Capote's study, though similar to Gerald Frank's *The Boston Strangler* in some respects, was more profound, especially with respect to the murderers' psyches; indeed, Capote's revelations about the characters' strange behavior were unquestionably informative and of interest not only to the lay reader, but to criminologists, sociologists, psychologists, historians, and legislators.

The success of the book encouraged several production companies to adapt some of Capote's short stories for television and his nonfiction novel for theater. Capote also revised his play *House of Flowers,* but the 1968 Broadway production was severely criticized. Capote returned to short stories, essays, and reportage.

In the mid-1970s he published several chapters of a novel entitled *Answered Prayers* in *Esquire,* and in 1980 a collection of short stories and a nonfiction novella appeared under the title *Music for Chameleons.* Capote died in 1984.

WORKS: *Local Color* (1950); *The Muses Are Heard* (1956); *In Cold Blood* (1966); *Music for Chameleons* (1980).

NOTES

1. Truman Capote, *Music for Chameleons* (New York: Random House, 1980), p. xiii.

2. Ibid., pp. xiii–xiv.

3. Everette E. Dennis and William L. Rivers, *Other Voices: The New Journalism in America* (San Francisco: Canfield Press, 1974), p. 35.

Bob Casey
(1890–1962)

Bob Casey, a journalist who worked for the *Chicago Daily News,* was born in Beresford, South Dakota, in 1890. Attending the Armour Institute of Technology (Illinois Institute of Technology) in Chicago and St. Mary College in Kansas, he was not particularly interested in journalism until he sold a short story to *Adventure* magazine. Immediately he obtained a position editing sports on the Des Moines *Register and Leader,* then spent two years on the Houston *Post.* Eventually he got a job with the *Inter-Ocean* of Chicago, where he remained until its demise. He worked for the *Chicago Evening Journal* as automotive editor, then moved to the *Chicago Evening American* until the United States entered World War I.

Casey enlisted in the army and before the war was over had become somewhat of a hero, receiving three citations for bravery under fire and the Silver Star Medal. When he was released he returned to the *Chicago Evening American.* He moved to the city's *Daily News* in 1920, where he became one of the paper's best reporters. His feature stories appeared on the front page. Unusually gifted at elaborating on the least important details, Casey could increase a story's importance by his untiring style. Whether covering animals or gangsters, his stories mirrored his attitude toward the subject. Animal stories would have a human interest quality; gangster stories, on the other hand, would belittle the subjects, not make heroes of them.

In addition to his features, Casey wrote several travel books in which he included photographs as well as tales and legends. In 1931 he published *Easter Island,* which dealt with the island's mysterious past and present. He also wrote adventure and detective novels and stories.

In 1933 he covered the revolution in Cuba for the *Daily News,* and when World War II began he flew to France, where he wrote dispatches filled with fact and fiction. After France fell to the German Army, he flew to London, where he bypassed censors in order to report on the city's destruction. In 1940 he sailed to Africa, where he filed dispatches on battle after battle until he was pushed by Egyptians from a train. His leg crushed, he returned to Chicago. *I Can't Forget,* a book of his war experiences, was immediately published.

When Pearl Harbor was bombed, Casey went to Hawaii. He reported on numerous naval battles in the Pacific, including Midway. His eyewitness accounts were startling, and when he returned to Chicago in 1942 his book *Torpedo Junction* was ready for publication.

His books on World War II were perhaps his best. Not only were battle scenes accurately and descriptively depicted, but everyday conversations and minute details of soldiers' lives added realism.

In 1943, with the aid of the United States Navy, Casey gathered information on submarines and wrote *Battle Below: The War of the Submarines,* which was suppressed by the navy until 1945. The book's style was simple and direct. The use of direct quotations gave it authenticity. That same year he wrote *Such Interesting People,* which concerned his humorous experiences as a reporter. He then returned to London to report on the war.

When the war ended he returned to Chicago and wrote more books, including *This Is Where I Came In, More Interesting People,* and *Chicago Medium Rare.* He died in 1962.

WORKS: *I Can't Forget* (1941); *Torpedo Junction* (1942); *Battle Below: The War of the Submarines* (1945); *Such Interesting People* (1945); *This Is Where I Came In* (1945); *More Interesting People* (1947); *Chicago Medium Rare* (1952).

Robert Christgau
(1942–)

Robert Christgau, senior editor of the *Village Voice,* was born in New York City in 1942 and graduated from Dartmouth College in 1962. In 1969 he contributed a column, "Rock & Roll &," to the *Village Voice,* which he produced until he joined *Newsday* three years later.

Christgau, a critic who reviewed not only music but the artists and the individual characteristics that enhanced their music, returned to the *Village Voice* in 1974, a year after his colorful book *Any Old Way You Choose It: Rock and Other Pop Music, 1967–1973* appeared. It was a collection of witty and sometimes acerbic essays and columns about rock and roll's place in society originally written for *Newsday* and other publications.

He wrote the column "Consumer Guide" for the *Voice,* and contributed features on music and musical personalities. He also wrote a "Consumer Guide" column for *Creem,* a popular music magazine, and a "Secular Music" column for *Esquire.* He reviewed films for other periodicals.

As he wrote in his 1981 guide, *Christgau's Rock Guide: Rock Albums of the Seventies:*

When I became *Esquire*'s "secular music" columnist in early 1967, I didn't know I'd found a vocation—I was just staking my journalistic claim to a subject I'd been passionately analytic about since Alan Freed hit New York in 1954. . . . When the column dried up two years later, I quickly hustled down to *The Village Voice,* where I was allotted one 2500-word piece per month, a deal that quartered my rock-related income as it tripled my workload. And still I craved more.[1]

Christgau, unlike most critics who reviewed popular music, listened to albums that were seldom played on the air and, as a result, created the "Consumer Guide," which provided prospective buyers with ratings of albums. As he put it, "I conceived the CG as complementing my monthly essay. It was criticism with an immediate, undeniable practical function—criticism in a pop form, compact and digestible.''[2] His guide was a compilation of new as well as old commentary and ratings of several hundred recordings from the 1950s, 1960s, and 1970s.

Christgau's collection of reviews from the *Village Voice* was published in 1990. Titled *Christgau's Record Guide: Rock Albums of the '80's*, it contained reviews of some 2,500 albums. Christgau also included introductory essays about trends and developments in music during the 1980s. *Christgau's Record Guide: The '80s*, which also rated recordings, was published in 1991.

WORKS: *Christgau's Record Guide: Rock Albums of the Seventies* (1981); *Christgau's Record Guide: Rock Albums of the '80's* (1990); *Christgau's Record Guide: The '80s* (1991).

NOTES

1. Robert Christgau, *Christgau's Record Guide: Rock Albums of the Seventies* (New York: Ticknor and Fields, 1981), p. 3.

2. Ibid., p. 4.

Irvin S. Cobb
(1876–1944)

What Damon Runyon would do later, Irvin S. Cobb, who was born in Paducah, Kentucky, in 1876, did years before. Cobb, a newspaperman, author, lecturer, speaker, radio personality, screenwriter, and actor, attended William A. Cade's Academy in Kentucky until he was 16 years of age. Forced to leave school to support his family, he became a reporter for the *Paducah Daily News*. Within three years he was managing editor. In 1898 he wrote for the *Cincinnati Post*, then the *Louisville Evening Post*, where he entertained readers with a satirical column titled "Kentucky Sour Mash." In 1901 he was offered the managing editor's position at the *Paducah Daily Democrat*, which he occupied for three years.

Cobb had learned how to improvise when a story lacked the essentials needed to make it an arresting and entertaining piece. Therefore, it was only natural for him to go to New York City. In 1904, practically out of money, he succeeded in securing a position with the *New York Evening Sun*, for which he covered, in a style original to himself, the 1905 Russo-Japanese peace conference at Portsmouth, New Hampshire. His accounts, published under the title "Making Peace at Portsmouth," described the personalities of the negotiators rather than routine deliberations. The accounts earned Cobb a reputation as well as an offer to join Joseph Pulitzer's *New York Evening* and *Sunday World*.

For six years, he wrote a daily column titled "Through Funny Glasses," a series titled "Hotel Clerk," a humor page for the Sunday color section, and humor for the McClure syndicate. In 1907 he covered at length the trial of Harry K. Thaw, who had been accused of murdering architect Stanford White. His reportage was unique; indeed, it had personality. Through careful description and authentic dialogue, Cobb captured for the reader the environment of the courtroom. What he produced was an example of literary journalism.

Although his newspaper reporting days ended in 1911 when he accepted a position at the *Saturday Evening Post,* he was sent to Europe as a correspondent when World War I began three years later. He reported on the war for a year, then returned to New York City. His personalized accounts were collected and published under the title *Paths of Glory* (1915). When the United States entered the war, he returned to the front and wrote descriptive human interest stories. Two additional books, *Speaking of Prussians* and *The Glory of the Coming,* appeared in 1917 and 1918, respectively.

In addition to amassing war stories, Cobb wrote fiction for various magazines, including the *Saturday Evening Post.* In fact, his first collection, *Back Home,* which introduced perhaps his most famous character from the South, Judge William Pittman Priest, an amalgam of a Paducah judge and Cobb's father, had been published in 1912. Like Mark Twain, Cobb wrote several stories about one character. His judge, for example, also appeared in *J. Poindexter, Colored* (1922), which featured the judge's intellectual servant.

Cobb published several volumes of fiction. He also wrote *Stickfuls* (1923), an account of his early newspaper days. Filled with humorous anecdotes, the book was well received by critics.

Cobb left the *Post* for a similar position at *Cosmopolitan* in 1922. He continued to write for magazines, but the material for his books was haphazardly collected, and consequently his books failed to sell well. In 1929 Cobb suffered severe financial losses in the stock market crash; after that he wrote few stories. In 1932 he resigned from *Cosmopolitan;* radio was calling him, he believed, and he performed on syndicated radio shows that entertained families from coast to coast. He moved to Hollywood in 1934, where he wrote screenplays and worked as an actor until he was hospitalized five years later. His autobiography, *Exit Laughing,* was published in 1941. As his health deteriorated, he realized that Hollywood was not his home; he returned to New York City just a few months before his death in 1944.

WORKS: *Paths of Glory* (1915); *Speaking of Prussians* (1917); *The Glory of the Coming* (1918).

Elizabeth Cochrane
(1867–1922)

Elizabeth Cochrane, known as "Nelly Bly," or Bly, was born in Pennsylvania in 1867. Educated at home by her father until she was 13, she was sent to a boarding school in Indiana, Pennsylvania, where she remained for a year. In 1881 she moved to Pittsburgh, where she responded to an article in the Pittsburgh *Dispatch* titled "What Girls Are Good For." George A. Madden, although he did not publish her letter, enjoyed her direct style and suggested that she contribute an article on girls and life. Immediately she started writing. One article followed another; her article "Divorce," at the suggestion of Madden, appeared under the pseudonym Nelly Bly.

It was the period of "yellow" journalism, and newspapers were furiously competing for extraordinary investigative stories. Using her pseudonym, Nelly investigated practically any business or municipal operation she desired. She investigated factories and wrote indignant articles. She wrote articles about Pittsburgh society, including the theater as well as art. She traveled through the West and Mexico and wrote of her travels.

Upon her return, Madden offered to increase her salary to $15 a week, but she had grown tired of Pittsburgh. She had seen part of the world, and she was determined to see more. She moved to New York City and finally, through trickery, was employed by Joseph Pulitzer's New York World. Pulitzer allowed Nelly to write whatever she wanted in order to prove herself. One of her first efforts involved having herself committed to the insane asylum on Blackwell's Island, which resulted in two of the most sensational and controversial stories of the period:

She told of the cold, the poor food and the cruelty to which the patients were exposed. She found the asylum a "human rat trap, easy to get into, impossible to get out of." She charged the nurses with goading their patients. She saw demented and gray-haired women dragged shrieking to hidden closets, then cries being stifled by force as they were hustled out of sight.[1]

As a result of these stories, Blackwell Island was investigated and subsequently improved. Immediately Nelly's name was known by thousands of readers.

She continued her investigations, exposing political lobbyists such as Edward R. Phelps of Albany, the conditions of city prisons, the mistreatment of invalids, the conditions of old women's homes, the mashers of Central Park, and male and female work relationships.

In 1889 Pulitzer allowed Nelly to race Jules Verne's fictional Phileas Fogg, which ultimately became her greatest feat. Sailing on the Augusta Victoria, she wired her stories and tried to make the journey as interesting as possible. In New York, the World published her stories and added others. Comments on fog, storms, travelers, and food entertained readers every day for months. Nelly wrote of her experiences, including her visit with Jules Verne. She saw London, Boulogne, Brindisi, Port Said, Aden, Colombo. She wrote about the Cunnainon Gardens, the elephants, and the attractions of Kandy. She visited Singapore and Hong Kong, where she encountered a monsoon. She saw Canton, Yokohama, and Tokyo, and sailed to the West Coast. On the West Coast she boarded a special train which brought her to Manhattan, Brooklyn, and finally Jersey City, where crowds had gathered to greet her. Her race was successful; she had completed the trip in 72 days, 6 hours, and 11 minutes.[2]

Having performed a feat with which no one could compete, she returned to the *World* and continued to write exposés, including articles that helped the Salvation Army. In 1895 she married Robert L. Seaman, a wealthy businessman who was 72. They were together for 15 years, until his death in 1910. Nelly had given up journalism and had become somewhat of a recluse. When her husband died, however, and the factory he had owned became bankrupt because of employee embezzlement, Nelly opened another. Unfortunately, it, too, went bankrupt. She had little business sense, but she was unwilling to admit it. After failing a third time, she traveled to Austria to visit friends. She could not face defeat and humiliation or her creditors' charges of fraud.

When she returned she was hired by Arthur Brisbane of the *New York Journal,* for which she reported the execution of Gordon Hamby at Sing Sing. But her article about capital punishment received little attention. Readers, it seemed, had changed. Nelly Bly died of pneumonia at the age of 55.

NOTES

1. Ishbell Ross, *Ladies of the Press: The Story of Women in Journalism by an Insider* (New York: Harper and Brothers, 1936), p. 51.

2. Ibid., pp. 52–56.

Robert Conot
(1929–)

Robert Conot, who was born in 1929, was reared in several southern states, including Alabama, Louisiana, and Mississippi. He served in the U.S. Army in the late 1940s, then entered Stanford University, from which he received his bachelor's degree in 1952. From 1952 to 1960 he worked in the media, first as a newspaper reporter and editor, then as a television scriptwriter.

His first book, *Ministers of Vengeance,* published in 1964, received little attention. When *Rivers of Blood, Years of Darkness* was published three years later, however, Conot's ability as an investigative journalist of considerable merit was immediately recognized by his peers. An in-depth account of the Watts riot of 1965, it depicted the incident that ignited the confrontation not from a journalist's point of view, but from the perspective of the participants. When Marquette Frye, a black youth, was stopped for speeding, he not only failed to produce a driver's license, but failed a sobriety test. His arrest sparked verbal and physical abuse between patrolmen and black bystanders. As Nicolaus Mills noted, Conot undeniably did his homework in investigating the spark that ignited the fire, a fire that spread to other cities months and years later.

To reconstruct the arrest scene on Avalon Boulevard, Conot has gone to the Los Angeles Court District Attorneys' records, court transcripts, interviews with police officers and witnesses to the arrest, and then has woven his information into a drama that moves between what people were thinking and what was actually happening.[1]

Rivers of Blood, Years of Darkness exemplified the force with which Mills wrote. Dialogue mixed with a moving narrative led the reader to the ultimate climax.

Conot, who was a consultant to the National Advisory Commission on Civil Disorders in 1967 and 1968, also wrote *American Odyssey* (1974), a well-researched history of Detroit and its relationship to regional and national trends, and *A Streak of Luck: The Life and Legend of Thomas Alva Edison* (1979), which depicted the inventor's weaknesses candidly and cynically.

WORKS: *Ministers of Vengeance* (1964); *Rivers of Blood, Years of Darkness* (1967); *American Odyssey* (1974).

NOTE

1. Nicolaus Mills, *The New Journalism: A Historical Anthology* (New York: McGraw-Hill, 1974), p. 2.

Frank Conroy
(1936–   )

Frank Conroy expressed his feelings about his environment in the autobiographical novel *Stop-time,* using the elements of literary journalism to depict the mood of the 1950s and 1960s. Conroy was born to Francis Philip and Helga Conroy on January 15, 1936, in New York City, and was educated at Haverford College in the 1950s. His father had been a successful literary agent before he suffered a nervous breakdown and had to spend several years in convalescent homes. He died of cancer when Conroy was 12. Conroy's mother, who had gotten a divorce, married Jean Fouchet of New Orleans.

Although Conroy had contributed to periodicals, including the *New Yorker, New Times,* and *Harper's,* among others, he was not generally recognized as a major writer until his autobiographical novel was published in 1967.

The book was reviewed widely. Most critics found it to be uniquely different; indeed, several suggested that Conroy had created a new genre, part autobiography, part novel. As Thorpe Menn wrote:

He accomplishes, in fact, what many writers attempt in first novels—to show in various details yet always in the same way how each life is unique, different, unusual in its similarity to other lives. None has succeeded better than Conroy in conveying, through a prolonged, comfortable edge-of-sleep feeling, the meaning of adolescent experience.[1]

One learned that Conroy suffered from a serious illness when he was very young. One also learned that he was the yo-yo champion of Ft. Lauderdale when he was 13. Yet Conroy was not typical of those who wrote autobiographies. As Menn pointed out, he just got by—"in school, in jobs, with companions, with his mother and step-father, as a runaway, in discovering sex, and as the only American in a Danish International Folk High School."[2] Although it became evident that Conroy was a loner, he was not like Holden Caulfield. Instead of going to a sanitarium, he went to Haverford College. *Stop-time* illustrated Conroy's use of description and dialogue—two elements found in fiction and literary journalism.

Although Conroy subsequently contributed short stories as well as various forms of journalism to numerous publications, his next book did not appear until 1985. Titled *Midair,* it contained eight short stories, several of which had been published in the *New Yorker.* Conroy, who had taught at several universities, was serving as director of the literature program at the National Endowment for the Arts when the collection was published. Several critics, even though they appreciated the realistic stories, were surprised that he had not written something more substantial.

In 1991 he selected and edited *The Iowa Award: The Best Stories from Twenty Years.* Conroy had become the director of the University of Iowa Writers Workshop several years earlier and, for this book, selected the best story from each of the award-winning collections.

Two years later he wrote *Body and Soul,* a novel about a pianist's rise to glory. Conroy, who enjoyed playing jazz on the piano, had penetrated a world few novelists had explored. However, the novel, even though it was noticed by several reviewers, was not acknowledged by the reading public.

WORK: *Stop-time* (1967).
NOTES
1. Thorpe Menn, "To Be Alive Is All," *Saturday Review,* February 24, 1968, p. 43.
2. Ibid.

Stephen Crane
(1871–1900)

Born to Reverend Jonathan Townley Crane and Mary Peck Crane on November 1, 1871, in Newark, New Jersey, Stephen Crane attended various schools, including the Hudson River Institute, Lafayette College, and Syracuse University. He contributed anonymously to articles his mother published in the *New York Tribune,* the *Philadelphia Press,* the *Detroit Press,* and several Methodist newspapers. He also gathered news for his older brother, who operated a news agency in Asbury Park, New Jersey. Before he left Syracuse in 1890, he had worked as a correspondent for the *New York Tribune,* had written for the school newspaper, and had published a Sullivan County sketch, "A Tent in Agony," in *Cosmopolitan.*[1]

For the next two years he struggled to become a writer in New York City. He contributed three New York City sketches to *Truth,* a humor magazine, wrote occasionally for the *New York Herald* and *Tribune,* and published at his own expense *Maggie: A Girl of the Streets,* his first realistic novel. Using the pseudonym Johnston Smith, Crane gave away some copies, sold only a few, and piled the remaining copies in his room.

Thomas A. Gullason said of the novel:

[*Maggie*] presents the essence of Crane's art and vision, where he flourishes a radically new lifestyle in writing and seeing and feeling. Its avant-garde techniques of impressionism, symbolism, and irony, and its perception of reality signal the spirit of modern American literature found in Crane's disciples of the 1920s—Sherwood Anderson and Ernest Hemingway. It is the first major naturalistic novel in America.[2]

One year later Crane completed his classic, *The Red Badge of Courage,* which portrayed the realities of war. Although Crane had not had any war experience, the novel, first serialized in the *Philadelphia Press* and then published in 1895, was instantly successful.

Crane traveled through the West and wrote for the Bacheller Syndicate in 1895. He used incidents he had witnessed as the basis for such stories as "The Blue Hotel" and "The Bride Comes to Yellow Sky." His publisher, however, demanded more war stories, and in 1896 *The Little Regiment and Other Episodes of the American Civil War* was published.

In order to convince himself that his stories of war mirrored reality, Crane had to observe the various opposing forces of man. In 1896 he set sail for Cuba aboard the *S.S. Commodore,* which contained a contraband cargo of guns and ammunition for General Maximo Gomez. The vessel sank off the Florida coast, and Crane experienced what he later described in "The Open Boat."

Crane met Cora Taylor, who operated a brothel in Florida, and grew to love her. The following year he reported on the Greco-Turkish War from Greece, where he became ill. Taylor was by his side. His reports were published in the *New York Journal,* the *World,* and the *Westminster Gazette.* A year later he was in Cuba reporting on the Spanish-American War for the *World.* He filed literary sketches that not only reported the war but enabled readers to understand battle and what it does to men. Crane used description and realistic dialogue to enhance his reports from Cuba, which contained the elements found in literary journalism. These sketches were collected and published in 1900 under the title *Wounds in the Rain.* Crane, like Twain in *The Innocents Abroad,* had put life on paper.

Tired out, Crane returned to New York City. Because he was young, people could not understand why his health was so poor. Gossip about him being a degenerate eventually forced him to move to England in 1899. He and Taylor entertained guests in their manor, Brede Place, until Crane was almost bankrupt. He died of tuberculosis a year later while en route to Germany. He was 28.

WORKS: *Maggie: A Girl of the Streets* (1893); *The Red Badge of Courage* (1895); *The Little Regiment and Other Episodes of the American Civil War* (1896); *Wounds in the Rain* (1900).

NOTES

1. R. W. Stallman and E. R. Hagemann, eds., *The New York City Sketches of Stephen Crane (and Related Pieces)* (New York: New York University Press, 1966), p. xvi.

2. Thomas A. Gullason, ed., *Maggie: A Girl of the Streets,* by Stephen Crane (New York: W. W. Norton, 1979), p. xi.

D

Robert Daley
(1930–)

Robert Daley was born on May 10, 1930, to Arthur Daley, a newspaper columnist, and Betty Daley, and received his bachelor's degree from Fordham University in 1951. Although he did not begin a career as a reporter upon graduation, he did begin writing in 1953 when he became publicity director for the New York Giants football team, a position he held until he moved to the *New York Times* in 1959. Daley, who served as a foreign correspondent in Europe, wrote his first book in 1960. Titled *The World Beneath the City*, it was an informative document on various problems most readers never considered; gas leaks, poor subway systems, and alligators in sewers, among other things, were indeed beneath the city's streets and away from readers' view. In several books thereafter, he focused on European sports, including the Grand Prix and bullfights. He explored the former in narrative and photography in *The Cruel Sport*, published in 1963, and the latter in *The Swords of Spain*, published in 1966.

When he returned from Europe he left the *Times* to become a novelist. Several of his novels were critically and commercially successful. In 1971, however, he became a deputy police commissioner with the city of New York, a position from which he resigned a year later. The experience served him well. When his *Target Blue: An Insider's View of the N.Y.P.D.* was published in 1973, critics considered it one of the best, most revealing books ever written on police corruption and graft. Daley, who was not interested in a career in muckraking, returned to writing novels and subsequently published *Strong Wine, Red as Blood* (1975), *To Kill a Cop* (1976), and *The Fast One* (1977).

In 1977 he recorded Mel Fisher's search for the sunken galleon *Atocha* in *Treasure.* One year later he wrote *Prince of the City: The Story of a Cop Who Knew Too Much,* an engrossing piece of literary journalism that presented the actual story of undercover police officer Robert Leuci, who had been specially assigned to the Knapp Commission, established to investigate corruption within the New York City Police Department. The subject had been discussed in Peter Maas' *Serpico.* Daley's book was a critical and commercial success.

Daley, who contributed articles as well as photographs to *Life, New York, New York Times Magazine, Newsweek, American Heritage, Saturday Evening Post, Esquire, Reader's Digest, Playboy, Cosmopolitan, Vogue,* and other magazines, wrote another nonfiction book in 1980. *An American Saga: Juan Trippe and His Pan Am Empire,* which was favorably reviewed, was unlike his literary journalism in the sense that it was pure biography and history. His next five books were crime novels: *Year of the Dragon* (1981), *The Dangerous Edge* (1983), *Hands of a Stranger* (1985), *Man with a Gun* (1988), and *A Faint Cold Fear* (1990).

In 1991 he explored France—its people, its culture, the country—in narrative and photography in *Portraits of France.* Daley blended history, travel writing, autobiography, and criticism of food and wine to characterize the country he embraced as his second home. In the style of an old-fashioned reporter, he described arresting scenes and incidents, captured picturesque images, and presented the various riches that made up France. The book was another example of literary journalism.

His 1993 novel *Tainted Evidence,* which focused on a trial, featured a female assistant district attorney named Karen Hening who worked for the city of New York. *Wall of Brass,* a suspense novel about a New York City police commissioner being murdered, followed in 1994.

WORKS: *The World Beneath the City* (1960); *Target Blue: An Insider's View of the N.Y.P.D.* (1973); *Prince of the City: The Story of a Cop Who Knew Too Much* (1978); *An American Saga: Juan Trippe and His Pan Am Empire* (1980); *Portraits of France* (1991).

Sara Davidson
(1943-   )

Sara Davidson was born in Los Angeles in 1943. She received her bachelor's degree from the University of California at Berkeley in 1964 and her master's degree from Columbia University in 1965. She worked as a reporter as well as a film reviewer for the *Boston Globe* from 1965 to 1967 and served as the newspaper's New York correspondent from 1967 to 1969. Davidson, a young, intuitive reporter, covered in fresh prose the alternative ways of life in the late 1960s. From rock groups and the counterculture to radical activists and the Robert Kennedy assassination, her bright, colorful phrases filled the *Globe's* columns.

When she resigned from the newspaper to become a freelance writer, she turned her journalistic talent to similar articles for various periodicals, including *Ms, Harper's, Life, Esquire,* the *Atlantic Monthly, Rolling Stone, Ramparts, New York, McCall's, Nova,* and the *New York Times Magazine.* Some of these articles were based on journals that she had kept while living in Venice, California.

She received attention from critics in 1977 when her fact-based book, *Loose Change: Three Women of the Sixties,* was published. An account of the experiences of three women who had lived together during the tumultuous 1960s, it attempted to trace their lives from the 1960s to the mid-1970s in an effort to record historically the effects of those scarred years and concurrently to present some insight into what happened in individual lives as well as in the nation. Although some critics enjoyed her descriptive passages and praised her perceptive eye for ironic, even bizarre details, they claimed that she had failed to understand the reasons for the social and political turmoil that swept the country. The book was popular nonetheless, and justifiably so, for it presented the period from a unique perspective. The book was also an example of literary journalism.

In 1985 she wrote the novel *Friends of the Opposite Sex.* One year later, she published the controversial but perceptive biography *Rock Hudson: His Story,* which not only described Hudson's life but his sexuality. The book was a bestseller primarily because Hudson died of AIDS.

WORKS: *Loose Change: Three Women of the Sixties* (1977); *Rock Hudson: His Story* (1986).

Richard Harding Davis
(1864–1916)

A journalist, playwright, and author, Richard Harding Davis used some of the techniques of the literary journalist when he reported on the Johnstown flood disaster, the West, the Mediterranean, the Spanish-American War, the Greco-Turkish War, the Boer War, the Russo-Japanese War, and World War I. Davis was born in Philadelphia in 1864 to prominent parents. His father was editor of the Philadelphia *Public Ledger;* his mother was a popular novelist. Davis attended the Episcopal Academy at Swarthmore and Ulrich's Preparatory School at Bethlehem before entering Lehigh University and later Johns Hopkins.

At 22 he was employed by the *Philadelphia Record.* Later he worked for the *Philadelphia Press.* His reporting on the Johnstown flood of 1889 earned him a reputation; consequently, he was offered more money by the *Telegraph.* In 1889 he moved to the *New York Sun.* Davis wrote news stories and features and also contributed articles to *Scribner's Magazine.* His style was simple and direct, and bordered on the sensational or adventurous. In 1890 he left the *Sun* to become managing editor of *Harper's Weekly,* for which he traveled through the West, the Mediterranean, and Europe. He wrote numerous accounts of his exploits, which were later collected in *The West from a Car Window, The Rulers of the Mediterranean, Our English Cousins,* and *About Paris.*

In 1896 he reported on the conflicts in Central America, particularly the hotbed regions surrounding the Canal Zone. His reports appeared in book form under the title *Three Gringos in Venezuela and Central America.*

Concurrently, Davis contributed fiction to newspapers and magazines. In 1890, for instance, he had written "Gallagher" for *Scribner's Magazine.* This title was subsequently used for a collection of short stories that appeared a year later. Readers enjoyed his fiction. "Gallagher" was followed by another interesting character named Van Bibber. In addition to his short stories, Davis wrote several novels which enjoyed a wide audience, followed by several plays. Although some of his plays were successful, his greatest literary contribution was his foreign correspondence work for several New York and London newspapers.

Whenever he covered a war he looked for action that could be described sensationally; in short, it had to be dramatic so that he could write vivid, picturesque scenes easily visualized by the reader. Unfortunately, because of the influence of "yellow" journalism, his stories were often colored and sentimental.

Davis, who had earned $100,000 a year, left his second wife, the musical comedy star Bessie McCoy, almost penniless when he died in 1916.[1]

WORKS: *The West from a Car Window* (1892); *The Rulers of the Mediterranean* (1894); *Our English Cousins* (1894); *About Paris* (1895); *Three Gringos in Venezuela and Central America* (1896).

NOTE

1. Stanley J. Kunitz and Howard Haycraft, eds., *Twentieth Century Authors: A Biographical Dictionary of Modern Literature* (New York: H. W. Wilson, 1942), p. 355.

Daniel Defoe
(1660–1731)

Daniel Defoe was not just one of England's most prolific writers devoted to writing realistic, fact-based stories and to entertaining the public and making enemies by writing political criticism. He was a literary journalist who wrote for the masses. In 1701 his poem "True-Born Englishman," which defended William III, was immediately successful and catapulted him to national prominence. This success was short-lived, however. In 1702 he wrote *The Shortest Way with the Dissenters,* which criticized Dr. Henry Sacheverell, a High Church priest, who failed to notice the subtle humor. Sacheverell had Defoe imprisoned, for the Church had political clout.

Robert Harley, the speaker of the House of Commons, knowing of Defoe's abilities as a writer, had him released in 1703. Harley realized that Defoe's talents could be used to shape public opinion; consequently, in 1704 he helped support the *Review,* a journal Defoe published intermittently until 1714. The journal served Harley's purposes on numerous issues.

England's political atmosphere was intense at the time. Indeed, it was hard to distinguish Tories from Whigs, and in reality each party controlled the House of Commons intermittently from 1679 to 1722. During this period there were 17 elections. Instability was rampant, so much so that in 1695, after years of not being enforced, the Licensing Act, which had been established to regulate printers and what was published, was a law of the past. As clashes between the King and Parliament increased, each realized the significance of printers in terms of their ability to shape public opinion. To license them, each believed, would be politically unsound. In addition, the rise of the two-party system made it difficult to enforce the act, since no particular person or party remained in power long enough to oversee its implementation. Consequently, since there was no effective pre-publication censorship, "an explosion of polemical literature in the form of newspapers, newsletters, journals, pamphlets, broadsides, lampoons, and so forth" resulted.[1]

Defoe, of course, was one of the better writers, and the *Review* was one of the most popular publications. Laura Ann Curtis emphasized:

He was an enthusiastic supporter of the Revolution: of the hereditary Protestant monarchy it prescribed, of the fundamental rights of Parliament and people it recognized, not to be dispensed with by royal prerogative, and of the legal toleration it entailed for Protestant Dissenters. . . . He advocated . . . negotiations for the union of England and Scotland. An outspoken opponent of the theories of divine right and of passive obedience professed by adherents of the Stuart dynasty, a ridiculer of Jacobites (supporters of James II and of his son, the Pretender), Defoe contributed to turning England away from its Stuart past to the present of its revolution settlement.[2]

However, it was his partisanship—his loyalty to Harley—that caused the decline in readers and ultimately the demise of the *Review*. When Harley ousted Godolphin and the Whigs in 1710, Defoe supported him; Defoe was considered by many to be a traitor. After having supported the war with France, he advocated peace; after having regarded France as England's economic rival, he advocated commercial trade. People did not know which side he favored because of his chameleon-like personality.

Defoe supported Harley well. More important, he served England well. He realized that progress would only be made if advocates such as himself raised issues and then persuaded the masses as well as certain political figures to act appropriately on those issues. As an advocate he had no rival. Unfortunately, he brought about his own fall by his own contrariness. Political propaganda replaced logic in his writing, and his credibility as a journalist suffered. As an advocate, however, his political conviction enabled him to present his point of view without having to contemplate the consequences. After all, any journalist who claims to be an advocate must have political convictions to present his side of an issue.

In addition to advocacy reporting, Defoe wrote realistic, fact-based stories such as *Robinson Crusoe,* which was inspired by Alexander Selkirk's unfortunate lengthy stay on the island of Juan Fernandez in 1704, and *Moll Flanders,* which described in intimate detail the lower orders of London society. However, his realistic stories merely introduced him to another form of journalism: the literary or nonfiction novel. Indeed, Defoe amplified his talent in the dramatic account *A Journal of the Plague Year,* which accurately recorded the history of the Great Plague in London. Although Defoe had been five years old at the time of the Great Plague, he made use of what he remembered and what other survivors told him. Unquestionably fiction based on fact, the book was read by many who believed that the author had witnessed countless deaths; ironically, it was written 56 years after the disease ravaged England. Defoe based his book on contemporary accounts of the plague. According to Watson Nicholson:

From these he got not only the facts concerning the origin, symptoms, and treatment of the distemper, but also the effects of the calamity on trade, on the appearance of the town and on the spirits of the people, as well as many illustrative stories. The newspapers of the times furnished him with the weekly Bills of Mortality, the progress of the contagion, weather conditions, movements of the court, proclamations regarding fasts, inhibitions of fairs in various parts of the kingdom, the building of fires in the streets in an attempt to check the spread of the disease, orders and prescriptions of the College of Physicians, the activities of the Mayor and Aldermen, advertisements of the quacks, the lists of charitable contributions, the alarms raised by the comets of 1664, together with the numerous interpretations of their meaning, accounts of other prodigies, stories about victims of the Plague, etc., etc.[3]

Defoe described the horror from the point of view of a citizen who recounted what he saw and heard. His style, simple and direct, added to "the awe-inspiring nature of the catastrophe."[4]

Parts of *A Journal of the Plague Year* contained scene-by-scene construction, the third person point of view, and dialogue—elements found in literary journalism. The reader learned about certain characters, including their economic status and their personality.

Since *A Journal of the Plague Year* is an undeniable historical record of the Great Plague, its importance to historians of the period is unquestionably great. As a piece of literature, the work should be considered by scholars and journalists as a serious document.

Thus, Defoe practiced advocacy journalism as a result of the political and social turmoil that confronted England. Then he turned to literary journalism when his popularity as an advocate started to decline. Defoe died in 1731.

WORKS: "True-Born Englishman" (1701); *The Shortest Way with the Dissenters* (1702); *Robinson Crusoe* (1719); *Moll Flanders* (1722); *A Journal of the Plague Year* (1722).

NOTES

1. Laura Ann Curtis, ed., *The Versatile Defoe* (Totowa, N.J.: Rowman and Littlefield, 1979), p. 4.

2. Ibid., pp. 5–6.

3. Watson Nicholson, *The Historical Sources of Defoe's Journal of the Plague Year* (Boston: Stratford Co., 1919), p. 98.

4. George A. Aitken, ed., *The Tatler* (New York: Hadley and Mathews, 1899), p. ix.

Charles Dickens
(1812–1870)

Charles Dickens was born on February 7, 1812, in Portsmouth, England. His father, John Dickens, was a clerk in the naval pay office. His mother, Elizabeth Barrow Dickens, stayed at home and raised Charles and his brothers and sisters.

Because of his job, John Dickens had to move his family to London in 1814, then to Chatham in 1817, then back to London in 1822. Eventually, the family faced financial misfortune in London, and Charles had to find employment in a blacking warehouse, where he pasted labels on shoe-blacking pots; he was 12. His father was arrested, then incarcerated for debt for three months. When his father was gainfully employed, Charles enrolled at the Wellington House Academy in London, where he learned to write stories suitable for newspapers. He submitted stories about accidents, fires, and police reports to the *British Press,* where his father worked and the editor accepted them for publication.

Dickens left the academy several years later and served as a law clerk. In 1828 he became a freelance reporter; he covered the courts as well as the streets of London. In his spare time, he read works by Oliver Goldsmith, Henry Fielding, Tobias Smollett, Joseph Addison, Samuel Johnson, William Hazlitt, Walter Savage Landor, Leigh Hunt, Charles Lamb, and Thomas De Quincey.

From 1832 to 1834 he worked as a parliamentary reporter for the *Mirror of Parliament,* which had been founded by his uncle John Henry Barrow. Dickens observed Parliament during a very important period. Indeed, the reform movement enlivened Parliament, and the ensuing debates affected Dickens.

In 1832 he also submitted fact-based sketches to the *Monthly Magazine,* which accepted them unconditionally, and later to *Bell's Weekly Magazine* as well as to *Bell's Life in London and Sporting Chronicle.* Published under the pseudonym "Boz," the sketches grew in popularity.

Dickens became a staff writer for the *Morning Chronicle* in 1836; he was assigned to cover the courts and Parliament. The *Chronicle* now published his sketches, and, at the suggestion of the publisher, the first volume of *Sketches by Boz* appeared. The book was an immediate success, and Dickens not only wrote more sketches but added the serial "The Posthumous Papers of the Pickwick Club," which became *The Pickwick Papers.* Within weeks readers knew the true identity of "Boz" and "Pickwick." Thea Holme wrote:

Here was Boz, reflecting a completely new outlook, the outlook of the man in the street; setting down in his *Sketches* all the small events in the everyday life of common persons ...; directing his powers of observation and description upon scenes and characters within the daily scope of any loiterer in London.[1]

These sketches graphically portrayed the ugliness of the crime, poverty, and disease that characterized nineteenth-century London. Concurrently, the sketches revealed the pomposity of the new families of wealth. Boz looked at both worlds and reported what he saw. Holme commented:

But Boz is no objective reporter; the facts he presents are invested with his own reaction to them, and in some cases are lifted by his imagination into tragedy or fantasy.... With a swift stroke of invention he brings to life a whole cast of characters, imagines their relationships one with the other, and sets them before us in a sort of comic ballet.[2]

The Pickwick Papers occasionally depicted fact in the guise of fiction. For instance, in covering a divorce for the *Morning Chronicle,* Dickens learned that Lord Melbourne had been accused of adultery with the wife of the Honorable George Nathan. Dickens used some of the material in the farcical trial of Bardell versus Pickwick. *Sketches by Boz* and *The Pickwick Papers* were examples of literary journalism.

Later in 1836 Dickens left the *Morning Chronicle.* He was hired by Richard Bentley to edit a new monthly journal of humor, fiction, and verses. The first issue of *Bentley's Miscellany* appeared in January 1837. Dickens' *Oliver Twist* was serialized in the journal beginning with the second issue; the novel, which was inspired by the author's disgust with the New Poor Law, was eventually published in three volumes in 1838. Although Dickens enjoyed editing a journal, he disagreed with Bentley over editorial control and resigned in 1839.

One year later his weekly publication, *Master Humphrey's Clock,* which he had arranged with publishers Edward Chapman and William Hall, appeared. The journal contained essays, short stories, and an occasional serialized novel by Dickens. In 1841, however, Dickens discontinued the magazine, even though he continued to publish his novels in monthly installments.

The following year Dickens traveled to America. His letters to friends, at first filled with enthusiasm, then with disillusionment about the United States, appeared in *The Life and Adventures of Martin Chuzzlewit,* which was published monthly from 1842 to 1844. His *American Notes for General Circulation,* which appeared in 1842, was a journalistic account of various American institutions, including asylums, factories, and prisons, and showed his use of literary techniques in his journalism. For instance, Dickens was the observer, and he used scene-by-scene construction as well as the third person. Dickens described the characters, their speech, their physical reactions to questions, and their comments. The dialogue revealed another aspect of the characters.

Two years later Dickens traveled to Italy, then wrote *Pictures from Italy.* The book first appeared in the *Daily News,* of which he was founding editor, in 1846. Again, his descriptions were faithfully realistic.

At this time, Dickens critiqued numerous institutions. He wrote letters to newspapers endorsing a bill introduced by Lord Ashley that, if enacted, would bar women from working in mines. He criticized American publishers who pirated books published in England and other countries. He attacked the High Church for its preposterous rules and customs. He attacked capital punishment.

His tenure as founding editor of the *Daily News* was brief, lasting only 17 issues. In 1850 he contracted with publishers William Bradbury and Frederick Evans to bring out an inexpensive weekly magazine titled *Household Words.* Dickens maintained editorial control and was involved in every aspect of production; he provided the magazine's imaginative editorial philosophy. This was reflected in articles that explained various production processes—from the manufacturing of glass plates to the workings of London's post office. Dickens also serialized novels, including his own *Hard Times.* He contributed articles advocating improvements in housing, education, sanitation, and safety. In short, *Household Words* attempted to inform as well as entertain.

In 1859, however, he severed his relationship with Bradbury and Evans, who had been critical of his extramarital affair with Ellen Ternan and purchased total interest in the magazine just to stop its publication. He started *All the Year Round* the same year. The magazine contained a mix of articles and fiction similar to that found in its predecessor, except for the series of essays about "The Uncommercial Traveler," who wandered through London and described in depth the deplorable conditions as well as the shady characters he saw and met. The essays were written by Dickens and were more literary than polemical. He also serialized *Great Expectations* in the magazine. Dickens published *All the Year Round* until his death in June 1870. His son, Charley, who worked at the magazine, became sole owner by the terms of Dickens' will.

Dickens recorded for history an accurate picture of London in his *Sketches by Boz.* He gave the reader an accurate portrait of the United States in his *American Notes for General Circulation.* Both volumes, because they depicted the milieu and the people, including their dress and speech, are undoubtedly valuable to those interested in learning about London of the 1830s or America of the 1840s.

WORKS: *Sketches by Boz, Illustrative of Every-Day Life and Every-Day People* (1836); *The Posthumous Papers of the Pickwick Club, Edited by "Boz"* (1836–1837); *American Notes for General Circulation* (1842); *Pictures from Italy* (1846).

NOTES

1. Charles Dickens, *Sketches by Boz,* with Introduction by Thea Holme (London: Oxford University Press, 1957), pp. vi–vii.

2. Ibid., pp. viii–ix.

Joan Didion
(1934–)

Joan Didion was born on December 5, 1934, in Sacramento, California, to Frank Reese and Eduene Jerrett Didion. She attended the University of California at Berkeley, where she majored in English literature, and entered *Vogue*'s Prix de

Paris contest. Her essay about architect William Wilson Wurster won first prize, and Didion moved to New York City on her graduation from Berkeley in 1956. She worked at *Vogue* as a promotional copywriter, then as an associate feature editor for almost 10 years. In addition to her contributions to that periodical, she contributed articles and short stories to such magazines as *Harper's Bazaar, Mademoiselle,* the *American Scholar,* and the *National Review.* While in New York Didion met John Gregory Dunne, whom she eventually married, and they contributed columns and articles to the *Saturday Evening Post* and *Esquire.*

Didion published the novels *Run River* in 1963, *Play It as It Lays* in 1970, *A Book of Common Prayer* in 1977, and *Democracy* in 1984. She received considerable praise when her first collection of literary journalism appeared in 1968. *Slouching Towards Bethlehem* took its title from William Butler Yeats' poem "The Second Coming." In the preface, Didion said of the collection's title piece:

"Slouching Towards Bethlehem" . . . was for me both the most imperative of all these pieces to write and the only one that made me despondent after it was printed. It was the first time I had dealt directly and flatly with the evidence of atomization, the proof that things fall apart: I went to San Francisco because I had not been able to work in some months, had been paralyzed by the conviction that writing was an irrelevant act, that the world as I had understood it no longer existed. If I was to work again at all, it would be necessary for me to come to terms with disorder. That was why the piece was important to me.[1]

The article was filled with vignettes of hippiedom, including characters and their varied ideas, and kaleidoscopic scenes. Didion captured their unusual lifestyles; indeed, she brought out the flavor of the culture and questioned its spirit. In the other articles, she presented her ideas and philosophy on life; she penetrated the California lifestyles; she criticized Las Vegas marriages; she wrote of New York, Newport, Hawaii, and Alcatraz; she wrote about John Wayne, Michael Laski, and Howard Hughes; and she explored the San Bernardino Valley and its people.

In 1979 her second collection of literary journalism appeared. *The White Album* was distinctive in that each essay characterized Didion's life—from her breakdown in 1968 to her impressions on societal and political disorders from the late 1960s to the late 1970s. From student strikes, Eldridge Cleaver, and Linda Kasabian (a Charles Manson follower) to the mansions built by Ronald Reagan and J. Paul Getty, Didion used her unique form of literary journalism to characterize each subject. *The White Album* was personal and confessional, and perhaps for that reason some critics did not grasp the message or approve of the literary journalistic style. The essays in her first two collections had originally been published in the *American Scholar, Esquire,* the *Saturday Evening Post, Travel & Leisure, Life,* the *New York Review of Books,* the *New York Times Book Review,* the *Los Angeles Review of Books, New West,* and *Holiday.*

In *Salvador* (1983) Didion chronicled the two weeks she and her husband spent in the war-torn country of El Salvador. The book revealed the horror of senseless and aimless killing in a country that was grappling with progress. Some reviewers criticized Didion for not suggesting solutions to the problems she discussed. Most, however, praised Didion for her candidness. She had written an accurate but disturbing essay about a country in turmoil and informed the reader what two Americans saw and felt.

Four years later she wrote *Miami*, which not only recounted the relationship between the United States and Cuba but examined Washington's seduction and betrayal of Cuban exiles. The seduction took the form of training Cuban exiles so they could invade their country and topple Fidel Castro. The betrayal occurred during the 1961 Bay of Pigs invasion, specifically when President John F. Kennedy broke his promise by not providing air support. Didion compared the rhetoric of the Kennedy and Reagan administrations. Joan Zseleczky said of the book: "*Miami* is . . . proof of the thesis that enough lies from the rich and powerful can cover over anything, no matter how compelling the argument against whatever distortions someone is attempting to promote."[2]

In 1992 Didion published another collection of literary journalism to mixed reviews. The essays in *After Henry* examined the residents of Los Angeles as well as the media's coverage of the 1988 presidential election and a rape in Central Park, among other subjects. They were well written, direct, and easily interpreted.

Sentimental Journeys, another collection of literary journalism, was published a year later. In it Didion explored three media worlds—Washington, D.C., California, and New York City—during the 1980s. She examined the Reagan White House, the social rites of the Hollywood studio system of a bygone era, the 1988 election campaigns, and the Central Park incident about a jogger who was gang-raped. Some reviewers found this collection inferior to her other collections, especially *Slouching Towards Bethlehem.*

WORKS: *Slouching Towards Bethlehem* (1968); *The White Album* (1979); *Salvador* (1983); *Miami* (1987); *After Henry* (1992); *Sentimental Journeys* (1993).

NOTES

1. Joan Didion, *Slouching Towards Bethlehem* (New York: Simon and Schuster, 1968), pp. xi–xii.

2. Joan Zseleczky, "Joan Didion," *Modern American Women Writers,* edited by Elaine Showalter (New York: Charles Scribner's Sons, 1991), p. 95.

John Dos Passos
(1896–1970)

Born in a Chicago hotel on January 14, 1896, John Roderigo Dos Passos (actually John Roderigo Madison at the time of his birth) traveled extensively with his mother, Lucy Madison, a southern woman from Maryland who was not married. His father was John Randolph Dos Passos, a prominent lawyer who worked for a corporation.

Dos Passos attended a private school in England before he returned to the United States in 1907 to attend the Choate School in Connecticut. Dos Passos was an outstanding student. When he was 14, his father's legal wife died, leaving him free to marry Dos Passos' mother, which he did. His father died in 1917.

Dos Passos was accepted at Harvard in 1911; he was 15. He enjoyed Cambridge, even though World War I was looming on the horizon. He made friends, but they were like him in the sense that they paid no attention to what was occurring in Europe; after all, it had nothing to do with them. After he received his bachelor's degree in 1916, he traveled to Spain, a country he found fascinating, to study agriculture. He joined the Norton-Harjes Ambulance Group and sailed to France. Dos Passos drove an ambulance for a year, until he was dishonorably discharged from the American Red Cross in 1918 for writing antiwar statements. During that time, however, he had met Robert Hillyer and Ernest Hemingway.

Dos Passos returned to the United States dismayed by what had happened. His desire to return to Europe was so great that he joined the Medical Corps. He toured France again and, in 1919, was released to attend classes at the Sorbonne. By this time he had completed his first novel, *One Man's Initiation— 1917,* which was based on his experiences in the war. The novel was published in England in 1920, but it did not sell. The same year he finished *Three Soldiers,* another novel about the war. The main character, in actuality based on Dos Passos, embraced the writer's positive opinions and attitudes toward the French. The novel was published in 1921.

For the next several years Dos Passos traveled and wrote, even though he spent much of 1922 in New York. He saw Hemingway again, and got to know F. Scott and Zelda Fitzgerald, Malcolm Cowley, John Peale Bishop, John Howard Lawson, and others who wrote about life in the 1920s, a decade when many writers traveled, especially to Paris, and tried desperately to put on paper the dramatic changes occurring in society. In 1922 his *Rosinante to the Road Again* was published. Considered by many a travel book about Spain, it was a work of literary journalism in the sense that Dos Passos employed devices and techniques found in fiction to dramatically enhance a work of nonfiction. Melvin Landsberg said of it, ''Essays on Spanish literary men are strung on a thread of narrative reflecting Dos Passos' bewitchment with Spanish life.''[1] As Landsberg put it, the reader believed he had been exposed to much more than a few essays.

Telemachus and Lyaeus, two explorers, appeared through the book. These explorers, especially Telemachus, were searching in part for their own identity, although Telemachus' behavior was solemn, while Lyaeus' behavior was carefree. The explorers traveled to the same places Dos Passos and his friend, e.e. cummings, had traveled in 1921. Thus, Dos Passos was relating his experiences as well as those of his friend. The theme of Spanish life versus industrial life ran throughout the book in characters Dos Passos had met but had disguised by slightly changing their names.

The essays concerned novelists Pio Baroja and Blasco Ibanez, poets Antonio Machado and Juan Maragall, the theater in Madrid, and certain incidents in the fight of Giner de los Rios and his followers for academic freedom in Spain. The latter essay, according to Landsberg, "is a comment on infringement of and assaults upon academic freedom in the United States."[2] Telemachus (Dos Passos) attempts to understand himself through his reactions to others as well as through his reactions to the places and events he observes.

Dos Passos revised an early novel and published it in 1923. Titled *Streets of Night,* it, too, was autobiographical in that the main character represented Dos Passos. In 1925 *Manhattan Transfer* appeared. Here, too, characters representative of American social orders were confronted with alienation, frustration, loneliness, and loss of individuality. The book realistically portrayed New York and its environs through a cinematic technique he later perfected in the trilogy *U.S.A.*

In another travel book, *Orient Express* (1927), Dos Passos critically examined the Soviet Union, specifically the Bolsheviks who seized Kronstadt and executed so-called rebels. Then he examined Persia, which suffered primarily because of its lack of modernization. Industry, it seemed, had passed it by. Dos Passos did not condemn this antiquated society. Rather, his character respected, if not appreciated, the value system the Persians had adopted. Dos Passos also examined Iraq as well as other countries, almost always comparing these nations to more affluent Westernized countries. This book, too, was an example of literary journalism because Dos Passos presented his views through the major character. Dos Passos also had two plays published before 1929.

He married Katherine Smith in 1929, the year *The 42nd Parallel,* the first volume of his *U.S.A.* trilogy, appeared. Set in pre–World War I America, the book explored the collapse of the American Dream. A powerful indictment of the social unrest that gripped the nation, the book weaved an interesting story about five characters. To make the story even more believable, Dos Passos incorporated "Newsreels," which included headlines, news stories, and songs; "Camera Eyes," which included sketches based on the author's experiences; and biographies of actual Americans. The additional material provided the reader with candid as well as historical glimpses of what was occurring during this period.

The second novel in this trilogy, *1919,* published in 1932, focused on America's disappointments and insecurities from a European perspective. The third novel, *The Big Money,* appeared in 1936, and centered on New York and the moral decay of American society after the war. In both, Dos Passos interweaved newsreels, camera eyes, and biographies with the story. The reader learned about Frank Lloyd Wright, William Randolph Hearst, Jack Reed, Rudolph Valentino, Thomas Edison, Theodore Roosevelt, and Woodrow Wilson as well as fictional characters. The series was perhaps Dos Passos' masterpiece because it employed unusual techniques to tell a realistic and accurate story of America.

In the late 1930s, Dos Passos traveled to Spain to see what had become of this once beautiful country as a result of the Spanish Civil War. He returned dismayed and angry over what facism and communism had done to Spain in particular and to Europe in general. His novel *Adventures of a Young Man* (1939) explored these issues. It was much simpler in style and tone than his previous three novels and consequently criticized. *Number One,* published in 1943, was also considered an inferior work. *The Grand Design* (1949) examined the New Deal from a critical perspective. Dos Passos was not necessarily in favor of the government shaping the national destiny. Of these three novels, the latter was closer to his earlier novels in its overall design and development.

Katherine, his wife, had been killed in an automobile accident in 1947. Although Dos Passos remarried in 1949, his first wife's death was reflected in his writing for much of the 1950s. Indeed, *Chosen Country* (1951), *Most Likely to Succeed* (1954), and *The Great Days* (1958) were more personal. For instance, in *Chosen Country* Katherine was portrayed as Lulie while Dos Passos was portrayed as Jag Pignatelli. These novels examined the author and the world in which he lived.

In the 1960s, Dos Passos wrote *Midcentury* (1961), which employed the techniques he used in the *U.S.A.* trilogy, including biographies of actual persons. Almost 500 pages, the book focused on the labor movement.

Dos Passos died September 28, 1970. Although hailed principally as a novelist because of his trilogy, his travel books were works of literary journalism.

WORKS: *Rosinante to the Road Again* (1922); *Orient Express* (1927); *In All Countries* (1934).

NOTES

1. Melvin Landsberg, *Dos Passos' Path to U.S.A.: A Political Biography 1912–1936* (Boulder: Colorado Associated University Press, 1972), p. 87.

2. Ibid., p. 89.

Theodore Dreiser
(1871–1945)

Born on August 27, 1871, in Terre Haute, Indiana, Theodore Dreiser chronicled American life in newspapers, magazines, and novels. His family, which was of German descent, moved constantly. Impoverished though they were, Dreiser's father, a Catholic, somehow earned enough to send his children to parochial schools.

In 1879, however, Dreiser's parents decided that the family had to separate in order to survive. Dreiser and the younger children went with their mother. For five years they lived briefly in several Indiana towns, then in Chicago, and finally in Warsaw, Indiana, where Dreiser and the other children were allowed to attend public schools. When he became 16 he left to go to Chicago; the desire to find work and make money was irresistible to him. He remained there until one of his high school teachers, Mildred Fielding, learned of his whereabouts and persuaded him to accept her gift to attend Indiana University.

Dreiser studied, but found higher education grueling. After a year he returned to Chicago, where he was employed by real estate offices and collection agencies. Although he did not particularly enjoy the work, he was not going to starve. He had seen enough of privation and was determined to make ends meet.

In 1891 he was employed as a reporter for the *Chicago Globe.* J. C. Levenson said of him: "Straight reportage was never to be his strong point, but his observation and retentiveness and, in his feature writing, reflection on scenes of success and failure helped him rise as he went from one newspaper to another in Chicago, St. Louis, and elsewhere."[1]

Three years later he met perhaps the most influential person of his career. Arthur Henry, the city editor of the *Toledo Blade,* hired Dreiser to cover a streetcar strike which lasted only four days. Within those four days the two had discussed their ambitions to be writers of fiction. Dreiser had met someone who had similar interests, but without a job he had to move on, first to Cleveland, then Buffalo, then Pittsburgh, where he gained employment as a reporter for the *Pittsburgh Dispatch.* For several months he lived and worked in Pittsburgh until he had saved enough money to travel to New York City. Immediately, Dreiser learned that New York City was filled with reporters and hopeful novelists and that if he received any assignment whatsoever he would be paid very little. His brother, Paul Dresser, who had found success as a songwriter, aided Dreiser on more than one occasion. In return, Dreiser suggested that his brother's partners publish a monthly magazine filled with songs and articles about the music industry. *Ev'ry Month* was the result. Dreiser edited and wrote most of the candid articles. When he left two years later, the magazine had become a success. By now Dreiser's name was known by other magazine editors, and he began to write for such periodicals as *Munsey's, Success,* and *Cosmopolitan.* He corresponded with Arthur Henry, who had visited him in 1897. Two years later he visited Henry in Ohio and at Henry's suggestion began to write short stories and a novel.

Sister Carrie was more than a realistic novel in the sense that Dreiser not only knew the main characters but had lived with them; indeed, he was the main character's brother. As James L. W. West III wrote,

Dreiser . . . drew much material from his childhood experiences and from the checkered and impoverished lives of members of his own family. Particularly important was his sister Emma's involvement with L.A. Hopkins in a scandalous affair on which Dreiser based the story of Carrie and Hurstwood.[2]

Dreiser had to alter the story to pass it off as fiction, because Hopkins was married and a father. When Hopkins' wife learned of his infidelity, he immediately stole $3,500 from his employer and fled to Montreal with Emma. Of course, the newspapers published the affair, and Hopkins ultimately returned most of the money, and then moved with Emma to New York City.

The novel had been accepted by Frank Norris of Doubleday, Page and Company, but its realism offended Frank Doubleday, the publisher, who was about to stop the book's publication when he learned that Dreiser had already signed a contract. The company failed to advertise the book, and Dreiser made no money on it.

Dreiser became overly depressed and his marriage suffered as a result. For the next several years he forgot writing altogether. At one point he tried to commit suicide; fortunately, his brother, Paul, got him into a sanitarium, where he slowly recovered.

When he was released he was unfit for any form of work that required concentration. He realized that he would have to regain his strength to function properly at a newspaper or magazine. He worked for a railroad to regain his physical fitness. Once he had the energy, he went to work as an assistant editor for the *New York Daily News*. In 1904 he worked for Street and Smith, a paperback publishing company, where he became editor of *Smith's Magazine* a year later. Although he saw the magazine's circulation increase to 125,000, he obtained a higher paying position with *Broadway Magazine* in 1906. A year later he saw his first novel reissued by B. W. Dodge; it was both a critical and a commercial success. But business, not literature, occupied Dreiser's life. He was hired by the Butterick Publishing Company to handle three women's magazines. His salary was a staggering $5,000 a year. Although he displayed superior ability in managing a large staff, he was dismissed several years later when his employer learned that he was having an affair with a 17-year-old girl.

Free from his editing obligations, Dreiser separated from his wife and devoted his time to writing fiction. In *Jennie Gerhardt* (1911) he depicted womanly devotion with an objectivity completely different from that of *Carrie*. He apparently relied on more than his immediate family's experience. According to Levenson:

As he explored the relation between daughter and father with sympathy for both, he evidently groped toward an understanding of his own past. He also rendered in detail the barriers that fell between his working-class heroine and her upper-middle-class lover, and thus broke through the American assumption that social class was nonexistent or inessential.[3]

The novel *The Financier* followed in 1912. Dreiser's character Frank Cawperwood, based on the street railway magnate Charles Tyson Yerkes, reappeared in *The Titan,* which came out two years later. In 1915 *The "Genius"* was published, but not without criticism. Dreiser, it seemed, had gone too far in his portrayal of artistry and candid sexuality. For 10 years he failed to have another novel published. He did, however, produce poems, plays, short stories, and articles. He even wrote several books of travel and his memoirs.

In 1925 *An American Tragedy,* a novel based on a murder case, was published. Clyde Griffiths, the protagonist, was modeled on Chester Gillette, who had killed his pregnant girlfriend, Grace Brown, in 1906. The other characters, such as Griffiths' father, were based on people Dreiser had seen or known.

In *An American Tragedy,* the murder of Roberta by Clyde was undeniably realistic. Dreiser created suspense through the use of interior monologue and action. Extensive description, scene-by-scene construction, and dramatic dialogue enabled the reader to visualize not only the tragic scene on the lake, but the characters, especially Clyde. In the guise of fiction, Dreiser weaved a revealing portrait of reality.

The novel confirmed Dreiser's position in American literature and made enough money to allow him to retire to the country. He devoted the remaining years of his life to writing *The Bulwark* and *The Stoic,* published posthumously in 1946 and 1947, respectively, and to public and political causes. He died of a heart attack in 1945.

WORKS: *Ev'ry Month; Sister Carrie* (1900); *Jennie Gerhardt* (1911); *The Financier* (1912); *The Titan* (1914); *The "Genius"* (1915); *An American Tragedy* (1925); *The Bulwark* (1946); *The Stoic* (1947).

NOTES

1. J. C. Levenson, "Dreiser, Theodore," *Dictionary of American Biography: Supplement Three, 1941–1945,* edited by Edward T. James (New York: Charles Scribner's Sons, 1973), p. 233.

2. James L. W. West III, "Sister Carrie: Manuscript to Print," in *Sister Carrie,* by Theodore Dreiser (Philadelphia: University of Pennsylvania Press, 1981), p. 506.

3. Levenson, "Dreiser, Theodore," pp. 235–236.

W.E.B. DuBois
(1868–1963)

W.E.B. DuBois was born on February 23, 1868, in Great Barrington, Massachusetts, to Alfred DuBois and Mary Sylvina Burghardt. His father, who was of French as well as African descent, deserted his family soon after his son was born.

While growing up DuBois had little experience of racial prejudice, primarily because he and his mother lived in a small town that had few blacks. He was usually the only African-American child attending school as well as the Congregational Church.

At 15, he learned about journalism; he worked as the western Massachusetts correspondent for the *New York Globe,* a progressive weekly African-American newspaper. This experience encouraged him to serve his race for most of his life.

In 1885 DuBois entered Fisk University in Nashville, Tennessee. Barbaric behavior by bigoted whites toward African Americans was prevalent in the South, and DuBois learned instantly that people like him were considered inferior by whites. DuBois enjoyed Fisk University, however, for several reasons: the university had a dedicated faculty, the student body was black, and he served on the editorial board of the monthly paper. DuBois taught school in Tennessee during the summers, an experience he found rewarding.

When he graduated in 1888, he entered Harvard University as a junior. Two years later he graduated with honors. DuBois stayed at Harvard and received his master's degree in 1891. DuBois studied under George Santayana, Albert Bushnell Hart, Barrett Wendell, and William James. Although he was interested in the sciences, he majored in philosophy at the bachelor's level and in political economy and history at the master's level. Then he studied toward the doctorate. In 1892 he left Harvard to study economics and sociology at the University of Berlin; he remained in Europe two years, long enough to learn about Marx and communism. Upon returning to the United States he taught Latin and Greek at Wilberforce University, an African American Methodist Episcopal college in Ohio, for two years. During this time, he completed his doctoral dissertation, "The Suppression of the African Slave-Trade to the U.S.," which was later published. He earned his doctorate in 1895, the first African American to do so at Harvard University.

In 1896 he married Nina Gomer, a student at Wilberforce, and later moved to Philadelphia to conduct research for the University of Pennsylvania. This one-year assignment included interviewing more than 5,000 persons about African Americans living in Philadelphia. *The Philadelphia Negro* (1899) was the result. Perhaps the first of its kind, the book used sociological methods to paint an accurate portrait of African Americans living and working in Philadelphia. DuBois relied on environmental and historical factors rather than genetic or biological factors to define his topic. This approach was relatively new and untried.

DuBois moved to Atlanta University in 1897. In addition to teaching economics, sociology, and history, he was responsible for the annual Atlanta University Conference for the Study of the Negro Problems, and was specifically in charge of publishing the proceedings as well as conducting research. DuBois stayed at Atlanta University for 13 years and produced countless studies of the Negro condition in America as well as articles for several mass circulation magazines like the *Atlantic Monthly*. In addition, he spoke at various conferences, and blamed whites and the attitude of Booker T. Washington, who advocated vocational education as the primary means for African Americans to improve themselves, for the African Americans' dilemma in America, particularly in the South.

In 1903 his analysis of this dilemma appeared in *The Souls of Black Folk*. Consisting of autobiography, biography, journalism, poetry, history, sociology, and fiction, the book was unlike anything yet published. Epigraphs and bars of music from spirituals reflecting African-American culture began each chapter. The book was an example of literary journalism because DuBois mixed various literary and journalistic forms to create a single colorful document.

DuBois organized the Niagara Movement in response to the jailing of William Monroe Trotter, the editor of the *Boston Guardian,* for disrupting a speech by Booker T. Washington. Concurrently, DuBois founded the *Moon Illustrated Weekly* in Memphis, Tennessee, to spread his beliefs regarding African Americans. The weekly lasted a year. DuBois founded the *Horizon,* a monthly, in Washington, D.C., a year later to promote the Niagara Movement. This publication lasted several years, until the Niagara Movement failed in 1910.

DuBois' position at Atlanta University was threatened by his adamant opposition to Booker T. Washington's philosophy. Tuskegee Institute, where Washington played a major role, was nearby, in Alabama, and consequently had tremendous support. Many African Americans as well as whites in the South respected both Washington and Tuskegee.

When the National Association for the Advancement of Colored People (NAACP) was established in 1910 to fight segregation in America, DuBois played an important role. He was named director of publications and research and founded the organization's monthly organ, *Crisis,* in which he espoused his philosophy, condemned those who lynched African Americans, applauded those who had made a difference in society, and instilled pride in those of African descent by teaching them about their roots. DuBois edited the magazine for more than 20 years, even though he disagreed on occasion with the leaders of the organization over its contents. The monthly grew in popularity, as circulation increased from 1,000 copies in 1911 to more than 100,000 in 1919.

The magazine's purpose was to examine the hatred caused by ignorance that led to racism. Later, when DuBois realized that African Americans might never be accepted by mainstream America, he called for a separate Negro culture—a concept not unlike that proposed by Booker T. Washington. This call for a Negro nation within a white America was too much for the directors of the NAACP. Indeed, the organization had been founded on the principle of integration. Conflicts between DuBois and the directors ensued, and DuBois resigned in 1934.

While DuBois edited the magazine, he also wrote about African Americans in articles, novels, and book-length works of nonfiction, including *The Quest of the Silver Fleece* (1911), a novel; *The Negro* (1915), a serious scholarly analysis; *Darkwater: Voices from Within the Veil* (1920), a work similar to *The Souls of Black Folk;* and *Dark Princess* (1928), another novel. In addition, he visited the Soviet Union, with which he was impressed, as well as countries in Europe.

In 1934 he returned to Atlanta University, where he taught and conducted research. *Black Reconstruction: An Essay Toward a History of the Part Which Black Folk Played in the Attempt to Reconstruct Democracy in America, 1860–1880* was published a year later. DuBois examined the role of African Americans in the Civil War, specifically arguing that they revolted and consequently forced a confrontation between the Confederacy and the Union.

For the next several years he contributed a weekly column to predominantly minority-owned newspapers and contributed occasional articles to other newspapers and magazines. His book *Black Folk: Then and Now* was published in 1939 and included sections from *The Negro.*

From 1940 until his retirement from the university four years later, he edited the university magazine, *Phylon,* a scholarly journal that published studies of minorities. In 1940 the first of his two autobiographies was published. In *Dusk of Dawn: An Autobiography of a Concept of Race,* DuBois examined racial theory as it related to his life.

In 1944 he was hired by the NAACP as director of special research, a position he held for four years. DuBois wrote extensively and published critiques of capitalism, including *Color and Democracy: Colonies and Peace* in 1945 and *The World and Africa* in 1947. DuBois leaned more toward communism than ever before, and in 1949 addressed the Conference for World Peace. Always seeking a platform on which he could express his controversial views, he became chair of the Peace Information Center, which was formed primarily to spread the Stockholm Peace Appeal, which opposed the proliferation of nuclear weapons.

In 1951, a year after his wife had died, he married Shirley Graham, whom he had known for several years. The same year he was indicted for being an agent for a foreign power. He was later acquitted by a federal judge, but he was not allowed to leave the country for several years. In addition to contributing articles to the radical newspaper *National Guardian,* he wrote three novels in the mid- to late-1950s. In 1958 he toured Europe, the Soviet Union, and Asia. In 1959, in Moscow, he received the Lenin Peace Prize.

Until his death on August 27, 1963, DuBois opposed the United States. He became a member of the Communist party in 1961, and shortly before his death he renounced his citizenship. He died in Accra, Ghana, where he had lived for two years.

As noted, DuBois experimented with literary journalism in *The Souls of Black Folk.* Shelley Fisher Fishkin said of it, "A mixture of journalism, social science, autobiography, fiction, poetry, musicology, and history, *The Souls of Black Folk* resembled nothing that had come before."[1] Indeed, his use of "Sorrow Songs"—lines from Negro spirituals—reflected, if not summarized, the themes with which he was concerned: pain, suffering, and the aspirations of African Americans.

In one section of the book, DuBois employed the elements found in fiction, including realistic dialogue, description, and a certain poetic style to depict accurately one African American's experience with a white person.

WORK: *The Souls of Black Folk* (1903).

NOTE

1. Shelley Fisher Fishkin, "The Borderlands of Culture: Writing by W.E.B. DuBois, James Agee, Tillie Olsen, and Gloria Anzaldua," in *Literary Journalism in the Twentieth Century,* edited by Norman Sims (New York: Oxford University Press, 1990), p. 138.

Finley Peter Dunne
(1867–1936)

Finley Peter Dunne was born in Chicago on July 10, 1867, and was reared in a large home. His parents were from Ireland; like most Irish immigrants they believed in Catholicism and the Democratic party. Finley was the fifth of seven children. His twin brother, John, died shortly after birth.

Dunne attended schools in Chicago. At West Division High School, he contributed humorous and satiric commentary to the school newspaper, which the editors sometimes used. However, Dunne was not a very good student. His mother died a year before he graduated from high school, and his father insisted that he go to work upon graduation.

In 1884 Dunne began his career in journalism with the *Chicago Telegram;* he was hired as an office boy and police reporter, for which he was paid $5 a week. Dunne knew Chicago well. Several of his stories attracted attention, and he was hired by the *Chicago Evening News,* where he wrote features and learned from Henry Ten Ezck White, the editor, how to write brief editorial paragraphs filled with satiric humor. His work was soon appearing on the editorial page.

When he was 20 he was assigned to cover the Chicago White Stockings, a baseball team. Dunne, together with Charles Seymour, created the modern-day sports story by writing a news story about a baseball game. This assignment allowed him to travel around the country, which he enjoyed.

Like other journalists of his day, Dunne seldom let opportunities pass him by. In 1888 he was working as a political writer for the *Chicago Times.* Soon he was promoted to city editor. Within a year management changed, and Dunne no longer had a job. Twenty-four hours later he was working as a reporter for the *Chicago Tribune,* a position he did not enjoy even though he was an excellent reporter. In 1890 he was promoted to editor of the newspaper's Sunday edition. A year later he moved to the *Chicago Herald,* where he worked as a political writer. In 1892 he moved to the company's other newspaper, the *Evening Post,* where he served as editor of the editorial page. Dunne enjoyed writing satiric editorials, especially those that contained dialect and dialogue, devices he had incorporated into his stories about city government and sports. In December 1892 he wrote his first Irish dialect piece, and it was well received. The column's character, Malachi McNeary, was based on the real-life bartender James McGarry who owned a saloon on Dearborn Street. McGarry finally asked Dunne to stop using him and his saloon as models for the column. Dunne agreed; however, he realized that the bartender and saloon were popular among readers, so he kept the basic premise.

In October 1893 Martin Dooley, who operated a saloon on Archey Road in Bridgeport, was introduced to readers. A philosopher as well as an observer of the human condition, Dooley relied on the newspaper to discuss important topical issues. Again, dialect was evident. Dooley spoke like an Irish immigrant

who had lived in a small section of Chicago for several decades. As Franklin
P. Adams wrote:

The expression of that social consciousness as articulated in the ''Dooley'' sketches,
would never have been printed unless they had been written in dialect. For editors, fearful
of calling names, feel that the advertisers and the politicians and the social leaders—
money, politics, and social ambition being the Achilles heels of editors and publishers—
are journalism's sacred cows. But if pretense and hypocrisy are attacked by the office
clown, especially in dialect, the crooks and the shammers think that it is All in Fun.[1]

In essence, Dunne discussed questionable characters, sometimes referring to
them as crooks and con men, through Mr. Dooley. The discussion was presented
in a humorous manner, and names were changed. Nonetheless, the columns were
examples of literary journalism because of Dunne's use of description and dialogue to discuss actual events, situations, and people. The reader learned about
Bridgeport and its various citizens, institutions, and customs: Father Kelly, Timothy Hogan, William J. O'Brien, and numerous families as well as Dooley's
saloon, Saint Bridget's Church, and Finucane Hall. Dunne steered the characters'
discussions to issues he deemed relevant and important. In short, he editorialized
through the column.

In 1896 Dunne was no longer free to editorialize because the *Post* and its
sister paper, the *Times-Herald,* were purchased by a Republican who demanded
that Dunne curb his creativity. Dunne deleted the Irish Republican politician
McKenna from the column and introduced Mr. Hennessy, an Irish Catholic
Democrat.

In 1897 Dunne became the managing editor of the *Chicago Journal;* he introduced the *Journal*'s readers to his column in 1898. Dunne's column opposed
what the newspaper supported—from the Spanish-American War to the American military. The column grew in popularity as a result of predicting certain
events with incredible accuracy, such as the defeat of the Spanish fleet in Manila
Bay. Other newspapers, including the *Boston Globe,* published Dunne's columns. *Mr. Dooley in Peace and in War* was published in 1898 and was an
immediate success, and some critics considered Dunne a genius.

Dunne toured Europe to gather information for his columns; however, Dooley
was not a character who could be moved from Archey Road. By October 1899
Dunne had returned to the *Journal,* and Dooley had returned to Archey Road.
The same year, *Mr. Dooley in the Hearts of His Countrymen,* another collection
of columns, appeared, much to the delight of fans as well as critics. The book
was a success.

In 1900 Dunne moved to New York. The same year *Mr. Dooley's Philosophy*
was published. Although the critics liked the book, readers were slow to purchase it. Dunne's column, which appeared in numerous newspapers, was also
published in *Harper's Weekly.*

In 1901 *Mr. Dooley's Opinions* appeared, and a year later Dunne again traveled to Europe, including Venice, where he proposed to Margaret Abbott. Dunne

was 35 when they married later that year. *Observations by Mr. Dooley,* another collection of columns, was published in 1902.

Dunne accepted the position of editor of the *New York Morning Telegraph,* which was offered to him by his friend William Whitney. Dunne spent time with Whitney, especially over lunch. When Whitney died in 1904, Dunne retired from newspapers. Depressed, Dunne missed a number of deadlines, and consequently did not have enough columns for another collection that year, which his publishers had grown to expect.

Finally, in 1906, he produced *Dissertations by Mr. Dooley.* The same year he helped establish the *American Magazine,* which was founded by several muckraking journalists. Dunne contributed commentary to the magazine as well as a weekly Dooley column for a newspaper syndicate. Dunne stayed at the magazine until 1913. He contributed a column to the *Metropolitan Magazine* for about six months. In 1910 another collection of columns, *Mr. Dooley Says,* was published. It did not sell well.

Dunne moved to *Collier's,* where he wrote commentary. In 1917 he became editor. Although he was given an interest in the magazine when Robert Collier died, Collier's widow sold the publication in 1919, and Dunne no longer had a job. He turned to editing another collection of columns; *Mr. Dooley on Making a Will and Other Necessary Evils* was published in 1919. Critics, it seemed, had had enough of Dooley. Even though they liked Dunne's writing, they thought he should discuss current topics.

Dunne wrote several Dooley columns about the 1924 presidential campaign, then weekly columns for the magazine *Liberty.* In 1927 one of his friends, Payne Whitney, died and left Dunne half a million dollars. With a fortune, Dunne no longer needed to write columns about Dooley. However, before his death in 1936, Dunne started writing his autobiography; his son, Philip, worked with him.

WORKS: *Mr. Dooley in Peace and in War* (1898); *Mr. Dooley in the Heart of His Countrymen* (1899); *Mr. Dooley's Philosophy* (1900); *Mr. Dooley's Opinions* (1901); *Observations by Mr. Dooley* (1902); *Dissertations by Mr. Dooley* (1906); *Mr. Dooley Says* (1910); *Mr. Dooley on Making a Will and Other Necessary Evils* (1919); *Mr. Dooley at His Best,* edited by Elmer Ellis (1949); *Mr. Dooley: Now and Forever,* edited by Louis Filler (1954); *The World of Mr. Dooley,* edited by Filler (1962); *Mr. Dooley on the Choice of Law,* edited by Edward J. Bander (1963).

NOTE

1. Finley Peter Dunne, *Mr. Dooley at His Best,* edited by Elmer Ellis, with a foreword by Franklin P. Adams (New York: Charles Scribner's Sons, 1938), p. xvii.

John Gregory Dunne
(1932–   )

John Gregory Dunne was born to Richard and Dorothy Dunne on May 25, 1932, in Hartford, Connecticut. He attended the elite Catholic Portsmouth Priory School, a boarding school, before entering Princeton University. On his graduation in 1954, he served two years in the U.S. Army. When he was released he moved to New York City to work first for an advertising agency, then a trade journal, and then *Time* magazine, where he remained as a staff writer for five years.

During his years in New York City, Dunne met Joan Didion, another journalist who worked for a magazine; after five years, they moved into an apartment together. According to *Current Biography,* "In April 1964, three months after their marriage, the couple took tentative leave from their jobs to visit Southern California. Dunne became 'an instant Westerner,' and they decided to remain in Los Angeles and make their living by free-lance writing."[1]

They contributed columns and articles of considerable merit to the *Saturday Evening Post* and *Esquire.* One article by Dunne concerned Cesar Chavez, the Chicano labor leader, and the grape-pickers' strike. Chavez's effort to organize the National Farm Workers' Association for the nonunionized California farm workers was honestly reconstructed by Dunne's objectivity: In Michael Adams words:

Dunne depicts the economic and social history of the region, Chavez's background, the efforts of priests and civil rights workers to help the laborers, and conflicts between the NFWA and unions from the AFL-CIO and the Teamsters. Dunne is objective about all these matters, trying to be fair to all parties.[2]

The article was expanded into a book in 1967. *Delano: The Story of the California Grape Strike* was praised by critics for its distinctive, nonobtrusive literary style; and although it was but one of many books on the subject it was considered by many critics to be the most informative.

Two years later his style of writing was powerfully exemplified in the hilarious but honest report *The Studio,* written after he had observed for a year the mechanics of Twentieth Century-Fox and its attempts to produce large-scale musicals such as *Dr. Doolittle, Star!,* and *Hello, Dolly!,* which would, the company executives hoped, be huge box-office successes. Dunne's clever exposé, even though much of the material focused on *Dr. Doolittle,* mercilessly penetrated the glamour of Hollywood.

In one section of *The Studio* Dunne honestly portrayed what happened during a showing of *Dr. Doolittle.* The writing was concise and illustrated Dunne's ear for accurate conversation. The humor, although subtle, was ever present.

Dunne mixed fact with fiction in his 1974 *Vegas: A Memoir of a Dark Season,* in which he used three "composites" (characters drawn from several real persons)—Artha Ging, a prostitute; Jackie Kasey, a comedian; and Buster Mano, a midwestern police officer—as well as himself to depict the loneliness and aloofness of the city.

Dunne, who wrote the novels *True Confessions* (1977), *Dutch Shea, Jr.* (1982), *The Red White and Blue* (1987), and *Playland* (1994), and, with his wife, the screenplays "Panic in Needle Park," "Play It as It Lays," and "True

Confessions," also contributed articles to publications such as the *Atlantic,* the *National Review, New York, Life, Holiday, Harper's,* and the *New Republic.* More than 30 of his articles and essays were collected and published in 1978 under the title *Quintana and Friends.*

Harp, his autobiographical examination of being raised a Catholic and of his time in the army, was published in 1989. One year later, essays that originally appeared in the *New York Review of Books* were published under the title *Crooning: A Collection.* In the volume Dunne examined Daniel James, a writer of screenplays and Broadway plays, who transformed himself into Danny Santiago, a prize-winning young Chicano novelist. He discussed the Kennedy brothers and the incident at Chappaquiddick. Dunne was criticized by some for discussing old material.

WORKS: *Delano: The Story of the California Grape Strike* (1967); *The Studio* (1969); *Vegas: A Memoir of a Dark Season* (1974); *Quintana and Friends* (1978); *Harp* (1989); *Crooning: A Collection* (1990).

NOTES

1. Charles Moritz, ed., *Current Biography* (New York: H. W. Wilson, June 1983), p. 10.

2. Michael Adams, "John Gregory Dunne," *Dictionary of Literary Biography Yearbook: 1980,* edited by Karen L. Rood, Jean W. Ross, and Richard Ziegfeld (Detroit: Gale Research, 1981), p. 190.

E

Gloria Emerson
(1929?–)

Gloria Emerson was born in the late 1920s. Her parents, a prominent pair who had invested in oil, lived in Manhattan. Emerson was raised in an atmosphere of opulence. Unlike her friends, who upon graduation from high school enrolled at the most prestigious universities, Emerson learned about life by experiencing it; then she wrote about what she had experienced.

When she was 21 she obtained an editorial position at *Promenade,* a magazine that was distributed to hotels in New York City. This experience helped her get a job as a reporter with the *New York Journal-American.* In 1956, when she was about 26 or 27, she left the paper to go to Vietnam. A close friend was in the Marine Corps and was serving in Saigon. Emerson worked as a freelance writer.

By 1957 she was married and living in New York City. Hired as a reporter by the *New York Times,* she wrote numerous stories for women. When her husband was transferred to Europe in 1960, she left the paper. Her marriage ended in divorce several years later. Emerson worked as a freelance writer in Europe, then joined the Paris news bureau of the *New York Times* in 1965. She covered the Paris fashion collections and was eventually sent to the Trucial States in the Middle East, West and East Africa, and Eastern Europe. She reported on the Nigerian civil war in 1968 as well as the civil war in Northern Ireland in 1969. She wanted to cover the war in Vietnam and requested an assignment there. Finally, James Greenfield, the foreign editor, assigned her to Vietnam in 1970. Emerson covered the war in a style that was typically literary, contributing a series of articles, often longer than the editors desired, about the effects of war on the South Vietnamese. These articles required hundreds of lengthy interviews; Emerson realized that she was presenting a side of the war that most journalists overlooked. The series earned the George Polk Award for excellence in foreign reporting in 1971.

In 1972, after being criticized for her lengthy, almost anti-American stories, she left the *Times*. "After Vietnam it wasn't possible to function as a foreign correspondent," she said, "because I could not possibly conceal my own views and beliefs."[1] Emerson decided to write a book. She had notes and tapes from the war, but she needed additional information. For the next several years she traveled throughout the United States, interviewing veterans, people who had lost loved ones in the war, draft dodgers, deserters, former prisoners of war, members of various antiwar movements, members of draft boards, and mayors of small towns. From these interviews, notes, and tapes she attempted to write a critical but accurate document about the Vietnam War and its effect on America. *Winners and Losers: Battles, Retreats, Gains, Losses and Ruins from the Vietnam War* was published in 1976 and won the National Book Award a year later. Emerson reported that American officers had overestimated the numbers of North Vietnamese killed and wounded. Friendly villagers, including women and children, had been included in their totals. She revealed, too, how enlisted men in the Awards and Decorations Office at Bien-hoa bestowed medals on officers who may or may not have done anything to deserve them; no one in the office had verified the stories.

The book received mixed reviews, but Walter Clemons claimed that Emerson's book, C.D.B. Bryan's *Friendly Fire,* and Ron Kovic's *Born on the Fourth of July* were the three best books about the effects of the Vietnam War on Americans. Clemons found Bryan's and Kovic's books "more moving than Emerson's. But the breadth and adventurousness of her coverage are astonishing. Her book is filled with voices, each of them distinct: angry, regretful, puzzled, complacent and—some of them—officially pompous."[2]

The book was an example of literary journalism, as Maria S. Bonn pointed out:

Michael Herr's *Dispatches* and Gloria Emerson's *Winners and Losers . . .* are fully engaged in the slippery relationship of fact, fiction, documentation and reportage and how these categories become infinitely entangled when applied to the historical, political, and experiential chaos of war.[3]

In one section of the book, Emerson described in detail how she and Luong, a Vietnamese friend and interpreter, behaved somewhat awkwardly when confronted by Vietnamese officers who were also physicians. Indeed, through Emerson the reporter, the reader not only learned of the conflict between her and the physicians but understood why it occurred. Using the first person point of view and pacing her story, Emerson allowed the scene to unfold before the reader's eyes.

Emerson, a tall, attractive woman who smoked too much, married a second time; this marriage, like her first, ended in divorce. Other problems entered her life, too. For instance, her parents lost most of their fortune and subsequently became alcoholics. However, Emerson persevered. She contributed articles to various magazines before and after her book was published, and even presented a lecture at the U.S. Naval War College.

In the early 1980s Emerson moved to Princeton, New Jersey, where she taught a course in journalism at Princeton University. In 1985 she published *Some American Men,* in which she presented more than a dozen essay-style profiles of men of different races, classes, and stages of life. The profiles were interesting, and the reader learned that men had changed, even though they were proud, or troubled, or brave. The book was dismissed by most reviewers.

Six years later her book *Gaza: A Year in the Intifada: A Personal Account from an Observer* was published. Emerson said of it: "This small book, a record of the life of Gazans for only one year, was not written in the hope of denigrating the Jewish state, only to illuminate, as so many others have done, why there is a revolution that will persist for years until the Palestinians have their nation."[4] Some reviewers questioned Emerson's reporting, which was not balanced, as well as her methodology. Others questioned the book's historical context, while still others faulted her for not including references. Emerson dismissed these criticisms, claiming that the book was a literary one, not a historical analysis.

Paul Hendrickson wrote: "She begins with what she observes at her hotel, . . . and then moves outward to hospitals, prisons, refugee camps. She tells the stories . . . of Palestinian lawyers, doctors, students, priests, merchants."[5] The book described a subtropical landscape populated partly by thousands of refugees living in camps. Emerson recorded an all too familiar downward spiral, a test of wills in which Palestinian mutiny led to Israeli repression, which in turn led to increased insurgency and severer repression. *Gaza,* like *Winners and Losers,* was about conflict. The reporting was personal rather than objective, another example of literary journalism.

WORKS: *Winners and Losers: Battles, Retreats, Gains, Losses and Ruins from the Vietnam War* (1976); *Some American Men* (1985); *Gaza: A Year in the Intifada: A Personal Account from an Occupied Land* (1991).

NOTES

1. Julia Edwards, *Women of the World: The Great Foreign Correspondents* (Boston: Houghton Mifflin, 1988), p. 234.

2. Walter Clemons, "Lest We Forget," *Newsweek,* January 10, 1977, p. 67.

3. Maria S. Bonn, "The Lust of the Eye: Michael Herr, Gloria Emerson and the Art of Observation," *Papers on Language and Literature: A Journal for Scholars and Critics of Language and Literature,* Winter 1993, p. 28.

4. Gloria Emerson, *Gaza: A Year in the Intifada. A Personal Account from an Occupied Land* (New York: Atlantic Monthly Press, 1991), p. xxi.

5. Paul Hendrickson, "The Shriek of a Woman from the War Zones: Gloria Emerson's Piercing Views of Vietnam and Gaza," *Washington Post,* June 5, 1991, pp. B1, B8–9.

Joseph (Joe) Eszterhas
(?–   )

Joe Eszterhas was born in Csakanydoroszlo, Hungary, where he was reared in a refugee camp until he immigrated to the United States several years later. He grew up in a slum in Cleveland, Ohio.

During the protest years of the late 1960s and early 1970s, he worked as a reporter for the *Cleveland Plain Dealer*, for which he wrote traditional, inverted pyramid–style stories. His success as a reporter did not go unnoticed. The editor of *Life* magazine wanted him to do a feature article about the My Lai massacre, in which several U.S. servicemen in Vietnam executed innocent citizens of all ages. The article featured dialogue, but it was not an example of literary journalism; Eszterhas merely reported what others had given to him. However, his ability to describe scenes based on the information he was given was uncanny.

In 1970, at Kent State University in Kent, Ohio, four students were killed by members of the Ohio National Guard. Eszterhas, together with Michael Roberts, another reporter, investigated the unrest that led to the shootings. Speaking to literally hundreds who had been involved or had seen what occurred, Eszterhas and Roberts presented with incredible accuracy a widely praised scene-by-scene analysis of youth assembled on a university campus rebelling against an establishment-approved war. In *Thirteen Seconds: Confrontation at Kent State* (1970) the two reporters incorporated lengthy quotations that revealed not only the characters involved but to an extent their motivations. After this, Eszterhas' journalism changed. Conventional journalism was too restricting, he realized.

When he went to work for *Rolling Stone* in 1971, he rebelled against the traditional forms of reporting, turning to the devices and techniques of the novelist to paint a more accurate picture of his subject. His dialogue became more realistic, for instance, and he employed scene-by-scene construction as well as first-person narration. In his investigation of Charlie Simpson, a 25-year-old small-town hippie who killed at least two police officers and a dry-cleaning store manager before killing himself, he showed, according to Annie Gottlieb,

how both sides of Harrisonville (Missouri) seized on the shooting as a sign that the real, ridiculous, hokum Revolution was upon them. Seized on it almost gleefully: for both sides come across as equally lazy in their prejudices, equally eager to provoke each other, equally ready to turn to violence as an antidote to boredom and an alternative to thought.[1]

Eszterhas, through interviews, depicted the characters and situations. But in this analysis Eszterhas himself seemed to have witnessed everything, including the shootings by Simpson. Thus the reader was drawn into the story. *Charlie Simpson's Apocalypse* was published in 1974.

Nark!, another investigative piece, also appeared in 1974. The book gave a disturbing but accurate picture of agents of the Federal Bureau of Narcotics/

Drug Enforcement Administration. Eszterhas presented the corruption as well as the inhumanity exhibited by various narcotics agents, and argued that these agents enjoyed busting small-time marijuana users and pushers rather than hard drug dealers.

Eszterhas left *Rolling Stone* in the 1970s to pursue a career as a freelance writer. He authored or co-authored several screenplays, including "F.I.S.T.," "Flashdance," "Jagged Edge," and "Music Box." Films made from these screenplays were, for the most part, successful.

WORKS: *Thirteen Seconds: Confrontation at Kent State* (with Michael Roberts, 1970); *Charlie Simpson's Apocalypse* (1974); *Nark!* (1974).
NOTE
1. Annie Gottlieb, "Charlie Simpson's Apocalypse," *New York Times Book Review,* January 27, 1974, p. 5.

F

Clay Felker
(1925-)

Clay Felker was born in St. Louis in 1925 and graduated from Webster Groves High School in 1942. He attended Duke University, but his education was interrupted by World War II. After the war he took a position with the New York Giants before eventually returning to Duke, where he edited the college newspaper and ultimately graduated in 1951. For six years he worked with Time-Life, writing sports and political copy for *Life* magazine and later *Sports Illustrated*. In 1957 he joined *Esquire* magazine as features editor, but left five years later when Harold Hayes was appointed chief editor. Felker believed he should have been promoted to the position.

Felker, who wanted to run a magazine, became a consulting editor to Viking Press and edited the photography organ *Infinity*. However, the magazine, a publication of the American Society of Magazine Photographers, did not have a large circulation. Hired as a consultant by the *New York Herald Tribune* in 1963, he became editor of the newspaper's Sunday supplement, *New York,* within a year. Immediately, Felker's ideas for stories appeared on the Sunday magazine's pages. What he had done for *Esquire* from 1957 to 1962 he did for *New York. Time* said of him:

Felker is an idea editor, not a pencil editor. He has had remarkably accurate antennae for coming fashions—and a knack for catchy headlines. . . . The list of writers for whom he has provided a springboard is also impressive. . . . he helped steer Norman Mailer into reportage and published some of the first so-called New Journalists, most notably Tom Wolfe.[1]

The *Herald Tribune* merged with the New York *World-Telegram and Sun* and the New York *Journal-American* in 1966, and Felker became an associate editor of the new *World Journal Tribune* and a supervisory editor of *Book Week*, a Sunday literary supplement, in addition to editing *New York.* After a year and a half, the paper ceased publication. *New York,* which had given space to such literary journalists as Jimmy Breslin, Tom Wolfe, Dick Schaap, Gail Sheehy, Gloria Steinem, and George "Adam Smith" Goodman, among others, was no more, or so many professionals in the media assumed. Felker, however, purchased the rights to the magazine's name with his severance pay and financial help from others. With publisher George Hirsch and members from the original staff, he produced the first weekly issue in April 1968. Although the magazine was at first criticized for a lack of identity, the problems with editorial matter and graphics were corrected within several months. Indeed, not only were the articles relevant to readers in New York City and other large metropolitan areas, but the graphics were expressive and energetic, reinforcing the editorial matter. Articles were mixed, from how-tos and guides on entertainment, shopping, transportation, living, and health, to in-depth investigative reportage on such issues as marriage, homosexuality, the assassination of President John F. Kennedy, prostitution, and the Black Panthers.

The magazine failed to make a profit in its first two years even though the circulation more than tripled. Through its affiliation with Armand Erpf and Aeneid Equities, however, it survived. In 1969, 20 percent of the magazine's stock was sold on the market, and in 1970 it finally made a profit. Erpf died a year later, and George Hirsch, who had been named publisher by Erpf, eventually resigned when Felker made a power play for his position. The same year, Jimmy Breslin, Peter Maas, and Gloria Steinem, who became editor of *Ms,* left the magazine because of disagreements over editorial policy. Nonetheless, the magazine continued to be an inspirational force to other periodicals. City magazines from coast to coast copied *New York*'s editorial matter and graphics. Articles like "The Ten Worst Judges in New York," "An Evening in the Nude with Gay Talese," "A Buying Guide to Country Acreage," and "100 Ways to Keep Warm" entertained and informed readers, while the magazine's columns discussed books, music, and films.

In 1974 the New York Magazine Company, which Felker headed, purchased the *Village Voice.* Felker, who had given Carter Burden, the owner of the *Village Voice,* 23.8 percent of the New York Magazine Company's stock, was fulfilling his dream. Two years later the company suffered a loss when Felker spent approximately $4 million to launch *New York*'s equivalent *New West.* Of course, the company's board of directors was unhappy. In fact, tensions between Felker and members of the board were so heated that Felker foolishly asked Rupert Murdoch, the Australian press lord, to help him purchase stock from some board members. Murdoch, seeing a money-making opportunity, asked to be given control of the company. Felker refused to relinquish his power. After all, it had taken him years of hard work to get where he was. Murdoch had amassed his fortune from two newspapers and a radio station left to him by his father. Unfortunately, Felker seemed unaware of Murdoch's shrewdness and the fact that he could purchase stock from board members without having to go to others for help.

In 1977 Murdoch amassed more than 50 percent of the company for a mere $7.6 million. When he held a director's meeting, he requested Felker's position as president, which he received, and asked Felker to remain with the magazine. Felker refused. He had other ideas.

New York changed dramatically. When Felker left, many of his staff members left, too. As a result, the magazine's taste, quality, and appearance deteriorated.

Felker was approached by Vere Harmsworth, head of the Associated Newspapers Group, Ltd., one of Britain's largest newspaper chains, about purchasing a magazine. Felker liked the idea, and together they purchased *Esquire,* which had been popular among readers and advertisers but now was stumbling. Felker changed the magazine's focus by targeting predominantly male executives. The content became more timely and topical. However, these changes were not enough to recapture the readers the magazine had lost, and Felker left the magazine several years later.

By the summer of 1980 he was editing the new afternoon edition of the *New York Daily News* as well as creating the new section called "Manhattan," which eventually became another *New York* in the sense that it identified trends. Felker was also responsible for the business news section, which had been expanded. Publisher Robert Hunt saw the afternoon edition as a means to offset the loss of thousands of readers suffered by the morning edition. However, the afternoon edition faced numerous major problems, and Felker returned to magazines in 1983, becoming the founding editor of *M,* a fashion and topical magazine targeted to men. For almost 10 years, Felker put his knowledge about readers and publishing into the magazine, until the publication died in 1992.

WORKS: *Esquire; New York; M.*

NOTE

1. "Felker: 'Bully . . . Boor . . . Genius,' " *Time,* January 17, 1977, p. 55.

Frances FitzGerald
(1940–)

Frances FitzGerald was born on October 21, 1940, in New York City. Her father, the late Desmond FitzGerald, was a lawyer on Wall Street and later a deputy director of the Central Intelligence Agency. Her mother, Marietta Endicott Peabody FitzGerald, was very prominent in the Democratic party during the 1950s and 1960s and served with Adlai Stevenson at the United Nations. She divorced Desmond FitzGerald in 1947 and married Ronald Tree, a British multimillionaire, shortly thereafter.

Frances FitzGerald met numerous well-known political figures at a very early age, primarily through her mother. Indeed, she was active in Adlai Stevenson's unsuccessful campaign for the presidency in 1952.

FitzGerald graduated from the prestigious Dalton School, then attended the Foxcroft preparatory school in Virginia, where she was allowed to keep a horse. She was an excellent student, and writing occupied much of her time. After she graduated from Foxcroft, she attended Radcliffe College, where she majored in Middle Eastern history. She graduated magna cum laude in 1962. At one time she had wanted to study law at Harvard but dismissed the idea after talking to George Plimpton. Instead, she moved to Paris to write a novel. She gained employment with the Congress of Cultural Freedom, an organization that published periodicals and conducted seminars for noncommunist intellectuals. Fitz-Gerald grew frustrated with trying to write a novel.

In 1964 she returned to New York City, where she focused on nonfiction. Her profiles and other articles appeared in the *New York Herald Tribune, Vogue, Village Voice, New York Review of Books,* and the *New York Times Magazine.*

In 1966 she went to Saigon (Ho Chi Minh City) to experience the Vietnam War. FitzGerald thought she would do some research, conduct a few interviews, leave, then write a few articles. However, as she grew to learn more about Vietnam, particularly its culture, she stayed for months. She read documents, interviewed officials and others, and grew to realize that the United States was involved in a civil war that it could not win. The Vietnam War was a war of two cultures. One was communistic; the other was democratic. One was based on the ideas of Marx and Confucius; the other was based on the ideas of Locke and Adam Smith. FitzGerald wrote several articles before she returned to the United States, then wrote a more comprehensive article for the *Atlantic Monthly,* which won an award from the Overseas Press Club.

For the next several years, she researched the war, even returning to Vietnam for a brief period. In 1971, she published *Fire in the Lake: The Vietnamese and the Americans in Vietnam.* FitzGerald's incisive and perceptive examination of the war was critically acclaimed for its disturbing but accurate presentation. Even her opinions regarding America's involvement, which were predominantly negative, were appreciated for their candor. The journalist in this instance had become more than just a reporter; she had become involved in the story—not so much as an observer but as an activist who was in pursuit of reality. The work, because of the elements employed, was an example of literary journalism. The book sold extremely well and earned its author several prestigious awards, including the Pulitzer Prize and a National Book Award.

FitzGerald spoke out against the war and in behalf of the Indochina Peace Committee, and she resumed writing. In 1973 she reported on Cuba for the *New Yorker.* A year later she was in Iran interviewing government officials for another article. Based on the information she obtained, FitzGerald predicted that the Shah would fall. The article, which appeared in *Harper's,* received considerable recognition.

Her next book examined how the United States had been presented in history books adopted by school systems across the country. In *America Revised: History Schoolbooks in the Twentieth Century* (1979), FitzGerald accused publishers of forcing their writers and editors to revise these texts every few years for monetary reasons, and also of neutralizing the copy to avoid giving offense to persons or groups or placing blame on anyone for the various problems discussed. Although insightful and sound in its logic, the book was not liked by those in educational administration, even though numerous educational groups invited FitzGerald to speak.

For several articles and, later, a book, FitzGerald examined four distinct communities: the homosexual community in the San Francisco neighborhood called Castro; the Thomas Road Baptist Church in Lynchburg, Virginia, where Moral Majority leader Jerry Falwell preached; an all-adult community in Florida; and Rajneeshpuram, a controversial commune in Oregon. *Cities on a Hill: A Journey Through Contemporary American Cultures* (1986) examined each community in depth, primarily to show how the white middle class had changed in the 1960s and 1970s. Even though the cultures examined seemed different on the surface, there were, she assured the reader, striking similarities. Some critics praised her unbiased perspectives of minorities. Diane Johnson wrote:

Her method is to visit each of the communities at intervals, talk with people, look around, read, and report. Because she is thoughtful, intelligent, detached, and learned, she is a reliable observer, and her method seems admirably adapted to the complex subject, especially when compared to pretentious works of political science or sociology.[1]

Indeed, FitzGerald gave a sympathetic ear to her subjects because she had become indirectly involved. No longer was she a mere reporter writing about facts. Like other new journalists, she had become an ardent observer and to a certain extent a participant. She used the first person point of view as well as in-depth description. Elements usually reserved for fiction were employed to reveal actual individuals and their situations.

FitzGerald wrote about the Oliver North trial for the *New Yorker*. This article contained the same trademarks as her other work. In addition to her work for the *New Yorker*, FitzGerald became a member of the *Nation*'s editorial board.

WORKS: *Fire in the Lake: The Vietnamese and the Americans in Vietnam* (1972); *America Revised: History Schoolbooks in the Twentieth Century* (1979); *Cities on a Hill: A Journey Through Contemporary American Cultures* (1986).
NOTE
1. Diane Johnson, "Playtime," *New York Review of Books,* January 29, 1987, p. 3.

Janet Flanner
(1892–1978)

Janet Flanner was born in Indianapolis in 1892 and attended Tudor Hall, a private school, and the University of Chicago, which she was asked to leave after her sophomore year because of her rebellious behavior. She returned to Indianapolis and worked as a movie critic for the *Indianapolis Star* before accepting a position at a girls' reformatory in Pennsylvania.

When World War I ended she moved to New York City, then traveled abroad, finally settling in Paris in 1922. At the time Paris was attracting many American writers. (Indeed, Gertrude Stein, a realistic novelist who later turned to cubistic surrealistic writing, was an attraction for several American writers such as Ernest Hemingway, Thornton Wilder, Sherwood Anderson, and F. Scott Fitzgerald.) Flanner, like her contemporaries, was interested in the political, literary, and artistic movements of France. She met Colette, the French novelist, Djuna Barnes, Gertrude Stein, Margaret Anderson, Ernest Hemingway, and F. Scott Fitzgerald, among others. The information she gathered from her acquaintances served her well when she began writing for the *New Yorker* in 1925.

Her column was informative. American readers learned of Paris, the country, and its people, especially the leaders of various political, literary, and artistic movements. Flanner discussed and critiqued novels, musical compositions, and French magazines. She included profiles of writers, artists, performers, and socialites; and in each her prejudices appeared. Sometimes her comments were full of praise; sometimes they bordered on ridicule.

Her only novel, *The Cubical City,* was published in 1926. The characters were based on her family, and the novel severely criticized sexual puritanism. Unfortunately, the novel suffered from narrative passages in which the characters' personalities were described rather than conveyed through action.

In 1934, in addition to her "Letter from Paris," she began writing a "Letter from London." In 1940 she published *An American in Paris,* a book of profiles and crime accounts. One selection, "The Murder in Le Mans," skillfully used dialogue and description. Other elements of literary journalism were used throughout, making fact read like fiction.

When France was invaded she fled the country, returning to the United States. She continued writing for the *New Yorker* during the war, and when France was liberated in 1944 she returned to continue her "Letter from Paris," which appeared until her retirement in 1975. She died in New York City in 1978.

WORK: *An American in Paris* (1940).

Marshall Frady
(1940–)

"I grew up not only a Southern Baptist; but a Southern Baptist minister's son, in the small cities and towns of my father's nomadic pastorates over the inland South,"[1] Marshall Frady said of his childhood. Born on January 11, 1940, in Augusta, Georgia, Frady attended public schools and, like most Protestants who were raised in southern churches, savored the Bible and the hymns, even though he questioned certain passages of the former. His father was the pastor of the

Second Baptist Church, and it became like a second home to Frady. While other children were playing or going to the movies on Sunday, Frady was attending church.

Although he enjoyed reading, his choice of material was limited to poets like Longfellow and Lowell, and the romantic pageants of Lloyd Douglas. When he was 12 he read John Steinbeck's *East of Eden,* which shook the foundation beneath Frady's feet; he had never read such an earthy and realistic novel. Several years later, he read Mencken, Tarkington, and Dickens, among others, and argued with his father about religion.

When he turned 16 he moved with his family to Anderson, South Carolina. Frady read about some guerrillas in Cuba in a news magazine and was determined to join them. He left school and traveled by bus to Florida several times, finally reaching Havana on his third try. Unfortunately, the guerrillas were several hundred miles away, and Frady was almost out of money. He stayed in Havana a few days, then returned to Anderson. Although his attempt to join the guerrillas had been unsuccessful, he had experienced more than most boys his age.

After graduating from high school he attended Furman University, his father's alma mater. He graduated in 1963 and worked briefly in the Atlanta bureau of *Newsweek,* where he heard about a new form of journalism that incorporated elements usually applied to fiction. He was attracted to this form of writing, but he left his job to write a biography of George Wallace. Before *Wallace* was published in 1968, Frady had also pursued postgraduate work at the University of Iowa and worked as a correspondent for *Newsweek.*

During the next several years, Frady worked for one magazine, then another. He was a staff writer with the *Saturday Evening Post* in the late 1960s, a contributing editor for *Harper's* in the late 1960s and early 1970s, and a writer for *Life* from 1971 to 1973.

For the next several years he gathered material for a biography of Billy Graham, which he published in 1979. A year later, after he had become chief correspondent for ABC News' "Closeup," he published *Southerners: A Journalist's Odyssey,* a compilation of articles that had appeared in various magazines years earlier. The articles focused on such luminaries as Wilbur Mills, Jesse Hill Ford, Julian Bond, Mendel Rivers, Lester Maddox, Jimmy Carter, Lyndon Johnson, and Sam Ervin, to mention a few. Because of Frady's cultural as well as professional experience, his insight into these popular figures was acknowledged by various critics. Alan L. Miller said of the book: "The Atlanta-based journalist writes with a sweep that transcends the boundaries of simple description. He is simultaneously chronicler, philosopher, and poet—melding the subtlety of literary allusion with a jeweler's eye for human imperfections."[2] Robert Sherrill said of Frady, "He's one of the few Southern nonfiction writers left with the guts to try the literary equivalent of a triple-somersault with twist and jacknife off the low board."[3] The articles, because of Frady's use of vivid description, realistic dialogue and expressions, as well as other elements and devices usually exhibited in fiction, were representative of literary journalism.

In 1985, he published *To Save Our Schools, to Save Our Children,* his adaptation of a nationally acclaimed television documentary. The book provided an incisive analysis of the crisis that confronted public schools in America; it included profiles of a number of alienated and apathetic students who reflected socioeconomic factors of poverty, broken homes, and cultural impoverishment; also profiled was a group of aging, demoralized teachers who were poorly paid, suffered from a lack of respect from students and communities, and were subjected to oppressive work conditions. The book was a well-researched piece of muckraking journalism. Frady became a correspondent for ABC News' "Nightline" in 1986.

WORKS: *Southerners: A Journalist's Odyssey* (1980); *To Save Our Schools, to Save Our Children* (1985).

NOTES

1. Marshall Frady, *Southerners: A Journalist's Odyssey* (New York: New American Library, 1980), p. xv.

2. Alan L. Miller, "True Accounts," *National Review,* March 20, 1981, p. 301.

3. Robert Sherrill, "People from Georgia and Nearby Places," *New York Times Book Review,* September 28, 1980, p. 47.

Gerold Frank
(1907–   )

Best-selling author Gerold Frank was born in Cleveland in 1907 and received a bachelor's degree from Ohio State University and a master's degree from Western Reserve University (Case Western Reserve University). He began what was to become a long, rewarding career in journalism in 1933 when he accepted a reporting position with the *Cleveland News.* Four years later he moved to New York City, where he worked as a reporter for the *New York Journal-American.* During World War II, he served as a correspondent in the Middle East. The experience enabled him to become a correspondent for the Overseas News Agency; he covered Europe and later the United Nations. Although he enjoyed his position, he resigned after a few years.

In 1952 he became a senior editor with *Coronet Magazine,* a general interest periodical. During his six years with the publication, he wrote the best-selling *I'll Cry Tomorrow* with Lillian Roth and Mike Connally, *Too Much Too Soon* with Diana Barrymore, and *Beloved Infidel* with Sheilah Graham. Another biography, *My Story,* written in cooperation with Zsa Zsa Gabor, appeared in 1960.

Frank turned his attention to international terrorism and political assassination in *The Deed.* His major work, however, appeared three years later. An in-depth documentary of what happened to Boston during the horror-filled months of the early 1960s, *The Boston Strangler* had the power of literary journalism. The book was published in 1966, after Frank had conducted an exhaustive investigation for more than two years. His purpose was not to devote a book to the stranglings, however, but to depict a city gripped with fear.[1]

The book's journalistic style was characterized by short, precise sentences and simple language. Frank used abundant dialogue, careful description, the third-person point of view, and interior monologue. He revealed the characters' actions and reactions. More important, he revealed their thoughts and emotions.

The Boston Strangler, because it was an in-depth study of several murders, the police investigation, and the eventual apprehension of the suspect, was of great importance to criminologists, sociologists, psychologists, and historians. It also showed the lay reader how a city reacted to a series of murders—from fear to courage.

In 1975 he wrote *Judy,* a definitive biography of Judy Garland. Frank interviewed members of her family, including associates in the film industry and her husbands, and presented an accurate portrait of her life.

Frank contributed numerous articles to various publications, including the *New Republic,* the *Nation, McCall's,* the *New Yorker, Look,* and *Life.*

WORKS: *I'll Cry Tomorrow* (1954); *Too Much Too Soon* (1957); *Beloved Infidel* (1958); *My Story* (1960); *The Boston Strangler* (1966); *Judy* (1975). NOTE

1. Gerold Frank, *The Boston Strangler* (New York: New American Library, 1966), pp. ix–x.

Lucinda Franks
(1946–)

Prize-winning literary journalist Lucinda Franks was born in Chicago in 1946 and raised in Wellesley, Massachusetts. She graduated from Vassar College in 1968 and worked as a journalist for United Press International from 1968 to 1974. Franks, an enterprising investigative reporter, was fired upon in Belfast, lived among deserters in Sweden, and heard the painful cries of the Israeli athletes assassinated in 1972 at the Munich Olympics. In 1971 she received the Pulitzer Prize for her UPI articles on the tragic life and death of Diana Oughton, a young member of the radical terrorist group known as the Weathermen.

She joined the staff of the *New York Times* in 1974, the year her book, *Waiting Out a War: The Exile of Private John Picciano,* was published. In this journalistic account of a young army draftee who deserted the military, Franks traced his lower-middle-class upbringing, his brief period of basic training, and finally his self-imposed exile in Sweden, where he eventually learned the realities of life. Jack Forman found "especially interesting . . . her account of the Army's continual harassment of the Picciano parents, who, after their initial doubt about the wisdom of John's desertion, gradually came around to actively supporting him."[1]

Franks contributed numerous articles to periodicals throughout the 1970s and

1980s, and in 1991 wrote her first novel, *Wild Apples,* a moving, realistic account of two sisters and their mother struggling to overcome a crippling past. Said Franks, "My novel is about how to save history while breaking the patterns of the past: the repetition of family dysfunctions, cycles of behavior, and emotional life that get handed down from generation to generation."[2]

WORK: *Waiting Out a War: The Exile of Private John Picciano* (1974).

NOTES

1. Jack Forman, "Franks, Zwinda," *Library Journal,* May 15, 1974, p. 1402.
2. Celia McGee, "Novel Harvest," *New York,* August 26, 1991, p. 32.

G

Paul Gallico
(1897–1976)

A sports columnist who eventually turned to fiction and screenplays, Paul Gallico was born in New York City in 1897. Gallico, the author of the novels *The Adventures of Hiram Holiday, Trial by Terror, Mrs. 'arris Goes to Paris,* and *The Poseidon Adventure,* attended Columbia College of Columbia University, from which he graduated in 1921. Paying his way through college was not easy, however. He worked as a longshoreman, usher at an opera house, factory employee, physical education instructor, and tutor. He had a huge frame and engaged in several sports at Columbia, including swimming and rowing. His desire to experience the physicality of each sport benefitted him later in his writing; indeed, as Boyd Litzinger pointed out, "participation in physical competition provided him with the sense of conflict and the metaphor of the individual-against-the-odds which marks much of his writing."[1]

After a brief stint with the National Board of Motion Picture Review, he joined the staff of the *New York Daily News* in 1922. Initially assigned to review theatrical releases, he was transferred to the sports department within six months; Joseph Medill Patterson, the founder and publisher, had not enjoyed Gallico's reviews. The sports department was a logical place for Gallico's talents.

In *Further Confessions of a Story Writer,* Gallico tells about being assigned to write about Jack Dempsey, the heavyweight boxer, as he trained at Uncle Tom Luther's at Saratoga. Gallico asked Dempsey if he would let him into the ring to learn firsthand what it was like to box the heavyweight champion. Dempsey agreed. Gallico wrote, "After one minute and twenty-seven seconds I was flat on my back with a cut lip and a prize headache. But I also had a story."[2]

For the next 14 years Gallico covered sports both as an editor and as a columnist, writing stories on Babe Ruth, Helen Wills, Ty Cobb, Johnny Weismuller, and others. His reporting had a sense of authenticity. He tried some three dozen sports, including piloting planes, and persuaded professional athletes to either compete with him or allow him to accompany them: he played against tennis stars Helen Wills and Vincent Richards; swam against Johnny Weismuller; tried to catch pitches thrown by Dizzy Dean and Lefty Grove; played golf with Bobby Jones; and rode with Gar Wood in his speedboat and with Cliff Berger in his Indianapolis race car. Gallico's reporting was filled with insight and realism. Readers learned not only about the sport, but about the athlete.

In 1936 Gallico resigned to devote his time to writing fiction and nonfiction. Although he worked briefly for the *Daily News* a year later and for *Cosmopolitan* in 1944, for the most he worked as a freelancer. He contributed articles and short stories to such periodicals as the *Saturday Evening Post, American Magazine, Reader's Digest, Esquire, True, Collier's, Good Housekeeping, Vogue, Liberty,* and the *New Yorker.* His nonfiction appeared between hard covers in *Farewell to Sport,* a popular success.

Gallico traveled extensively and lived in different countries. He averaged a book a year until his death in 1976.

WORK: *Farewell to Sport* (1938).

NOTES

1. Boyd Litzinger, "Paul Gallico," *American Novelists, 1910–1945: Part 2: F. Scott Fitzgerald–O. E. Rolvaag,* edited by James J. Martine (Detroit: Gale Research, 1981), Vol. 9, p. 43.

2. Paul Gallico, *Further Confessions of a Story Writer* (New York: Doubleday, 1961), p. 12.

Brendan Gill
(1914-   )

Brendan Gill was born on October 4, 1914, in Hartford, Connecticut. His father, a physician, was determined that his son would be well educated. During the early to mid-1930s, when few could afford a college education, Gill attended Yale University, from which he graduated in 1936.

Almost immediately, he went to work at the *New Yorker,* a high quality magazine. Each issue contained columns about literature, dining, the theater, music, architecture, film, and other topical subjects, and at least one or two short stories. Gill was a regular contributor for several decades. From 1960 to 1967 he served as the periodical's film critic. In 1968 he became the drama critic, a position he held until 1987, when he started contributing a column on architecture. In addition to his regular assignments, he contributed articles for the "Talk of the Town" section.

Gill's short stories were published in various magazines, and he wrote several novels and book-length nonfiction works. It was his book about the *New Yorker,* however, that caused thousands of readers to notice him. Partly autobiographical, partly anecdotal, *Here at "The New Yorker"* was a literary and commercial success.

The book contained numerous memories about his writing as well as about those with whom he worked. In a narrative saturated with humor, Gill presented the foibles of the editors and writers who were responsible for an attractive if not overrated publication. Filled with funny memos that had circulated throughout the various offices, old cartoons that had appeared in the magazine, photographs of famous writers who had worked or written for the magazine, and numerous anecdotes, the book was labeled a new form of autobiography by critics. Yet Gill's arrangement of these various physical forms of communication did not detract from the book's cohesiveness. Parts of the book contained elements found in fiction, that is, realistic dialogue, in-depth description, first-person point of view, and interior monologue or thoughts. These various elements, when added to the other physical forms of communication, enhanced the book's overall worth. As one read the book, one tended to forget that it was about the making of a magazine; indeed, because of anecdotes and other forms of slice-of-life, the magazine seemed to take human form.

Gill published a second book that was partly autobiographical in 1990. *A New York Life: Of Friends and Others* presented portraits of other interesting literary personalities Gill had met during his career at the *New Yorker.*

WORK: *Here at "The New Yorker"* (1975).

Ralph J. Gleason
(1917–1975)

Born on March 1, 1917, in New York City, Gleason lived with his parents in Chappaqua, New York, where he attended public schools. At age 15, when he contracted measles and could not attend high school for several days, he became a devotee of jazz music.

After graduating from high school, he attended Columbia University for several years, writing a column about jazz music for the student newspaper. Although he failed to graduate, his experience as a music critic was instrumental in his co-founding the first magazine in the United States devoted solely to jazz music. *Jazz Information* was attractive in design, but failed to attract enough readers to remain financially healthy. After two years the publication ceased to exist.

During World War II, he worked for the Office of War Information. When he was discharged he got a job with the Columbia Broadcasting System (CBS), then with the American Broadcasting Company (ABC). In 1950 he moved to San Francisco, where he remained for the rest of his life.

Gleason wrote reviews and later columns, including "On the Town," about jazz and popular music for the *San Francisco Chronicle,* as well as a syndicated column about jazz and popular music for the *New York Post* and other newspapers. He served as a correspondent for *Variety* and as a contributing editor and writer for *Hi/Fi Stereo Review.* He worked as an associate editor and columnist for *Down Beat,* another music magazine. This position lasted 12 years.

In addition, Gleason contributed articles to other publications, including the *New Statesman, Evergreen Review, Saturday Review, Playboy, Esquire,* and the *New York Times.* In 1957 he founded and edited *Jazz: A Quarterly of American Music.* Like his previous publication, it, too, died after two years, for primarily the same reason.

During the 1960s Gleason served as an editor for *Ramparts,* one of the first alternative magazines to publish several forms of new journalism; worked as a disc jockey for two radio stations; and served as an advisor for the Monterey Jazz Festival, the Stanford Jazz Year (1966–67), and the Monterey Pop Festival. In addition, he taught at two universities and produced several programs and documentaries for National Educational Television.

In 1967 Jann Wenner, who wanted to publish a revolutionary popular music magazine, approached Gleason about the idea. Gleason grew enthusiastic and financed at least 20 percent of the publication's costs. Wenner noted:

Ralph named this magazine. He had written an essay for the *American Scholar* in the summer of 1967, titled "Like a Rolling Stone," trying, as usual, to explain what was going on in music and with the people. Anyone who read it saw the most coherent, fun and eclectic explanation of "the reality of what's happening today in America." . . . The article became the philosophical, ethical and cultural base on which *Rolling Stone* still operates.[1]

Gleason served as the magazine's consulting editor and, later, senior editor. He also contributed the column "Perspectives." He helped or influenced numerous staff members over the years, including Wenner. The magazine published as much new journalism as any other publication at the time.

In 1969 he wrote *The Jefferson Airplane and the San Francisco Sound,* which related the development of rock journalism to the growth of FM underground radio in San Francisco. He also interviewed various members of the group and presented their responses in a question and answer format.

Before his death on June 3, 1975, he wrote *Celebrating the Duke: And Louis, Bessie, Billie, Bird, Carmen, Miles, Dizzy, and Other Heroes.* Although he preferred covering jazz musicians as well as their music, he had a considerable influence on popular music, particularly on how it was covered, primarily through his association with *Rolling Stone* and other alternative publications.

WORK: *The Jefferson Airplane and the San Francisco Sound* (1969).
NOTE
1. Jann Wenner, "Ralph J. Gleason in Perspective," *Rolling Stone,* July 17, 1975, p. 39.

Albert Goldman
(1927-)

Born on April 15, 1927, in Dormont, Pennsylvania, Albert Goldman attended Carnegie-Mellon University, the University of Chicago, from which he received his master's degree in 1950, and Columbia University, from which he received his doctorate in 1961.

A former professor of English, Goldman wrote music reviews for the *New Leader,* a leftist magazine that had been a tabloid weekly before 1950, programs for television, and music reviews for *Life.* While working at *Life,* he published a collection of his columns and articles in 1971 under the title *Freakshow: The Rocksoulbluesjazzsickjewblackhumorsexpoppsych Gig and Other Scenes from the Counterculture.* In addition, he edited the magazine *Cultural Affairs.*

In 1973, after three years with *Life,* he resigned to devote more time to writing books. His in-depth biography of comedian Lenny Bruce, *Ladies and Gentlemen—Lenny Bruce!!,* appeared in 1974. Candid and graphic, the book presented a side of Lenny Bruce that had for the most part been hidden from the public. Although he wrote other books during the 1970s, Goldman did not score another hit until his controversial biography of Elvis Presley appeared seven years later. Simply titled *Elvis,* the book was severely criticized for its seemingly demeaning tone and subsequently demoralizing portrait of a rock legend. Nonetheless, Goldman, who wrote numerous articles incorporating the elements of literary journalism, found that such devices, when used in biographies, helped make what would have been merely an interesting book intensive and almost artistic.

In his 1988 *The Lives of John Lennon* he again used the literary journalistic elements that he had successfully employed in *Elvis.* Filled with gossipy anecdotal material and vivid description, the biography was extremely critical of Lennon. However, like *Elvis,* it became an instant best-seller.

Four years later he published several essays written between 1968 and 1971 for *Life* and *New York* magazines under the title *Sound Bites.* Goldman examined the lives of rock musicians and singers, including Bob Dylan and Jim Morrison, as well as several kinds of music, including jazz and blues. The collection did not sell as well as his biographies.

WORKS: *Freakshow: The Rocksoulbluesjazzsickjewblackhumorsexpoppsych Gig and Other Scenes from the Counterculture* (1971); *Ladies and Gentlemen— Lenny Bruce!!* (1974); *Elvis* (1981); *The Lives of John Lennon* (1988); *Sound Bites* (1992); *Cultural Affairs* (editor).

Richard Goldstein
(1944-)

Born in New York City in 1944, Richard Goldstein received his bachelor's degree in 1965 from Hunter College of the City University of New York and his master's degree a year later from Columbia University. His first story, "One in Seven: Drugs on Campus," was published the same year by the *Saturday Evening Post.*

Goldstein, who eventually contributed columns to *Vogue* and *New York,* began his first column on rock music in the *Village Voice.* However, he also contributed articles to other periodicals on subjects of interest to him. According to Ellen Sander, "Richard Goldstein came to be recognized not only as the most astute rock critic of his times and one of the decade's most promising young writers but as one of the most creative, colorful, and scholarly American journalists alive."[1]

In 1968 he published *The Poetry of Rock,* a collection of rock lyrics; certain sections exhibited his talent as a writer. Two years later, perhaps for readers who missed his columns on rock music, *Goldstein's Greatest Hits: A Book Mostly About Rock 'n' Roll,* was published. A collection of previously published articles, it was among the best writing about rock during the late 1960s.

Goldstein served as editor of *US,* a quarterly magazine that contained cartoons, poetry, photographs, and personal journalism, in the late 1960s before he went to work at the *Village Voice.* Goldstein had disagreements with the editors at the *Voice* in the early 1970s, and moved to Clay Felker's *New York* magazine. When Felker purchased the *Village Voice,* he asked Goldstein to be senior editor; Goldstein accepted and eventually became executive editor.

The article "The Groovy Revolution: Fold, Spindle, Mutilate," which covered the uprisings at Columbia University, illustrated his use of personal comment. Goldstein believed that the radicals revolted because they were merely numbers to the administrators who controlled the university. The article was an example of literary journalism.

In 1989 he produced *Reporting the Counter-Culture.* A collection of essays written more than 20 years before, it gave the reader a glimpse of what writers thought about the sixties subculture in America.

WORKS: *The Poetry of Rock* (1968); *Goldstein's Greatest Hits: A Book Mostly About Rock 'n' Roll* (1970); *Reporting the Counter-Culture* (1989).
NOTE
1. Ellen Sander, "The Journalists of Rock," *Saturday Review,* July 31, 1971, p. 47.

George Goodman ("Adam Smith")
(1930–   )

George Goodman, who uses the pseudonym Adam Smith, was born to Alexander and Viona Goodman on August 10, 1930, in St. Louis. He graduated from Harvard University in 1952 and studied as a Rhodes Scholar at Oxford from 1952 to 1954. He served in the U.S. Army for two years, then began a career in journalism. After writing briefly for *Collier's* magazine, then *Barron's,* he was hired as an associate editor of *Time* and *Fortune* in 1958. In 1960 he served as vice president of the Lincoln Fund, a position he held for two years. He then moved to Los Angeles, where for three years he wrote screenplays. Although he gained experience as a writer, his career finally blossomed when he returned to New York City to become editor of *Institutional Investor* and contributing editor and vice president of *New York* magazine, for which he wrote most of *The Money Game* (1967), his best-selling book on finance.

"Adam Smith" captured Wall Street as no writer before him. Using scenes, dialogue, and description, he revealed who played the market and why. For the first time, perhaps, the mechanics of American finance were examined in terms readers could understand.

Goodman, who contributed articles to other periodicals, had also written several novels during the 1950s, but none were nearly as successful as his first book on finance. In the early 1970s he contributed an occasional column to *Newsweek* and lectured at Harvard University. In addition, he wrote *Supermoney,* another popular book, in 1972. Written in the same style as his first book, it, too, discussed complex information.

Goodman served as editorial chairman of the *N.J. Monthly* from 1976 to 1979, served as a member of the editorial board of the *New York Times* in 1977, and became executive editor of *Esquire* in 1978, a position he held for three years. He also served on various committees and on the boards of several companies and institutions, including universities, in the 1970s and 1980s.

In 1981 he published *Paper Money,* which explained the international monetary system and how the U.S. dollar seemed in peril. Although written using the same literary style as *The Money Game, Paper Money* lacked humor, primarily because of the numerous disasters that Goodman described.

Seven years later Goodman published *The Roaring Eighties,* in which he discussed the spending and resulting debt that occurred during the 1980s. Of course, Goodman mentioned that fortunes had been made as well as lost, but the economic climate, even though it had changed somewhat, was not necessarily an improvement on that of the past. The book was written in the same literary style as *The Money Game.*

WORKS: *The Money Game* (1967); *Supermoney* (1972); *Paper Money* (1981); *The Roaring Eighties* (1988).

Germaine Greer
(1939–)

Born in Australia to Eric and Margaret Greer on January 29, 1939, Germaine Greer left home at 18. She was educated at the Star of the Sea Convent in Gardenvale, close to Melbourne; the University of Melbourne, where she received a bachelor's degree in 1959; the University of Sydney, from which she obtained a master's degree two years later; and Newnham College, Cambridge, where she earned a doctorate in 1967. She taught English at the University of Warwick and contributed articles to alternative periodicals such as *Oz,* the *Spec-*

tator, the *Listener,* and *Esquire.* Before 1970 she co-founded the pornographic newspaper *Suck.*

Greer, who enjoyed the camaraderie of the musicians and actors of London, was somewhat of a celebrity before she wrote the best-selling feminist book *The Female Eunuch.* However, when the book appeared in 1970 she was sought after by the media on both sides of the Atlantic. Her book, which argued that women had been stereotyped "Eternal Feminine" by men and society who, in actuality, had castrated women's sexuality through such characteristics as "timidity, plumpness, languor, delicacy and preciosity," called for a revolution of spirit. As Greer put it:

Sex must be rescued from the traffic between powerful and powerless, masterful and mastered, sexual and neutral, to become a form of communication between potent, gentle, tender people, which cannot be accomplished by denial of heterosexual contact. The Ultra-feminine must refuse any longer to countenance the self-deception of the Omnipotent Administrator, not so much by assailing him as by freeing herself from the desire to fulfill his expectations.[1]

Greer appeared on radio and television programs throughout the United States, and debated Norman Mailer. Although her spark as a pronounced feminist was extinguished, her contribution to the movement undeniably served a purpose.

Greer published *The Obstacle Race: The Fortunes of Women Painters and Their Work* in 1979, in which she claimed that there were no great female artists like Titian or Poussin because women's egos had been damaged, their libidos had been driven out of reach, and their energy had been diverted into neurotic channels. The book, like her previous one, was an example of advocacy journalism.

In 1984 she published *Sex and Destiny: The Politics of Human Fertility,* an exhaustive inquiry into the Western world's attitudes toward children, family, recreational sex, and the ways these concepts had shaped policies around the world. Her discussion ranged from childbirth, sterilization, and family planning to eugenics and overpopulation. Greer claimed that the birth rate was falling in Western societies because of a prevailing antichild attitude. She approved of this attitude because the West consumed a disproportionate amount of natural resources. The book was criticized for its seemingly antifeminist perspective.

Two years later she wrote the scholarly biography *Shakespeare,* which discussed his life and work. This was followed in 1987 by *The Madwoman's Underclothes: Essays and Occasional Writings,* which collected articles and essays written for various publications between 1968 and 1985. Greer examined abortion, rape, pornography, and seduction, and each entry revealed her strengths and weaknesses both as a writer and as a woman in search of herself. Overall, the essays were about being white, middle-class, and extremely well-educated, as well as about certain minorities, the poor, and the less educated.

In 1989 she wrote an insightful biography of her father. *Daddy, We Hardly*

Knew You captured her father's life in Australia, as well as her search for who he really was. Greer also revealed how she confronted employees who worked in public offices for information about him.

Three years later she focused on menopause. In *The Change* she showed how attitudes toward menopause had changed—or not—over time, and urged women to question their ideas about the subject. The book seemed more personal than her other books on feminist issues.

Several of her articles were examples of literary journalism. For instance, "McGovern, the Big Tease" not only illustrated her literary journalistic style, but depicted what happened on a bus ride home. Her eye for minute details was evident; indeed, she captured accurately the arresting dialogue and mannerisms of the characters.

WORKS: *The Female Eunuch* (1970); *The Obstacle Race: The Fortunes of Women Painters and Their Work* (1979); *Sex and Destiny: The Politics of Human Fertility* (1984); *The Madwoman's Underclothes: Essays and Occasional Writings* (1987); *The Change* (1992).

NOTE

1. Germaine Greer, *The Female Eunuch* (New York: McGraw-Hill, 1971), p. 8.

John Howard Griffin
(1920–1980)

John Howard Griffin was born in Dallas in 1920 and was educated intermittently in France. He served in the U.S. Army Air Force from 1942 to 1945. He wrote syndicated columns for the International News Service and King Features Syndicate from 1957 to 1960 and he contributed numerous articles, short stories, and photojournalistic pieces to magazines. He also wrote novels, historical studies, and photographic volumes that depicted individuals' lives in words and pictures, and sociological and psychological volumes on blacks in America, including the critically acclaimed best-selling book *Black Like Me.*

Black Like Me, which was written after Griffin medically darkened the color of his skin so that he could tour the American South as an African American, was a revealing study of hatred and prejudice. When the book was published Griffin's life was threatened, but he was not deterred. Throughout the 1960s he visited cities and tried to improve relations between white and African-American leaders. Concurrently, his health suffered from the numerous injections he had undergone to darken his skin.

Black Like Me used dialogue and interior monologue to effectively depict the differences between good and evil. Griffin's experiences were not pleasant. His reporting revealed how many whites in the South thought of and treated African Americans. Though he posed as an African American and indeed tricked the whites he encountered, his revelations were honest. He used the first person point of view since he was involved in what he reported. He made dramatic use of description and dialogue to record scenes, moods, and startling if not ugly sides of human nature.

WORK: *Black Like Me* (1961).

Kenneth Gross
(1939–   )

A former reporter for the *Newark Evening News,* Kenneth Gross co-authored, with Bernard Lefkowitz, *The Victims: The Wylie-Hoffert Murder Case—And Its Strange Aftermath,* a literary journalistic account of the Janice Wylie and Emily Hoffert murders. Gross, who was born in New York City in 1939, attended City College of the University of New York and served in the U.S. Army from 1956 to 1959. He worked as a copy boy for the *New York Times* before moving to the *News* in 1962. A year later he joined the *New York Post.* Although he was a contributor to such periodicals as *Esquire* and the *Nation,* among others, his writing was not recognized nationally until *The Victims* appeared in 1969.

The book was a stirring dramatization that showed readers, through frequent changes of scene, dialogue, action, and interior monologue, the victims before they were murdered, the police officers involved in the investigations, and the various suspects. Why was the book written? According to the authors:

The social standing of the victims and the savage cruelty of the crimes made it one of the most sensational stories in the history of American journalism. Yet, like most other reporters who covered this pursuit of truth, we were dissatisfied with our efforts. We suspected that there were two investigations, one that was publicized and one that was concealed.[1]

In 1975 Gross wrote the gripping *The Alice Crimmins Case,* an account of the sad, lurid trials of a Queens, New York, woman who was accused of murdering her two young children in 1965. The convictions, however, did not seem to be based on conclusive evidence, as Gross pointed out. The book was intriguing and revealing.

WORK: *The Victims: The Wylie-Hoffert Murder Case—And Its Strange Aftermath* (with Bernard Lefkowitz, 1969).

NOTE

1. Bernard Lefkowitz and Kenneth Gross, *The Victims: The Wylie-Hoffert Murder Case—and Its Strange Aftermath* (New York: G. P. Putnam's Sons, 1969), p. 7.

H

David Halberstam
(1934–)

Former political reporter and war correspondent David Halberstam gained considerable recognition for his interpretive reporting of the Vietnam War, which appeared frequently in the *New York Times* in the early 1960s. Halberstam, who was born on April 10, 1934, in New York City, was reared in Rochester, Minnesota, Winsted, Connecticut, and Yonkers, New York, where he attended Roosevelt High School and worked as a reporter for the school newspaper.

In 1951 he entered Harvard University. Before he graduated four years later he had served as managing editor of the college newspaper and had contributed to the *Boston Globe*. When desegregation became an important public issue during the Eisenhower administration, Halberstam moved to the South. For a year he worked as a reporter for the *West Point Daily Times Leader* in Mississippi; then for four years, from 1956 to 1960, he worked as a reporter for the Nashville *Tennessean*. After five solid years of reporting, Halberstam migrated to Washington, D.C., where he became a member of the *New York Times'* capital bureau, for which he reported on John F. Kennedy's inauguration and the first few months of his administration.

Although Halberstam proved himself a capable journalist when he was assigned to the Congo (Zaire) wars later that year, perhaps his best reporting appeared after he was sent to South Vietnam in 1962. Revealing the atrocities, the political corruption, and the undeniable fabrications that had been reported, Halberstam candidly presented what he observed. Predictably, his reports were attacked by some government bodies and journalists as being inaccurate, sensationalized, and biased, perhaps with the aim of arousing reader interest. Eventually, the U.S. government, particularly the Pentagon, monitored Halberstam's activities in Vietnam. After a year and a half he returned to the United States. *The Making of a Quagmire,* an insightful book about his experiences in the Congo and Vietnam, was published in 1965. In 1965 he was also assigned to Warsaw. Halberstam, who had set a precedent for candidly reporting what he witnessed, wrote about the hostile atmosphere of Poland and was subsequently ordered out of the country. He remained in Europe, however, until 1966, when he returned to the New York offices of the *Times* to work on the metropolitan staff.

A year later he resigned. Willie Morris had become editor-in-chief of *Harper's* and was hiring writers. Halberstam became a contributing editor and wrote interpretive articles on Vietnam, which he revisited; profiles of Robert S. Mc-Namara, Richard J. Daley, and Robert F. Kennedy, among others; and interpretive articles on politics, including the 1968 presidential campaign. In addition, he wrote a novel and interpretive books on two disparate political figures, *The Unfinished Odyssey of Robert Kennedy* and *Ho.* When Willie Morris resigned from the magazine in 1971 as a result of a philosophical dispute, Halberstam and six other editors resigned too. He contributed articles to various magazines, including *Esquire,* the *Atlantic,* and *McCall's,* and finished *The Best and the Brightest* (1972), his monumental study of the Kennedy and Johnson administrations and their failure to recognize the inevitable consequences of America's involvement in the Vietnam War. Halberstam interviewed some 500 persons directly involved and based the book primarily on the interviews. Some critics accused him of presenting a superficial account which supported his thesis. Others claimed that he had overlooked or failed to take into account information contrary to what he had gathered or reported. Nevertheless, the book, which was an example of literary journalism, sold exceptionally well.

In 1979 he published *The Powers that Be,* a massive study of Time Incorporated, CBS, the *Los Angeles Times,* and the *Washington Post.* Halberstam discussed without reservation the mechanics of each. His study, which presented not only the history but the various personalities of each company, was candidly written. Halberstam recorded more than mere facts; indeed, he recorded what his subjects thought. The book, which became a best-seller, was another example of literary journalism.

Two years later he published *The Breaks of the Game,* a book about sports. In 1985 he covered the manic scramble for positions on the U.S. Olympic rowing team in *The Amateurs.* The book described the sport and the athletes who were addicted to it. Halberstam enjoyed writing about sports and would return to the subject later in his career.

He presented an accurate and candid history of the U.S. and Japanese automobile industries in 1986 in *The Reckoning.* Halberstam traced the fall of Detroit and the rise of Japan through those who worked at the Ford Motor Company and the Nissan Motor Company. Vignettes and anecdotes humanized and dramatized the story. Halberstam claimed that Detroit lost the first round because the Big Three automakers failed to spend enough on modernizing their plants, thus dooming them to failure. Japan's relatively young industry, on the other hand, succeeded in manufacturing and selling cars that people wanted. Engineers in Japan were interested in designing cars, not airplanes. The book, which was a best-seller, was an example of literary journalism.

In 1989 he captured the 1949 pennant race between the Boston Red Sox and the New York Yankees in his best selling book *Summer of '49.* Halberstam saw this as the season when baseball changed from being a game to being show business. Radio, which had created heroes, had to move over and make room for television, which created celebrities. Halberstam's writing was filled with vigor. Full of wonderful dugout vignettes and anecdotes, the book captured Joe DiMaggio of the Yankees and Ted Williams of the Red Sox.

In *The Next Century,* published in 1991, Halberstam warned about problems confronting the American economy. Through memories, ideas, and insights from his life's work, he not only presented warnings but offered hope for American businesses and manufacturers. He examined other countries such as Japan and found that they suffered from similar problems. He claimed that change had to come—that is, quality had to become an important goal of businesses and manufacturers again, and without cooperation at home and abroad some problems would become much worse. The book was a departure to a certain extent; Halberstam the literary journalist had become Halberstam the philosopher.

His book *The Fifties,* published in 1993, was a very candid examination of the decade presented through a series of mini-biographies of politicians, from Harry S. Truman, Dean Acheson, and Adlai Stevenson to Richard Nixon, Dwight Eisenhower, and Joe McCarthy, among others. He showed the warts as well as the credos, and discussed various subjects besides politics and politicians. Indeed, he even examined rock and roll. The book was a best-seller.

October 1964, published in 1994, dealt with the 1964 baseball season, specifically the World Series between the New York Yankees and the St. Louis Cardinals, which pitted Mickey Mantle and company against Bob Gibson and company. The Yankees lost, and Halberstam attempted to define the Yankees' downfall as a reflection of the social changes of the 1960s. Social analysis was not a major part of the book, however. Indeed, it was similar to his *Summer of '49* in the sense that he depicted accurately the speech, actions, and mannerisms of the players and managers of both teams. Thus, the book was an example of literary journalism.

WORKS: *The Making of a Quagmire* (1965); *The Unfinished Odyssey of Robert Kennedy* (1969); *Ho* (1971); *The Best and the Brightest* (1972); *The Powers that Be* (1979); *The Breaks of the Game* (1981); *The Amateurs* (1985); *The Reckoning* (1986); *Summer of '49* (1989); *The Fifties* (1993); *October 1964* (1994).

Pete Hamill
(1935-   )

Born on June 24, 1935, in Brooklyn, Pete Hamill said that he grew up in a state of rage. As he wrote in the introduction to his collection of *New York Post* columns, *Irrational Ravings* (1971), "I had won a scholarship to a Jesuit high school called Regis. . . . Most of the students were upper-middle-class, and I spent the first few months there in a stage of desperate unhappiness."[1]

Hamill was reared in poverty and consequently learned early the ugliness of life, including injustice and bigotry. At 16 he dropped out of school to work in the Brooklyn Navy Yard, where he remained until he entered the navy. Hamill studied art and became familiar with the literature of Fitzgerald and Hemingway and was determined to return to school once he was discharged. He applied to Columbia University but was refused admittance. He tried to get a job as a copy boy at three New York City newspapers before he finally accepted a position as a messenger with an advertising agency. Eventually, he moved to another agency and enrolled in advertising design courses at the Pratt Institute. Although advertising appealed to him at first, he grew bored with it by the time he reached 25. In 1959 *Atlantis,* a Greek-language monthly magazine, published his first article. Hamill read the *New York Post* every day, especially Murray Kempton and Jimmy Cannon:

I didn't always understand Kempton, but there was something both elegant and passionate about his style that moved me and fed my angers. He had refined the great weapon of the fifties—irony—into something private and supple. But it was Cannon who made me want to be a newspaperman.[2]

In 1960 Hamill joined the *New York Post,* where he learned the fundamentals of journalism. Three years later he became a contributing editor to the *Saturday Evening Post,* for which he traveled throughout Europe and wrote mostly about actors and actresses. He remained with the magazine until he was offered the chance to write a column for the *Post* two years later. Hamill said he would have become a minor league Damon Runyon if it had not been for Vietnam: "The killings in Asia made it impossible to be Damon Runyon, and I started warring with myself in the column, torn between descriptive narratives and polemics."[3]

Hamill's column reflected what he sincerely believed about the war in Vietnam, the racial question, the differences between Brooklyn and Manhattan, the question of New York City being separated from New York, and the relationship between Arthur Goldberg, Secretary of Labor during John F. Kennedy's presidency, and U.S. policy in Vietnam, among other issues. If he decided to praise the Mets and criticize Mendel Rivers, Chairman of the Armed Services Committee, even though Rivers was dead, readers eagerly read his views.

"Going Away," one of his columns, was indicative of his impressionistic style, which mixed narrative with dialogue. In simple, direct sentences, he not only realistically depicted scenes and characters, but gave the reader homespun ideas to contemplate. Many of his columns were examples of literary journalism.

In 1967 he resigned from the *Post* when Bill Moyers, who had left the Johnson administration to become publisher of *Newsday*, asked him to become a Washington columnist. But when Hamill wrote a column attacking the president, an editor at *Newsday* prevented it from being published. Hamill resigned and completed his first novel, *A Killing for Christ*, which was published in 1968. Later, he contributed to the *Village Voice*, but when his friend Robert Kennedy was murdered he suffered from writer's block. In 1969 he returned to the *Post*, and also contributed articles to *New York*, of which he eventually became a contributing editor, *Ramparts*, *Playboy*, *Cosmopolitan*, *Life*, and *Esquire*, of which he also became a contributing editor.

In addition to articles, several collections of short stories, including *Tokyo Sketches: Short Stories* (1993), and novels, including *Loving Women: A Novel of the Fifties* (1988), about an Irish kid from Brooklyn who journeyed through the South in the 1950s, he wrote several screenplays and scripts for television, including "Report from Engine Co. 82" and "Death at an Early Age."

In 1994 he published his highly acclaimed autobiography, *A Drinking Life: A Memoir*, which affectionately told of the artist as a boy and as a young man and his thirst for alcohol. William Hamill, Pete's father, used to take his son to several bars. Pete was eight at the time. Anne Hamill, Pete's mother, never drank. She encouraged her son to draw cartoons, which he enjoyed. Hamill recalled his life at 8, at 16, and at other ages. He talked about life in Greenwich Village in the early 1950s. He explained that he joined the navy to see the world, but saw the bottom of numerous liquor bottles. He recalled his life as an art student in Mexico and as an apprentice reporter for the *New York Post*. He told about his nights on the town. He claimed that his marriage deteriorated because he was addicted to alcohol. In 1972 Hamill examined his life and realized that he had to change. He put the bottle down on the counter and never picked it up again. The memoir was well written and proved that Hamill had the skill of a journalist and the insight of a novelist.

WORKS: *Irrational Ravings* (1971); *A Drinking Life: A Memoir* (1994).
NOTES
1. Pete Hamill, *Irrational Ravings* (New York: G.P. Putnam's Sons, 1971), pp. 15–16.
2. Ibid., p. 25.
3. Ibid., p. 27.

Hutchins Hapgood
(1869–1944)

Hutchins Hapgood was born on May 21, 1869, in Chicago, but grew up in Alton, Illinois, which bordered the Mississippi River. His parents were affluent, especially for this small community. Unlike his three brothers, who grew to be tall, Hapgood was medium in height and somewhat stocky, and suffered from an undiagnosed illness throughout most of his childhood. As a result, he played by himself most of the time.

He attended the University of Michigan for a year, then transferred to Harvard University, which his older brother, Norman, had attended. At Harvard, Hapgood's mysterious illness practically disappeared. Indeed, the world seemed to open its arms to him while he was there. The likes of William James, George Santayana, and Barrett Wendell illuminated the classrooms, and Hapgood swallowed what they said. He graduated magna cum laude in 1892.

Hapgood traveled abroad and spent two years in Germany, where he learned about life firsthand. Then he returned to Harvard, where he worked as an assistant to George Pierce Baker, and earned a master's degree in 1897. Hapgood taught English composition at Harvard and, later, at the University of Chicago. However, he forgot about pursuing a career in academia when his brother Norman urged him to join the staff of the *New York Commercial Advertiser.*

The *New York Commercial Advertiser* was guided by Lincoln Steffens, the city editor. On the staff were several prominent journalists, including Abraham Cahan, who wrote literary journalism. Several of these journalists, including Steffens, eventually left the *Commercial Advertiser* to go to more prestigious newspapers or magazines. Hapgood wrote impressionistic pieces, usually 500 words in length, about the various individuals who lived in the city. He wrote about the Jewish immigrants who flocked to New York's Lower East Side. Cahan, a close friend, introduced him to the Jewish way of life. These vivid sketches of individuals and their customs were collected in the book *The Spirit of the Ghetto.*

In 1903 Hapgood left the newspaper and toured Italy for several months. His book *The Autobiography of a Thief* appeared the same year. When he returned to the United States he joined the *New York Morning Telegraph,* which specialized in covering sporting events. He moved to Chicago after a year or so and worked as the drama critic for the *Chicago Evening Post.* Then he returned to Italy for several months. When he returned to the United States he became a salesman for a company in Indianapolis owned by his younger brother. Although he appreciated what his brother had done for him, he grew disgruntled within a few months. Selling was not in him, and he missed working for a newspaper. Finally he was hired to write editorials for the *New York Evening Post;* later he sought employment at the *New York Globe and Commercial Advertiser,* the new name of the first newspaper for which he had worked. Many of the original journalists, including Steffens, had left the paper by this time. The same year Hapgood published another collection of sketches originally written for newspapers. *Types from City Streets* was similar to *The Spirit of the Ghetto,* except that the sketches concerned various individuals from different ethnic groups.

For four years, until 1914, Hapgood wrote several columns a week. Unfortunately, because of his involvement with bohemian circles and revolutionary members of the labor movement, his creativity suffered. In short, Hapgood spread himself too thin. He enjoyed traveling abroad, drinking with others in bars, and discussing popular topics with friends until morning.

In 1915 he was one of the original Provincetown Players of Provincetown, Massachusetts. He and his wife, Neith Boyce, a former journalist whom he had married in 1899, wrote and performed one of the group's early plays, *Enemies,* in 1916.

After World War I, Hapgood seemed spiritually adrift. His son, Boyce, died in 1918 from influenza, and the revolutionaries of the labor movement were growing docile or becoming conformists.

No longer employed as a newspaper columnist, Hapgood wrote nonetheless, if only sporadically. *The Story of a Lover,* for instance, appeared anonymously in 1919. Somewhat erotic for the period, it presented a different view of life.

In 1922, after several years of frustration and despair, Hapgood sold his house and moved with his wife to Europe, where they lived for two years. When they returned to the United States they lived part of the year in Richmond, New Hampshire, part in Provincetown, and part in Key West, Florida.

When the stock market crashed in 1929 Hapgood's inheritance was affected, and thereafter he had to support his family on a meager income. Although he hoped for a great literary success, it never came. Unlike his friend Lincoln Steffens, who enjoyed literary fame and financial success, especially after his *Autobiography* was published, Hapgood failed in his efforts. His autobiography, *Victorian in the Modern World,* published in 1939, failed to attract much attention. Critics, though kind, felt that Hapgood's creative ability had dissipated after 1914. Hapgood acknowledged that he had wasted time on alcohol and women. He died of a cerebral hemorrhage on November 18, 1944; he was 75 years old.

The Spirit of the Ghetto, more than any other work, captured Hapgood's creative ability. In it he presented an authentic portrait of an American immigrant community, free of the usual stereotypes. As Moses Rischin wrote:

Here were objects neither of commiseration nor outrage, neither financial titans nor merchant princes, neither a mystical people nor a tenement proletariat, neither comics nor grotesques. Instead, these Jews were not types at all but real individuals identified by name and physical appearance, distinct in their personalities and accomplishments, part of a vital Jewish world working out its own destiny and oblivious of Christian categories or rhetoric.[1]

When he wrote about individuals, Hapgood described them in a way that allowed the reader to visualize them, and his use of dialogue allowed the reader to hear how they spoke. Although he incorporated these basic elements of literary journalism, he remained objective. In Irving Howe's words: "Hapgood wrote with that precise restraint which is the mark of the serious reporter and he never allowed his prose to slip into the kind of emotional indulgence that subjects places and people to the journalist's ego."[2]

WORKS: *The Spirit of the Ghetto* (1902); *Types from City Streets* (1910).
NOTES

1. Hutchins Hapgood, *The Spirit of the Ghetto,* edited by Moses Rischin (Cambridge, Mass.: Belknap Press of Harvard University Press, 1967), p. xxi.

2. Irving Howe, "The Subculture of Yiddishkeit," *New York Times Book Review,* March 19, 1967, p. 7.

William Hard
(1878-1962)

William Hard was born on September 15, 1878, in Painted Post, New York. His father, Clark Pettengill Hard, was a Methodist minister and served as a missionary. When Hard was four, he moved with his parents to India, where his father served in the field.

Hard attended the Philander Smith Institute in Mussoorie, India, and University College in London. He returned to the United States and completed his bachelor's degree in 1900 at Northwestern University. Upon graduation, he was granted a fellowship by the university and taught a course in medieval history for a year. In 1901 he moved to the university's Settlement House, in Chicago, and wrote about reform issues for the house's newsletter. He enjoyed advocating ideas, especially those concerning labor, in print.

In 1902 he was hired by the *Chicago Tribune* to write editorials, a position he held until 1905. He married Anne Scribner, an editor for the *Chicago Post,* a rival newspaper, in 1903. The same year the magazine *Commons* published his first article. Hard, who was devoted to the organized labor movement, covered the stockyards strike in 1904 for *Outlook,* another periodical.

After serving as an assistant to Joseph Medill Patterson, the commissioner of public works in Chicago, Hard worked as an editor for *Ridgway's Weekly,* founded by Erman J. Ridgway, the publisher of *Everybody's Magazine,* from 1906 until the magazine ceased publication in 1907. Ridgway then hired Hard to write muckraking and advocacy articles for *Everybody's.* Hard wrote about unsafe conditions in industry and, in 1908, about the exploitation of newsboys by Chicago newspaper publishers. His article influenced legislators to write and pass legislation to protect children in the workplace. Many of his articles were published in *Injured in the Course of Duty,* which appeared in 1910.

Hard wrote the first of several articles about women and their role in society in 1908, analyzing the social, political, legal, and economic issues they faced. These articles appeared in *Everybody's* and other publications until about 1914, and many were collected in *The Women of To-morrow,* published in 1912.

Hard examined national and international issues, particularly those of a political and economic nature, during World War I. He focused on these topics for the rest of his life. He moved his family to Washington, D.C., where he worked as a correspondent for the *Metropolitan*. Later, he moved to the *New Republic*, where he remained until 1920. He wrote in opposition to the League of Nations and debated over Bolshevik Russia. Hard based *Raymond Robins' Own Story*, which was published in 1920, on the experiences of a friend who had spent 18 months in Russia.

Hard contributed the "Weekly Washington Letter" to the *Nation* from 1923 until 1925. In addition, he contributed articles to numerous magazines, and through at least two news services, including his own, provided various newspapers with information about Washington and the national agenda.

In 1928 he wrote a biography, *Who's Hoover*, primarily to promote Herbert Hoover's presidential campaign. From 1929 until 1937 Hard worked as a correspondent and commentator for the National Broadcasting Corporation, which had a popular radio network. Hard participated in the first international broadcast in 1930 when he summarized daily events from the Naval Arms Conference in London. The same year he provided weekly reports from Washington, D.C. Hard enjoyed these assignments because both allowed him to speak to politicians. In 1932 he summarized daily events from the Republican National Convention in Chicago. Later he covered several international conferences, including those from Berlin and Geneva.

Hard entertained Republicans with 15-minute commentaries on the New Deal and the presidential campaign of 1936, and was appointed to the Republican National Committee in 1937. He served as an assistant to the chairman and, later, as secretary of the Republican Program Committee. In 1938, however, he resigned; he missed writing and reporting.

Hard returned to his favorite profession in 1939, when he became an editor for *Reader's Digest*, a position he held until his death on January 30, 1962. His contributions to the magazine were consistently about public issues. He was fair as well as open and humorous. And although he was creative, his articles were based on facts.

One of his earlier articles, " 'De Kid Wot Works at Night,' " which appeared in the January 1908 issue of *Everybody's*, examined the lives of children who sold newspapers after dark. Many were exploited by their employers, putting in long hours and frequently missing school, if they had not stopped attending altogether.

Hard used elements often found in fiction to bring the characters to life. As Donald McQuade and Robert Atwan wrote:

The attractiveness of the kids who work at night and Hard's reluctance to render them merely in sociological terms prompt him to fictionalize their lives, treating them more like characters in a short story than as subjects to be documented. He takes us beyond the limits of factual observation by vividly imagining many details of the newsboys' behavior in situations that must have been annoyingly inaccessible to him.[1]

Hard opened the article with a detailed description of Chicago during the early hours of evening. Then he introduced the major characters and their jobs.

Hard described what the characters saw as well as what they did, presenting realistic situations and revealing how the characters were affected. He provided analysis and reasons for much-needed regulation. Like other articles he wrote, it was an example of literary journalism, because he used vivid description and authentic dialogue.

WORKS: *Injured in the Course of Duty* (1910); *The Women of To-morrow* (1912).

NOTE

1. Donald McQuade and Robert Atwan, *Popular Writing in America: The Interaction of Style and Audience* (New York: Oxford University Press, 1993), p. 252.

Harold Hayes
(1926–1989)

Harold Hayes, perhaps one of the more influential editors in terms of encouraging the work of literary journalists in the 1960s and early 1970s, was born in Elkin, North Carolina, on April 18, 1926. Hayes, who graduated from Wake Forest in 1949, worked on the public relations staff of the Southern Bell Telephone Company and later as a reporter for United Press International, both in Atlanta. In 1952 he moved to New York City, where he worked as an assistant editor, then as an associate editor for *Pageant* magazine. A year later he was hired as an associate editor at *Tempo*. Before he moved to *Esquire* in 1955, he was editor of *Picture Week*. Although his association with each periodical was rewarding, the experiences he had with *Esquire* were undoubtedly the most rewarding and challenging. He explained:

At *Esquire* our attitude took shape as we went along, stumbling past our traditional boundaries of fashion, leisure, entertainment and literature onto the more forbidding ground of politics, sociology, science and even, occasionally, religion. Any point of view was welcome as long as the writer was sufficiently skillful to carry it off, but we tended to avoid committing ourselves to doctrinaire programs even though advised on occasion that we might thereby serve better the interests of mankind. None of the programs available would permit us consistently to keep our lines open to the reader, so we stayed loose.[1]

Hayes worked as an assistant to the publisher until 1959. That year he became articles editor, a position he held until he was advanced to managing editor and editor in 1962 and 1963, respectively. From 1970 to 1973 he served as senior vice president. The most significant years, however, were those from 1959 to 1970. As an editor, he encouraged such writers as Gay Talese, Martin Mayer, Garry Wills, Tom Wolfe, Robert Benton, John Berendt, Norman Mailer, John Lardner, Thomas B. Morgan, Dan Wakefield, Jessica Mitford, Brock Brower, Tom Wicker, John Sack, Eldridge Cleaver, Ovid Demaris, Murray Kempton, Rex Reed, Susan Sontag, Susan Brownmiller, Michael Herr, J. Anthony Lukas, and James Baldwin, among others, to break away from the traditional forms of writing. Indeed, Hayes, who realized that magazines had become relics in the sense that circulations had dropped consistently for several years, encouraged new forms of writing. The combination of reporting and fiction not only became the new form of journalism that filled *Esquire*'s pages, but helped increase circulation. In 1960, for example, its circulation was approximately 800,000; in 1970 about 1.2 million copies were sold. Articles like "Joe Louis: The King as a Middle-Aged Man," "When Demirgian Comes Marching Home Again (Hurrah?) (Hurrah?)," "Looking for Hemingway," "Khesanh," "Lester Maddox as a Leader of Men," "In the Red Light: A History of the Republican Convention in 1964," "The Last Night," "The Marvelous Mouth," "There Goes (Varoom! Varoom!) That Kandy-Kolored Tangerine-Flake Streamlined Baby," and "A Short, Bumpy Ride with Steve McQueen" left readers clamoring for more.

When Hayes left *Esquire* in the early 1970s, the magazine changed. Many ideas for articles originated with Hayes. Now writers had to come up with their own. By the early 1980s, the magazine's circulation had decreased by 500,000.

Hayes first hosted the television program "Roundtable," then turned to writing articles for such magazines as the *New Yorker, New Statesman,* and the *New Republic,* and to writing nonfiction, including *The Last Place on Earth* (1977) and *Three Levels of Time* (1980). In addition, he worked as a consultant to various periodicals.

In the early 1980s he served as vice president of the editorial department of CBS Publications. He completed a captivating biography of Dian Fossey, the dedicated primatologist who was murdered in Rwanda in 1985, before he died from a brain tumor in 1989. Critically acclaimed, *The Dark Romance of Dian Fossey* was published posthumously in 1990 and emphasized Fossey's emotional and sexual history as well as her life. Hayes paid slight attention to her interest in gorrillas, however.

WORKS: *Esquire* (various positions); *The Last Place on Earth* (1977); *Three Levels of Time* (1980); *The Dark Romance of Dian Fossey* (1990).
NOTE
1. Harold Hayes, ed., *Smiling Through the Apocalypse* (New York: McCall Publishing, 1969), pp. viii–ix.

William Hazlitt
(1778–1830)

Predominantly an essayist, William Hazlitt, who was born in 1778 in Maidstone, Kent, wrote articles that contained elements found in literary journalism. His father, a Unitarian minister who believed that William should be educated for the ministry, sent him to Hackney College in London. After three years William had had enough of religion and returned home, where he read works by the writers of his day.

Like his older brother, John, who was an artist in London, William turned to painting. He painted portraits of his father, Samuel Taylor Coleridge, William Wordsworth, and Charles Lamb, and visited picture galleries in Paris. If he had remained an artist, he would have unquestionably excelled; but he turned to writing.

In 1805 he published *An Essay on the Principles of Human Action; Free Thoughts on Public Affairs* followed a year later, and in 1807 three of his books appeared.

In 1808 he moved to Winterslow, where he wrote two books that were later published. In 1812 he moved to London and worked as a reporter for the *Morning Chronicle.* He was dismissed two years later because of his attitude, which was at odds with the publisher's. Hazlitt contributed articles about literature, art, the stage, and politics to the *Examiner,* the *Champion,* and the *Edinburgh Review.* Together with Leigh Hunt of the *Examiner,* he wrote the essays later collected in *The Round Table,* a volume published in 1817. The same year *Characters of Shakespeare's Plays* was published and was an instant success.

During 1818, in addition to writing for periodicals and newspapers, Hazlitt lectured at the Surrey Institution; his *Lectures on the English Poets* was published the same year. A second series of lectures was collected and published as *English Comic Writers* in 1819. A year later, after writing *Political Essays,* he collected a third series of lectures, *The Dramatic Literature of the Age of Elizabeth.*

For the next several years he wrote for the *London Magazine.* The pieces were ultimately collected and published in *Table Talk* and in *Plain Speaker.* In 1822 he wrote a series of essays for the *New Monthly Magazine* and the *Liberal.* A year later he revealed his love affair with Sarah Walker, whom he had intended to marry, in *Liber Amoris.* Unfortunately, she would not marry him.

In 1824 he married Isabella Bridgewater, a widow who had a yearly income. To Hazlitt this was glad tidings; he traveled frequently, and the money he earned did not last. After the marriage they traveled to Paris and remained there at least three months, during which time Hazlitt visited the Louvre and wrote essays. In 1825 they went to Italy; Hazlitt recorded the details in *Notes of a Journey Through France and Italy,* which was published the same year. They returned to France a year later so that Hazlitt could work on his *Life of Napoleon.* In 1827 he returned to London; his wife remained behind.

Before his death in 1830 he had finished his four-volume treatise on Napoleon and had written articles of criticism for the *Examiner.*[1] One article, "The Fight," revealed his ability to describe, round-by-round, a major boxing match. Because of the elements used, the article was an example of literary journalism.

WORKS: *An Essay on the Principles of Human Action* (1805); *Free Thoughts on Public Affairs* (1806); *The Round Table* (1817); *Characters of Shakespeare's Plays* (1817); *Lectures on the English Poets* (1818); *English Comic Writers* (1819); *The Dramatic Literature of the Age of Elizabeth* (1820); *Liber Amoris* (1823); *Notes of a Journey Through France and Italy* (1825).

NOTE

1. Geoffrey Keynes, ed., *Selected Essays of William Hazlitt* (London: Nonesuch Press, 1934), pp. xi–xix.

Lafcadio Hearn
(1850–1904)

Lafcadio Hearn, born in 1850 on the Ionian island of Santa Maura, had an unfortunate life. Abandoned by his parents, he was reared by his father's aunt, who paid for his education. At first he had private tutors; then he attended Catholic schools in England and France. While he was attending school in England, he became blind in his left eye after an accident. He was determined to use his right eye as much as possible and, as a result, it swelled enormously. His peculiar appearance gave him an inferiority complex he never overcame.

Before he reached 19 his great-aunt's fortune had diminished. He had no job and no security. He had not been an appreciative child; indeed, he had been dismissed from one school and had run away from another. His great-aunt was determined to rid herself of his presence by sending him to New York City, then Cincinnati.

In 1869 he arrived in New York City. After two years of misery he had earned enough money to travel to Cincinnati. Unfortunately, misery met him there. Not finding employment, he suffered from malnutrition; he slept in doorways, alleys, vacant lots, and haylofts. Finally, he obtained some menial jobs such as running messages and peddling mirrors. Henry Watkin, a printer who allowed him to sleep in his shop, was instrumental in helping Hearn earn a living. He taught Hearn everything he knew about printing and helped him obtain a position with the *Trade List*. Hearn worked during the day and wrote articles at night. Eventually the *Cincinnati Enquirer* published most of his articles in its Sunday edition, and these early contributions helped him obtain a position with the newspaper a year later. He wrote feature articles, one of which vividly described a murder victim whose corpse had been burned beyond recognition. The story not only hypnotized readers, but earned Hearn a reputation among his peers.

Until his involvement with Althea Foley, a black woman, cost him his job, he wrote other macabre articles for the *Enquirer* as well as for his own short-lived publication, *Ye Giglampz*. Also, he wrote short sketches on Cincinnati's poor blacks and whites, prostitutes, and criminals. These sketches, like his macabre articles, were excitingly graphic, for Hearn captured the characters' dress, manners, thoughts, and speech. The characters became instantly human. For instance, in "Dolly," one of numerous stories he wrote about blacks, Hearn described a character accurately and realistically. Though the story was sad, since it concerned Dolly's love for Aleck, who accepted her love willingly but married another, and Dolly's subsequent tragic death, Hearn commented appreciatively on Dolly's pleasing personality and femininity. Hearn's extensive description of Dolly's beauty and favorable characteristics was illustrative of literary journalism. The story also used dialogue, scene-by-scene construction, the third person point of view, and interior monologue. Perhaps no other writer of this period used these devices so effectively.

After Hearn lost his job with the *Enquirer,* the *Cincinnati Commercial* immediately hired him, but at a lower salary. In 1877 he was sent to New Orleans to cover the Hayes-Tilden presidential campaign; Hearn became intrigued with the city itself and wrote colorful descriptions on Creole life, which the editor of the *Commercial* did not particularly want. Dismissed for not fulfilling his duties, he was stranded in New Orleans without a job. Fortunately, he obtained a position with the *Item,* a struggling newspaper that paid him $10 a week. Hearn wrote articles criticizing child abuse, lynching, and police extortion. He wrote reviews and columns, and even did translations of foreign literature for the *Democrat.* When the *Democrat* and the *Times* merged in 1881, Hearn was offered a position writing editorials and a column, "Foreign Press." Before resigning from the newspaper six years later, he had written a number of books: *One of Cleopatra's Nights, Stray Leaves from Strange Literatures, Gombo Zhebes, La Cuisine Creole,* and *Chita: A Story of Last Island,* the latter based on fact. He published stories and articles in *Harper's Weekly, Century Magazine,* and *Harper's Bazaar,* and his reputation had spread to the Northeast.

In 1887 he traveled to New York City and persuaded the editor of *Harper's* to send him to the West Indies, where he wrote sketches of the country and its people. He was so enchanted and fascinated with the country that he later returned at his own expense. For two years he lived in Martinique, half starving, perhaps euphoric because of the immense pleasure of the "waspcolored" people and the warm sun.

In 1889 he returned to New York City and *Harper's.* In 1887 *Harper's* had published Hearn's *Some Chinese Ghosts,* a book of Oriental legends, and was going to publish in book form his West Indies sketches and *Youma,* a novel. Now Hearn decided to see Japan and describe its beauty for the world. In 1890 he sailed to Japan, where he broke off his relationship with *Harper's,* obtained a teaching position, and married within two years. He lectured at the Government College, and a year later published *Glimpses of Unfamiliar Japan.* For a brief period in 1894 he wrote for the *Kobe Chronicle;* he resigned, however, to teach English literature at the Imperial University, where he remained until 1903. A year later he was dead.

Hearn wrote candidly about segments of society, including the poor and minorities, readers knew little about. More important, he brought to America portraits of other lands. Hearn's revelations about other countries, particularly Japan, were of special interest.

WORKS: *One of Cleopatra's Nights* (1882); *Stray Leaves from Strange Literatures* (1884); *Gombo Zhebes* (1885); *La Cuisine Creole* (1885); *Chita: A Story of Last Island* (1886).

Ben Hecht
(1894–1964)

Ben Hecht, who was born in New York City in 1894, was a journalist, novelist, playwright, and screenwriter. He attended schools in New York and in Racine, Wisconsin, where he graduated from high school. Although he entered the University of Wisconsin, the desire to experience what the world had to offer brought him to Chicago, where he ultimately made his mark in newspapering He obtained a position as a reporter on the *Chicago Journal* in 1910, but his reputation for capturing the reality of Chicago's senseless brutality was not made until he moved to the *Chicago Daily News* four years later.

Hecht, who read voraciously the works of Gautier, Baudelaire, Mallarme, and Verlaine, developed a style that was extraordinary and imaginative. The use of metaphor, imagery, and vivid phrases made his writing distinct.

In 1918 he served as a correspondent in Berlin. When he returned to Chicago a year later he wrote a daily column on the seamier side of life in Chicago, covering subjects such as murder, brothels, and the bizarre. According to Louis L. Snyder and Richard B. Morris, "Again and again Hecht showed an uncanny ability to picture the strange jumble of events in strokes as vivid and touching as the brushmarks of a novelist."[1] Perhaps his best book, *1001 Afternoons in Chicago,* a compilation of his columns, was published in 1922.

Eventually Hecht became associated with the writers Sherwood Anderson, Theodore Dreiser, Maxwell Bodenheim, Carl Sandberg, and Pascal Covici. He knew Margaret Anderson and contributed to her *Little Review,* the magazine of the Chicago "literary renaissance," and to *Smart Set.*

In 1923 he founded the *Chicago Literary Times,* which lasted a year. A year later he moved to New York City, where he became known as an able playwright. Although he had written several novels, such as *Erik Dorn, Gargoyles,* and *The Florentine Dagger,* his play *The Front Page,* which opened in 1928, enabled him to pursue other interests. In addition to novels and plays, he wrote approximately 60 screenplays.

Though his literary interests were varied and earned him both wealth and fame, his greatest contributions were his columns. The stories told in them, he confessed in *A Child of the Century,* had been untrue.

The "news stories" I brought back . . . gave Mr. Finnegan, Mr. Dunne and Mr. Hutchens all the delusion that they had hatched a journalistic wonder. . . . I made them all up. I haunted police courts, the jails, the river docks, the slums. I listened to the gabble of sailors, burglars, pimps, whores, hop-heads, anarchists, lunatics and policemen. Out of their chatter I wove anecdotes worthy of such colorful characters. And to give reality to the people of my "scoops" I raided the family album in my Taute Chasha's flat.[2]

Hecht admitted that all of his relatives, particularly the women, appeared as spies, heiresses, and queens in the columns of the *Journal.*

Ben Hecht died in New York City in 1964.

WORKS: *1001 Afternoons in Chicago* (1922); *A Child of the Century* (1954).

NOTES

1. Louis L. Snyder and Richard B. Morris, *A Treasury of Great Reporting* (New York: Simon and Schuster, 1949), p. 374.

2. Ben Hecht, *A Child of the Century* (New York: Simon and Schuster, 1954), pp. 132–133.

W. C. Heinz
(1915–   )

W. C. Heinz was born on January 11, 1915, in Mount Vernon, New York, and graduated from Middlebury College in 1937. He began his career in journalism the same year with the *New York Sun* as a copy boy, and advanced quickly to reporter, feature writer, war correspondent, and sports columnist. In 1950 he left the *Sun* to devote his time to writing books as well as articles and short stories for such magazines as the *Saturday Evening Post, Cosmopolitan, Life, Collier's, Esquire, Look, True, Coronet, Reader's Digest,* and *Sport.*

His first book, *The Professional,* published in 1958, was a vivid, authentic account of boxing. *The Surgeon* (1963) concerned a doctor who performed lung surgery and saved countless lives. Heinz examined the everyday operations of an emergency room in *Emergency,* which was published in 1974. *Once They Heard the Cheers* (1979) depicted 19 sports heroes he had known. Like his other books, it was graphic, authentic, entertaining, and informative. His most recent book, *American Mirror,* was published in 1982.

Heinz said of his work:

What I attempt to do in my writing is to set the scene and put the characters in it and let them talk. When I can do this with sufficient accuracy and sensitivity the reader experiences the impression, very real, that I have not been telling him something and that he is getting it second-hand, but that he himself saw it and heard it for he was there.[1]

"Death of a Race Horse" had the elements of a short story. Heinz's descriptive sentences were characteristic of sports reporting. However, in this story, the descriptive paragraphs were separated by dialogue that was not only accurate but dramatic. Heinz effectively used both elements to capture the inevitable tragic climax. Though the article read like fiction because of its use of description, dialogue, scene-by-scene construction, and the third-person point of view, and was therefore representative of literary journalism, the reader realized that it was fact. If this story had been written like a traditional news story, the emotional impact would have been lost. Only by using devices usually reserved for fiction could the pathos be shown.

WORKS: *The Professional* (1958); *The Surgeon* (1963); *Emergency* (1974); *Once They Heard the Cheers* (1979); *American Mirror* (1982).
NOTE
   1. Ann Evory, ed., *Contemporary Authors: New Revision Series* (Detroit: Gale Research, 1981), Vol. 4, p. 294.

Ernest Hemingway
(1899–1961)

Ernest Hemingway, one of America's great novelists, was born on July 21, 1899, in Oak Park, Illinois, and graduated from Oak Park High School in 1917. He learned his craft as a reporter for the *Kansas City Star,* then volunteered to serve with the Red Cross in Italy. Hemingway was wounded and subsequently shipped home.

   In 1920 he contributed stories to the *Toronto Star,* and the paper gave him an assignment as a European correspondent. Although he and his new wife Hadley Richardson traveled throughout Europe, Paris was home to him. The numerous American writers living there inspired him, and he filled notebook after notebook with descriptive sketches. In 1923 his *Three Stories and Ten Poems* was published, followed by *In Our Time* a year later; both were published in Paris.

   A more inclusive *In Our Time* was published in New York City in 1925. Hemingway was considered a major literary artist by Gertrude Stein, Sherwood Anderson, and F. Scott Fitzgerald, and other writers and critics. When *The Sun Also Rises* was published in 1926, Hemingway's reputation was internationally established; with each realistic short story or novel his style bordered on perfection.

   Although his position as a correspondent ended in 1924, Hemingway remained in Paris until 1928. Then he and his second wife, Pauline Pfeiffer, moved to Key West, Florida. *A Farewell to Arms,* loosely based on his experiences in World War I, appeared a year later and sold exceptionally well.

   During the next decade his life was filled with adventure, from hunting and deep-sea fishing to covering the Spanish Civil War for the North American Newspaper Alliance. Hemingway nevertheless found time to write short stories, a play, a novel, and two volumes of nonfiction, including the descriptive *Green Hills of Africa* (1935).

   In 1940 *For Whom the Bell Tolls* was published, his second marriage ended, and he and his third wife, Martha Gellhorn, a reporter, moved to Cuba. Four years later he became a correspondent for *Collier's* magazine and traveled to Europe, where he participated in World War II. Two years later he divorced Martha and married Mary Welsh.

   Across the River and into the Trees was published in 1950 to mixed reviews. Two years later, when *The Old Man and the Sea* appeared, Hemingway won the Pulitzer Prize. He received the Nobel Prize in 1954. A year later he was severely injured in a plane crash. These injuries, together with others he had sustained in previous incidents, forced him to realize that he was not invincible. Indeed, he was suffering both physically and mentally.

When Fidel Castro came to power in Cuba, Hemingway and his wife moved to Idaho, where he died from a self-inflicted gunshot wound in 1961.

Hemingway's writing stemmed from his journalistic experience. Some of his short stories, for example, were mere news accounts. As William White noted, several news stories he wrote for the *Toronto Daily Star*—"A Silent, Ghastly Procession," "Refugees from Thrace," "Christmas on the Roof of the World"—were transformed into short stories and published in *In Our Time* and *Two Christmas Tales*. White wrote:

But the blurring of the distinction between his news writing and his imaginative writing is most evident in these three instances: "Italy, 1927," a factual account of a motor trip through Spezia, Genoa and Fascist Italy, first published in *The New Republic* . . . as journalism, then used as a short story in *Men Without Women* (1927) with a new title, "Che Ti Dice La Patria," and in *The Fifth Column and the First Forty-Nine Stories* (1938); "Old Man at the Bridge," cabled as a news dispatch from Barcelona and published in *Ken* . . . and also put into [*The*] *First Forty-Nine Stories* without even a new title; and "The Chauffeurs of Madrid," originally sent . . . by the North American Newspaper Alliance . . . to subscribers of its foreign service as part of Hemingway's coverage of the Spanish Civil War, and which was included by Hemingway in *Men at War* (1942), which he edited and subtitled "The Best War Stories of All Time."[1]

WORKS: *In Our Time* (1924; 1925); *Green Hills of Africa* (1935); *The Fifth Column and the First Forty-Nine Stories* (1938); *Men at War* (1942).
NOTE
   1. William White, ed., *By-line: Ernest Hemingway* (New York: Charles Scribner's Sons, 1967), p. xi.

Michael Herr
(1940–   )

Michael Herr, born in 1940, wrote perhaps the most perceptive book about the Vietnam War. Entitled *Dispatches,* the book was an example of literary journalism. Reviewer William Plummer called it

ostensibly a conjunction of war stories, profiles, mini-dramas, and set pieces that appeared as reports from "over there" in *Esquire* and elsewhere. In its bound incarnation, *Dispatches* seems rather a force of memory that has taken these several years—Herr left Indochina in 1968—to be understood, and that still, blessedly, remains radiantly enigmatic.[1]

Herr captured the war's frightful atmosphere. With death all around, he nonetheless revealed to the reader what soldiers believed, said, dreamed, and thought. Alfred Kazin wrote:

Herr caught better than anyone else the kooky, funny, inventively desperate code in which the men in the field showed that they were well and truly in shit. "Some people just wanted to blow it all to hell." He catches the hatred between fellow grunts that the daily unstopping fear could produce: "Good luck" meant "Die, motherf---er".[2]

As Plummer noted, sections of *Dispatches* appeared in *Esquire* in the late 1960s. Herr also contributed his realistic, gruesome accounts to *Rolling Stone* and *New American Review* during the same period. Unlike most correspondents, he enjoyed Vietnam; to him it was an experience he would in all likelihood not have again. Perhaps for this reason the writing in *Dispatches* surpassed other Vietnam accounts. In other words, Herr grew close to the subject and allowed the subject to speak for itself. As Tom Wolfe pointed out, Herr did not make the story autobiographical. He penetrated the psyches of soldiers and recorded their thoughts.[3]

Herr skillfully and accurately captured the language of the combat soldier. At times his writing was extremely personal, much more so than that of John Sack in *M*. For instance, in one scene, Herr used the pronouns "we," "me," and "I," and focused on how he and others, particularly an African-American soldier, reacted to the death of Martin Luther King, Jr. The killing of King became their most important concern, especially for the African-American soldier, who questioned his role not only in Vietnam, but at home in the United States. The war in Vietnam was temporarily forgotten.

Dispatches, like Sack's *M,* revealed the ugliness of Vietnam. It showed that, unlike most wars, the Vietnam War forced the military to engage in battles without the essential support of civilian and governmental groups in the United States.

In 1990 Herr wrote *Walter Winchell,* a novel about the life and times of the gossip columnist.

WORK: *Dispatches* (1977).

NOTES

1. William Plummer, "Ecstasy and Death: Dispatches by Michael Herr," *Saturday Review,* January 7, 1978, p. 36.

2. Alfred Kazin, "Vietnam: It Was Us vs. Us: Michael Herr's *Dispatches:* More than Just the Best Vietnam Book," *Esquire,* March 1, 1978, p. 120.

3. Tom Wolfe, *The New Journalism,* with an anthology edited by Tom Wolfe and E. W. Johnson (New York: Harper and Row, 1973), p. 85.

John Hersey
(1914–1993)

Hersey was born on June 17, 1914, to American parents who were missionaries living in China. He did not live in the United States until his family returned

10 years later. The environment in which Hersey was reared was often reflected in his novels, in which the American philosophy of life, with its stress on progress, democracy, and education, figured prominently. He attended public schools for a few years, then, when he received a scholarship, Hotchkiss, a private prepatory school. He worked part time to make up for what the scholarship did not cover. After Hotchkiss, he enrolled at Yale. He graduated in 1936, and his excellent study habits earned him the opportunity to attend Clare College, Cambridge. When he returned to the United States he worked briefly for Sinclair Lewis. Then he joined *Time* magazine, for which he served as correspondent in China and Japan in 1939; he also served as a writer, an editor, and later as a war correspondent in the South Pacific, in the Mediterranean, and in Moscow. When the war ended he became an editor and correspondent for *Life* and later for the *New Yorker*. In 1945 and 1946 he covered Japan and China for both magazines, and in the latter year published his literary journalistic classic, *Hiroshima*, which appeared first in the *New Yorker*, then in book form. According to Sam B. Girgus:

The dropping of the bomb is experienced through the eyes of six survivors—two doctors, a widow with two children, a German priest, a Japanese pastor, and a woman clerk— whose experiences become personal events for the reader. He does this simply by showing rather than telling what each of the six was doing when the bomb was dropped, how they reacted to it, how they behaved afterward, and how they felt throughout their ordeals. Interior emotions and attitudes are illustrated by external action.[1]

Hersey had written other journalistic accounts of World War II, such as *Men on Bataan* (1942) and *Into the Valley* (1943), but *Hiroshima* was extraordinarily different. The previous books had been explorations into war and its effects on soldiers; the latter was an indictment of man's revolutionary power to annihilate multitudes of people.

In one section of the book, Hersey showed Mrs. Nakamura, a Japanese widow, looking for her children. Hersey's extensive use of description enabled the reader to visualize Mrs. Nakamura's agony as she searched for her two children. Dialogue, though slight, played an important role, since through what was said Mrs. Nakamura learned that her children were alive. Description was not only the dominant element but the most important, since Hersey used it to create suspense. The reader observed not only Mrs. Nakamura's movements but the devastation, the ripped buildings, the ugly environment that had resulted from the bomb. Hersey succeeded in contrasting man's will to survive against the greatest weapon ever created.

Hiroshima, since it depicted accurately the effects of the atomic bomb, was without question not only a disturbing document but a necessary reminder of man's power to kill and destroy.

In addition to nonfiction, Hersey wrote several critically acclaimed novels, including *A Bell for Adano* (1944), which won a Pulitzer Prize, *The Wall* (1950),

The War Lover (1959), *The Child Buyer* (1960), *White Lotus* (1965), *The Walnut Door* (1977), *The Call* (1985), and *Antoinetta* (1991). He died of cancer in 1993.

WORKS: *Men on Bataan* (1942); *Into the Valley* (1943); *Hiroshima* (1946).

NOTE

1. Sam B. Girgus, "John Hersey," *American Novelists Since World War II: Second Series,* edited by James E. Kibler, Jr. (Detroit: Gale Research, 1980), Vol. 6, p. 139.

J

Alva Johnston
(1888–1950)

Alva Johnston was born in Sacramento, California, on August 1, 1888, and was educated in public schools. When he graduated from high school he was hired as a reporter by the *Sacramento Bee,* where he worked for several years.

Johnston was hired by Carr V. Van Anda, the managing editor of the *New York Times,* in 1912. He was assigned the usual beats. As he proved himself, his by-line appeared over numerous articles, particularly those written for the Sunday edition. Johnston wrote about various subjects, including science. He covered the American Association for the Advancement of Science convention in 1922, reporting in scientific as well as everyday terms the theories discussed. This story brought him recognition and the Pulitzer Prize in 1923. As a reporter for the *New York Times* wrote, "It was Mr. Johnston's extraordinary faculty for making difficult subjects comprehensible to the average reader, combined with his tireless enthusiasm in research, that won him the coveted Pulitzer Prize."[1]

In 1922 Johnston moved to the *New York Herald-Tribune.* He returned to the *New York Times* two years later and remained until 1928, when he went back to the *Herald-Tribune,* for which he wrote a series of articles on racketeering as well as several articles on the citizens of a small town in Indiana who ignored the 18th Amendment, which prohibited the sale of alcohol.

In 1932 Johnston left the *Herald-Tribune* to write full time for several magazines, including the *Saturday Evening Post* and the *New Yorker.* To the former he contributed articles that explored the insurance business of James Roosevelt, the oldest son of Franklin D. Roosevelt, and the grammar of Samuel Goldwyn. To the latter he contributed sketches of personalities for the "Biographical Profiles'' section. Some of these appeared as chapters in his books, *The Great Goldwyn,* published in 1937; *Wilson Mizner, the Legend of a Sport,* published in 1943; and *The Case of Erle Stanley Gardner,* published in 1947.

Johnston wrote a number of stories based on court cases, including the famous Snyder-Gray murder case, that could be considered literary journalism; his articles and profiles for the *New Yorker* certainly contained the elements necessary to be literary journalism. Johnston died on November 23, 1950.

WORKS: "Biographical Profiles" (*New Yorker*); *The Great Goldwyn* (1937); *The Case of Erle Stanley Gardner* (1947).

NOTE

1. "Alva Johnston, 62, Noted Writer, Dies," *New York Times,* November 24, 1950, p. 35.

Jill Johnston
(1929–   )

Jill Johnston was born on May 17, 1929, in London to an American mother. Her father, who rejected his daughter as well as her mother, was an English aristocrat. Johnston grew up thinking that she was more like an orphan than a child who had parents.

Although Johnston was married for several years to Richard Lanham and had two children, she realized that a heterosexual lifestyle was not for her. Indeed, it was because of this realization that she was able to write so convincingly about the women's movement and lesbianism for the *Village Voice.*

In 1959 she started writing "Dance Journal," an artistic and critical column about avant-garde dance. Later, she explored herself through articles about feminists. What and how she wrote reflected her opinions and attitudes. Occasionally, she became personally involved in what she wrote, almost to the point that her own and the subject's belief systems were one and the same.

In 1971 she published a compilation of her columns under the title *Marmalade Me.* A year later she wrote about the women's movement in "The March of the Real Women." This and other articles focused on the divisions within the women's movement, especially between the straights and the lesbians. Johnston advocated having lesbians lead the women's movement because they were not as confused sexually as straights.

In 1973 this idea and others were further explored in *Lesbian Nation: The Feminist Solution,* a book about lesbianism as well as feminism. Johnston then turned inward and examined herself in relation to others in articles and, later, a book. Her *Gullibles Travels* was favorably reviewed by Susan Braudy in *Ms:*

Jill Johnston elides thoughts, "vaginates verbs," avoids paragraphs, and thinks better than most people do. This overly sensitive, unsettling, disruptive wonderwoman, this "recalcitrant daughter" in "high-denim dyke gear," is one of our most original open-to-the-gut feminist writers.[1]

The essays in this book focused on women such as Agnes Martin and Bella Abzug. In addition, Johnston depicted herself, almost lifelike and on canvas, as she employed one persona, then another. This book, more than any other, exhibited her creative ability. The essays were examples of literary journalism because of the author's role in what was reported. In one, Johnston used lowercase letters, particularly when she referred to herself. She also played with language.

In 1983 she wrote the first volume of her autobiography, *Mother Bound*. In it Johnston explored herself and her relationship with her parents. Two years later she wrote the second volume, *Autobiography in Search of a Father: Paper Daughter,* in which she continued her soul-searching and obsession with her parents. As in the first volume, she explored her life during the 1960s. She recounted her emotional breakdowns, her lesbianism, and her newly acquired fame. Both volumes were written in the same stream-of-consciousness literary style used in *Gullibles Travels.*

WORKS: *Marmalade Me* (1971); *Lesbian Nation: The Feminist Solution* (1973); *Gullibles Travels* (1974); *Mother Bound* (1983); *Autobiography in Search of a Father: Paper Daughter* (1985).
NOTE
1. Susan Braudy, "The Johnston Papers," *Ms,* October 1974, p. 36.

K

Roger Kahn
(1927–)

Roger Kahn, born in Brooklyn in 1927, attended New York University from 1944 to 1947, then worked for seven years as a reporter for the *New York Herald Tribune.* Switching from newspapers to magazines, he became a contributing editor to *Sports Illustrated* in 1955. This experience, along with his previous work at the *Herald Tribune,* enabled him to become sports editor of *Newsweek* within a year, a position he held until 1960. For the next several years he devoted his time to writing articles and books about sports. From 1963 to 1968 he was editor-at-large at the *Saturday Evening Post.* In the latter year he published *The Passionate People: What It Means to Be a Jew in America.* This book was followed in 1970 by *The Battle for Morningside Heights: Why Students Rebel,* which explored in depth the 1968 student rebellion at Columbia University's Morningside Heights campus. That year he also became a sports columnist for *Esquire.*

In 1972 *The Boys of Summer,* a book about the old Brooklyn Dodgers baseball team, appeared. Basically written out of love for baseball and the Dodgers, Kahn's book was successful with critics and readers, who liked its incisive information and its informal composition. Filled with anecdotes, dialogue, and sports trivia, the book was an exercise in literary journalism. Kahn had interviewed every player he could locate and recorded with incredible accuracy what each had said. The prose, which was simple and direct, captured incidents without overplaying the subjects.

Kahn's next book, *How the Weather Was* (1973), was a collection of articles about various sports heroes, including Babe Ruth and Willie Mays, as well as other celebrities such as Robert Frost.

Kahn became a columnist for *Time* in 1976. He also contributed articles to other periodicals, including the *Nation* and *American Scholar*. Articles that had appeared in *Sports Illustrated* were expanded and published in 1977 under the title *A Season in the Sun,* another book about baseball.

Kahn wrote two novels before publishing his next piece of nonfiction, *Good Enough to Dream* (1985). In it Kahn discussed his brief experience as president and part-owner of the Utica Blue Soxs of the New York–Pennsylvania League, one of only 16 minor leagues in the country. Interesting because of the numerous colorful characters it described, the book was another example of literary journalism.

Joe and Marilyn: A Memory of Love followed a year later. To say the least, Kahn's version of Joe DiMaggio and Marilyn Monroe's love affair and ultimate marriage was compassionate and elegant.

Although Kahn collaborated with Pete Rose on *My Story* in 1989, he later stated that he would not do another book with a sports legend. He believed that such efforts required writers who were perhaps better than he at handling such assignments.[1]

In 1992 he published a collection of articles written between 1954 and 1990 under the title *Games We Used to Play: A Lover's Quarrel with the World of Sport.* Each article illustrated that Kahn not only enjoyed watching sports, but loved writing about sports as well.

The Era: 1947–1957: When the Yankees, the Giants, and the Dodgers Ruled the World (1993) dealt with the "golden age" of baseball. Kahn covered the 11 seasons from 1947, when Jackie Robinson began playing for the Brooklyn Dodgers, to 1957, when the Dodgers and the Giants moved to California. Of course, Kahn had been in a position to see and hear what he recounted, having been a reporter for the *New York Herald Tribune* during most of the 11 seasons. The book provided a colorful history filled with anecdotes, much like his earlier *The Boys of Summer.*

WORKS: *The Battle for Morningside Heights: Why Students Rebel* (1970); *The Boys of Summer* (1972); *Good Enough to Dream* (1985); *Joe and Marilyn: A Memory of Love* (1986); *The Era: 1947–1957: When the Yankees, the Giants, and the Dodgers Ruled the World* (1993).

NOTE

1. Craig Little, "PW Interviews: Roger Kahn," *Publishers Weekly,* October 4, 1993, p. 50.

Murray Kempton
(1918–)

Journalist and author Murray Kempton was born in Baltimore in 1918 and attended public schools and Johns Hopkins University. Interested in history and political science, he became a member of the Socialist party. When he received his degree in 1939, he remained in Baltimore for a few months, then moved to New York City, where he first worked as an organizer for a noncommunist American youth congress, the Campaign for Youth Needs, then as an organizer for the International Ladies' Garment Workers' Union. Experience at these positions enabled him to become publicity director for the American Labor party and a writer for both the Young People's Socialist League and the Workers' Defense League in 1941.

A year later he was hired by the *New York Post* to report on labor, but his assignment was abruptly interrupted when he enlisted in the U.S. Army. For two years he was engaged in combat in the Pacific; he returned to the United States unharmed.

For the next several years he worked first as a reporter for the Wilmington, North Carolina, *Star,* then as assistant to Victor Riesel, the labor editor of the *New York Post.* In 1949 he became the paper's labor editor and focused his attention on the relationships between union officials and members of organized crime. As a columnist he covered civil rights and politics, including domestic and foreign policy as well as presidential campaigns. He was deeply concerned with the Red Scare created by Senator Joseph McCarthy, which he denounced. His attitude toward communists was not necessarily favorable, but he believed that members of the Communist party had rights. His book, *Part of Our Time: Some Monuments and Ruins of the Thirties,* explored this attitude and belief in depth.

During the 1950s Kempton covered with equal candor the problems confronting blacks. He addressed the problem of segregation, a practice deemed unjust. He covered Antherine Juanita Lucy's first day at the University of Alabama as well as the controversial trial of two white men who were charged with the murder of a black youth. These dispatches were so elegant in style that they were almost short stories. Indeed, they were examples of literary journalism.

Toward the end of the decade he covered Nikita Khrushchev's tour of the United States, and in 1960 the presidential campaign. A year later he traveled to the South again and wrote about Dr. Martin Luther King, Jr.'s desegregation campaign. The same year he defended Carmine DeSapio, New York's Tammany Hall leader. Kempton, who strongly believed in human rights, was severely criticized not only for having supported DeSapio, but for having defended another columnist, Westbrook Pegler, who had been dismissed from the Hearst empire in 1962 for his right-wing philosophy.

A year later Kempton left the *Post* and moved to Washington, D.C., where he worked as an editor and as a columnist for the *New Republic.* Kempton, who worked for over a year for the liberal weekly, wrote numerous articles about controversial issues and persons, including the "Warren Report," Jack Ruby, John F. Kennedy and his administration, and Joe Valachi. His second book, *America Comes of Middle Age: Columns 1950–1962,* published in 1963, was a collection of columns that had appeared in the *New York Post.*

From 1964 to 1966 he wrote columns for the *New York World Telegram and Sun.* He returned to the *Post* shortly thereafter and contributed a column through most of the 1970s. In addition, he contributed to numerous magazines and wrote *The Briar Patch: The People of the State of New York Versus Lumumba Shakur, et al.* in 1973. Kempton explored the deplorable injustice with which the U.S. court system treated the Black Panthers.

Although he threatened to leave the *Post* more than once throughout the 1970s, he remained with the paper until 1981, when he left to join New York *Newsday,* where his column appeared at least four times a week. In addition, he contributed essays to various periodicals throughout the 1980s and early 1990s, including *House and Garden,* the *Saturday Evening Post,* and the *New York Review of Books.* Kempton became a member of the editorial advisory board of the *Washington Monthly* during this time.

Kempton met numerous prominent people as well as members of organized crime during his 50-plus years in journalism, from Adlai Stevenson, Alger Hiss, Richard Nixon, Daniel Patrick Moynihan, Nancy Reagan, George Bush, and Ross Perot to Malcolm X, Martin Luther King, Jr., Louis Armstrong, Huey Newton, Frank Costello, Carmine Persico, Jimmy Hoffa, John Gotti, Jean Harris, and William F. Buckley.

Rebellions, Perversions, and Main Events, which contained his columns and stories from the *Post* and *Newsday,* as well as lengthy essays from the *New York Review of Books,* was published in 1994. Together, the columns and essays exhibited Kempton's affection for the radical, the rebel, the rascal, the misfit, and the loser. Indeed, he complimented Alger Hiss for being a good comrade at Lewisburg Prison; he praised Lillian Hellman for her defiance of the House Committee on Un-American Activities. He examined with sarcastic criticism several presidents, including Truman, Eisenhower, and Nixon, who was a friend. Kempton also discussed Italy, Italians, and certain members of the Mafia, as well as jazz and art. Like most of his work, this collection revealed his ability to advocate worthy causes, defend the accused, and criticize individuals for unprofessional or unethical conduct, all in a literary and elegant style.

WORKS: *Part of Our Time: Some Monuments and Ruins of the Thirties* (1955); *America Comes of Middle Age: Columns 1950–1962* (1963); *The Briar Patch: The People of the State of New York Versus Lumumba Shakur, et al.* (1973); *Rebellions, Perversions, and Main Events* (1994).

Tracy Kidder
(1945–)

Tracy Kidder was born on November 12, 1945, in New York City. His father, Henry, was a lawyer, and his mother, Reine, was a teacher. Kidder studied English at Harvard University and wrote short stories in his spare time. He graduated in 1967, then served in Vietnam as an intelligence officer in the U.S.

Army. When he was discharged he moved to Iowa City, where he continued his education at the University of Iowa's Writers Workshop. He noted: "I got a little fellowship there and it was wonderful for me. First of all, being there made me realize that there were an awful lot of other people in the world who were trying to do what I was attempting to do. It was good in that way. Humiliating, so to speak."[1]

Before he received his master of fine arts degree in 1974, he met Dan Wakefield, a contributing editor at *Atlantic Monthly*. Wakefield wrote to the editor of the magazine on Kidder's behalf, and Kidder was assigned an article about Juan Corona's murder trial. Corona, a farm labor contractor in California, had been accused of murdering 25 migrant farm laborers. To do the article justice, Kidder went to California and traced the steps of the workers. Unfortunately, many of them had been hobos; if they were not working, they rode trains. Few, if any, had homes. Kidder's attempts to unravel their lives were, for the most part, futile. The article suffered as a result. Kidder expanded the article into a book, *The Road to Yuba City: A Journey into the Juan Corona Murders,* which was published in 1974. The book suffered from his inexperience as well as his inability to penetrate the world of migrant workers. Although he rode trains like hobos, ate what they ate, rested where they rested, and worked where they worked, he was an outsider, and many sources were suspicious of his intentions. Thus he was not able to cover Juan Corona and his world thoroughly. The book also suffered from Kidder's use of the first person point of view.

The book failed to stir much discussion, even among critics. Nonetheless, it was an example of literary journalism because Kidder employed devices typical of fiction, such as vivid description and authentic dialogue. In addition, he was more than just an observer; he was a participant.

Although Kidder published several short stories, including at least two in the *Atlantic Monthly,* he focused primarily on articles, publishing about a dozen in the *Atlantic.* Kidder wrote about the Caribbean, politics in Washington, D.C., American railroads, disabled Vietnam veterans, water pollution, nuclear power, Long Island real estate, and solar energy. His writing improved with each article.

His next book, *The Soul of a New Machine,* which chronicled the development of a super mini-computer by Data General Corporation engineers, was published in 1981. The book was critically acclaimed by reviewers. Jeremy Bernstein wrote:

For readers who would like to know what it takes to make one, . . . how they are organized, and who the people are who put them together, I strongly recommend Tracy Kidder's book. I do not know anything quite like it. It tells a story far removed from our daily experience, and while it may seem implausible, it has the ring of truth.[2]

In *The Soul of a New Machine,* Kidder allowed various characters to speak directly to the reader. Kidder, the observer, provided just enough description to whet the reader's appetite.

The book became a best-seller because Kidder had explained a very complex subject in everyday terms. He had entered the world of the engineers and watched them work; he had observed how their ideas sometimes clashed. In short, he had learned about computers, particularly their design, and about the individuals who created them, then presented in detail what he had learned. These detailed explanations were the book's primary strength. Kidder received the Pulitzer Prize and the American Book Award in 1982, the year he became a contributing editor at the *Atlantic Monthly*.

In 1985 he published his third book. Titled *House,* it was similar to *The Soul of a New Machine* in the sense that he examined another project—the building of a house—from conception to completion. He presented the individuals involved—from the Yale-educated architect to the Harvard-educated owner to the experienced builders. Kidder observed the progress of the project, depicting with accuracy the problems that cropped up along the way, some of which were the result of personalities clashing.

The story progressed logically from the time the contract was signed to the time when the owners moved into their new home. Kidder included explanations of building terms and references.

Kidder's fourth book, *Among Schoolchildren,* was published in 1989. Chris Zajac, the book's primary subject, taught fifth grade in Holyoke, Massachusetts. Zajac, as Kidder observed, was more than a teacher. She was a psychologist in the sense that she inspired confidence in her students as much as she aroused their curiosity. Although Kidder learned more about Zajac perhaps than any other subject about which he had written, he also learned about her students and their families. Kidder presented Zajac's thoughts as well as her words and deeds. However, he was an omniscient observer, just as in *House;* he was not one of the participants.

Like other literary journalists, Kidder researched his subjects for months, then presented the characters and their stories to the reader. He knew the characters well: their thoughts, their mannerisms, and their expressions.

His fifth book, *Old Friends,* was published in 1993. It detailed quite candidly the friendship between Lou Freed, 90, and Joe Torchio, 72, as they lived from day to day in a new nursing home, Linda Manor, in Northampton, Massachusetts. Kidder's prose was uplifting, to say the least, as he humanized what most individuals consider a very depressing environment. The book was another example of literary journalism.

WORKS: *The Road to Yuba City: A Journey into the Juan Corona Murders* (1974); *The Soul of a New Machine* (1981); *House* (1985); *Among Schoolchildren* (1989); *Old Friends* (1993).

NOTES

1. Jean W. Ross, "CA Interview," *Contemporary Authors,* edited by Hal May (Detroit: Gale Research, 1983), Vol. 109, p. 251.

2. Jeremy Bernstein, "Modern Times," *New York Review,* October 8, 1987, p. 41.

Larry L. King
(1929–)

Larry L. King, who wrote a humorous, raucous *Playboy* article about a whorehouse in Texas which eventually became the subject of a Broadway play and a film, was born in Putnam, Texas, on January 1, 1929. He served in the U.S. Army Signal Corps as a writer and later as a staff sergeant for two years, then attended Texas Technological College (Texas Tech University) until 1950. He began to work as a newspaper reporter in 1949, however. He explained:

In my early twenties I was a police reporter in Texas and New Mexico. There I saw, and wrote about, all manner of gore and small-bore corruptions; hot-blooded killings and cold-blooded ones, fatal accidents ranging from automobile crashes to lightning bolts, passionate trials, crooked cops, racist judges; thieves and thugs and con men.[1]

King, unlike most reporters, impersonated authorities, paid little attention to regulations, and confronted both "cops and robbers" to obtain information. He frequented beer joints not only because he liked beer, but because he learned from various persons, including criminals, hookers, con men, dope traffickers, double-crossers, and police informers, how corruption had infiltrated both the bottom rung and the top rung of society.

In 1955 King moved to Washington, D.C., where he worked for U.S. Congressmen J. T. Rutherford and James Wright, among others. In 1965 he became editor of *Capitol Hill* magazine. His knowledge of Washington was useful as well in his work as a correspondent and later contributing editor for the *Texas Observer*. His profiles, which usually contained anecdotes within a descriptive vignette, were published in the *Washington Post,* the *Washington Star, Atlantic, Esquire, Sport, American Heritage, Classic, Harper's,* the *Nation, True,* and the *Progressive.* His articles were collected and published as *... And Other Dirty Stories* (1968), *The Old Man and Lesser Mortals* (1974), and *Of Outlaws, Con Men, Whores, Politicians, and Other Artists* (1980).

King was a contributing editor to *Harper's* magazine in the late 1960s. Willie Morris, the magazine's guiding editor, enjoyed promoting the new journalism. In "The Authentic New Journalists," David McHam claimed that King may have been the magazine's best writer in the early 1970s: "His five articles ... were the kind that caused people who appreciate good writing to meet their friends with a 'Did you see the Larry King story on thus and so?' "[2]

King also became a contributing editor to *New Times* and *Texas Monthly* in the 1970s, as well as president of Texhouse Corporation in Washington, D.C., in 1979. He became a contributing editor to *Parade* magazine in 1983.

In addition to numerous articles, he wrote several books of nonfiction. In *Confessions of a White Racist,* published in 1971, King explored his own racism and that of other whites while he lived in Texas, Washington, D.C., and New

England. *The Whorehouse Papers* (1982) concerned the problems he encountered while writing the play "The Best Little Whorehouse in Texas." Indeed, King described in detail his numerous disagreements with collaborators, various personality clashes, and the powerlessness he felt as he watched his work being changed by others. He also told of his growing dependency on alcohol, which was aggravated by the many confrontations. *None but a Blockhead: On Being a Writer* and *Warning: Writer at Work* were published in 1986. The first was a memoir about his life as a writer and drinker, and, like his articles, was flooded with his redneck humor—that is, until he discussed the death of his second wife, Rosemarie Coumarias, a photographer who died of cancer in 1972. The second focused on his writing.

King also wrote *Because of Lozo Brown,* a children's book, in 1989, as well as the plays *The Night Hank Williams Died: A Play in Two Acts, with Incidental Music,* which was performed in the late 1980s and published in 1989, and *The Golden Shadows Old West Museum* (1992), which was based on a short story by Michael Blackman about the problems of aging and the impersonal treatment of the elderly.

WORKS: . . . *And Other Dirty Stories* (1968); *The Old Man and Lesser Mortals* (1974); *Of Outlaws, Con Men, Whores, Politicians, and Other Artists* (1980).

NOTES

1. Larry L. King, *Of Outlaws, Con Men, Whores, Politicians, and Other Artists* (New York: Viking Press, 1980), p. 71.

2. David McHam, "The Authentic New Journalists," in *The Reporter as Artist: A Look at the New Journalism Controversy,* edited by Ronald Weber (New York: Hastings House, 1974), p. 116.

Jane Kramer
(1931-   )

A native of Providence, Rhode Island, Jane Kramer received her bachelor's degree from Vassar College in 1952 at the age of 21 and her master's degree from Columbia University in 1961. Kramer, a writer who worked for the *Village Voice* and later the *New Yorker,* collected 24 articles that had appeared in the former publication for her first book, *Off Washington Square: A Reporter Looks at Greenwich Village, N.Y.* The articles discussed such celebrities as author Robert Gover, Raymond Auger and his robot, publisher J. David Stern, iconoclast Peter Cook, artist Salvador Dali, Jim Ross and Synanon, Marcel Marceau, poet e.e. cummings, and Hugh Hefner and his Playboy empire. The book appeared in 1963, the year she moved to the *New Yorker.*

Six years later she wrote a perceptive biography of the poet Allen Ginsberg. *Allen Ginsberg in America* was criticized by some reviewers for its lack of critical insight. However, Michael L. Johnson claimed that she captured the whole man as well as his environment.[1]

A year later she wrote *Honor to the Bridge Like the Pigeon that Guards Its Grain Under the Clove Tree,* an account of the kidnapping and assault of a 13-year-old Arab girl living in Morocco. Kramer, by using the techniques of the novelist, not only entertained readers but allowed them to experience Arabian beliefs and customs.

The Last Cowboy, which first appeared in the *New Yorker,* concerned Henry Blanton, who lived and worked on a ranch in the Texas panhandle; it was published in 1977. Kramer, through descriptive scenes, dramatic dialogue, and interior monologue, allowed the reader to hear, understand, and perhaps appreciate Henry Blanton, even though he was biased, rowdy, and chauvinistic. Indeed, Kramer presented a fascinating portrait of a bygone hero. As she wrote in the introduction: "He had settled into his life, but he could not seem to settle for it. He moved in a kind of deep, prideful disappointment. He longed for something to restore him—a lost myth, a hero's West."[2]

As in her other articles and books, Kramer presented an intimate personality profile with which few critics could find fault. She repeated the performance in *Unsettling Europe,* which was published in 1980. Its intimate sketches of four European families were written while she served as the *New Yorker*'s "Reporter in Europe." The families, although of different backgrounds, faced the same problem: they had been uprooted from their natural homeland because of political or economic pressure. When they settled in other countries they were ostracized by their new neighbors. Kramer had hope, nonetheless, that such integration of peoples would make Europe stronger, not the opposite.

Europeans, a collection of essays published in the *New Yorker* between 1978 and 1987, was published in 1988. The essays presented sides of Europe that most tourists never experience. Examples of literary journalism, the essays contained names and quotations and examined Germans, French, Italians, and other cultures and peoples.

WORKS: *Off Washington Square: A Reporter Looks at Greenwich Village, N.Y.* (1963); *Allen Ginsberg in America* (1969); *Honor to the Bridge Like the Pigeon that Guards Its Grain Under the Clove Tree* (1970); *The Last Cowboy* (1977); *Unsettling Europe* (1980); *Europeans* (1988).

NOTES

1. Michael L. Johnson, *The New Journalism: The Underground Press, the Artists of Nonfiction, and Changes in the Established Media* (Lawrence: University Press of Kansas, 1971), pp. 137–138.

2. Jane Kramer, *The Last Cowboy* (New York: Harper and Row, 1977), pp. vii–ix.

Mark Kramer
(1944–)

Mark Kramer was born to Esther and Sidney Kramer on April 14, 1944, in New York City. His father was an attorney and publisher, and his mother managed a bookstore. Kramer received his bachelor's degree from Brandeis University in 1966, then attended Columbia University, from which he received his master's degree in sociology in 1967. Although he continued his formal education at Indiana University the following year, he started writing for the Liberation News Service and contributed the column "Living in the Country" to *Real Paper.*

In 1969 he moved to western Massachusetts, where he learned to farm. This experience was presented in his columns, which were collected and published under the title *Mother Walker and the Pig Tragedy* in 1972. The book's freeform style enhanced the etchings scattered throughout the text.

Although Kramer contributed articles and reviews to several publications, including the *Atlantic Monthly, National Geographic,* and the *New York Times,* he devoted at least two years to his next book. He lived part of the time on a New England dairy farm, part of the time on a midwestern hog farm, and part of the time on a large California corporate farm. The result was *Three Farms: Making Milk, Meat, and Money from the American Soil,* published in 1980, the year he became writer in residence at Smith College in Northampton, Massachusetts. Based on experience, observation, and research, the book was divided into three sections: "Making Milk," "Family Farmer," and "The Farmerless Farm." From the small farm to the large one, Kramer explained what each required to be productive—newer and better technology. More important, however, he explored how those who operated the farms were affected by technology.

In 1983 his book *Invasive Procedures: A Year in the World of Two Surgeons* was published. In it Kramer explored the fascinating world of medical science, having spent almost two years conducting research. He interviewed surgeons and, after getting permission from at least two, observed them as they performed more than 100 operations. He also observed them with their patients after surgery and interviewed their staffs as well as their colleagues. In short, he learned as much as he could about them and their profession, and presented a vivid and dramatic portrait of surgical medicine. Joe McGinniss observed that "his reportorial skill, combined with a prose style that . . . is as clean and sharp as one of his subjects' scalpel blades, has produced a book that gives an intriguing and often insightful look behind the scenes of a world that both fascinates and repels."[1]

As he had in *Three Farms,* Kramer used the first-person point of view, but participated just enough to inform the reader of his whereabouts.

He also contributed to *The Literary Journalists,* which was edited by Norman Sims in 1985.

WORKS: *Mother Walker and the Pig Tragedy* (1972); *Three Farms: Making Milk, Meat, and Money from the American Soil* (1980); *Invasive Procedures: A Year in the World of Two Surgeons* (1983).

NOTE

1. Joe McGinniss, "Doctors, Operating," *New York Times Book Review,* September 18, 1983, p. 12.

James Simon Kunen
(1948–)

James Simon Kunen was born in 1948 in Boston. The author of perhaps the most personal account of the 1968 Students for a Democratic Society (SDS) strike against Columbia University's involvement in research for the Pentagon, *The Strawberry Statement*, Kunen was a student at the university when he wrote the informal, diary-like journal. Through vignettes, musings, and anecdotes, Kunen revealed himself as a conscientious and righteous person who was searching for a more humane society. The book was a critical and commercial success, and the film version was no less popular. Because sections had been published in the *Atlantic* and *New York* magazines, readers had been seduced by the author's charming wit before the book appeared.

By the time he graduated from Columbia in 1970, he had contributed columns to the *Boston Globe, Newsday,* and the *Washington Post.* In addition, he had written another book, *Standard Operating Procedure.*

In the 1970s Kunen contributed articles to such publications as *Esquire, US,* the *Atlantic, Life, New York,* and *Mademoiselle,* and a column to *New Times.* However, none had the power of his first book. Michael L. Johnson called him a "perspective reporter" who exercised "an articulate critical intelligence."[1]

In 1985 Kunen produced *"How Can You Defend Those People?" The Making of a Criminal Lawyer,* an autobiographical work that focused on his becoming a lawyer and practicing in Washington, D.C. Stylishly written, the book explored his innocence as an idealistic lawyer who worked in a not so idealistic world.

Reckless Disregard: Corporate Greed, Government Indifference, and the Kentucky School Bus Crash, published in 1994, dealt with a school bus accident that ultimately killed 27 people. The bus had been struck by a truck driven by a drunk driver. The impact forced the gas tank of the bus to explode. The book focused on the crash, the bus, and the parents of one of the victims and their suspicions that the bus had been unsafe. In fact, they believed that the bus, primarily because of its poor design, had been responsible for their daughter's death. Officials of Ford Motor Company, its manufacturer, knew that the bus was unsafe because of its design. The parents sued Ford to correct the problem. Their lawyer, however, advised them to take Ford's monetary offer of $5 million, which they eventually accepted. The book, which had been thoroughly and carefully researched, concerned corporate greed and an uncaring governmental bureaucracy.

WORKS: *The Strawberry Statement* (1969); *Standard Operating Procedure* (1970); *"How Can You Defend Those People?" The Making of a Criminal Lawyer* (1985); *Reckless Disregard: Corporate Greed, Government Indifference, and the Kentucky School Bus Crash* (1994).

NOTE

1. Michael L. Johnson, *The New Journalism: The Underground Press, the Artists of Nonfiction, and Changes in the Established Media* (Lawrence: University Press of Kansas, 1971), pp. 122–123.

L

John Lardner
(1913–1960)

John Lardner entered the world of American journalism when he accepted a job as a reporter with the *New York Herald Tribune*. It was 1931, and the Great Depression had started. Lardner was one of four sons of the late Ring Lardner. However, he was the only son who followed in his father's footsteps, by becoming a journalist who wrote mostly about sports. He was born on the South Side of Chicago, when his father was writing for the old *Chicago Examiner*. He attended the prestigious Phillips Academy, from which he graduated in 1929. Although he continued his formal education at Harvard, he left after a year to work as a reporter for the *Paris Herald,* then transferred to its parent paper, the *New York Herald Tribune,* where he worked for Stanley Walker, the city editor.

Lardner soon specialized in sports. From 1933 to 1948 he contributed a sports column to the North American Newspaper Alliance. In 1939 he joined the staff of *Newsweek* magazine; he contributed the column "Lardner's Week," which was devoted to sports, and, during World War II, served as one of the magazine's correspondents. During the war, he covered the North African campaign for the *New Yorker*. Although he remained with *Newsweek,* Lardner reviewed plays on Broadway first for the *New Yorker,* then for the old *New York Star*. His criticism was filled with sports analogies and humor.

In addition, he contributed articles to the *New York Times Magazine* as well as the *National Guardian*. Before his untimely death at the age of 47 in 1960, he had contributed a regular column about television to the *New Yorker* and had written five books: *The Crowning of Technology* (1933), *Southwest Passage: The Yanks in the Pacific* (1943), *It Beats Working* (1947), *White Hopes and*

Other Tigers (1951), and *Strong Cigars and Lovely Women* (1951). Although several of his books were entertaining because of his unusual writing style, his work for the *New Yorker* could be considered literary journalism because much of it contained the elements of fiction, particularly realistic or authentic dialogue.

WORKS: Articles (*New Yorker*).

Ring Lardner
(1885–1933)

Ring Lardner, perhaps better known as a sports reporter than as a literary journalist, was born on March 6, 1885, in Niles, Michigan. Although Henry and Lena Lardner had nine children, they were quite capable of providing for them. They had inherited a farm and considerable cash, and were considered to be one of the wealthiest families in Niles.

Ring, like the other children in the family, was educated at home by his mother, who was a voracious reader and a talented musician. In addition to learning about literature and music, he learned about baseball. In fact, before he entered Niles High School at age 12, he could recite the batting orders of each professional team.

Lardner graduated when he was 16 and for the next four years worked at a variety of jobs in Niles and Chicago. Finally, he was hired to write about sports as well as other topics by the *South Bend Times*. At the 1907 World Series he met Hugh Fullerton, who wrote about baseball for the *Chicago Examiner*. Fullerton was so impressed by Lardner's knowledge of baseball that he helped him obtain a job writing about sports at the *Chicago Inter Ocean*.

Within a year he was working at the *Chicago Examiner,* for which he covered the Chicago White Sox. He enjoyed traveling with the team and talking to the players. He learned their likes and dislikes and grew to understand their language. He played poker with them; he drank with them. He listened intently to what they said.

Lardner left the *Examiner* and went to the *Chicago Tribune,* where he covered the Chicago Cubs in addition to the White Sox. His coverage was unique. Most sports writers provided running accounts, inning by inning; Lardner gave readers information about the players or incidents that occurred during the game. He was a careful observer, and he employed humor in his stories.

Lardner became engaged to Ellis Abbott and found a job that required less travel editing the *Sporting News*. However, within two months, after he had realized that the owner was unethical, journalistically speaking, he left in search of another job.

Lardner worked briefly as a sports writer for the *Boston American* before he was named sports editor in 1911, the year he and Abbott married. Subsequently, he quit in protest when two sports reporters were fired.

After working as a copyreader at the *Chicago American,* he returned to the

Chicago Examiner, again as a sports writer. Lardner's writing was now filled with humor. At the same time, he experimented, using verse, for instance, and occasionally parodying popular songs. Because he used dialogue in the vernacular of baseball players as well as vivid description, some of his writing is considered literary journalism. The former allowed readers to visualize scenes, and the latter gave them accurate portraits of individuals and settings.

In 1913, after *Chicago Tribune* reporter Hugh E. Keogh died, Lardner was offered his column, "In the Wake of the News," a popular column about sports. Lardner made changes, however, in both content and style. Occasionally, he employed a one-paragraph comment or one-line joke. He used verse as well as dialogue to comment on numerous topics, including members of his immediate family. His columns about baseball players featured not only accurate descriptions but realistic dialogue. As a result, readers learned about various players and were entertained at the same time.

Lardner contributed short stories too. One was based on correspondence between a pitcher for the White Sox and his friends. Although rejected by the newspaper, the story was accepted by the *Saturday Evening Post.* Consequently, Lardner contributed short stories to other magazines, and many were eventually collected and published in book form.

During World War I Lardner worked as a correspondent in Europe. Even though his columns and articles were informative, Lardner's lack of familiarity with the subject matter showed; indeed, these columns and articles were inferior to his other material, particularly his sports reporting.

In 1919 he resigned from the *Chicago Tribune* and signed with the Bell Syndicate. For the next several years he covered major sports events in his column, and contributed short stories to periodicals. He tried writing plays for Broadway, but he enjoyed little success. He contributed autobiographical articles to the *Saturday Evening Post* in 1932, a year before he died of a heart attack.

WORK: *Some Champions: Sketches and Fiction by Ring Lardner,* edited by Matthew J. Bruccoli and Richard Layman (1976).

A. J. Liebling
(1904–1963)

Born in New York City in 1904, A. J. Liebling, one of journalism's most celebrated critics, attended Dartmouth College, Columbia University, from which he graduated, and later the Sorbonne in Paris. Upon his graduation from Columbia, he worked for the *New York Times,* the *Providence Journal,* and the *Evening Bulletin,* the latter two located in Providence, Rhode Island.

In 1926 he moved to Paris, where he grew lackadaisical toward his studies at the Sorbonne; Parisian culture attracted his interest. The young women, the cafés, the restaurants, the theater became his education. Unfortunately for Liebling, the year ended too soon.

When he returned to Providence he continued his duties for the *Providence Journal* and the *Evening Bulletin*. In 1930 he became a staff writer with the *New York World;* when the *World* merged with the *Telegram* one year later he became a feature writer. For four years he contributed lively, spirited articles to the paper. In 1935 he moved to the *New Yorker,* where he remained for the rest of his journalistic career. Beginning as a staff writer, Liebling eventually won journalistic prominence when he was sent to Europe in 1939 as the magazine's correspondent. From France, England, and North Africa his accounts came. Liebling covered the significant campaigns in Europe and North Africa, but his coverage was unlike that of other correspondents; he looked for minute details, finding them interesting and significant. His writing was equally interesting. A cross between objective reporting and fiction, the style allowed Liebling to become a participant, to report on the event from his perspective. Elements of literary journalism were present.

Liebling returned to New York City when the war ended and in 1946 began his "Wayward Press" column, in which he satirized popular issues, especially American journalism. In addition, he contributed numerous articles to the magazine. Many of his columns were collected and published in book form. Perhaps the best known were *The Wayward Pressman, The Sweet Science: A Ringside View of Boxing,* and *The Press. The Sweet Science*'s powerful descriptive sentences enabled the reader to visualize events and subsequently experience what Liebling observed. He died in 1963.

WORK: *The Sweet Science: A Ringside View of Boxing* (1956).

Robert Lipsyte
(1938–   )

Robert Lipsyte, a sports columnist, novelist, and author of screenplays, was born to Fanny and Sidney Lipsyte on January 16, 1938, in New York City. He received his bachelor's and master's degrees from Columbia University in 1957 and 1959, respectively, and began his newspaper career as a copy boy with the *New York Times* in the late 1950s. After being promoted to sports reporter and later sports columnist, he resigned from the *Times* in 1971 to write young adult and adult novels, which were based primarily on sports and the characters' struggles to compete. Ironically, his writing for the *Times* had not been dissimilar. Indeed, his skills as a journalist were unleashed in such award-winning articles as "The Long Road to Broken Dreams," "Where the Stars of Tomorrow Shine Tonight," and "Dempsey in the Window."

Using traditional sports writing techniques, Lipsyte captured honestly and critically not only a given sport, but the glorified athletes, whom he recognized as human beings first and heroes second. He penetrated the sports world in such books as *Assignment: Sports* (1970), which, through vignettes, went beyond the mere scores, wins, and losses to what made the athlete decide to pursue a particular sport. Lipsyte, in the style of the literary journalist, revealed more than the essential facts of an event; he presented the thoughts, mannerisms, and characteristics of the participants. In 1975, in *SportsWorld: An American Dreamland,* he presented believable portraits of Kareem Abdul-Jabbar, Muhammad Ali, Angelo Dundee, Bill Bradley, Jimmy Ellis, Billie Jean King, Sonny Liston, Joe Louis, Joe Namath, Floyd Patterson, Babe Ruth, and Tom Seaver, among others, and also criticized team owners, television executives, sports commentators, and newspaper and magazine journalists for selling and promoting spectator sports as necessities of life.

In addition to contributing to a variety of periodicals, including *TV Guide,* the *Nation, Harper's,* the *New York Times Book Review,* and the *New York Times Sports Magazine,* he contributed a column to the *New York Post* in 1977, a year before he wrote a brief but insightful biography, *Free to Be Muhammad Ali.* The same year he was diagnosed with cancer. After surgery and two years of chemotherapy, however, he had no signs of the disease.

From 1982 to 1986 he worked as a sports essayist for the program "Sunday Morning," which was produced by CBS. In 1986 he was hired as a correspondent by NBC, a position he held until he was hired to host the program "The Eleventh Hour," which aired on PBS in 1989.

From the early 1980s to the early 1990s, while he was employed by various television networks, he wrote three books: *Jock and Jill* (1982), *The Summerboy* (1982), and *The Brave* (1991). All three were novels for young readers.

In 1991 he left television altogether and returned to the *New York Times* to write at least one sports column a week. This position allowed him more time to write books. By 1994 he had written two novels and two biographies: *The Chemco Kid* (1992) and *The Chief* (1993), as well as *Arnold Schwarzenegger: Hercules in America* (1993) and *Jim Thorpe: Twentieth-Century Jock* (1993). All four books were for young readers. The Schwarzenegger biography placed him among the famous strong men in history, then examined his body-building mystique in the context of fitness crazes during the past several decades. It was well written and offered a balanced portrait of the subject. The biography of Jim Thorpe used his life story as a lens through which to examine the effects of racism on Native Americans. In short, Lipsyte placed Jim Thorpe, the all-around athlete, in the larger context of Native American history. Like the previous book, it was well written and provided a balanced portrait of the subject.

WORKS: *Assignment: Sports* (1970); *SportsWorld: An American Dreamland* (1975).

Jack London
(1876–1916)

Jack London was born John Griffith Chaney on January 12, 1876, in San Francisco, to Flora Wellman and her common-law husband, William H. Chaney, who abandoned her when she became pregnant. She married John London before Jack's first birthday. Jack attended public schools in Oakland. His parents were impoverished, and he was forced to work at numerous jobs before he was 14.

A year later, after hearing stories from sailors, his interest in adventure and intrigue led him to become an oyster pirate. He grew to enjoy robbing oyster beds in San Francisco Bay until he was asked to join the other side. Law enforcement was not to his liking, however. In 1893 he signed on the *Sophie Sutherland* as a seaman. London enjoyed his new occupation. Although he was a prodigious reader, nothing satisfied him more than traveling and the sea.

When he returned from his voyage later that year, he entered a writing contest, submitting an account of a typhoon the ship had encountered near Japan. The article won and was subsequently published in the *Morning Call.*

London had hoped he could make enough from writing to support himself, but a depression gripped the United States. In 1894 two of his stories were published in *Evenings at Home,* but London realized that such efforts were not enough; he also knew that the jobs open to him demanded too much work for too little pay. Like Jacob Coxey of Ohio, who led thousands of unemployed Americans to Washington, Charles T. Kelly of San Francisco had formed an army. London was determined to be a member. He missed the train, but tramped on another until he caught up with Kelly in Iowa. London, like others who were starving, deserted Kelly's army in Missouri and journeyed to Chicago, Washington, New York, and Niagara Falls, where he was arrested on a charge of vagrancy. For 30 days he labored in the Erie County Penitentiary, seeing another side of life there: "He saw men whipped, tortured, and beaten to death. He became the friend and confidant of hardened criminals, listened to their yarns, their gripes and their philosophies, all of which became a part of the literary luggage that he was later to draw on."[1]

When he was released he went to Canada and tramped to Vancouver, where he boarded a vessel to San Francisco. King Hendricks and Irving Shepard wrote: "The experience 'on the road' was a turning point in his life. He saw, and lived, the life of the underprivileged at its worst. He mingled with men who were physically strong and capable of productive labor but to whom society or social conditions denied any opportunity."[2]

After these exploits, London entered high school, where he wrote several articles for the school newspaper. London concluded that only socialism would help the poor. Concurrently, he realized the importance of an education. He passed the entrance examination to the University of California but attended for only one semester. His family needed financial help.

In 1897 London, like others who had dreams of finding a fortune, journeyed to the Yukon, where he became ill with scurvy. Although he did not find gold, his experiences would be useful later; he turned to writing as soon as he was home. The *Overland Monthly* accepted "To the Man on Trial" in 1898, and the *Atlantic Monthly* accepted "An Odyssey of the North" a year later. Houghton Mifflin published a collection of his stories, *The Son of the Wolf,* in 1900, the year he married Elizabeth Maddern. London's reputation as a writer of merit began to spread, and in 1901 another collection was published. Most of these stories were based on his experiences. His first novel, *A Daughter of the Snows,* appeared a year later.

In 1902 London traveled to England for the American Press Association, where he lived among the poor in the slum districts of London. He recorded his experiences in *The People of the Abyss,* a work of literary journalism. According to Marie L. Ahearn:

The narrative "I," Jack London, continues to observe, to describe, to question, to listen, and to live the life of the East End. He is neither a remote observer nor an adventurous participant; on the contrary, he is vulnerable, and participation is often an ordeal for him. It is not a lark to be hungry and homeless, and it is this human ordeal that the reader shares.[3]

The book moved rapidly from one scene to another, and in most chapters the narrator was involved in at least one scene. However, as Ahearn pointed out, he often interrupted the narrative to explain a term, to provide background information or statistics, to record a conversation, or to comment about something.[4]

The People of the Abyss was based on observation and conversation. However, London used what he had seen and heard in his fiction, too. His highly acclaimed novel, *The Call of the Wild,* was published in 1903. Writing novels was not enough for him, however. He missed the excitement of adventure. In 1904 he covered the Russo-Japanese War for the *San Francisco Examiner,* but soon returned. His first marriage ended in divorce in 1905. Immediately he married Charmian Kittredge and purchased land in California, where he eventually made his home. Two years later, along with his second wife and four crewmen, he sailed to Hawaii and other South Sea islands, and then to Australia. London became extremely ill, and they returned home in 1909.

In the remaining years of his life, he produced short stories, essays, and novels, and sailed his yacht, *The Roamer,* in San Francisco Bay and other waters. Although sailing, his ranch, and his wife had filled a void in his life, his last seven years were not always satisfying. In 1910, for instance, his second child, a boy, died at birth. Three years later London sued the Balboa Amusement Company for making a film based on one of his books; at the time copyright laws were unclear because the film industry was relatively new. London won his suit and set a precedent, but his health deteriorated. That same year his almost completed home was destroyed by fire.

In 1914 he signed on with *Collier's* magazine as a war correspondent and went to Vera Cruz, Mexico, where his health grew much worse. When he developed uremia, doctors warned him to stop drinking alcohol, but it was too late. London had abused his body too long. At the time of his death in 1916 he had written about 50 books, making him one of the most prolific writers of his day.

WORKS: *The Son of the Wolf* (1900); *The People of the Abyss* (1903).

NOTES

1. Jack London, *Jack London Reports,* edited by King Hendricks and Irving Shepard (New York: Doubleday, 1970), pp. x–xi.

2. Ibid.

3. Marie L. Ahearn, *"The People of the Abyss:* Jack London as New Journalist,'' *Modern Fiction Studies* 22, no. 1 (Spring 1976): 76–78.

4. Ibid.

J. Anthony Lukas
(1933–)

Born to Elizabeth and Edwin Lukas on April 25, 1933, in New York City, J. Anthony Lukas attended the coeducational Putney School in Vermont before enrolling at Harvard University, from which he graduated in 1955. Before he entered journalism as a city hall correspondent for the *Baltimore Sun* in 1958, he attended the Free University of Berlin, then served in the U.S. Army. Lukas, an able reporter who wrote political stories, eventually moved to the *New York Times* in 1962, where he served in the Washington and United Nations bureaus. Within weeks, however, he found himself assigned to the Congo (now Zaire) and West Africa, where he remained until 1965. For the next two years he was assigned to India, Ceylon, and Pakistan. After spending most of his career with the *Times* overseas, Lukas was assigned to the metropolitan desk upon his return to New York.

In 1969 and 1970 Lukas covered the Chicago-Seven conspiracy trial for the *Times,* then wrote *The Barnyard Epithet and Other Obscenities: Notes on the Chicago Conspiracy* (1970), based on the information he had gathered on the trial. The book concerned American youth and their radical nature. Through vignettes filled with intensity, he conveyed the courtroom's carnival atmosphere, the traits of the judge and some of the jurors, and the personalities of the Chicago Seven.

Perhaps his most important story while serving as a general assignments reporter was "The Two Worlds of Linda Fitzpatrick," a sensitive story about a girl from an upper-class family who became involved in the psychedelic scene of Greenwich Village and was eventually murdered. The story won a Pulitzer Prize, among other awards, and was included in his 1971 best-selling book *Don't Shoot: We Are Your Children!* An example of literary journalism, it was similar to his earlier book in the sense that it explored the alternative lifestyles of young men and women. Lukas wrote it because he believed he was out of touch with American youth:

Linda's story nagged at me. It made me realize that after five years abroad I was just as out of touch with American young people as most of the parents I'd been talking to.

The assumptions I had voiced only a week before seemed shallow and insensitive. Yet, in the weeks that followed, I came to distrust most of the other generalizations about "youth" or "hippies" or "radicals" which journalism and sociology were then producing.[1]

In *Don't Shoot: We Are Your Children* Lucas used a subtle literary style and provided contrasting impressions of Linda throughout to reveal her personality.

In the early 1970s Lukas became a staff writer for the *New York Times Magazine*, then left the magazine several months later to devote his time to writing articles and books. He also co-founded *MORE*, a critical journal that targeted the news media, and served as its senior editor, then as associate editor, until the journal collapsed in 1978. During this period, he was a contributing editor to *New Times*, an alternative news magazine that also folded in 1978.

Lukas, who contributed to *Esquire*, the *Atlantic*, *New Times*, *Harper's*, *Saturday Review*, the *Nation*, and the *New Republic*, among others, wrote *Nightmare: The Underside of the Nixon Years* in 1975. The book was a departure for him. Instead of examining social unrest, he focused on Richard Nixon and the political turmoil caused by Watergate. The book was praised by critics for its candid historical presentation of that complex period.

Lukas received a contract for another book in 1976, but the project occupied his time for several years. Finally, in 1985 his *Common Ground: A Turbulent Decade in the Lives of Three American Families* was published to critical acclaim. The book concerned Boston during the tumultuous decade from 1968 to 1978 and began with reactions to Martin Luther King's death. More specifically, it focused on the school integration crisis of the mid-1970s and captured the events of the period by examining three families: a young upper-middle-class couple, Joan and Colin Diver, who had two sons; a struggling but devoted African-American mother of six, Rachel Twymon; and a young widow of Irish descent, Alice McGoff, who was trying to raise seven children in the community of Charlestown. Lukas also focused on Judge W. Arthur Garrity, Jr., who issued the court order mandating busing; Kevin White, the mayor; Thomas Winship, editor of the *Boston Globe;* Richard Cardinal Cushing and his successor, Humberto Cardinal Medeiros; and Louise Day Hicks, a member of the Boston School Committee who opposed busing. As a result of busing, the liberal-minded Divers fled to the suburbs. Rachel Twymon endured as a daughter became pregnant and a son was charged with rape. And Alice McGoff watched helplessly as her community was partially destroyed by violent whites who opposed the busing of African Americans to their all-white school. *Common Ground* was well researched and presented the historical events by combining flashbacks with a chronological narrative. The book, another example of literary journalism, received a Pulitzer Prize in 1986.

WORKS: *The Barnyard Epithet and Other Obscenities* (1970); *Don't Shoot: We Are Your Children!* (1971); *Nightmare: The Underside of the Nixon Years*

(1975); *Common Ground: A Turbulent Decade in the Lives of Three American Families* (1985); *MORE* (co-founder and associate editor).
NOTE
1. J. Anthony Lukas, *Don't Shoot: We Are Your Children!* (New York: Random House, 1971), p. 4.

Michael Lydon
(1942-   )

Michael Lydon was born in Boston in 1942. He majored in history at Yale University, from which he graduated in 1965. From 1965 to 1968 he was a bureau correspondent in San Francisco and London for *Newsweek,* for which he wrote about the young rock music–inspired magazine publisher Paul Williams, whose *Crawdaddy* launched the careers of several journalists, including Jon Landau and Richard Goldstein.

The atmosphere Lydon encountered inspired him to literally drop out of the conservative world of *Newsweek* and to concentrate on pieces which were impressive literary journalistic accounts of rock stars, black artists, and, of course, the music itself.

His book *Rock Folk: Portraits from the Rock 'n' Roll Pantheon,* which was published in 1971 and reissued in 1990, contained articles that originally appeared in *Rolling Stone, Ramparts,* and the *New York Times.* Chuck Berry, B. B. King, Smokey Robinson, Janis Joplin, the Rolling Stones, and the Grateful Dead, as well as the music business and the history of popular music, were covered. According to Ellen Sander:

His writing is piquant and full of incidental delight. He has Carl Perkins as an amiable has-been "reading *The Power of Positive Thinking* . . . like Mr. Peepers reading Charles Atlas." Lydon always uses his subject as an opportunity to illuminate the scene in general, and his insights are always right-on.[1]

Lydon's *Boogie Lightning: How Music Became Electric* was published in 1974. Its purpose was to document a historic event: the marriage of music and electricity. Lydon presented the history from the 1940s, when African-American musicians recorded rhythm and blues on independent labels, to the 1950s and beyond, when they began to play electrically. He told the story through various kinds of music—from rhythm and blues, folk, and gospel to blues, soul, and rock 'n' roll—and through the geniuses who produced music with electric guitars and other electrical instruments and microphones, such as John Lee Hooker, Ray Charles, Bo Diddley, Aretha Franklin, and James Brown. The book was reissued in 1980.

Lydon wrote about show business in the same illuminating style. Although he was merely one among many rock journalists, his writing was undeniably superior to that of his peers.

WORKS: *Rock Folk: Portraits from the Rock 'n' Roll Pantheon* (1971; 1990); *Boogie Lightning: How Music Became Electric* (1974; 1980).

NOTE

1. Ellen Sander, "The Journalists of Rock," *Saturday Review,* July 31, 1971, p. 49.

M

Peter Maas
(1929–)

Peter Maas was born in New York City in 1929 and received his bachelor's degree from Duke University 20 years later. He served in the U.S. Navy from 1952 to 1954, then began his career in journalism as a reporter in Paris for the *New York Herald Tribune*. He moved to *Collier's* in 1955, a year before the magazine ceased publication. Although he enjoyed writing for newspapers and magazines, he worked several years on a lobster boat before resuming his professional career in 1959 as a senior editor at *Look*.

Four years later he joined the *Saturday Evening Post* as a senior writer. While at the *Post* he first learned of Joseph Valachi, a Mafia hitman who had informed the FBI of the Cosa Nostra's existence. Maas seized the opportunity to learn everything he could about Valachi and subsequently wrote a series of articles for the *Post*. Maas, who was later retained by the Justice Department to edit Valachi's memoirs, was eventually granted permission to speak to the hitman. Maas was unaware, however, that 12 prominent Italian Americans had intended to prevent Valachi's memoirs from being published. They persuaded the Justice Department to file suit against Maas in 1966; the court ruled two years later that although Valachi's memoirs could not be published, Maas could indeed write a book about the subject.

In 1969 *The Valachi Papers* was published; it ultimately became a best-seller and the basis for a popular film. Even though Maas had written more than a hundred articles (including muckraking exposés, profiles, and political reportage) for such periodicals as *Look, Collier's, Saturday Evening Post,* and *Esquire,* as well as a modest selling nonfiction book, *The Rescuer,* and had become a contributing editor as well as a columnist at *New York,* he was now known as a writer for the masses. In short, he had become a marketable property.

His next book, about the rise and fall of an honest New York City police detective, Frank Serpico, appeared in 1973. *Serpico,* another best-seller that subsequently became a popular movie, was thoroughly researched. According to B. Hal May, Maas "conducted six months of tape-recorded interviews with Serpico at his Greenwich Village apartment and spent six months corroborating the detective's story. He combed the files and inter-office memos kept on Serpico, questioned hundreds of witnesses, and visited the scenes of crimes."[1]

His third best-seller, *King of the Gypsies,* which was published in 1975, caused a stir among the gypsies for its overemphasis on so-called gypsy practices such as con games, shams, revenge, and violence. Nonetheless, through a story as old as time, Maas had succeeded once again in illuminating another culture within American society.

In 1978 he contributed a sports column to the *New York Times,* and a year later saw his first novel, *Made in America,* in bookstores. Dino De Laurentiis purchased the film rights for almost $500,000.

Maas became a contributing editor to *Esquire* in the 1980s. He returned to nonfiction in *Manhunt* (1986), which dealt with the case against Edwin P. Wilson, who had profited considerably from selling illegal military equipment to Libya. Wilson had worked for the CIA as well as the U.S. Navy. Maas revealed that Wilson's personal connections to Hubert H. Humphrey actually helped him establish a working relationship with the CIA. For instance, he opened an international shipping company, actually a CIA "proprietary" operation, which allowed him to make friends in high places and earn a sizable fortune by misappropriating funds. As Maas implied, Wilson's greed was his undoing. After years of accumulating wealth, he was caught.

In 1989 Maas wrote *Father and Son,* a political action thriller about the IRA. A year later in *In a Child's Name: The Legacy of a Mother's Murder,* he passionately explored the custody battle over Philip Andrew Taylor, whose father, Dr. Kenneth Z. Taylor, had murdered the boy's mother, Teresa. Dr. Taylor's parents wanted custody of the child; so did the child's aunt, Celeste White, Teresa's sister. The case dragged on for months. Finally, the aunt was granted custody. Maas covered the trial as well as the custody battle. The book was an example of literary journalism, employing literary devices such as scene-by-scene construction and authentic dialogue. In 1994 Mass explored the new American underworld in the action novel *China White.*

In 1995 he wrote *Killer Spy,* about the FBI's pursuit and ultimate capture of Aldrich Ames, who sold secrets to the KGB. One of several books about Ames, it was informative as well as entertaining.

WORKS: *The Rescuer* (1968); *The Valachi Papers* (1969); *Serpico* (1973); *King of the Gypsies* (1975); *Manhunt* (1986); *In a Child's Name: The Legacy of a Mother's Murder* (1990).

NOTE

1. B. Hal May, "Maas, Peter," *Contemporary Authors: Volumes 93–96,* edited by Frances C. Locher (Detroit: Gale Research, 1980), p. 326.

Norman Mailer
(1923–)

The existentialist, radical, left-wing novelist, essayist, and hero of several autobiographical, literary journalistic accounts, including *Armies of the Night* and *Miami and the Siege of Chicago,* Norman Mailer first experimented in literary journalism when he contributed columns to the *Village Voice* (at the time an alternative newspaper, although now considered an established paper), which, together with Daniel Wolf and Edwin Fancher, he helped found in 1955.

Mailer, who was born on January 31, 1923, grew up in Brooklyn, where he attended Boys High School. At 16 he entered Harvard University. Though he majored in engineering, his talent for creative writing was soon recognized when one of his short stories, "The Greatest Thing in the World," was judged the best entry of *Story* magazine's 1941 college contest. In 1943 he received his degree, then served in the U.S. Army. Mailer, who saw action in the Philippines and Japan, was released in 1946. His experiences were graphically depicted in the realistic novel *The Naked and the Dead,* which appeared two years later. Hailed by critics as a masterpiece, the book was immediately successful.

Mailer was young, however, and was influenced by perhaps too many "isms" pervading his chosen environment. Indeed, as his novel's main characters combatted internal and external forces, so, too, did Mailer. His next novel, *Barbary Shore,* which was published in 1951, reflected these internal and external forces. *Barbary Shore* was not as well received as his first novel. Nonetheless, Mailer continued to write. In 1952 he left his first wife and moved to Greenwich Village in New York City, where he became intrigued with the "hip" or "beat" way of life. In 1955 *The Deer Park* appeared. Although Mailer strongly believed that the book would be well received, the critics dismissed it as a minor effort. Frustrated, Mailer turned to the *Village Voice,* which was losing hundreds of dollars a week. He wrote:

For weeks I lost face in a drift of bold programs and dull resolutions, and all the while my partners and I were coming to see that there were different ideas of how the paper should develop. They wanted it to be successful; I wanted it to be outrageous. They wanted a newspaper which could satisfy the conservative community—church news, meetings of political organizations, so forth. Before the paper could be provocative, went their argument, it must be established. I believed we could grow only if we tried to reach an audience in which no newspaper had yet been interested. I had the feelings of an underground revolution on its way, and I do not know that I was wrong.[1]

Mailer contributed to the paper for several weeks. He confessed later that the time he had spent writing for the *Village Voice* could have been used on another novel.

In 1957 Mailer wrote "The White Negro" for *Dissent,* a New Left literary magazine. "The White Negro" reflected a change in Mailer's focus. Philip H. Bufithis noted:

This demonic rebel is for Mailer the essence of "hip" and the model for "a new breed of adventurers, urban adventurers who drifted out at night looking for action with a black man's code to fit their facts. The hipster had absorbed the existentialist synapses of the Negro, and for practical purposes could be considered a white Negro."[2]

Mailer returned to writing articles, essays, and fiction for such publications as *Esquire,* the *New York Review of Books,* and *Commentary;* his next major book did not appear until 1959. A volume devoted to short stories, plays, articles, excerpts from novels, columns from the *Village Voice,* poems, essays, interviews, and letters, *Advertisements for Myself* was just that. The "Advertisements," which were critical commentaries, not only linked the short stories, plays, and excerpts from novels, but revealed another side of Mailer. The negative, radical philosophy that he had so expertly espoused in *Dissent* was now evident in a piece of literature.

Unfortunately, Mailer's frustrations continued to haunt him throughout the 1960s, and he became a pawn of the media. Indeed, Mailer became known for his actions rather than for his words. In 1960, for example, he stabbed his wife, Adele Marales, after an all-night party at their apartment. Although seriously wounded, she did not press charges. She recovered, and they lived together until their divorce in 1962. Mailer soon married Lady Jeanne Campbell. After a year the marriage ended in divorce, and Mailer married Beverly Bentley. He was arrested for arguing with police officers in Provincetown and for arguing with the management over a liquor bill in a New York nightclub.

His writing during this period included *The Presidential Papers* (1963), a collection of articles criticizing President Kennedy's shortcomings; *Cannibals and Christians* (1966), a collection of short stories, political essays, interviews, and reportage on professional boxing; and *An American Dream* (1965) and *Why Are We in Vietnam?* (1967), two novels that explored metaphorically the ugly side of human nature.

In 1968 *Armies of the Night: History as a Novel, the Novel as History* was published. Similar to his 1960 article for *Esquire,* "Existential Hero: Superman Comes to the Supermarket," which concerned the presidential nomination of John F. Kennedy and had the flavor of literary journalism, *Armies* depicted Mailer's activist role in the antiwar march on the Pentagon and how the march affected him. Through the use of the names Mailer, the Existentialist, the Historian, the General, and the Novelist, among others, Mailer explained quite humorously what happened to him, the other demonstrators, and the soldiers. The reader gained insight not only from a participant who was eventually arrested, but from an observer who questioned and analyzed the events as they happened.

The book was widely acclaimed and received both the National Book Award and the Pulitzer Prize. Mailer's gift as a chronicler of events was seen the same year in his *Miami and the Siege of Chicago,* a personal account of the presidential nominating conventions of 1968.

In 1969 he ran in the New York City Democratic mayoralty primary election, but failed, due partially to his proposal to make the city the fifty-first state. The same year he wrote a series of articles for *Life* that philosophically analyzed and questioned the U.S. space program. From these articles came the book *Of a Fire on the Moon,* published in 1970.

A year later he was attacked for being a male chauvinist by feminists such as Kate Millett. Mailer explored his relationship with women in *The Prisoner of Sex* (1971), a counterattack treatise in which he criticized Millett's attacks on Henry Miller and D. H. Lawrence. His other writing in the 1970s included the biographical novel *Marilyn: A Biography* (1973), *The Fight* (1975), and *The Executioner's Song* (1979), which he called "a true life novel" about the executed murderer Gary Gilmore. In one section, Mailer's depiction of the execution was concise, like the execution itself. However, he increased the suspense with extensive description, describing the scene as if he were there recording every second. Each person present, it seemed, was observed by the writer; some mental or physical reaction by each was dramatically depicted.

In 1980 Mailer married and divorced Carol Stevens, then married Norris Church. Two years later he received national attention from the media when Jack Henry Abbott, an ex-convict whom Mailer had helped get released from prison, was accused of murder.

In 1983 *Ancient Evenings,* a long novel about ancient Egypt, was published to mixed reviews. *Tough Guys Don't Dance,* a short, seamy murder mystery with psychic overtones, appeared a year later. A film version of the book was released several years later.

His *Harlot's Ghost,* a long novel about the CIA during the Cold War was published in 1991. Although the book was favorably reviewed, the topic was not particularly timely, for the Cold War was for the most part over between the United States and the former Soviet Union.

Mailer wrote an intriguing article about Madonna, the popular entertainer, in 1994. Madonna, like Mailer, had been chameleon-like in her professional career, frequently adopting new personas and projecting new images.

In 1995 he wrote the impressive, artistic book *Oswald's Tale: An American Mystery,* which concerned not only the assassination of John F. Kennedy but the mysterious personality of his accused assassin, Lee Harvey Oswald. The book was based on hundreds of interviews and official documents. *Portrait of Picasso as a Young Man,* which focused on Picasso's love for Fernande Olivier, was published the same year.

WORKS: *Armies of the Night: History as a Novel, the Novel as History* (1968); *Miami and the Siege of Chicago* (1968); *Of a Fire on the Moon* (1970); *Marilyn: A Biography* (1973); *The Fight* (1975); *The Executioner's Song* (1979).

NOTES

1. Norman Mailer, *Advertisements for Myself* (New York: G. P. Putnam's Sons, 1959), pp. 277–278.

2. Philip H. Bufithis, "Norman Mailer," *American Novelists Since World War II: Dictionary of Literary Biography,* edited by Jeffrey Helterman and Richard Layman (Detroit: Gale Research, 1978), Vol. 2, p. 283.

William Manchester
(1922-)

William Manchester, the author of *The Death of a President: November 20-November 25, 1963,* was born in Attleboro, Massachusetts, on April 1, 1922, and moved with his family to Springfield seven years later. He graduated from Classical High School in 1940 and entered the University of Massachusetts. When the United States entered World War II he enlisted in the Marine Corps and served from 1942 to 1945. Before he resumed his education, he worked briefly for the *Daily Oklahoman;* this experience served him well later.

In 1946 he received his bachelor's degree from Massachusetts State College (now University of Massachusetts), and a year later he earned his master's degree from the University of Missouri. He did his master's thesis on the literary criticism of H. L. Mencken, and then moved to Baltimore and obtained a position with the *Baltimore Sun,* the paper on which Mencken was employed. First as a police reporter, then as a foreign correspondent stationed in Europe, the Middle East, and Asia, Manchester covered world events for the *Sun* until he resigned to become Mencken's secretary in 1954. Mencken, who had suffered a stroke, lived until 1956.

Manchester, having written articles for magazines, an authorized biography of Mencken, and several minor novels, soon found employment as a managing editor of Wesleyan University's publications and later as a member of the faculty.

He wrote two political books before his literary journalistic account of President Kennedy's death: *A Rockefeller Family Portrait: From John D. to Nelson* (1959) and *Portrait of a President: John F. Kennedy in Profile* (1962). Neither contained the insight, the emotion, or the literary power of his 1967 work.

The fact that *The Death of a President* was published was in itself a feat, for the Kennedy family had contracted the book with the stipulation that it be approved by members of the family before publication. Robert Kennedy, on behalf of the family, gave his approval. Manchester's agent accepted more than $600,000 from the publishers of *Look* magazine for the rights to serialize the book. However, the Kennedys subsequently changed their minds about the project and withdrew their permission to publish the book. Deborah A. Straub wrote:

Several months later . . . Jacqueline filed suit against Manchester, Harper & Row, and *Look,* claiming that the publication of the book would cause her "great and irreparable injury'' and would result in ''sensationalism and commercialism'' (despite the fact that most of the profits from the sale of the book had been designated for the Kennedy Memorial Library).[1]

The editors at *Look* and at Harper & Row agreed to change certain passages that concerned Jacqueline Kennedy. As a result, the suit was settled out of court.

The book was divided into four parts. Manchester used two narrative techniques. The first, which Donald Pizer termed ''simultaneous narrative,'' was devoted to important or emotional events. The second, ''sequential narrative,'' was used to not only produce action in a chronological order, but to interweave the actions of the various participants. As a result, Manchester produced an accurate, engaging documentary similar to a novel.[2]

Manchester's talent as a literary journalist was also evident in *The Arms of Krupp* (1968), about the Krupp family of Germany and its role in manufacturing munitions before, during, and after the Third Reich. The major portion of the text concentrated on the Krupps' role during Hitler's rise to power and World War II. Critics praised the book for its abundant research and melodramatic narrative.

The same literary journalistic style was exhibited in *The Glory and the Dream: A Narrative History of America, 1932–1972*, which was published in 1974. Manchester chronicled the foibles, triumphs, and tragedies of the generation that grew up during the Depression. He identified the heroes as well as the villains, and focused on numerous struggles and events, including World War II, the death of President Roosevelt, and the resignation of General MacArthur, as well as popular icons, including Frank Sinatra, Elvis Presley, and the Beatles.

In 1978 he told the dramatic story of General Douglas MacArthur in the authoritative biography *American Caesar: Douglas MacArthur, 1880–1964*, which was praised by critics for its hypnotic effect. Manchester examined his own life as a sergeant in the Marine Corps during World War II in *Goodbye Darkness: A Memoir of the Pacific War* (1980). Manchester was wounded in the Pacific and was awarded a Purple Heart.

Manchester published *The Last Lion: Winston Spencer Churchill: Visions of Glory: 1874–1932* in 1983 and *The Last Lion: William Spencer Churchill: Alone: 1932–1940* in 1987. The first volume of the projected three-volume biography covered Churchill's life up to his fall from the Cabinet in 1931. The second volume recounted the wilderness years, before he became one of the major political figures of World War II.

In 1992 Manchester examined medieval superstition and obscurantism under the brilliant illumination of the Renaissance in *A World Lit Only by Fire: The Medieval Mind and the Renaissance: Portrait of an Age*. Manchester concluded that Magellan's voyage around the world broke forever the power of the medieval mind. Several reviewers criticized the author for inaccuracies.

WORKS: *The Death of a President: November 20-November 25, 1963*

(1967); *The Arms of Krupp* (1968); *The Glory and the Dream: A Narrative History of America, 1932–1972* (1974); *American Caesar: Douglas MacArthur, 1880–1964* (1978); *Goodbye Darkness: A Memoir of the Pacific War* (1980).

NOTES

1. Deborah A. Straub, "Manchester, William," *Contemporary Authors: New Revision Series*, edited by Ann Evory (Detroit: Gale Research, 1981), Vol. 3, p. 359.

2. Donald Pizer, "Documentary Narrative as Art: William Manchester and Truman Capote," *Journal of Modern Literature*, September 1971, p. 108.

Greil Marcus
(1945–   )

Greil Marcus was born on June 19, 1945, in San Francisco. His father, Gerald Marcus, an attorney, was determined that his son would get a good education. Marcus attended the University of California, Berkeley, where he earned the bachelor's and master's degrees in 1966 and 1967, respectively.

A follower of rock music most of his life, he started writing about it in 1966. His work was not published in a professional publication, however, until 1968, when he joined the staff of the underground newspaper *Express-Times*. Although he enjoyed writing for the paper, he moved to *Rolling Stone*, where he was made an associate editor in 1969. The same year he saw two books he had edited and co-written published. *Rock and Roll Will Stand* was a book of essays; *Woodstock*, co-written with Jan Hodenfield and Andrew Kopkind, was a splashy pictorial book about one of the greatest musical events in the history of rock music.

In 1970 he moved to *Creem*, where he was given considerable freedom with respect to what and how he wrote. Two years later he and Michael Goodwin wrote *Double Feature: Movies and Politics*, which proved that he had other interests besides rock music. Indeed, he contributed essays and articles on film and politics to various periodicals.

In 1975, the year *Mystery Train: Images of America in Rock 'n' Roll Music* was published, he was made book editor at *Rolling Stone*. Marcus wrote the biweekly column "Undercover" until 1980. He contributed several articles to *The Rolling Stone Illustrated History of Rock and Roll*, edited by Jim Miller and published in 1976. He contributed the monthly column "Real Life Rock" to *New West Magazine* from 1978 until 1982 and contributed the same column to *Music Magazine*, a publication in Japan. He edited *Stranded: Rock and Roll for a Desert Island*, a book of essays, in 1979.

Marcus left *Rolling Stone* in 1980, but kept writing about music, books, politics, and other subjects for the *New York Times, New York Times Book Review, Los Angeles Times,* the *New Yorker, TriQuarterly, Newsday,* and *New Musical Express,* among other periodicals.

In 1983 he started writing the monthly column "Speaker to Speaker" for *Artforum;* the column lasted until 1987. From 1986 to 1990 he produced the monthly column "Real Life Rock Top Ten" for the *Village Voice*. In addition, he contributed a column about books to *California Magazine* intermittently in the 1980s. He started a column about music and other topics for *Artforum* in 1990, and started another about popular culture for the *San Francisco Focus* in 1991.

Marcus wrote *Lipstick Traces: A Secret History of the Twentieth Century,* which was published by Harvard University Press in 1989. The concept for the book germinated when Marcus heard the song "Anarchy in the U.K." by the Sex Pistols in 1976. Marcus, who toured Europe, particularly France, primarily to gather information about punk recording artists, blended anecdote, popular culture analysis, and personal confession as he jumped backward and forward in time, from Sid Vicious of the Sex Pistols to the Surrealists, from Alexander Trocchi of the 1950s avant-garde group Lettrist International to George Grosy, from Daniel Cohn-Bendit, Danny the Red of the French Student rebellion, to the Anabaptists of the sixteenth century. Why had he included these historical figures from the past? According to Marcus:

In tracing the sources of punk, especially the Sex Pistols, I'd done a lot of reading into Dada and also the situationists—a small group of Left Bank prophets in the '50s and '60s. I knew the book was going to be about a spectral tradition, beginning with Dada, moving through other voices in the 20th century and ending with punk.[1]

The book evolved over a nine-year period and changed considerably from the author's initial concept.

In 1991 his *Dead Elvis: Chronicle of a Cultural Obsession* appeared. Although he had devoted a lengthy chapter to the popular singer in *Mystery Train: Images of America in Rock 'n' Roll Music,* Marcus realized that he had to write a book when his files on the performer began to overflow. The result was a perverse, noisy, gleeful, blasphemous book that was filled with pictures. According to Marcus, "I knew the book was going to be full of the strange illustrations I'd collected, and that it would include lots of different voices, including some that I didn't agree with."[2] To say the least, the book was about American culture and how the dead Elvis came to be appreciated by many who had not appreciated him when he was alive. The book was an example of literary journalism because of the different voices used, including Marcus' own.

In 1993 two collections of previously published material appeared: *Ranters and Crowd Pleasers: Punk in Pop Music, 1977–92* and *In the Fascist Bathroom: Writings on Punk 1977–92.* The former contained lively, insightful pieces about punk artists as well as Ronald Reagan and Margaret Thatcher. The latter contained well-written, thoughtful articles and essays about punk artists such as the Mekons, Gang of Four, The Clash, and Liliput, among others, and about punk music in general. Marcus claimed that punk music was about newness; however, it was more than just a different style or kind of music.

Although he had written about other subjects, his popularity was based on his reviews, essays, and articles about music, particularly rock music. In fact, his book *Mystery Train* was nominated for a National Book Critics Circle Award and was widely praised by reviewers. Some, in fact, claimed that it was one of the best books about rock music. Mark Crispin Miller called *Mystery Train* ''an impressive book, well-informed and frequently hilarious.''[3] The book was an example of literary journalism. Marcus first analyzed the two ''ancestors'' of rock, Harmonica Frank and Robert Johnson, then proceeded to examine more modern artists, including The Band, Sly of the Family Stone, Randy Newman, and, of course, Elvis Presley. The essays in the book captured on paper a rarely defined slice of American culture. Indeed, his writing was perceptive and unusually brilliant.

In several sections of the book, the amount of attention focused on one personality, then another, was reflected in the length of the sentences. Indeed, Marcus cut from one personality to another just like a television camera on a talk show. In addition, he employed authentic dialogue that enabled the reader to visualize the personality. These techniques, as well as others, personalized the writing.

WORKS: *Woodstock* (with Jan Hodenfield and Andrew Kopkind, 1969); *Rock and Roll Will Stand* (editor, 1969); *Double Feature: Movies and Politics* (with Michael Goodwin, 1972); *Mystery Train: Images of America in Rock 'n' Roll Music* (1975); *Stranded: Rock and Roll for a Desert Island* (editor, 1979); *Lipstick Traces: A Secret History of the Twentieth Century* (1989); *Dead Elvis: Chronicle of a Cultural Obsession* (1991); *Ranters and Crowd Pleasers: Punk in Pop Music* (1993); *In the Fascist Bathroom: Writings on Punk 1977–92* (1993).

NOTES

1. William C. Brisick, ''PW Interviews: Greil Marcus,'' *Publishers Weekly,* November 15, 1991, p. 54.

2. Ibid., p. 53.

3. Mark Crispin Miller, ''Where All the Flowers Went,'' *New York Review of Books,* February 3, 1977, p. 35.

Dave Marsh
(1950–)

Dave Marsh, a literary journalist, has written extensively and exclusively about rock music and rock musicians. He was born in Pontiac, Michigan, on March 1, 1950. His father, O. K., was a railroad brakeman on freight trains. Marsh spent the first 13 years of his life on East Beverly Street, which was near a Pontiac Motors assembly line plant.

In 1964, when he was 14 and finishing the eighth grade at Madison Junior High, General Motors offered a reasonable amount of money for their property to each home owner on the street, including Marsh's father. Marsh was saddened. Where would they live? What about his friends? Marsh had thought his father would refuse, and was crushed when he accepted the offer.

Marsh moved with his parents to the suburbs, which disturbed him. "This was catastrophic to me. I loved the city, its pavement and the mobility it offered even to kids too young to drive."[1] In the suburbs, cars were necessary. When Marsh changed schools something was wrong. He excelled in school, just as he had at Madison Junior High; his new classmates, however, were underachievers. Thus, until he graduated, Marsh kept to himself.

Although he had listened to rock music on the radio, it had not meant that much to him. When he heard "You Really Got a Hold on Me" by Smokey Robinson he thought the song was speaking for him as well as to him, and it changed his life. Indeed, Marsh was affected by the racial bigotry exhibited by many whites. Integration became a major topic throughout the nation. Marsh listened intently to other popular songs, primarily to infer what the artists were saying. Berry Gordy, Jr., the founder of Motown Records, was producing hit after hit, and Marsh realized that Motown artists were not necessarily saying the same thing to their audiences as other performers were to their audiences. Marsh began to question much of what he had been taught; he realized that racism had clouded numerous issues.

After he graduated from high school he attended Wayne State University for a year. He dropped out primarily to edit *Creem* magazine, which was devoted to rock music, although he had written for a variety of publications while attending college. Four years later, in 1973, he moved to Boston, where he worked as a music editor for *Real Paper*. He got to know Jon Landau and Bruce Springsteen. Marsh then joined the staff of *Newsday*, for which he wrote about music. This position lasted about two years, until he joined *Rolling Stone* in 1975. Marsh served as a record reviews editor as well as a writer; for instance, he contributed the column "American Grandstand" from 1976 until 1979, the year he left the magazine to write full time.

Marsh wrote several biographies, including the best-selling *Born to Run: The Bruce Springsteen Story* (1979), *Elvis* (1981), *Before I Get Old: The Story of the Who* (1982), *Trapped: Michael Jackson and the Crossover Dream* (1985), and *Glory Days: The Bruce Springsteen Story Continues* (1987), but his book *Fortunate Son: Criticism and Journalism by America's Best-Known Rock Writer*, which was published in 1985, exemplified his personal literary journalistic style. It collected articles he had written for several publications, including *Creem* magazine and *Rolling Stone*, in which he demonstrated not only his writing ability but his belief in rock music as a cultural and political force in modern society. As Wendy Smith wrote in *Publisher's Weekly*,

What makes Marsh a provocative writer is the way he's created a coherent world view uniquely his own by fusing several disparate elements that at first glance don't necessarily seem connected: a traditional working-class radicalism: . . . the very different political ideals of the 1960s; and a profound love for rock and roll, which for Marsh is more than just music.[2]

Although Smith was discussing a different book, what she wrote applied to his other work primarily because the "disparate elements" became the fabric that linked the articles and books.

"The Daring Young Man and the Flying Chimpanzees/Call to A.R.M.S.," one article republished in *Fortunate Son,* contained the elements essential to literary journalism. Indeed, Marsh, the careful observer, recorded every incident and described with incredible accuracy not only the what and where but the who. He employed authentic dialogue that realistically depicted the scenes.

Marsh founded *Rock and Roll Confidential,* a newsletter targeted to the serious rock music listener, in 1983. A year later he became the music critic for *Playboy.*

Marsh's *The Heart of Rock and Soul: The 1001 Greatest Singles Ever Made* (1989) contained brief essays on his favorite singles of the past 30-plus years. Marsh mixed history and criticism, and argued that the single, not the album, was the most important unit of measure for music in the era of rock 'n' roll.

His *50 Ways to Fight Censorship and Important Facts to Know About the Censors,* which was published in 1991, was a departure from music criticism. Marsh presented 50 practical steps individuals could follow to fight the growing trend toward censorship in the United States. The same year he became a contributing editor to *Entertainment Weekly.*

In 1993 he co-wrote *Merry Christmas, Baby: Holiday Music from Bing to Sting* with Steve Propes. The book was a thorough survey of recorded Christmas music—from mainstream hits such as Nat King Cole's "Christmas Song" to efforts by Spike Jones, Jimi Hendrix, and Madonna. The same year he analyzed the song "Louie, Louie" in *Louie, Louie: The History and Mythology of the World's Most Famous Rock 'n' Roll Song; Including the Full Details of Its Torture and Persecution at the Hands of the Kingsmen, J. Edgar Hoover, and a Cast of Millions; and Introducing, for the First Time Anywhere, the Actual Dirty Lyrics.* The song had exploded onto the charts in 1963 and subsequently influenced the development of garage rock, psychedelic rock, and punk rock. The book was part rock criticism and part cultural analysis. Marsh also recounted the FBI's attempts to find the song obscene.

WORKS: *Born to Run: The Bruce Springsteen Story* (1979); *Elvis* (1981); *Before I Get Old: The Story of the Who* (1982); *Fortunate Son: Criticism and Journalism by America's Best-Known Rock Writer* (1985); *Trapped: Michael Jackson and the Crossover Dream* (1985); *Glory Days: The Bruce Springsteen Story Continues* (1987); *Louie, Louie: The History and Mythology of the World's Most Famous Rock 'n' Roll Song; Including the Full Details of Its Torture and Persecution at the Hands of the Kingsmen, J. Edgar Hoover, and a Cast of Millions; and Introducing, for the First Time Anywhere, the Actual Dirty Lyrics* (1993).

NOTES
1. Dave Marsh, *Fortunate Son: Criticism and Journalism by America's Best-Known Rock Writer* (New York: Random House, 1985), p. xix.
2. Wendy Smith, "PW Interviews: Dave Marsh," *Publisher's Weekly,* October 21, 1983, p. 69.

John Bartlow Martin
(1915–1987)

Born in Hamilton, Ohio, in 1915, John Bartlow Martin attended DePauw University. He edited the college newspaper, worked as a stringer for the *Indianapolis Times,* and briefly worked as a copy boy for the Associated Press before getting his first full-time job as a reporter shortly after leaving college in 1937. After working for about a year at the *Times,* Martin left Indianapolis and moved to Chicago, where he eventually became a freelance writer. His articles concerned actual crimes, and most were published in *True Detective.* Occasionally *Esquire* accepted an article, and in 1943 *Harper's* published one. His first book, *Call It North Country: The Story of Upper Michigan,* was published a year later.

Martin contributed articles to *Harper's* and *Reader's Digest,* and wrote a second book devoted to a specific region (Michigan). However, it was *Butcher's Dozen,* stories of actual crimes, that launched Martin's literary career, for in it he used the techniques of the novelist to present arresting factual stories. His 1952 *My Life in Crime,* about a criminal's life, used the same techniques employed in *Butcher's Dozen.* Martin's story about a criminal grabbed readers' attention and affected their conscience.

From 1952 to 1956 Martin served as a staff member to Adlai Stevenson, but continued to write books in his spare time. *Why Did They Kill?,* a literary as well as a sociological account of a murder by three juveniles, was published in 1953. The book employed the techniques of the journalist and the novelist. Martin used scene-by-scene construction to depict the murder. Furthermore, through incidentals, he created a suspenseful atmosphere; indeed, the reader learned that it was night, that a nurse was walking home, that a murderer was stalking her, that a woman heard something, that a police officer who lived nearby heard nothing, that two couples observed something in the road, and that two men found the victim lying in the road with her head crushed.

Why Did They Kill? was undoubtedly an important work, dealing as it did with youthful violence. More important, however, it traced the movements of the murderers as well as the authorities, and revealed, to a certain extent, the sociological and psychological motivations for the crime. The book could be considered a forerunner to Truman Capote's *In Cold Blood.* In 1954 the journalistic *Break Down the Walls,* about the ridiculous state of America's prisons, was published. Martin explored the myth that rehabilitation had been implemented in prisons across the country.

Martin also wrote an in-depth biography of Adlai Stevenson, a book on foreign policy, and several novels. He served on the staffs of John F. Kennedy, Lyndon Johnson, and Hubert Humphrey as well as teaching at several universities. Martin died in 1987.

WORKS: *Butcher's Dozen* (1950); *My Life in Crime* (1952); *Why Did They Kill?* (1953).

Peter Matthiessen
(1927-)

Peter Matthiessen is known more as a novelist than as a literary journalist, even though he employed devices characteristic of literary journalism in his 1978 book *The Snow Leopard.* Born on May 22, 1927, in New York City, Matthiessen was one of three children. His father, Erard Matthiessen, was an architect and a trustee of the National Audubon Society. Matthiessen was reared in rural New York and Connecticut. He attended Hotchkiss, a private prepatory school, where he contributed articles to the school newspaper.

In 1945, after he had graduated from school, he went into the U.S. Navy. While stationed at Pearl Harbor, he contributed stories to the *Honolulu Advertiser.* When he was released in 1947 he enrolled at Yale University, where he and a friend contributed a column to the campus newspaper. During his junior year, he attended the Sorbonne in Paris, a city that he thoroughly enjoyed.

Matthiessen returned to Yale, from which he received his bachelor's degree in 1950. That year his short story "Sadie" was published in the *Atlantic Monthly.* Matthiessen remained at Yale and taught creative writing.

In 1951 he married Patsy Southgate, whom he had met while at the Sorbonne, and returned with her to Paris. The same year, after extensive discussions with Harold Humes and other expatriates, he and Humes founded the prestigious literary journal *Paris Review.* Matthiessen became one of the magazine's editors. Even though his apartment was a meeting place for numerous writers, including James Baldwin, George Plimpton, Terry Southern, William Styron, and Irwin Shaw, he still found time to write his first novel, *Race Rock.*

The Matthiessens returned to the United States before the novel appeared in 1954. Matthiessen worked as a commercial fisherman on Long Island and, in his off hours, continued to write. His next novel, *Partisans,* was published in 1955 to mixed reviews.

In 1956 Matthiessen loaded his car with textbooks, clothes, and a sleeping bag, and visited every wildlife refuge in the United States. Three years later, after extensive study and writing, his encyclopedia *Wildlife in America* was published. Matthiessen's efforts were acknowledged by critics.

Matthiessen and his first wife were now divorced, and he spent the next several years traveling, observing, and learning about wildlife and about himself. *The Cloud Forest: A Chronicle of the South American Wilderness,* published in 1961, was an informative and objective account of his journey in the wilderness of South America. Matthiessen once again depicted the wildlife with incredible accuracy. *Under the Mountain Wall: A Chronicle of Two Seasons in the Stone Age,* which described the Kurelu, a small tribe in New Guinea, followed in 1962.

Matthiessen's next project was the novel *At Play in the Fields of the Lord,* which was set in a remote village in the jungles of South America. Published in 1965, the novel received favorable reviews. He devoted the next several years to researching various subjects and writing about them. For instance, *Oomingmak: The Expedition to the Musk Ox Island in the Bering Sea* was published in 1967; *Sal Si Puedes: Cesar Chavez and the New American Revolution* was published in 1970; *Blue Meridian: The Search for the Great White Shark* was published in 1971; and *The Tree Where Man Was Born/The African Experience,* which conveyed Matthiessen's impressions of East Africa, was published in 1972.

In 1975 Matthiessen's surrealistic novel *Far Tortuga* was published. Unusual in the sense of the devices employed—blank spaces, ink blots, wavy lines, unattributed dialogue—the novel explored the lives of nine crew members on a Caribbean schooner. It was considered by numerous critics to be Matthiessen's finest novel, even if it was somewhat unorthodox.

The Snow Leopard, which described the incredible journey Matthiessen made with naturalist George Schaller as he explored the remotest areas of Nepal, was published in 1978. In this book, Matthiessen searched inwardly as much as he searched the unfamiliar terrain for the snow leopard. Deborah Love, whom he had married in 1963, had died of cancer in 1972. According to John L. Cobbs:

Matthiessen's thoughts were very much on his wife and he made of the trip a deliberate attempt to confront the primal mysteries of life and death. The arduous trek through much beauty, but also much squalor, hardship, and loneliness, is the journal of an introspective man whose consciousness is hypersensitive to the meaning of the natural world and its importance for man.[1]

The Snow Leopard was part autobiography and part philosophy, particularly Zen, which Matthiessen had studied. Thus the book, because of the personal observations of the author as well as the literary devices used, was an example of literary journalism. Robert M. Adams wrote:

The author has dealt frequently and knowingly with natural scenery and wild life; he can sketch a landscape in a few vivid, unsentimental words, capture the sensations of entering a wild, windy Nepalese mountain village, and convey richly the strange, whinnying behavior of a herd of wild sheep. His prose is crisp, yet strongly appealing to the senses; it combines instinct with the feeling of adventure.[2]

The book earned a National Book Award and an American Book Award, and was critically acclaimed for its unusual literary and philosophical mixture.

Matthiessen published *Sand Rivers* in 1981, *In the Spirit of Crazy Horse* in 1983, *Indian Country* in 1984, and *Men's Lives: The Surfmen and Baymen of the South Fork* in 1986. These books were similar in the sense that all essentially explored the virtues of various lost cultures.

He explored his fascination with Zen in *Nine-Headed Dragon River: Zen Journals 1969–1982,* which was published in 1986. Four years later he wrote the fact-based historical novel *Killing Mister Watson,* about Edgar J. Watson, who had taken the law into his hands around the turn of the century in South Florida. As railroads brought civilization closer, people in the community realized that Watson's brand of justice was passé, so they murdered him.

Shadows of Africa, a large book filled with sketches about Africa and its splendid creatures, was published in 1992. The same year *Baikal: Sacred Sea of Siberia,* about the largest, deepest, and oldest freshwater lake in the world, appeared. Much of its ecosystem is also unique, and Matthiessen claimed that the lake had become a cause for an emerging conservation movement primarily because of the pollution affecting it. In *African Silences,* also published in 1992, Matthiessen described three journeys he had made that had been devoted to wildlife surveys in Africa. The first two had been made in West Africa in 1978 and were general in scope. The third had been made in the Congo Basin in 1986 and had focused primarily on elephants. Matthiessen discussed how the inhabitants and intruders affected the climate and animal populations, as well as how animals affected their own habitats. To say the least, the book was well researched.

In addition, Matthiessen contributed numerous short stories and articles to various periodicals, including *Esquire,* the *Atlantic, Harper's, Newsweek, Audubon,* the *New Yorker,* and the *Saturday Evening Post.*

WORK: *The Snow Leopard* (1978).

NOTES

1. John L. Cobbs, "Peter Matthiessen," *Dictionary of Literary Biography: American Novelists Since World War II: Second Series,* edited by James E. Kibler, Jr. (Detroit: Gale Research, 1980), Vol. 6, p. 223.

2. Robert M. Adams, "Blue Sheep Zen," *New York Review of Books,* September 28, 1978, p. 8.

Mary McCarthy
(1912–1989)

Born in Seattle, Washington, on June 21, 1912, Mary McCarthy was the oldest of four children. Her parents, Roy Winfield and Therese McCarthy, died of influenza when she was six years old. She and her brothers spent the next five years in Minneapolis with their great-aunt and her husband, an extremely stern couple who denied the children material comforts other children took for granted. In 1923 her maternal grandfather, Harold Preston, put two of her brothers, Kevin and Preston, in Catholic boarding schools, left Sheridan with his great-aunt, and took Mary back to Seattle. McCarthy's life there was more pleasant; her grandparents were nice to her. However, what had happened to her and her brothers in Minneapolis was vividly recalled in *Memories of a Catholic Girlhood,* published in 1957.

McCarthy attended the Forest Ridge Convent School during the week and studied rhetoric, English history, religion, and French literature. She attended a public high school before she was sent to the Anne Wright Seminary in Tacoma. McCarthy excelled in her courses. On graduation, she enrolled in a school for dramatic arts; later, she enrolled in Vassar College, where she studied the Elizabethans. She graduated in 1933.

One week later she married Harold Johnsgrud, an aspiring actor and playwright whom she had met at the dramatic arts school in Seattle. They moved to New York City, and McCarthy contributed book reviews to the *New Republic* and the *Nation.* In 1936 she worked as an editor for a publishing firm, then in 1937, after she and her husband divorced, she moved to the *Partisan Review,* for which she reviewed plays. McCarthy met other intellectuals in New York. Although she leaned to the left, she was not a participant in any movement.

In 1938 she married Edmund Wilson, a writer and critic of distinction. Wilson encouraged McCarthy to write fiction. Her short stories appeared in *Southern Review.* "Cruel and Barbarous Treatment" became the first chapter of *The Company She Keeps,* a novel published in 1942 and based in part on McCarthy's life. Indeed, through the strong personal elements in this as well as her other novels, McCarthy's own story was revealed to the reader.

McCarthy's satiric, ironic style was praised by critics. However, they disagreed over the merits of the book, some citing its lack of continuity as a major problem.

McCarthy and Wilson had a son, Reuel; they separated in 1945 and divorced a year later. She then married Bowden Broadwater, whom she had met earlier in Paris. McCarthy had taught at Bard College in 1945 and 1946, but found the job exhausting. She and Broadwater, who worked for the *Partisan Review,* lived in New York City. In 1948 McCarthy taught at Sarah Lawrence. She disliked the job so much that she did not complete the academic year.

Her novel *The Oasis,* which was first serialized in *Horizon,* appeared in 1949. The book, based in part on her experiences with different European-American groups after World War II, was attacked for its lack of action and its episodic structure.

The same year Broadwater left the *Partisan Review;* together, they purchased a house in Rhode Island. McCarthy's *Cast a Cold Eye,* a book of seven stories, was published in 1950.

McCarthy examined the paranoid atmosphere of the early 1950s in *The Groves of Academe,* which appeared in 1952. The critics disagreed over the book's literary merit. The same year she and Broadwater sold their house in Rhode Island and purchased one on Cape Cod. McCarthy wrote part of her next novel, a satire, on Cape Cod, part of it in Portugal, and part of it in Capri. Titled

A Charmed Life, it appeared in 1955. Readers and critics tried to identify the book's characters.

McCarthy and Broadwater sold the house on Cape Cod and moved to Europe. Broadwater, along with McCarthy's son, returned to New York City in late 1955; McCarthy did not return until 1956. For the next several years the family traveled back and forth. During these years, McCarthy wrote several pieces of nonfiction, including *Venice Observed* (1956), *Memories of a Catholic Girlhood* (1957), and *The Stones of Florence* (1959). Traveling and separation from one another put a strain on the marriage; in 1961 they were divorced.

McCarthy subsequently married James West, who worked for the State Department. She had met him while touring Poland. West was reassigned to Paris, where McCarthy continued to write. In 1963 her novel *The Group* appeared. It traced the lives of eight Vassar women as they confronted life after college. The novel became a best-seller but was dismissed for the most part by critics. Many failed to recognize parody, as they critiqued her use of clichés, indirect speech, and interior monologue.

McCarthy turned to nonfiction to examine the Vietnam War in a series of personal essays. First published in the *New York Review of Books,* these essays were later collected in the books *Vietnam* (1967) and *Hanoi* (1968). McCarthy, who journeyed to Vietnam at least twice, expressed her opposition to America's involvement in Vietnam by exposing the war's effect on Americans:

If one describes landscapes once filled with life now pitted and scarred from bombing and shelling, "free fire zones" in which anything moving constitutes a target, one is told that war is hell, that terrible things inevitably happen. The United States, one is assured, regrets this deeply.[1]

McCarthy's books about Vietnam were examples of literary journalism because, in addition to employing elements usually associated with fiction, she included herself—not merely as an observer, but as a participant in the sense that she recorded her thoughts about what she observed. And she observed plenty—from the pollution of the jungle to the squalor of the refugee camps.

During the early 1970s she followed the "war crimes" trial of Captain Ernest Medina, Lieutenant William Calley's company commander in Vietnam. The trial and Medina's acquittal furnished McCarthy with additional material about Vietnam. *Medina* was published in 1972. McCarthy followed Watergate and its aftermath for the *London Observer.* Her articles were published as *The Mask of State: Watergate Portraits* in 1974. Although books of McCarthy's essays had appeared previously, including *On the Contrary* (1961), these books were different in the sense that they dealt with political topics, not literary philosophy.

Before her death on October 25, 1989, McCarthy wrote *Birds of America* (1971), a comic novel that critics unfairly compared to other, more famous coming of age novels. *Cannibals and Missionaries* followed in 1979. A novel of ideas, it, too, was dismissed by critics. She responded to her critics in the defensive *Ideas and the Novel* (1980), in which she explained the theory behind her work, but the critics cared little for her explanations.

WORKS: *Vietnam* (1967); *Hanoi* (1968).

NOTE

1. Jonathan Mirsky, "The War in Vietnam," *New York Times Book Review,* November 26, 1967, p. 12.

Joe McGinniss
(1942–   )

Columnist Joe McGinniss, formerly a reporter, wrote one of the most insightful books on how a presidential candidate could be packaged and sold by professionals in marketing and advertising. Titled *The Selling of the President, 1968,* it concerned President Nixon's campaign and its effective use of the media.

McGinniss, who was born on December 9, 1942, in New York City, received his bachelor's degree from Holy Cross College in 1964. From 1964 until 1966 he worked as a reporter for the *Port Chester Daily Item,* the *Worcester Telegram,* and the *Philadelphia Bulletin.* From 1967 to 1968 he was a columnist for the *Philadelphia Inquirer.*

Although McGinniss wrote other books after *The Selling of the President, 1968,* including several novels, and contributed articles to *Harper's, Sports Illustrated, TV Guide,* and other periodicals, his capabilities as an informative, penetrating journalist were recognized immediately upon the book's publication in 1969, for both critics and readers enjoyed his candid reportage.

In one section, McGinniss described the process of Richard Nixon making campaign commercials, each of which had required numerous takes. McGinniss recorded every take, showing the mechanics of marketing a politician and at the same time revealing Nixon's character.

In 1983 McGinniss wrote *Fatal Vision,* about Jeffrey MacDonald, a doctor who was eventually convicted of killing his pregnant wife and two children. McGinniss was criticized for befriending MacDonald even when he had doubts about his innocence. Nonetheless, the book was praised by critics for its exhaustively detailed chronological reconstruction of the brutal slayings, the unusually tense courtroom trial, and its aftermath.

Blind Faith, another book about crime, was published in 1989. McGinniss traveled to Toms River, New Jersey, where a popular couple had supposedly been robbed and the wife murdered. The police suspected the husband, who had been having an affair, of being involved in her murder. Although the jury convicted the husband, the actual murderer—the man who had been hired to pull the trigger—was acquitted. This book was another example of literary journalism.

In 1991 McGinniss wrote a third book about crime, *Cruel Doubt.* Bonnie Von Stein was a suspect in the death of her husband, who had been bludgeoned and stabbed to death while he lay in bed beside her. The actual murderer turned out to be the couple's son, who was eventually tried and sentenced.

The Last Brother: The Rise and Fall of Teddy Kennedy, published in 1993, examined Ted Kennedy's life from birth to after Chappaquiddick. The book became somewhat controversial shortly after publication when some accused the author of using made-up quotes, especially in the first 100-plus pages. The book was another example of literary journalism.

WORKS: *The Selling of the President, 1968* (1969); *Fatal Vision* (1983); *Blind Faith* (1989); *Cruel Doubt* (1991); *The Last Brother: The Rise and Fall of Teddy Kennedy* (1993).

St. Clair McKelway
(1905–1980)

St. Clair McKelway was born in Charlotte, North Carolina, in 1905 and reared in Washington, D.C. From 1919 to 1922 he worked for the *Washington Times,* and from 1922 to 1933 he worked as a reporter for the *Washington Herald,* the *Philadelphia Daily News,* the *New York World,* and the *New York Herald-Tribune,* and as a correspondent for the *Chicago Tribune.*

In 1933 he began working for the *New Yorker,* for which he wrote numerous accounts under the headings "Annals of Crime," "Reporter at Large," and "Profiles." These arresting pieces of nonfiction contained the elements of literary journalism. McKelway illuminated his subjects through incidents they confronted every day. For instance, in the story "Average Cop," originally published in the *New Yorker,* then collected in *True Tales from the Annals of Crime and Rascality* (1950), Williams, a police officer, confronted and, to a certain extent, comforted a mother and father whose son was accidentally killed. Written in the third person, the story described not only the characters' actions and reactions to the incident, but the characters themselves. The reader learned that the parents were immigrants, that the father was a baker, that they lived in a flat. More important, McKelway described their features. Through the use of dialogue, he conveyed characteristics that were difficult to describe, such as Williams' inability to express in words how he reacted to the incident. McKelway used scene-by-scene construction to present what occurred.

In 1936 he became managing editor of the *New Yorker,* a position he occupied until 1939. Except for a three-year, rather heroic stint with the Army Air Force during World War II, he remained with the magazine as an editor and as a writer. In addition to his articles and short stories for the *New Yorker* and other magazines, he wrote several books, including *Gossip: The Life and Times of Walter Winchell* and *The Edinburgh Caper.* He died in 1980.

WORK: *True Tales from the Annals of Crime and Rascality* (1950).

Don McNeill
(1944–1968)

A chronicler of events and a reporter who carefully observed and then recorded the sights and sounds of the hippie world, Don McNeill covered in impressionistic vignettes "the story of a year, running roughly from the big beginning Be-In at Central Park in the spring of 1967 to the bloody Yip-In at Grand Central Station in March of 1968."[1]

McNeill, who was born in 1944, attended the University of Washington for three years, then moved to New York City, where he became a staff writer for the *Village Voice* in 1966. His articles, invariably turned in at the last moment, were factual. As Paul Williams wrote, "Don's only interest was in the compassionate truth—the contribution that truth told in print could make to the growth of his world—and, yes, the well-tuned phrase, he always enjoyed his words and sentences, conscious of the music he could set free."[2]

In 1968 McNeill accidentally drowned while swimming in a lake in upstate New York. His articles on such subjects as underground slogans, street theater, Abbie Hoffman, free concerts, Sweep-Ins, East Village, the Lower East Side, acid, Gary Snyder, Country Joe and the Fish, and Haight-Ashbury had become popular features of the *Voice;* they were collected and published posthumously in 1970 under the title *Moving Through Here.* The article "The Serenos" exemplified McNeill's ability to candidly report, through dramatic dialogue and realistic description, an incident of the streets.

WORK: *Moving Through Here* (1970).
NOTES
1. Don McNeill, *Moving Through Here* (New York: Alfred A. Knopf, 1970), p. vii.
2. Paul Williams, Epilogue to *Moving Through Here,* by Don McNeill (New York: Alfred A. Knopf, 1970), p. 234.

John McNulty
(1896?–1956)

John McNulty was born in Lawrence, Massachusetts. His father died when John was young. His mother operated a small store, from which she earned enough to support her family.

McNulty attended public schools. When World War I broke out, he joined the infantry and served in several major battles, including Fere-en-Tardenois. After the other sergeants in his company were killed in combat, McNulty was made a sergeant. During the fighting at Fere-en-Tardenois, he was wounded in the leg. When he was discharged he spent about a year in a hospital.

McNulty then attended the Columbia School of Journalism while he worked for the Associated Press. Upon graduation, he was employed by the *New York Post.* This position did not last, however, and at the age of 25 he moved to

Columbus, Ohio, where he worked as a reporter for the *Ohio State Journal.* McNulty remained in Columbus more than 10 years and learned about everyone he met, whether they were taxi drivers or bellboys. He even wrote speeches for a gubernatorial candidate who eventually won the election.

In 1935 he returned to New York City, where he worked as a reporter for the *Daily Mirror,* the *Daily News,* and the *Herald Tribune,* and then briefly as a staff writer for *Time* magazine. In 1937 he was hired by the *New Yorker;* except for about a year spent in Hollywood, he remained at the magazine until his death in 1956. His first assignment for the *New Yorker* was a "Reporter at Large" piece, and eventually he wrote for other sections of the magazine as well. However, his favorite pieces were affectionate articles that concerned the everyday folks of Third Avenue. As James Thurber, his friend, wrote:

Nothing, however commonplace, that he touched with words remained commonplace, but was magnified and enlivened by his intense and endless fascination with the stranger in the street, the drinker at the bar and the bartender behind it, the horseplayer, the cabdriver, the guy at the ball game, the fellow across the room, the patient in the next hospital bed.[1]

McNulty's reportage rang true. Indeed, his articles presented his subjects in every detail. He used realistic or authentic dialogue and careful description to allow the reader to hear their voices and to visualize their appearance. Some Third Avenue characters appeared in several pieces. For instance, Paddy Ferrarty (a bartender), Dinny (a waiter), Little Marty and Little Mike (hackies), Grogan (a horseplayer), and Grady (a cabby) were popular among readers. Several of his articles were collected and published under the title *Third Avenue, New York* in 1946. Another collection, *A Man Gets Around* (1951), concerned Bellevue Hospital, the blue-grass region of Kentucky, and Ireland. A posthumous collection of his articles, *The World of John McNulty,* was published in 1957. A reviewer for *Time* said of the latter:

Like a true narrowback, McNulty in his heart hungered for the lost village—and he found it in Third Avenue's vestiges of Irish life, in the awful cooking, the hatred of machinery, the acid yet basically gentle manner of one man to another. This last quality crops out in many stories.[2]

"Don't Scrub Off These Names," collected in *Third Avenue, New York,* exemplified McNulty's ability to carefully describe his characters. "The Slugger Comes Into His Own," collected in *The World of John McNulty,* revealed McNulty's sense of humor and illustrated his ability to use authentic dialogue. John McNulty died of a heart attack on July 29, 1956.

WORKS: *Third Avenue, New York* (1946); *A Man Gets Around* (1951); *The World of John McNulty* (1957).

NOTES

1. John McNulty, *The World of John McNulty* (Garden City, N.Y.: Doubleday, 1957), pp. 9–10.

2. "Street Scene," *Time,* November 4, 1957, p. 113.

John McPhee
(1931–   )

John McPhee, who was born to Mary and Homer McPhee on March 8, 1931, in Princeton, New Jersey, attended Princeton High School, Deerfield Academy, a private school in Massachusetts, Princeton University, from which he graduated in 1953, and Cambridge University. Although he excelled in sports while attending school, he also enjoyed writing, especially creative writing. When he returned home in 1954, he taught in a local school and saved his earnings. If he was going to make a career of writing, he would have to go to New York City, or so he thought.

In New York City, McPhee soon fulfilled his desire to be a professional writer. From 1955 to 1957 he wrote several television scripts for "Robert Montgomery Presents," a popular dramatic series. McPhee, who had had one article published in the *New York Times Magazine* in 1952, wrote and contributed articles to various magazines, including his favorite, the *New Yorker.* Although at first his articles were rejected for one reason or another, he persisted. Eventually he began to receive acceptances from periodicals like the *Saturday Evening Post* and the *Transatlantic Review.* In 1957 he joined *Time* as a staff reporter. McPhee worked in "the back of the book" area of the magazine. According to William L. Howarth, "Mostly he wrote assigned material on films or stage shows, and some book reviews. As writer of the 'Show Business' section, his cover stories on various stars ranged from Jackie Gleason to Richard Burton."[1]

The editors recognized McPhee's talent and subsequently offered him the "National Affairs" section; McPhee declined. Although his salary would have increased, he would have had less time to spend on other articles and short stories.

In 1963 his article "Basketball and Beefeaters" was accepted by the *New Yorker.* The magazine's editors refused his next idea, a profile of All-American basketball star Bill Bradley. However, McPhee persisted, and the magazine finally accepted and published his article on Bradley in 1965; an expanded version appeared the same year under the title *A Sense of Where You Are: A Profile of William Warren Bradley.* As a result of its favorable reception, William Shawn, the editor-in-chief of the *New Yorker,* offered McPhee a position he could not refuse. According to Howarth: "The *New Yorker* has a first option on all of McPhee's work. He is free to choose a subject and estimate its length; the editors are equally free to criticize, accept, or reject his proposal. If rejected, he may still write the piece and sell it elsewhere."[2]

McPhee, who contributed articles to other periodicals, including the *Atlantic, Vogue, Holiday, Playboy,* and *Horticulture,* wrote on subjects such as drink, art, science, history, sports, food, and education. Indeed, he wrote about nuclear power plants, oranges from Florida, Frank L. Boyden of Deerfield Academy and Henri Vaillancourt of New Hampshire, tennis, the development of a new plane, Alaska, and Florida, among other topics.

Some of his articles for the *New Yorker* were expanded and published as books. These included, in addition to the book on Bradley, *The Headmaster* (1966), *Oranges* (1967), *Levels of the Game* (1970), *The Deltoid Pumpkin Seed* (1973), *The Curve of Binding Energy* (1974), and *Coming into the Country* (1977), his best-selling authoritative book about Alaska, in which he described the developers, conservationists, and rugged individualists who often came into conflict over the land.

Howarth described McPhee's writing as "fresh, strong, unaffected, and yet entirely idiosyncratic."[3] Although Howarth claimed that McPhee was not a literary journalist, he acknowledged that his writing was neither straight reporting nor fiction, but a combination of the two.

In 1981 McPhee's first book about geology, *Basin and Range,* appeared. McPhee, accompanied by a geologist, traveled across the United States and subsequently explained how basins and ranges were formed, among other geological formations and wonders. Two years later, in *In Suspect Terrain,* he explored the geological relationships in urban areas, particularly those in the Midwest. In his third book about geology, *Rising from the Plains* (1986), McPhee recorded geologist David Love's explanations as they traveled by Ford Bronco through the Rocky Mountains in Wyoming. McPhee learned from Love about man and machine and how both were destroying nature and the state of Wyoming.

In 1989 he wrote about the Army Corps of Engineers and their attempts to control the Mississippi River, Icelanders and their attempts to stymie magma flows from a new volcanic eruption, and the people in California and their attempts to contain nature in *The Control of Nature.*

One year later McPhee recorded the loss of a livelihood as well as the loneliness of one practicing an obsolescent trade in *Looking for a Ship,* which recounted his adventures with first mate Andy Chase on board the *SS Stella Lykes,* one of the last ships of the dying American merchant fleet. McPhee and Chase journeyed from Charleston, South Carolina, through the Panama Canal to the west coast of South America.

His last book in the geology series was published in 1993. *Assembling California* described how California moved on shifting tectonic plates to become affixed to North America. McPhee also discussed the sobering implications for Californians living near the San Andreas fault. Nikki Finke wrote: "It's not just that McPhee paints an irresistible—and *understandable*—portrait of the San Andreas Fault that makes you want to jump in your Honda and go looking for signs of shifting plates. It's that he comes up with visual images that leap off the page.''[4]

Indeed, McPhee's skill at turning scientific jargon into everday language was evident in this book, and the reader not only learned about a dry subject but came to appreciate its logical theories.

McPhee's shorter articles from the *New Yorker* have been collected and published in several volumes, including *A Roomful of Hovings and Other Profiles* (1969), *Pieces of the Frame* (1975), *The John McPhee Reader* (1977), *Giving Good Weight* (1979), and *Table of Contents* (1985).

WORKS: *A Sense of Where You Are: A Profile of William Warren Bradley* (1965); *The Headmaster* (1966); *Oranges* (1967); *Levels of the Game* (1970); *The Deltoid Pumpkin Seed* (1973); *The Curve of Binding Energy* (1974); *Coming Into the Country* (1977); *Basin and Range* (1981); *In Suspect Terrain* (1983); *Rising from the Plains* (1986); *The Control of Nature* (1989); *Looking for a Ship* (1990); *Assembling California* (1993).

NOTES

1. William L. Howarth, ed., *The John McPhee Reader* (New York: Farrar, Straus and Giroux, 1976), p. x.

2. Ibid., pp. xi–xii.

3. Ibid., p. xvii.

4. Nikki Finke, "Shake it up, Baby!," *Los Angeles,* January 1993, p. 89.

H. L. Mencken
(1880–1956)

While Simeon Strunsky was writing in support of U.S. entry into World War I, H. L. Mencken marshalled opposing arguments in his *Baltimore Evening Sun* column, "The Free Lance." Mencken, born in Baltimore in 1880 into an affluent bourgeois German-American family, attended Professor Friedrich Knapp's Teutonic Institute and the Baltimore Polytechnic, where he excelled in chemistry and the natural sciences. He read both British and American literature voraciously, and learned to play the piano. These interests were later useful when he began writing essays and criticism.

In 1899 he obtained a position with the *Baltimore Morning Herald,* where he eventually took on the responsibilities of editor as well as reporter. In 1904 the *Morning Herald* was replaced by the *Evening Herald,* and Mencken rose to editor before the paper's demise two years later. Mencken immediately moved to the *Baltimore Evening News,* then the *Baltimore Sun.*

Mencken's writing was filled with agnosticism, elitism, and iconoclasm and drew on the works of thinkers and writers such as Charles Darwin, Thomas Huxley, Friedrich Nietzsche, Herbert Spencer, William Sumner, and James Huneker. Mencken's literary efforts included not only news reports, editorials, reviews, features, and humor, but short stories, articles of criticism, and several research studies, including *Philosophy of Friedrich Nietzsche* and *The American*

Language. Mencken, like realistic novelists, was able to observe life around him and then explain it vibrantly; indeed, color was in every sentence he composed.

In 1908 Mencken began reviewing books for *Smart Set,* a magazine published in New York City. His reputation as a critic spread. In 1914 Mencken and the magazine's drama critic, George Jean Nathan, became editors, and together they produced much of its material. Mencken's contributions, according to Douglas C. Stevenson, helped to keep alive the spirit of the aesthetic and moral rebellion of the 1890s:

He defied the genteel assumption that American letters must be primarily Anglo-Saxon, optimistic, and morally uplifting. He ridiculed literary commercialism, dramatized the view that an essential function of art is to challenge accepted axioms, and conducted a boisterous onslaught against the "snouters" who favored literary censorship.[1]

When his column "The Free Lance" appeared in the *Sun* in 1911 Mencken gave the readers of Baltimore something they had never seen. Indeed, he ridiculed municipal politics, public works, language, certain persons within the community, and national and international affairs. His *Smart Set* articles would be altered to suit the column, and vice versa. Eventually these articles and columns were collected and published.

When World War I began, his column was filled with venom. He attacked the pro-English Americans who ridiculed German Americans. His sentiment was so strong that he eventually became a partisan of Germany, and was severely criticized by other members of the press. In 1915 his column was stopped, and Mencken was soon sent abroad as a correspondent in the hope that his absence would quiet his critics. When he returned in 1917, however, criticism still confronted him. The United States was in the war, and Mencken's un-American attitude was unforgivable. His *Book of Prefaces,* for example, was unduly and viciously attacked by reviewers. *The American Language,* perhaps because it was published in a calmer climate, ultimately received critical acclaim and achieved popularity.

For the next several years Mencken wrote furiously for the *Sun, Smart Set, Atlantic Monthly,* and the *Nation,* taking on big business, big government, the "Red Scare," the Ku Klux Klan, education, sexual morality, and other issues. Between 1919 and 1927 his six-volume *Prejudices* series was published. Although many of the articles had been published previously, the series also included new material.

In 1923, because of financial and editorial problems, *Smart Set* ceased publication. A new critical review, backed by Alfred Knopf and edited by Mencken and Nathan, appeared a month later. Although the *American Mercury* was a better *Smart Set* in every respect, Nathan's and Mencken's personalities clashed, causing Nathan to leave before the magazine was a year old. Mencken's publication combined literary criticism, which the readers enjoyed and respected, with political criticism, which they questioned. Mencken's attitudes toward politics, for example, changed from one month to the next. His economic policy, which had been liberal to a certain extent, became conservative; and in the early 1930s he supported Franklin Roosevelt but attacked Roosevelt's New Deal policies. In 1933 he resigned from the magazine and devoted the rest of his life to writing for the *Sun* and collecting his essays and letters, which were published in several volumes.

In 1925 Mencken reported on the famous Scopes anti-evolution trial in Dayton, Tennessee. Among his dispatches was a descriptive account of an Erskine Caldwell–style revival meeting in which elements of literary journalism were quite visible. He was working for the *Sun* when he suffered a stroke in 1948; he died eight years later.

WORKS: *The American Language* (1919); *American Mercury* (1923–1933).
NOTE
1. Douglas C. Stevenson, "Mencken, Henry Louis," *Dictionary of American Biography: Supplement Six 1956–1960,* edited by John A. Garraty (New York: Charles Scribner's Sons, 1980), p. 444.

Larry Merchant
(1931–)

Larry Merchant was born in New York City in 1931 and received his bachelor's degree from the University of Oklahoma 20 years later. He was a "last string" halfback on Bud Wilkinson's Oklahoma football teams and never played in a game, but the experience was useful when, after serving two years in the army, he began to write sports columns. First published in the *Philadelphia Daily News* from 1957 to 1966, then in the *New York Post* for the next 10 years, Merchant's columns were entertaining as well as informative. Filled with behind-the-scenes stories of coaches and athletes, each column was a story in itself.

In 1971 he wrote *And Every Day You Take Another Bite,* which Arthur Cooper called "a funny, irreverent blitz of our national obsession with football in which he relegated the game to life's toy box . . . and demonstrated that football's celebrated complexities exist only in the minds of its bemused beholders."[1] The book was successful, and Merchant spent the advance placing bets on weekly National Football League games; that activity was the subject of his second hilarious book, *The National Football Lottery.* Cooper noted:

Merchant careens around the gambling circuit like a runty halfback scrambling to daylight. In Monte Carlo he practices "money management"—control of his emotions. . . . In Las Vegas he observes that losers "eat twice as much as winners (and) buy twice as many *objets d'art* as winners."[2]

Merchant's second book was successful both critically and commercially. *Ringside Seat at the Circus* published in 1976, did not receive as much praise as his first two books.

From 1977 to 1978 he worked as a reporter and editor for the National Broadcasting Company. When he left NBC he became a freelance television reporter, producer, and commentator. He wrote a column for the *Los Angeles Herald-Examiner* from 1979 to 1980.

WORKS: *And Every Day You Take Another Bite* (1971); *The National Football Lottery* (1973); *Ringside Seat at the Circus* (1976).

NOTES

1. Arthur Cooper, "Man Bites Ball," *Newsweek,* October 29, 1973, p. 104.
2. Ibid.

James Mills
(1932–   )

James Mills was born in 1932 and worked as a journalist for several newspapers, including the *Worcester Telegram and Evening Gazette* in Massachusetts and the *Corpus Christi Caller Times* in Texas. From 1960 to 1966 Mills worked as a reporter, writer, and editor at *Life* magazine. One article he wrote, "The Panic in Needle Park," which described the effects of drugs on people, took several months to investigate and write. Mills examined the topic at length in a book by the same name published in 1966. Edward M. Brown said of Mills, "By following and recounting the orbit of a young addicted couple he provides material accurate enough for a case study."[1]

In *The Panic in Needle Park,* Mills painted very realistic and accurate scenes. The use of description and authentic dialogue not only made the characters credible but helped the reader visualize them and their surroundings. The book was an example of literary journalism.

Mills also wrote an incisive account of Detective George Barrett, a police officer, in "The Detective."

The Prosecutor, another book based on fact, appeared in 1969. It was about an overworked district attorney attempting to prosecute a member of the Mafia. Mills, who as a reporter had covered the New York Police Department for United Press International in 1959, used a combination of elements usually found in fiction in his dogged, angry style of reportage, and the reader learned about the everyday problems that confront police officers and members of the legal profession.

Mills turned to the novel in the 1970s, 1980s, and 1990s. Most of his efforts focused on the topic he knew best—law and order. For instance, *Report to the Commissioner,* which was published in 1972, concerned a beautiful blonde undercover narcotics agent who was killed in the line of duty by another young police officer. The novel was written as if it were an actual confidential report prepared by the Internal Affairs Division of the New York City Police Department.

In 1986 his investigative exposé *The Underground Empire: Where Crime and Governments Embrace* was published. Mills described how a now defunct supersecret agency of the United States government, Centac, attempted to eliminate the international drug trade. However, during his investigation, Mills learned that without the sufferance of the federal government, the Underground Empire of drug traffickers could not exist. To say the least, the book was mind-boggling.

Four years later he wrote *The Power,* a spy thriller about psychic phenomena. His novel *Haywire,* about embittered former D.E.A. agent Doug Fleming, who agreed to smuggle $100 million worth of bonds from Peru to New York for international drug lords, was published in 1995.

WORKS: *The Panic in Needle Park* (1966); *The Prosecutor* (1969); *The Underground Empire: Where Crime and Governments Embrace* (1986).

NOTE

1. Edward M. Brown, "Addicts' Odyssey," *New York Times Book Review,* May 22, 1966, p. 10.

Joseph Mitchell
(1908–   )

Joseph Mitchell was born on July 27, 1908, near Fairmont, North Carolina. His parents owned a farm on which his father raised cotton. Mitchell, like his two brothers and three sisters, helped on the farm, but he could not learn basic mathematics, which he would have needed to become a successful cotton grower.

Mitchell attended the University of North Carolina from 1925 to 1929, but he failed to graduate. Instead of returning to the farm, however, he went to New York City, where he got a job as a crime reporter for the *New York World.* Mitchell was assigned first to Brooklyn, then to a precinct in Manhattan, and finally to Harlem. After several months, he moved to the *New York Herald-Tribune.* In 1931 he moved to the *New York World-Telegram,* for which he wrote numerous feature stories. He stayed at the paper until 1938, the year he joined the staff of the *New Yorker,* a very prominent literary magazine. Mitchell joined such writers as St. Clair McKelway, John McNulty, John Hersey, Lillian Ross, and Meyer Berger. The same year his first book, a collection of newspaper articles, was published. Titled *My Ears Are Bent,* it included accounts of people whom Mitchell had met.

Mitchell contributed articles to the *New Yorker,* but he attracted additional readers in 1943 when *McSorley's Wonderful Saloon* was published. Each of its 20 essays was devoted to a specific person or place. Mitchell celebrated the individuals about whom he wrote, even the unfortunate, and his power of observation was improving.

In 1948 *Old Mr. Flood* appeared. An example of literary journalism, the book contained three sketches about Hugh Flood, an old man who lived in a small hotel near the Fulton Fish Market. In actuality Flood was based on several old men, and was Mitchell's first composite character. The other characters in the book, on the other hand, were actual people, as were the locations. As Noel

Perrin wrote, "Inventing Mr. Flood seems to have given Mitchell the freedom to enter, when he himself was only forty, into the third phase of his celebration of rowdy life—the elegiac phase."[1]

It was 12 years before he produced another book. *The Bottom of the Harbor,* published in 1960, contained six articles about New York City: one about the bottom of the harbor; one about a seafood restaurant in one of the older buildings; one about the rats of the city; one about Ellery Thompson, the captain of a trawler; one about a minority community on Staten Island; and one about fishermen who lived in New Jersey. Mitchell's eye for details was uncanny. His description of places was accurate and realistic; his dialogue was authentic and captured the individuals' personalities. These articles, too, were examples of literary journalism because of the elements employed and because the author was one of the participants, even though he played a minor role for the most part. Some of the pieces were linked by the theme of mortality and what some have called graveyard humor, primarily because he wrote about old men and women.

Mitchell chronicled the life of Joe Gould, the son of a physician and a Harvard graduate, in *Joe Gould's Secret,* which was published in 1965. Unlike most Harvard graduates, Joe Gould had become a bohemian who visited bars on a regular basis. For drinks, he would entertain customers by demonstrating how he could converse with seagulls. Mitchell had met Gould in the early 1940s and wrote a profile of him for the *New Yorker* in 1942. Gould told Mitchell that he had been working on a major project: the Oral History of Our Time. Gould supposedly had collected information from almost everyone he met and had written it down in composition books. Mitchell had not seen the stack of composition books. When Gould died, Mitchell searched for the books. Only a few existed, and these were filled with repetitive information specifically about Gould's father. Mitchell realized that the oral history did not exist; this was Joe Gould's secret. The book was favorably reviewed by most critics.

Mitchell continued to work for the *New Yorker.* When his father died in 1976, he felt the need to help his brothers and sisters with the farm. He spent part of the year in New York City and part of the year in North Carolina. Mitchell will be remembered for Joe Gould and Old Mr. Flood, characters who allowed him to explore their lives and at the same time his own.

Mitchell's *Up in the Old Hotel,* a collection of four previously published books, including *McSorley's Wonderful Saloon, Old Mr. Flood, The Bottom of the Harbor,* and *Joe Gould's Secret,* was published in 1992.

WORKS: *My Ears Are Bent* (1938); *McSorley's Wonderful Saloon* (1943); *Old Mr. Flood* (1948); *The Bottom of the Harbor* (1960); *Joe Gould's Secret* (1965); *Up in the Old Hotel* (1992).

NOTE

1. Noel Perrin, "Paragon of Reporters Joseph Mitchell," *Sewanee Review,* Spring 1983, p. 177.

Thomas B. Morgan
(1926–)

Born in 1926 in Illinois, Thomas B. Morgan attended the University of Illinois for a year, then transferred to Carleton College, where he received his bachelor's degree in 1949. Upon graduation he became an associate editor at *Esquire*, a position he held for four years. From 1953 to 1958 he was a senior editor with *Look*, and from 1958 to 1969, until he became press secretary to the mayor of New York City, he wrote various articles for magazines, including *TV Guide*, *Cosmopolitan*, *Good Housekeeping*, *Holiday*, *Harper's*, *Redbook*, *Esquire*, and *Look*, and the books *Self-Creations: Thirteen Impersonalities*, *This Blessed Shore*, and *Among the Anti-Americans*.

His articles, which were predominantly personality pieces, were witty and entertaining as well as informative. His subjects included celebrities and politicians Gary Cooper, Roy Cohn, Teddy Kennedy, Alf Landon, Elia Kazan, John Wayne, Brigitte Bardot, Sidney Poitier, Nelson Rockefeller, Adlai Stevenson, and David Susskind. However, he also wrote about lesser known performers such as Tinker Bell and Blaze Starr, two burlesque queens, and about scientists, authors, and even people he met on the streets of New York City. His article about Sammy Davis, Jr., was unusual, as Morgan explained: "My very first post-novel effort, a chronicle of an encounter with Sammy Davis, Jr., for *Esquire*, came out virtually as a short story, using dialogue, atmosphere, and character development to explore Sammy's personality and self-created image of colorlessness."[1]

In other words, Morgan used techniques usually associated with fiction to candidly capture his subject. His article "Blaze Starr in Nighttown" also exhibited characteristics of literary journalism—that is, detailed description, dialogue, and an uncanny ability to obtain information overlooked by most interviewers or journalists.

In 1987 Morgan wrote *Snyder's Walk*, a realistic novel about a journalist and his profession.

WORKS: *Self-Creations: Thirteen Impersonalities* (1965); *This Blessed Shore* (1966); *Among the Anti-Americans* (1967).

NOTE

1. Thomas B. Morgan, *Self-Creations: Thirteen Impersonalities* (New York: Holt, Rinehart and Winston, 1965), p. 10.

Willie Morris
(1934–)

Journalist, editor, and novelist Willie Morris was born in Jackson, Mississippi, on November 29, 1934, and grew up in Yazoo City. In his autobiography, *North Toward Home*, Morris explained what the name meant to him: " 'Yazoo,' far from being the ludicrous name that others would take it, always meant for me something dark, a little blood-crazy and violent.''[1]

Morris enjoyed the atmosphere of Yazoo; however, he believed the town had not stimulated his intellect. Like a character in a Mark Twain novel, he played practical jokes, got into trouble, and taunted ''hell-fire and brimstone'' preachers who tried to convert him. He played sports, especially baseball, and wrote sports stories for the Yazoo *Herald.* Later he worked in various capacities at a radio station.

In 1952 he entered the University of Texas at Austin, where he eventually matured. Playing catch-up, he read every book he could and tried to improve his writing. Although he wrote a column for the *Daily Texan,* his penchant for muckraking journalism did not become evident until he was named editor of the newspaper in his senior year. After attacking as well as exposing the oil industry, Morris had to fight the university not only to keep writing for the paper but to keep his position as editor. He wrote:

The attempt to censor *The Daily Texan* in 1956 involved not a displacement of dissent, but the running roughshod over it by real power, and the more sophisticated kind of criticism that served as its forum—the kind of wealth which still encourages the idea in America that anything can be bought, including culture.[2]

Morris received his degree in 1956 and, as a Rhodes Scholar, attended Oxford University, from which he received a second bachelor's degree and a master's degree. Ronnie Dugger, whom Morris had known from his days at the University of Texas, asked Morris to return to Austin to take over the *Texas Observer,* a weekly muckraking newspaper Dugger had founded in 1955. Morris immediately responded. Although he was just 25 years old, he was not, in his words, ''the same self-righteous, moralistic boy'' he had been when he was editor of the *Daily Texan*:

I had the most earnest feelings that our little paper was somehow involved . . . in the great flow of history on this continent, and that to understand a place like Texas through its dissenters and its young rebels was to understand something of an older, vanished America; yet I also wished to be rooted in my own anxious time, a time when a new generation of young Americans would, for a tragically brief and poignant period, wield power.[3]

Morris, like Dugger, sustained the *Observer's* fighting spirit. Almost every day he visited state legislators to learn what was on the agenda; he traveled throughout Texas to learn what people wanted from their legislators; he followed John F. Kennedy's 1960 campaign tour in Texas; he revealed the corruption within the state's governing bodies; he criticized the collusion between legislators and representatives of the petroleum industry; he attacked the John Birch

Society as well as other right-wing organizations. In short, he not only presented the ills of Texas, but advocated various means to get rid of them.

After three years, however, he was glad to see Dugger return. Morris resigned as editor and left Texas. For a brief period he lived in California, where he attended Stanford University. Within several months he moved to New York City and obtained a position with *Harper's.* Morris became immersed in his work, so much so that he was advanced to executive editor in 1965. According to Joan Babbitt: "Morris . . . immediately began to put into practice his plan for establishing it as a truly *national* magazine. . . . The work of such new contributors as Larry King and William Styron infused vitality into a journal that had become pedestrian, stuffy, and uninspired."[4]

In 1967, at the age of 32, Morris became the magazine's editor-in-chief, a position that had not been occupied by anyone that young in its 167 years. His autobiography appeared the same year. The publishers approved of Morris' aggressive form of journalism, and he made the magazine one of the most discussed periodicals in the late 1960s: "With [David] Halberstam's dispatches from Vietnam and [Larry] King's coverage of Washington, *Harper's* consistently made news. In addition, it became a writer's magazine, offering some of the longest and most provocative pieces ever to appear in a periodical."[5]

Morris, who published writers such as Marshall Frady, Midge Decter, Michael Harrington, and Robert Coles, undeniably helped the magazine's circulation. When he began to pay contributing editors $25,000 a year and writers at least $1,000 for an article, the magazine's financial position drastically changed, and William S. Blair, the newly appointed president, did not approve. Blair, a former advertising specialist, together with John Cowles, Jr., whose company owned *Harper's,* questioned Morris' business sense. In addition, Blair cared little for Morris' philosophy of journalism. Therefore, when Morris published the controversial essay "The Prisoner of Sex" by Norman Mailer, Blair confronted him about his handling of the magazine. Morris, who had fought for what he believed was right, resigned in 1971.

His book *Yazoo: Integration in a Deep-Southern Town* appeared later the same year. The book concerned the 1969 U.S. Supreme Court ruling that Morris' hometown be desegregated. Morris, through interviews with citizens of Yazoo, wrote of the town's dedicated efforts to make segregation a stigma of the past.

When *James Jones: A Friendship* appeared in 1978 it was attacked by critics for not being objective. Morris, who contributed articles, vignettes, and essays to such periodicals as the *Nation, Commentary, Dissent,* and the *New Yorker,* published a collection of magazine pieces under the title *Terrains of the Heart and Other Essays on Home* in 1981.

In 1983 his *Always Stand in Against the Curve and Other Sports Stories* and *The Courting of Marcus Dupree* appeared. The first book contained autobiographical essays about his days as a high school baseball player and about the high school baseball tournament in Mississippi in 1952 in which his team was defeated. The second book presented the irony-rich story of football player Marcus Dupree. Morris mixed episodes from the early twentieth century with the history of Dupree's career. The book was a thorough examination of sports in the South.

Seven years later he collected several essays about people and situations familiar to most readers—from spending Christmas at grandmother's house to an unconventional professor whose teaching methods left an indelible impression on a student—in the book *Homecomings*. Morris also wrote about the terror that gripped a small community after a heinous crime had been committed. He described familiar feelings, sights, smells, sounds, and tastes. Art by William Dunlap accompanied the essays.

In 1991 Morris published a series of essays about William Faulkner's life in Oxford, Mississippi, in *Faulkner's Mississippi.* Photographs by William Eggleston accompanied the essays.

A year later the insightful collection *After All, It's Only a Game* appeared. It contained three memoirs and three short stories that captured his fondness for baseball and football and his role in each. The stories concerned other sports, including basketball. Morris focused on simple, everyday aspects of sports to which most readers could relate.

In 1993 he wrote *New York Days,* a worthy sequel to his autobiography, *North Toward Home.* As Gerald Parshall wrote, *"New York Days* is a melodrama with three protagonists: a man named Willie Morris, a place called Manhattan and a time called the 1960s.''[6] The book was filled with nostalgia as he examined his days as editor of *Harper's* in the late 1960s. According to Morris, the magazine mirrored and interpreted the nation as a result of the various writers it published. Morris had encouraged writers to contribute literary journalism as well as advocacy journalism.

Morris eventually left New York City and returned to Mississippi. Another memoir, *My Dog Skip,* about his relationship with his dog and, of course, Yazoo, Mississippi, was published in 1995.

WORKS: *North Toward Home* (1967); *Texas Observer* (editor); *Harper's Magazine* (editor-in-chief); *Yazoo: Integration in a Deep-Southern Town* (1971); *Terrains of the Heart and Other Essays on Home* (1981); *Always Stand in Against the Curve and Other Sports Stories* (1983); *The Courting of Marcus Dupree* (1983); *Homecomings* (1990); *After All, It's Only a Game* (1992); *New York Days* (1993).

NOTES

1. Willie Morris, *North Toward Home* (Boston: Houghton Mifflin, 1967), p. 4.

2. Ibid., p. 193.

3. Ibid., p. 203.

4. Joan Babbitt, "Willie Morris," *Dictionary of Literary Biography Yearbook: 1980,* edited by Karen L. Rood, Jean W. Ross, and Richard Ziegfeld (Detroit: Gale Research, 1981), p. 272.

5. Charles Moritz, ed., *Current Biography Yearbook 1976* (New York: H. W. Wilson, 1976), p. 273.

6. Gerald Parshall, ''The Yarn Spinner from Yazoo: At Home in the Land of Cotton, Willie Morris Plays Pranks, Haunts Cemeteries and Pens an Evocative Memoir of New York,'' *U.S. News & World Report,* September 13, 1993, p. 75.

Bill Moyers
(1934–)

Bill Moyers was born to Ruby and John Henry Moyers on June 5, 1934, in Hugo, Oklahoma, and grew up in Marshall, Texas. Before he graduated from high school he experienced the world of journalism as a reporter for the Marshall *News Messenger.* When he attended North Texas State University (University of North Texas) he contributed to the student newspaper and worked in public information. Moyers, who offered to support Senator Lyndon B. Johnson in his 1954 reelection campaign, was hired by Johnson during the summer of that year. Moyers' work was impressive, and Johnson took a special interest in his future. Instead of returning to North Texas State, Moyers transferred to the University of Texas at Austin, where he not only majored in journalism, but worked at KTBC-TV, a station owned by Lady Bird Johnson.

Two years later he received his bachelor's degree in journalism, then attended the University of Edinburgh. When he returned a year later he attended the Southwestern Baptist Theological Seminary in Fort Worth, from which he graduated in 1959. Moyers' interest in politics was rekindled several months later. Indeed, he spent months as Johnson's personal assistant, special assistant, and executive assistant. He coordinated Johnson's vice presidential campaign.

When Johnson became vice president, Moyers resigned to become the associate director of public affairs of the Peace Corps. When President Kennedy was assassinated, Moyers offered his services to President Johnson and subsequently became an advisor to the president on domestic affairs, the White House Chief of Staff, and the president's press secretary. In 1966, having grown disillusioned with Johnson's escalation of the war in Vietnam, he resigned to return to journalism. When offered the publisher's position at *Newsday,* Moyers immediately realized that his services could conceivably be more beneficial to a large newspaper. According to *Current Biography,* Moyers strengthened *Newsday*'s Washington bureau. He hired *Time*'s Nicholas Thimmesch, the *New York Post*'s Pete Hamill, Daniel P. Moynihan, and Saul Bellow. He published news analysis, investigative articles, and even ''soft news'' features.[1]

When Harry Guggenheim sold the paper to the Times-Mirror Company, Moyers resigned and several weeks later traveled by bus across the United States. His journey of some 13,000 miles was later reported in his best-selling book *Listening to America: A Traveler Rediscovers His Country.* The book, which was praised by critics, was filled with literary journalism techniques. Through visual description of cities, towns, countryside, and people, and through conversations on various subjects—from the Kent State killings to the Vietnam War—Moyers captured the intense beliefs and varied themes of American life.

In the 1970s Moyers turned to broadcasting, first as a host of National Educational Television's public affairs program "This Week," then as the editor-in-chief of "Bill Moyers' Journal," which later became "Bill Moyers' Journal: International Report." In addition, he contributed a "back-of-the-book" column to *Newsweek* for a year and anchored the Public Broadcasting Service program "USA: People and Politics." Moyers' programs were intriguing; he interviewed writers, economists, historians, and other public figures; he devoted shows to ideas and issues, including the Watergate scandal; he interviewed journalists and politicians from all over the world primarily to gain perspectives on international issues.

In 1976 he was hired by CBS, where he served as editor and chief reporter of "CBS Reports" for three years. Moyers made numerous documentaries, including "The Fire Next Door," which examined arson in the Bronx, and "The Vanishing Family: Crisis in Black America," which examined various cultural problems of African-American women.

Moyers returned to PBS in 1979, then moved back to CBS two years later to serve as a commentator on the "CBS Evening News." Concurrently, he produced documentaries for PBS, including the popular "Creativity" series. He left CBS in 1986 when the news program shifted its emphasis from hard news to entertainment.

Moyers produced several lengthy popular series for PBS in the late 1980s and early 1990s, including "The Secret Government," which examined the Iran-Contra scandal, "A World of Ideas with Bill Moyers," in which he interviewed numerous philosophers, "Joseph Campbell and the Power of Myth," and "Healing and the Mind." Several of these were turned into books: *The Secret Government* and *Joseph Campbell and the Power of Myth* were published in 1988, and *A World of Ideas: Conversations with Thoughtful Men and Women About American Life Today and the Ideas Shaping Our Future,* published in 1989, contained 41 interviews from the series. A year later *Global Dumping Ground: The International Traffic in Hazardous Waste* was published. Like the report on PBS, it made a strong case against the export of hazardous waste. However, as Moyers pointed out, exporting hazardous waste was a lucrative business and consequently difficult to stop. Furthermore, it was less expensive to ship toxic waste to another country than to dispose of it safely in the United States. In 1993 his *Healing and the Mind* was published. Moyers interviewed health experts and examined health practices all over the world, both for the series and for the book.

WORKS: *Listening to America: A Traveler Rediscovers His Country* (1971); *The Secret Government* (1988); *Joseph Campbell and the Power of Myth* (1988); *A World of Ideas: Conversations with Thoughtful Men and Women about American Life Today and the Ideas Shaping Our Future* (1989); *Global Dumping Ground: The International Traffic in Hazardous Waste* (1990); *Healing and the Mind* (1993).

NOTE

1. Charles Moritz, ed., *Current Biography Yearbook 1976* (New York: H. W. Wilson, 1976), p. 276.

N

Jay Robert Nash
(1937–)

Jay Robert Nash, who wrote several lengthy encyclopedia-style anthologies, including the best-selling *Bloodletters and Badmen: A Narrative Encyclopedia of American Criminals from the Pilgrims to the Present* (1973), was born in Indianapolis in 1937. When he returned from Europe in the late 1950s, he began a career in journalism when he accepted the position of editor with the *Milwaukee Literary Times* and *Antioch News*. From 1961 to 1970 he was editor and publisher of *Literary Times*. Concurrently, he edited *American Trade Magazines* (from 1962 to 1966), and *Chicago Land* and *FM Guide* (from 1967 to 1970).

Nash, together with Ron Offen, wrote the inquisitive *Dillinger: Dead or Alive?* (1970), which propounded the theory that Dillinger had not been killed outside a theater, as previously reported. In 1972 Nash's *Hoover and His FBI,* which discussed J. Edgar Hoover's undeniable power over the Federal Bureau of Investigation, was published. His first encyclopedic work, *Bloodletters and Badmen,* appeared a year later. In brief, graphic narratives, Nash presented not only the basic information concerning each criminal's acts, but recreated through descriptive scenes and dramatic dialogue the criminal's capture or arrest and sentencing.

In 1976 two additional encyclopedic works appeared. *Hustlers and Con Men: An Anecdotal History of the Confidence Man and His Games* and *Darkest Hours: A Narrative Encyclopedia of World-Wide Disasters from Ancient Times to the Present* were reminiscent of *Bloodletters and Badmen* both in format and in writing style.

Nash wrote *The Mafia Diaries,* a crime novel, in 1985, then returned to non-fiction with his six-volume *Encyclopedia of World Crime: Criminal Justice, Criminology, and Law Enforcement,* published in 1990. This encyclopedia covered every aspect of crime from biblical times to 1988. In 1992 a condensed version was published as *The World Encyclopedia of Organized Crime.* This version focused primarily on American mobsters. In addition, two additional volumes based on the six-volume encyclopedia were published: *Dictionary of Crime: Criminal Justice, Criminology and Law Enforcement* and *World Encyclopedia of Twentieth Century Murder.* Also in 1992, Nash wrote the *Encyclopedia of Western Lawmen and Outlaws,* which contained more than 1,000 biographical entries of outlaws and lawmen of the old West.

In 1993 he published *The World Encyclopedia of Organized Crime,* which was filled with mini-biographies of hardened criminals.

WORKS: *Dillinger: Dead or Alive?* (1970); *Hoover and His FBI* (1972); *Bloodletters and Badmen: A Narrative Encyclopedia of American Criminals from the Pilgrims to the Present* (1973); *Hustlers and Con Men: An Anecdotal History of the Confidence Man and His Games* (1976); *Darkest Hours: A Narrative Encyclopedia of World-Wide Disasters from Ancient Times to the Present* (1976); *Encyclopedia of World Crime: Criminal Justice, Criminology, and Law Enforcement* (six volumes, 1990); *Encyclopedia of Western Lawmen and Outlaws* (1992); *The World Encyclopedia of Organized Crime* (1993).

Jack Newfield
(1939–   )

Jack Newfield, a self-described American New Leftist, was influenced by Murray Kempton and Albert Camus in terms of style and ideas. Newfield, who became a senior editor at the *Village Voice,* was born on February 18, 1939, in New York City, and graduated from Hunter College in 1961. Although he contributed numerous articles to other publications, including *Playboy, Evergreen Review,* the *Nation, New York,* and *Partisan Review,* he wrote mainly for the *Village Voice*—about civil rights, lead poisoning, hippies, the 1968 Democratic Convention, Students for a Democratic Society, Vietnam, Nelson Rockefeller, John Lindsay, Theodore Sorensen, the media, poor whites, the legal system, Norman Mailer, Ralph Nader, Robert Kennedy, and any other politician, writer, or issue that affected him or his beliefs.

Newfield, an advocate of morality, laws, equal justice, and what was right for the good of society, criticized the wrongs in American society.

His first book, *A Prophetic Minority,* which discussed the rise of the New Left, was published in 1966. His critically acclaimed analysis of Robert Kennedy appeared in 1969. *Robert Kennedy: A Memoir* was not a biography per se, but rather a personal testament that criticized as well as praised its subject, detailed the insurgencies of the 1960s, which Kennedy eventually pronounced to be societal necessities.

Newfield produced a collection of his articles in 1971, *Bread and Roses Too: Reporting About America.* In one article Newfield captured his reactions and attitudes toward President Nixon after a televised presidential address. Like other pieces in the book, it was an example of literary journalism.

In 1972 he and Jeff Greenfield wrote the popular *A Populist Manifesto: The Making of a New Majority.* They stated in the preface:

This manifesto is a platform for a movement that does not yet exist. It is not a book about the 1972 campaign, or a blue-print for Utopia in 2001.

It is instead an effort to return to American politics the economic passions jettisoned a generation ago. Its fundamental argument is wholly unoriginal: some institutions and people have too much money and power, most people have too little, and the first priority of politics must be to redress that imbalance.[1]

The authors then elaborated on a number of issues, such as banking, insurance, utilities, taxes, regulatory agencies, land reform, the media, crime, health, unions, and foreign policy, and subsequently advocated reforms.

Newfield also wrote the arresting, controversial book *Cruel and Unusual Justice* (1974) and, with Paul Du Brul, *The Abuse of Power: The Permanent Government and the Fall of New York* (1977). His insightful book *The Education of Jack Newfield* appeared in 1984. With Wayne Barrett he exposed the men who surrounded Mayor Ed Koch in the penetrating, muckraking journalistic study *City for Sale: Ed Koch and the Betrayal of New York* (1989). The authors claimed that these men were not only corrupt but as crooked as a dog's hind legs, and that Koch turned over parts of City Hall to those he said he opposed. The book was not necessarily a balanced report. Nonetheless, the authors' claims were accurate.

WORKS: *A Prophetic Minority* (1966); *Robert Kennedy: A Memoir* (1969); *Bread and Roses Too: Reporting About America* (1971); *A Populist Manifesto: The Making of a New Majority* (with Jeff Greenfield, 1972); *Cruel and Unusual Justice* (1974); *The Abuse of Power: The Permanent Government and the Fall of New York* (with Paul Du Brul, 1977); *The Education of Jack Newfield* (1984); *City for Sale: Ed Koch and the Betrayal of New York* (with Wayne Barrett, 1989).

NOTE

1. Jack Newfield and Jeff Greenfield, *A Populist Manifesto: The Making of a New Majority* (New York: Praeger, 1972), p. ix.

Barry Newman
(1946?–)

Barry Newman was reared in Rockaway Beach, across the bay from Brooklyn. He studied political science at Union College in Schenectady, New York, before he got a job as a copy boy at the *New York Times.*

Eventually, he contributed stories to the religion department. In 1970 he moved to the *Wall Street Journal,* and traveled the world for stories. For instance, he was based in Singapore for several years, and his stories covered people and places in India, Indonesia, Australia, Malaysia, and various islands of the South Pacific. In 1981 he transferred to London; from there he roamed throughout most of Europe. Unlike many journalists, Newman was granted much freedom in his writing. Indeed, he was allowed to spend as much as two months on a story, even though the length was restricted to 2,000 words.

Newman rarely used the first person in his writing; he concentrated on the event and the characters involved. Seldom, if ever, did he concentrate on news value or timeliness. Like other literary journalists, he employed realistic or authentic dialogue and accurate description.

East of the Equator, a collection of his articles, was published in 1980.

WORK: *East of the Equator* (1980).

Roy Newquist
(1925–   )

Roy Newquist was born in Wisconsin in 1925 and attended Marquette University in the mid-1940s and the University of Wisconsin in the late 1940s. Principally a biographer, he began a career in advertising in the early 1950s, working as a copy supervisor. In 1963 he became the literary editor of Chicago's *American* and a book reviewer for a newspaper syndicate. In addition, he was a critic for the *New York Post* as well as a host of the radio program "Counterpoint."

His first book, *Counterpoint,* a collection of 63 interviews with publishers, columnists, and authors, was published in 1964. Although it was not written in a literary journalistic style—indeed, the interviews were in the traditional question-followed-by-answer format—Newquist nevertheless captured on paper arresting information that had been aired on his radio program. *Showcase,* a collection of 25 interviews with actors, actresses, writers, musicians, and others associated with motion pictures, the theater, and other forms of entertainment, appeared a year later. In 1967 a collection of more than 40 of his interviews with writers, editors, and publishers appeared under the title *Conversations.* As in earlier works, Newquist merely reported what each person said about his or her life and work.

Newquist, who contributed interviews to *Show* as well as newspapers, altered his approach to interviewing in the behind-the-scenes book *A Special Kind of Magic,* which appeared in 1968. An in-depth study of those involved in the filming of *Guess Who's Coming to Dinner,* including Stanley Kramer, Katharine Hepburn, Sidney Poitier, and Spencer Tracy, Newquist's insightful book was reminiscent of *Picture* by Lillian Ross, even though his approach was not exactly the same. Indeed, Ross knew what she was going to write; Newquist, as he admitted, did not.

I was present on the set throughout the filming of this movie . . . with the intention of doing a series of tape-recordings with the principals, interviews that were later to appear in various magazines.

Gradually, however, I began to realize that a particular set of circumstances and a curious procession of events made me feel as though I had been witnessing, through a juxtaposition of very special kinds of magic, a dramatic microcosm of what Hollywood has been, is, and will be.[1]

Newquist mixed vivid description with personal commentary; his informal approach to obtaining information from the producer and the actors and actresses was an improvement over the traditional question-and-answer formula.

His *Conversations with Joan Crawford,* a collection of interviews conducted with the actress before her death, appeared in 1980. Although it revealed other sides of Joan Crawford's life and work, the book failed miserably when compared to *A Special Kind of Magic.*

WORKS: *Counterpoint* (1964); *Showcase* (1965); *Conversations* (1967); *A Special Kind of Magic* (1968); *Conversations with Joan Crawford* (1980).

NOTE

1. Roy Newquist, *A Special Kind of Magic* (Chicago: Rand McNally, 1968), pp. 13–14.

O

John O'Hara
(1905–1970)

John O'Hara was born on January 31, 1905, in Pottsville, Pennsylvania. He attended Catholic schools, which he disliked, then he was dismissed from the Fordham Preparatory School and the Keystone Normal School (Kutztown State College), and failed to graduate from the Niagara Preparatory School. Rebellious and undisciplined, O'Hara had a taste for the opposite sex and liquor. His father, a prominent physician, eventually forced his son to find employment.

O'Hara worked for the *Pottsville Journal,* where he remained until he was fired in 1926. His father had died the year before, and the family needed an income. Unfortunately, O'Hara was not particularly adept at keeping a job. Although he succeeded in procuring a position with the Tamaqua *Courier,* he was fired three months later.

In 1927 he traveled to Europe as a waiter on the liner *George Washington.* When he returned to the United States, he left for the West in pursuit of a newspaper job, which he could not find. Despondent, he returned home. In 1928 he moved to New York City, where he worked for the *Herald Tribune,* contributed to the *New Yorker,* and worked for *Time, Editor and Publisher,* the *New York Daily Mirror,* the *New York Morning Telegraph,* and the *New Yorker* before 1932. His behavior was unchanged.

In 1933 he moved to Pittsburgh, where he tried managing the *Bulletin-Index;* four months later he returned to New York City. Fiction was his last resort. His career as a professional novelist began in 1934 with the publication of *Appointment in Samara.* The novel was set in Gibbsville, Pennsylvania (based on Pottsville) and concerned the last three days of Julian English, who could not face his insecurities; it was immediately successful. O'Hara returned to Gibbsville often; in fact, characters from Gibbsville filled many short stories and several novels. This devotion to the area he knew best gave his stories and novels a sense of realism; indeed, residents of Pottsville believed they knew certain characters. In fact, O'Hara's ability to depict reality applied to most sections of the country, not one town or area.

Butterfield 8 (1935), a roman à clef, was based on the sensational story of Starr Faithfull, a sexual denizen of Jazz Age speakeasies who drowned in 1931. The novel was published to an eager reading audience. *Hope of Heaven* appeared three years later. In addition, several volumes of his short stories, including *The Doctor's Son* (1935) and *Files on Parade* (1939), were published.

From 1940 to 1942 he wrote the column "Entertainment Week" for *Newsweek,* and saw Rogers and Hart's *Pal Joey* become a hit musical. O'Hara had written the book for the production, based on short stories that had appeared in the *New Yorker.*

In 1944 he was a war correspondent for *Liberty* magazine. When he returned he wrote numerous short stories, which were ultimately collected and published, and wrote several screenplays in Hollywood. His next novel, *A Rage to Live,* did not appear until 1949. It was set in a city based on Harrisburg, Pennsylvania, and depicted the exploits of Grace Tate, whose sexual infidelity ruined her husband.

In 1950 O'Hara accepted an assignment with the International News Service to cover the mercy-killing trial of Dr. Hermann Sander in Manchester, New Hampshire. Sander had been accused of injecting air into the veins of a cancer patient. According to Matthew Bruccoli, "O'Hara filed at least fifteen background articles. He was obviously in sympathy with Dr. Sander, and analyzed the New England town's attitude toward the trial."[1] Most of these articles were published by the *Boston Daily Record.* Unique in the sense that O'Hara employed the elements of fiction, they were early examples of literary journalism. During the 1950s O'Hara also wrote four novels: *The Farmers Hotel* (1951); *Ten North Frederick* (1955), which won the National Book Award; *A Family Party* (1956); and *From the Terrace* (1958). In addition, he wrote the columns "Sweet and Sour" for the *Trenton Sunday Times-Advertiser* and "Appointment with O'Hara" for *Collier's* as well as short stories and several screenplays.

In the 1960s several volumes of his short stories appeared, as did the novels *Ourselves to Know* (1960), *The Big Laugh* (1962), *Elizabeth Appleton* (1963), *The Lockwood Concern* (1965), *The Instrument* (1967), and *Lovey Childs: A Philadelphian's Story* (1969). In addition, he wrote the columns "My Turn" for *Newsday* and "Whistle Stop" for *Holiday.* O'Hara died in 1970.

Although known as a realistic novelist, O'Hara employed the elements of fiction in several newspaper articles. In his novels, a number of characters and events were based on actual individuals or actual incidents. Thus, he used the elements of fiction in some of his reportage, and real people and incidents in some of his short stories and novels.

WORKS: *Butterfield 8* (1935); *A Rage to Live* (1949); International News Service (articles).
NOTE
1. Matthew J. Bruccoli, *The O'Hara Concern: A Biography of John O'Hara* (New York: Random House, 1975), p. 203.

Tillie Olsen
(1913–   )

Tillie Olsen was born on January 14, 1913, in Omaha, Nebraska, to Samuel and Ida Lerner. She was the second of seven children. Her parents were Jewish immigrants from Russia, and her father labored at several jobs, including farming.

Olsen dropped out of high school when the Great Depression hit and worked in a slaughterhouse as well as in several factories. Her family needed the income. Like her father, she was active in political movements. She joined the Young Communist League, and later was arrested for attempting to organize laborers.

In 1933 she moved to California, where in 1934 she participated in the San Francisco Warehouse Strike. Olsen was arrested and spent time in jail. In 1936 she married Jack Olsen, a printer who was also a member of a union. Olsen eventually had several children and worked at a variety of jobs to help support her family. Even though she had published several poems, one or two short stories, and at least two essays in *The Partisan* (later the *Partisan Review*) and the *New Republic* in 1934, she did not consider writing as a career until another of her short stories was published in the *Pacific Spectator* 22 years later, the year she received a creative writing fellowship from Stanford University. Olsen wrote several short stories before her fellowship ended in 1957. Two years later, she received a Ford Foundation grant, which enabled her to edit the stories she had written and to write more short stories.

In 1961 her first book of short stories, *Tell Me a Riddle,* was published. The title story won the O. Henry Award for the best short story of 1961. The stories depicted people she had known—their marriages, their hardships, indeed, their simple, day-to-day lives. Her characters were not financially successful. Yet they had dreams, just like those who had achieved success. The book was favorably reviewed by numerous critics.

Olsen received several fellowships in the 1960s, including one in 1962 from the Radcliffe Institute for Independent Study and another in 1968 from the National Endowment for the Arts. From 1969 to 1974 she taught or served as writer-in-residence at Amherst College, Stanford University, Massachusetts Institute of Technology, and the University of Massachusetts.

In 1974 her novel *Yonnondio: From the Thirties* was published. Like Rebecca Harding Davis before her, Olsen graphically depicted the "despised people" of society. The novel was more focused than the short stories in her previous book. Indeed, Olsen presented the working class from a feminist perspective in the sense that most, if not all, of the characters injured on the job or in the home were women, not men. Concurrently, Olsen presented a political statement in the sense that she tried to make the reader understand the kind of conditions in which her characters lived as well as the causes of these conditions.

Olsen contributed short stories and essays to various periodicals, including *Ms., Harper's, College English,* and *Trellis.* Several of her short stories were reprinted in anthologies. In 1975 Olsen received a Guggenheim fellowship. Three years later her book *Silences* was published. An example of literary journalism, it was as unusual in appearance as in subject matter. Blank space was used to emphasize certain points by forcing the reader to pause and reflect on what had been read. Overall, the book focused on writers—men as well as women—who had been silent and/or silenced. Olsen explained:

This book is about such silences. It is concerned with the relationship of circumstances—including class, color, sex; the times, climate into which one is born—to the creation of literature.

It consists of two talks given nearly a decade apart—"Silences" (1962), "Women Who Are Writers in Our Century" (1971); an essay-afterword, "Rebecca Harding Davis," written in 1971 to accompany reprint of work by a forgotten nineteenth-century woman writer; and a long aftersection: "Silences—II," "The Writer-Woman—II," for essential deepenings and expansions.[1]

The first part of *Silences* contained three essays in which Olsen explored her premise—that many writers have problems in writing and therefore do not find themselves in print.

The second part, titled "Acerbs, Asides, Amulets, Exhumations, Sources, Deepenings, Roundings, Expansions," focused on various writers and their work. According to Shelly Fisher Fishkin, "In fact, one might argue that it is meant to be read as it was written, in bits and pieces, in time stolen between chores, allowing time to meditate on the significance of one passage before moving on to the next."[2]

The book ended with excerpts from Rebecca Harding Davis' *Life in the Iron Mills;* Davis was another writer who struggled to overcome her silence but was then silenced by the world. The book was critically acclaimed for its unusual humanitarian as well as feminist insight.

In 1979 Olsen was awarded an honorary degree of doctor of arts and letters by the University of Nebraska. Other awards followed.

She edited *Mother to Daughter, Daughter to Mother: Mothers on Mothering, a Feminist Press Daybook and Reader* in 1984. The book contained entries by more than 100 writers on mother and daughter relationships and how, sometimes, such relationships can be confusing. She discussed this theme further in 1990 in lengthy essays she contributed to *Mothers and Daughters: That Special Quality.* The book combined essays with black and white and color photographs. The photographs were accompanied by moving and revealing comments from the photographers about their respective photographs and about mother and daughter relationships.

WORK: *Silences* (1978).

NOTES

1. Tillie Olsen, *Silences* (New York: Delacorte Press/Seymour Lawrence, 1978), p. xi.

2. Shelley Fisher Fishkin, "The Borderlands of Culture: Writing by W.E.B. DuBois, James Agee, Tillie Olsen, and Gloria Anzaldua," in *Literary Journalism in the Twentieth Century,* edited by Norman Sims (New York: Oxford University Press, 1990), pp. 159–160.

Jane O'Reilly
(1936–   )

Jane O'Reilly, a feminist, was born on April 5, 1936, in St. Louis, Missouri. She attended Radcliffe College, from which she received her bachelor's degree in 1958.

O'Reilly, primarily a freelance writer, worked as a contributing editor from 1968 to 1976 for *New York* magazine when the periodical was guided by Clay Felker. She worked with other literary journalists, including Gay Talese, Gloria Steinem, Gail Sheehy, and Tom Wolfe. In 1976 she started the weekly newspaper column "Jane O'Reilly" for Enterprise Features; it lasted three years.

However, O'Reilly's reputation as a journalist was established when she contributed pro-feminist articles to numerous publications, including *Ms.* She contributed articles on other subjects to *McCalls, Woman's Day, Vogue, Esquire, Atlantic, New Republic, Oui, Viva, House and Garden,* and the *New York Times Book Review.* A collection of her articles about the feminist movement, *The Girl I Left Behind: The Housewife's Moment of Truth, and Other Feminist Ravings,* appeared in 1980. In an interview, O'Reilly said that

men should read [the book] from back to front because it ends with essays on political issues but starts on a personal level. And that's how men move, from being distant, objective and intellectual to the world of their emotions. Women, on the other hand, should read it from front to back because we are moving from our emotions and inner experience and apply it to our lives.[1]

Before the collection was published, O'Reilly became a contributing editor to *Time* magazine as well as a columnist for *Vogue.*

WORK: *The Girl I Left Behind: The Housewife's Moment of Truth, and Other Feminist Ravings* (1980).

NOTE

1. Stella Dong, "PW Interviews: Jane O'Reilly," *Publishers Weekly,* October 31, 1980, p. 11.

George Orwell
(1903–1950)

Although born in Bengal, India, in 1903, Eric Arthur Blair, better known as George Orwell, was reared in England, his parents' homeland. His parents were not wealthy, but they sent him to St. Cyprians, an expensive school, where he became aware of social class differences. Later he attended Wellington, then Eton, both private schools. In 1922 he passed the examinations for the Indian Imperial Police and became assistant superintendent of police in Rangoon, Burma. After five years he realized that such a career was not rewarding.

Returning to England in 1927, he soon tramped through the East End of London, where the poor, the despised, and the thieves congregated and barely survived. Whether Orwell was escaping his own social class, had read *The People of the Abyss,* or had been inspired to see for himself what Dickens had described, he made numerous visits during the next several years. In 1928 he moved to Paris; London was too expensive. During the next two years he wrote numerous short stories and articles as well as two novels. The stories and novels were rejected, but several of his articles were eventually published in *Progrès Civique* and *Monde.*

Before he returned in 1929 to his parents' home in Southwald, Orwell visited the worst sections of Paris. He combined his observations of Paris with those he had made of London, and from late 1929 to 1933 he added information and revised his manuscript. From 1930 to 1935 he contributed book reviews, articles, and poetry to *Adelphi* and other magazines, meanwhile supporting himself by teaching in private schools.

When *Down and Out in Paris and London* was published in 1933, the name George Orwell, one of four Blair had suggested to the publisher, appeared on the cover. Readers immediately realized that Orwell had written about actual occurrences in a novelistic fashion. The book was instantly successful.

His second book, *Burmese Days,* was finished in December 1933, just before he entered a hospital. Although he recovered from an apparent case of pneumonia, he did not return to teaching. Instead he devoted his time to writing and working in a bookstore. *Burmese Days* was followed by *A Clergyman's Daughter* in 1935. His third novel, *Keep the Aspidistra Flying,* appeared a year later.

The Road to Wigan Pier, a serious study of poverty and unemployment in England, was commissioned by Victor Gollancz in 1936. According to Richard H. Rovere:

The first half is exactly that. Orwell was never more brilliant as a journalist. The second part is an examination of socialism as a remedy. It was perhaps the most rigorous examination that any doctrine has ever received at the hands of an adherent. It was so tough, so disrespectful, so rich in heresies that Mr. Gollancz, who, as proprietor of the Left Book Club was the shepherd of a flock that scandalized as easily as any Wesleyan congregation, published the book only after writing an introduction that could not have been more strained and apologetic if he had actually been a Wesleyan minister who for some improbable reason found himself the sponsor of a lecture by George Bernard Shaw on the Articles of Religion.[1]

Orwell served as a journalist, then as a soldier in the Spanish Civil War. While fighting facism, he was wounded and subsequently brought back to England. What he had experienced and witnessed transformed his political philosophy from a weak belief in socialism to a strong one. In 1938 his *Homage to Catalonia* was published. A personal memoir of the war, the book was a forceful, descriptive account of a senseless social and political revolution. Although the book did not sell well, it contained the philosophy that he later presented in the allegory *Animal Farm* and in the dystopian *1984.*

Homage to Catalonia was characteristic of his personal style of reporting. Using the first-person point of view quite effectively, Orwell described the absurdities that seemingly plague every war. By speaking as a participant, Orwell enhanced his credibility as an observer. Orwell used anecdotes to convey the realities of war, more specifically, of the war he witnessed. Dialogue and scene-by-scene construction were used to present the truth as he saw it.

Orwell accurately described numerous incidents in the Spanish Civil War. Thus his work was an undeniable portrait of what a soldier experienced.

For the rest of his life, he wrote novels, essays, book reviews, articles, educational programs for the British Broadcasting Corporation, editorials, and World War II accounts. His writing appeared in *Horizon, Tribune, Time and Tide, New Statesman, Partisan Review, Observer,* and other publications. He died in 1950 of tuberculosis.

WORKS: *Down and Out in Paris and London* (1933); *The Road to Wigan Pier* (1936); *Homage to Catalonia* (1938).

NOTE

1. George Orwell, *The Orwell Reader,* with an introduction by Richard H. Rovere (New York: Harcourt, Brace and World, 1956), pp. xv–xvi.

P

Francis Parkman
(1823–1893)

Francis Parkman, who was born in 1823, was not a journalist or a novelist, although he attempted to write a novel on one occasion. Rather, he was a chronicler of history.

Parkman's parents and grandparents were exceedingly wealthy. In addition to owning land within Boston proper, his grandfather owned commercial enterprises that included shipping and foreign trade. Parkman's father, a minister, encouraged his son to attend Chauncy Hall, a highly regarded Boston school.

In 1840 Parkman entered Harvard College. In his senior year, he suffered a nervous breakdown. Writing history, which he had learned during his sophomore year, had to be postponed, or so he thought. He was persuaded by his parents to tour Europe. He sailed throughout the Mediterranean and visited Agrigento, Selinunte, Marsala, Trapana, and Segesta. He saw Naples and climbed Vesuvius; he saw Rome and the Pope. After traveling to Scotland, he returned home to take his final examination and to graduate.

During the summer he traveled in the Berkshires; the next summer he journeyed to the Great Lakes in order to write his first book, *Pontiac's Rebellion,* which was published six years later under another title, *History of the Conspiracy of Pontiac.*

Parkman's earliest published works had been adventure stories based on his experiences; these tales appeared in the *Knickerbocker Magazine* in 1845.

In 1846 he received his law degree from Harvard. Instead of settling down as his father had hoped, he journeyed to the Far West with his cousin, Quincy A. Shaw. Although he saw Pennsylvania, Ohio, Missouri, and the land in between, he did not stop. He and his cousin traveled the Oregon Trail and lived with the Oglala Sioux. When he returned home exhausted and partially blind, he had another nervous breakdown. For the next two years he tried to recuperate. In 1849 *The California and Oregon Trail*, later retitled *The Oregon Trail*, was published.

In 1850 he married Catherine Bigilow. Before she died eight years later, she offered the encouragement that Parkman needed; in addition, she read historical documents to him and took dictation. In short, her eyes and hands became his. This fact Parkman acknowledged without reservation.

For four years horticulture was his occupation. Then in 1862 he turned to studying and writing. Three years later *Pioneers of France in the New World* was published.

For the remainder of his life, except for contributing an occasional article or review to the *North American Review*, the *Nation*, or one of the horticultural journals, and a brief stint teaching horticulture at Harvard, he devoted his energy to history. Parkman died in 1893.

His historical treatises were representative of literary journalism. *The Oregon Trail* as well as the stories in the *Knickerbocker Magazine* explicitly illustrated his use of fictional devices to report factual experiences.

WORKS: *The California and Oregon Trail* (1849); *Pioneers of France in the New World* (1865).

Westbrook Pegler
(1894–1969)

Born in Minneapolis in 1894, Westbrook Pegler, one of the most critical columnists of this century, grew up in Chicago, where he graduated from grade school, but dropped out of Lane Technical School after a year and a half.

When he was 16 he was employed as an office boy by the United Press, where he eventually became a telephone reporter. Although he enjoyed reporting, his parents advised him to return to school. Enrolling at Loyola Academy, Pegler learned Latin, English composition, and even drawing. But he yearned for a newsroom, and left after two or three semesters. He worked for a year for the International News Service, which merged with the United Press.

In 1913 he worked for a newspaper in Des Moines, then returned to the United Press offices, first in New York, then in St. Louis, and finally in Dallas, where he worked as a reporter and bureau manager. Three years later he became a foreign correspondent and moved to London. When the United States entered World War I, he became a war correspondent with the American Expeditionary Force, which censored his stories. Eventually, dissatisfaction forced him to resign and enlist in the navy.

When the war was over he returned to the United Press in New York, for which he wrote and edited sports from 1919 to 1925. Pegler's sports reporting earned him a reputation. Like Damon Runyon, he presented minute but interesting details of every sports event. Jack Alexander wrote, "It was difficult to tell from his account who won the football game, but he gave a wry, readable picture of the raccoon coats, the traffic-jammed roads and the empty liquor bottles under the stadium."[1]

In 1925 Pegler moved to the *Chicago Tribune,* where he was highly paid for his sports reporting. As his commentaries on the hilarious or unusual side of sports and sports figures were read, Pegler's reputation spread. When in 1932 he was sent by the *Tribune* to Washington to write about politics and politicians, Pegler found his ultimate purpose in life. In 1933, as a result of his political reportage, he was hired by the Scripps-Howard organization to write a column. "Fair Enough" captured the attention of both readers and newspaper professionals, and caused numerous investigations into labor unions. For instance, in one of his columns he exposed William Bioff, a Hollywood union official, as an extortionist; when authorities were convinced that Pegler's accusations were true, Bioff was sentenced. In other columns, Pegler exposed George Scalise, the president of the Building Service Employees' International Union, as an extortionist and former criminal. Scalise was eventually sentenced. Pegler received the Pulitzer Prize for his efforts in 1941.

In addition to attacking labor union bosses, Pegler exposed or criticized other people and causes, including Elliot Roosevelt and John Hartford, Franklin and Eleanor Roosevelt, Upton Sinclair, Frank Sinatra, and Huey Long, as well as Nazism, communism, the income tax system, and the Newspaper Guild. Favoritism was not in his vocabulary; indeed, if he saw something wrong he exposed and criticized it in his column.

In 1944 he moved to the *Journal-American* and began writing "As Pegler Sees It." Although similar to his earlier column, he intermittently used a character named George Spelvin, American, or a member of George's family, to present information. These columns, often humorous and satiric, both informed and entertained readers.

Several of his George Spelvin columns were similar to his sports reportage in that he used techniques and devices found in fiction. Usually, the column presented his opinion in a satiric manner. His use of satire was effective in the sense that it allowed the reader to understand Pegler's position on an issue. If he had presented this position in a mere editorial, the message would soon have been forgotten.

In 1949 Pegler severely ridiculed Quentin Reynolds, a war correspondent and magazine writer who had reviewed a biography of Heywood Broun that had described how Broun had read a column by Pegler and had become fatally ill. Pegler had not particularly cared for Reynolds' review or his personality. Consequently, in perhaps one of his most scathing columns, Pegler belittled Reynolds as he had no one else. Reynolds sued Pegler for libel and won. Nonetheless, Pegler remained as critical as ever. From Harry Truman to his own employer, William Randolph Hearst, Jr., Pegler kept attacking and criticizing, until in 1962 the Hearst organization, which included King Features Syndicate, announced that it would not publish another column.

He wrote for *American Opinion* as well as other publications. Pegler died in 1969.

WORKS: "Fair Enough" (column); "As Pegler Sees It" (column).
NOTE

1. Jack Alexander, "He's Against," *Post Biographies of Famous Journalists,* edited by John E. Drewry (Athens: University of Georgia Press, 1942), pp. 385–386.

George Plimpton
(1927–   )

George Plimpton was born to Pauline and Francis Plimpton on March 18, 1927, in New York City. He attended Phillips Exeter Academy in New Hampshire, where he first became interested in journalism, and then Harvard University. Unfortunately, the calm life at Harvard was interrupted after a year. America's participation in World War II had cost the armed services not only millions of dollars but thousands of lives; the military needed men. Plimpton enlisted in the army in 1945. As a tank driver and infantryman, Plimpton witnessed the obscenities of war. When he was discharged he returned to Harvard; he received his bachelor's degree in 1950.

Having matured emotionally and intellectually, he immediately traveled to England to further his education. In 1952 and 1954 he received a bachelor's and master's, respectively, from King's College, Cambridge. However, he did not return to the United States after completing his formal education. Rather, he moved to Paris, where, together with friends, he founded the literary magazine *Paris Review.* When the magazine was recognized for its high literary appeal, he returned to New York City to broaden its base of operations and to contribute to other publications. In addition to editing the magazine, he wrote a children's book in 1955 and contributed articles to numerous periodicals. He taught at Barnard College from 1956 to 1958 and was an associate editor of *Horizon* from 1959 to 1961.

Plimpton, who had been interested in sports most of his life and who had fought in a bullfight in 1954, realized that readers of sports stories would not only be entertained by stories that mixed reporting with experience but would learn what the writer thought while participating in the activity. In 1959, for instance, he fought Archie Moore for three rounds. The excitement generated by the mere idea of an amateur boxing a professional was extraordinary. Plimpton knew he had to perform in other events. He played against tennis pro Poncho Gonzalez, swam against Don Schollander, and played a rubber of bridge with Oswald Jacoby. Of course, he lost, but that was not important. What mattered was the experience gained from each competitive event.

For *Sports Illustrated* he described quite humorously the humiliating experience of pitching to eight professional baseball players. The article was expanded and published as *Out of My League* in 1961. The new form of reporting was instantly praised, and the book became a best-seller. Two years later he joined the Detroit Lions and suffered through rookie training. When he played as a quarterback in an exhibition game, he lost almost 30 yards in five plays. The experience, of which he was proud, was recorded in *Paper Lion,* which was filled with humor. Plimpton told of a humiliating moment when his cleats apparently failed to connect with the earth. He described not only what happened but how embarrassed he was for falling down without being tackled. His approach to a story was similar to that of Paul Gallico, who competed against pros, then wrote about the experience. Plimpton's work was indeed literary journalism, since the necessary elements, including dialogue, were present.

In 1967 Plimpton became a contributing editor to *Sports Illustrated.* He enrolled as an amateur in three West Coast golf tournaments and contributed several witty articles to the magazine describing the disastrous experience. These articles were expanded and published as *The Bogey Man* in 1968.

Plimpton broadened his experiences in the 1960s, 1970s, and 1980s. In addition to playing and then writing about sports, he acted in several movies, including *Lawrence of Arabia, The Detective, Beyond the Law, Paper Lion,* and *Rio Lobo.* He became a percussionist with the New York Philharmonic. This experience culminated in performances with the Philharmonic in Canada and on NBC-TV's "Bell Telephone Hour" in 1968. In 1971 he conducted the Cincinnati Symphony Orchestra. His other experiences, including taming a lion, acting as a clown, and performing as a comedian, were recorded for television.

In 1972 he became an associate editor at *Harper's* and several years later a contributing editor at *Esquire.* He also wrote the insightful *One for the Record: The Inside Story of Hank Aaron's Chase for the Home Run Record* (1974), which described Aaron's attempts to break Babe Ruth's all-time record for the most home runs by any baseball player; *Shadow Box* (1977), about his experiences as a boxer; and *One More July: A Football Dialogue with Bill Curry* (1977), which, of course, focused on Bill Curry and football.

Fireworks: A History and Celebration, a departure for Plimpton in the sense that the book did not discuss his experiences at a particular sport, was published in 1984. It described the history of fireworks all over the world, from their invention to the present.

Plimpton returned to literary journalism the following year, however, when he penned *Open Net,* which described his exploits as a goalie for the Boston Bruins hockey team. Plimpton described his training and practice sessions with candor and humor, and the reader was richly rewarded by learning about the sport from a nonprofessional.

In 1987 he wrote *The Curious Case of Sidd Finch,* a humorous novel about a former Harvard man who pitched a perfect game for the New York Mets. However, Finch grew disillusioned with the game and eventually became a Buddhist monk. The novel received mixed reviews.

Three years later Plimpton wrote *The X Factor,* another example of literary journalism in which he described his horseshoe matches with George Bush. Plimpton also provided revelations about how one could become a successful horseshoe player based on advice received from various professionals. The book was similar to his other participatory sports books in the sense that he depicted his various exploits quite humorously.

A compilation of his work from three decades was published as *The Best of Plimpton* in 1991. The articles—about Marianne Moore; playing the triangle with the New York Philharmonic; boxing heavyweight Archie Moore; and visiting fireworks guru Orville Carlisle in his Norfolk, Nebraska, shoestore and fireworks museum—were examples of participatory journalism at its best.

WORKS: *Out of My League* (1961); *Paper Lion* (1966); *The Bogey Man* (1968); *Shadow Box* (1977); *Open Net* (1985); *The X Factor* (1990); *The Best of Plimpton* (1991).

Fred Powledge
(1935-)

Fred Powledge, sometimes an advocating if not a muckraking literary journalist, was born on February 23, 1935, in North Carolina. He attended the University of North Carolina, from which he received his bachelor's degree in 1957.

Powledge worked as an editor and writer for the Associated Press in New Haven, Connecticut, from 1958 to 1960, then went to work as a reporter for the *Atlanta Journal.* In 1963 he left the South to work as a reporter for the *New York Times;* this position lasted until 1966, when he received a Russell Sage fellowship in journalism and the behavioral sciences from Columbia University.

In 1967 his book *Black Power–White Resistance: Notes on the New Civil War* was published. Powledge's interest in race relations was evident in this book, which explored several demonstrations by blacks. Although the book was praised by some reviewers for its uninhibited style, others complained that Powledge's logic was occasionally muddled. Said Edwin M. Yoder, Jr.: "Mr. Powledge is at his best as a reporter. His almost lyrical evocation of the Albany [Georgia] demonstrations, his shrewd exploration of the 'style' of Atlanta's Mayor William Hartsfield are classic."[1]

However, Yoder criticized Powledge for his condescension and his belief in the "power structure" myth. Nonetheless, the book contained the elements of literary journalism, even though Powledge injected his beliefs about blacks and the reasons for their demonstrations.

Powledge lectured at the New School for Social Research in New York City from 1968 to 1969, then devoted his time to freelance writing. He contributed articles to various magazines, including the *New Yorker, Esquire, Penthouse, Playboy,* the *Nation,* and the *New Republic,* but the books that followed *Black Power* brought him attention from critics. For instance, *Journeys Through the South: A Rediscovery,* published in 1979, was favorably reviewed in the *New York Times Book Review* by Roy Blount, Jr.:

Deriving largely from a series of articles for *The Charlotte Observer,* it is that rare thing: a serious national book addressed most directly to Southern readers. William Faulkner wrote for the muses, whose vicars were concentrated in the Northeast. Fred Powledge is writing for people who want to make the best of their developing region, the rest of America please copy.[2]

Powledge traveled through the South in 1977 and recorded what he observed—from polluted waterways and exploited labor to unspoiled areas and interracial harmony. He met people who enjoyed their work as much as the towns and cities in which they lived. The book, somewhat of a departure for Powledge at the time, reminded the reader that the South had changed dramatically since the 1960s. The book was an example of literary journalism. Powledge employed description, authentic dialogue, and characterization based on observation.

Powledge explored pollution in *Water: The Nature, Uses, and Future of Our Most Precious and Abused Resource,* which was published in 1982. Two years later, in *Fat of the Land,* he argued that factory-prepared foodstuffs had taken the enjoyment out of food. He also examined waste, the cost of which was ultimately paid by consumers. He claimed that middlemen could be eliminated, and that more profit could be rightfully returned to those who farmed the land, ranched the plains, and harvested the lakes and oceans. He also suggested ways consumers could change the system.

In 1991 he published *Free at Last: The Civil Rights Movement and the People Who Made It,* which offered a journalistic, narrative history of the southern civil rights movement from the *Brown vs. Board of Education* decision in 1954 through the march from Selma to Montgomery in 1965. Powledge focused on the individuals responsible for the movement, including Charles Jones, Arthur Shores, and L. C. Dorsey, among others, interspersing long excerpts from interviews with them throughout the narrative. The book ended with a somewhat somber assessment of the movement's accomplishments.

Two years later he wrote about the movement's heroes in the children's book *We Shall Overcome: Heroes of the Civil Rights Movement.*

WORKS: *Black Power–White Resistance: Notes on the New Civil War* (1967); *Journeys Through the South: A Rediscovery* (1979); *Fat of the Land* (1984); *Free at Last: The Civil Rights Movement and the People Who Made It* (1991).

NOTES

1. Edwin M. Yoder, Jr., "Voices from Burning Slums," *Saturday Review,* August 26, 1967, p. 29.

2. Roy Blount, Jr., "Fresh Homebaked Goods," *New York Times Book Review,* August 12, 1979, p. 9.

R

Dotson Rader
(1942–)

Dotson Rader was born on July 25, 1942, in Minnesota, and attended Columbia University from 1963 to 1968. Like many other campuses during that period, Columbia experienced marches and demonstrations by students. Rader, an activist of the New Left movement, not only participated, but wrote about his experience in the book *I Ain't Marchin' Anymore!* It was published in 1969, the year he became the editor of *Defiance* magazine and a contributing editor of *Evergreen Review.*

In 1971 he became an editorial consultant to *New Politics,* and a year later a contributing editor of *Esquire.* He held the latter position until 1980, when he accepted a post as national correspondent with *Parade.* In 1982 he became a contributing editor of *Parade.*

While he worked at these publications, he produced several novels and another piece of nonfiction, *Blood Dues,* which was published in 1973. However, it was his first book that was an example of literary and advocacy journalism because he was personally involved in what he reported. Although widely reviewed, the book received its share of criticism primarily because Rader was young and, to a certain extent, naive about how the world functioned. As Steven V. Roberts pointed out, ''Mr. Rader and his friends display little real knowledge or understanding of contemporary politics.''[1] Yet Roberts appreciated certain sections of Rader's book:

The author, a 26-year-old contributer to *The New Republic* and the *Evergreen Review,* was on the scene at the Pentagon March, the Columbia Rebellion, and other highlights of radical protest. And, at least unconsciously, he reveals in spurts and fragments some interesting insights into the New Left.[2]

In the preface, Rader explained how the student organization, Students for a Democratic Society, came into existence. The rest of the book pertained to the movement and its revolutionary ideas. Rader employed scene-by-scene construction to present the confrontation between students at Columbia and the authorities. In addition, he depicted his movements after the confrontation; he used careful description and authentic dialogue.

In 1985 he published the gossipy biography *Tennessee: Cry of the Heart,* which presented in an impressionistic fashion a vivid and often fresh and revelatory portrait of Tennessee Williams. Rader showed that Williams lived a kind of reduced life after the death of his friend, Frank Merlo. Merlo had been the only man who loved Williams in the unconditional fashion that Williams desired. According to one reviewer, the book suffered from its jumbled time frame; indeed, Rader moved back and forth in time throughout the narrative.

WORKS: *I Ain't Marchin' Anymore!* (1969); *Tennessee: Cry of the Heart* (1985).

NOTES

1. Steven V. Roberts, "I Ain't Marchin' Anymore," *New York Times Book Review,* May 25, 1969, p. 31.

2. Ibid.

Julian Ralph
(1853–1903)

Julian Ralph wrote descriptive 11,000-word accounts for Charles A. Dana's *New York Sun.* These accounts were examples of literary journalism.

Ralph was born in 1853. His father was a doctor. Ralph worked as a full-time journalist for most of his life. At 15 he became a printer's apprentice for the Red Bank, New Jersey, *Standard.* After several years of reporting and editing for various newspapers in New Jersey and Massachusetts, he moved in 1872 to New York City to work for the *World.* A year later he was at the *Daily Graphic,* for which he reported the trial of Henry Ward Beecher in 1875. His style of reporting was superior to that of his peers, and Dana immediately offered him a position.

Ralph was a reporter and a writer of humor for the *Sun.* His "German Barber" sketches were collected and published as *The Sun's German Barber* in 1883. In addition, he traveled throughout Canada and the United States from 1891 to 1893 for *Harper's* magazine. The articles he wrote were extraordinarily vivid and picturesque.

Ralph wrote for the *Sun* for 20 years. In his spare time, he traveled and wrote articles for magazines. Between 1894 and 1897 he explored Russia and the Far

East, writing countless articles on what he saw and heard. He even covered the Sino-Japanese War.

Having been hired by William Randolph Hearst during one of his recruitment campaigns, Ralph became the *New York Journal*'s London correspondent in 1895. Two years later, when war broke out between Turkey and Greece, he reported on several campaigns. In addition, he reported on Queen Victoria's Diamond Jubilee and the Russian czar's coronation.

Remaining in London, he became foreign correspondent for the *New York Herald* and later the *Brooklyn Eagle.* Just before the turn of the century he began reporting for the London *Daily Mail,* for which he covered the Boer War.

According to Willard Bleyer, Ralph accompanied Lord Roberts in his victorious march to Blomfontein: "In the spring of 1900, Ralph with several English war correspondents issued a daily paper at Blomfontein for the British Army, called the *Friend,* to which Rudyard Kipling and Dr. A. Conan Doyle, both of whom were in South Africa, contributed poems and articles."[1]

Ralph returned to the United States in 1900; he died three years later. In addition to *The Sun's German Barber,* Ralph wrote *Dixie, or Southern Scenes and Sketches, People We Pass: Stories of Life Among the Masses of New York City, An American with Lord Roberts, War's Brighter Side: The Story of "The Friend" Newspaper,* and *The Making of a Journalist.*

Ralph used a vivid and picturesque style in reporting his observations. He was informative, but information per se was not as important to him as how the facts were presented. He wrote when "yellow" journalism was popular; consequently, he had to conform to some extent to keep a position. Whether his observations suffered as a result is anyone's guess. His writing, however, whether biased or not, was undoubtedly entertaining.

WORKS: *The Sun's German Barber* (1883); *Dixie, or Southern Scenes and Sketches* (1895); *People We Pass: Stories of Life Among the Masses of New York City* (1896); *An American with Lord Roberts* (1901); *War's Brighter Side: The Story of "The Friend" Newspaper* (1901); *The Making of a Journalist* (1903).

NOTE

1. Willard Bleyer, "Ralph, Julian," *Dictionary of American Biography,* edited by Dumas Malone (New York: Charles Scribner's Sons, 1935), Vol. 15, p. 332.

John Reed
(1887–1920)

John Reed, the radical, confused communist who died in Moscow after the Russian Revolution, was born on October 22, 1887, near Portland, Oregon. His father, U.S. Marshal Charles J. Reed, was a wealthy liberal. Reed attended Morristown Academy, a preparatory school in New Jersey, before he was accepted by Harvard.

Reed was extremely active at Harvard. He worked as a staff member of the

Monthly and the *Lampoon;* he was committed to the dramatic and musical organizations; he was a member of the water polo team; and he served as the
song-leader at the football games. He graduated in 1910 and spent the next six
months in Europe. When he returned, he was hired as assistant editor of the
American Magazine. Reed got to know New York City, and satirized bohemi-
anism in the poem *A Day in Bohemia,* which he published in 1912.

Reed learned about society from some of his assignments; however, his interest in social problems was sparked by his friend, Lincoln Steffens, who had
helped him get his first job. By 1913 Reed was eager to join the staff of *The
Masses,* a leftist publication edited by Max Eastman. Reed's approach to journalism was to observe, then record, using description and dialogue. When silk
workers went on strike in Paterson, New Jersey, Reed witnessed the thousands
who were hungry and bitter. When he attempted to participate, he was arrested.
As a result, he wrote two reports—one for *Metropolitan* magazine and one for
The Masses. The former concerned the oppressed who were incarcerated in filthy
cells. The latter focused on the confrontation between the strikers and the owners, backed by the police. Reed's reporting was not objective; indeed, he supported the strikers in no uncertain terms. The reader learned through
scene-by-scene construction as well as authentic dialogue how the oppressed
faced adversity.

The editor of *Metropolitan* magazine asked Reed to cover the Mexican Civil
War. Reed, who had read about Pancho Villa and his daring exploits, accepted.
He crossed the border and for four months lived and traveled with Villa's army.
Without question, Reed was impressed with Villa's valiant efforts. After all,
Villa represented the poorest people of Mexico in his fight against tyranny.
Although Reed wrote numerous reports about his experiences with Villa's army
for the magazine, he received additional recognition when his book *Insurgent
Mexico* was published in 1914.

Before Reed returned to New York City, he visited Ludlow, Colorado, where
strikers and members of their families had been burned alive by state officials.
Reed investigated the causes of the massacre, then wrote an insightful article
about the affair. Unfortunately, his articles and book about Mexico over-
shadowed his piece about Ludlow.

Reed was sent to cover the war in Europe in 1914. To say the least, he grew
disillusioned when he observed French and German soldiers alike die for their
respective governments. Instead of interviewing officers, Reed focused on the
opinions of common foot soldiers, many of whom survived by living like moles
in rain-filled trenches and dugouts. His reportage was unlike the accounts contributed by most other correspondents. Indeed, Reed was opposed to the war,
and his reports revealed as much; after all, he presented the squalor and the
senseless atrocities.

Reed returned to New York City and told the readers of *The Masses* that the
United States should not enter the war. The articles he wrote from Europe for

the *Metropolitan* were collected and published as *The War on the Eastern Front* in 1916.

Reed wrote fiction and poetry during this period, although neither attracted as much attention as his nonfiction. In 1917 President Woodrow Wilson, whom Reed had supported, finally realized that the country had to enter the war. Reed, now married to Louise Bryant, a journalist, sought solace in Russia. He and his wife observed the revolution; because of his opposition to capitalism, he enjoyed what he witnessed. He worked at the Bureau of International Revolutionary Propaganda, which issued papers and pamphlets for the armies of the Allies and the Entente. He spoke at the All-Russian Soviets in 1918. He wrote about his experiences in controversial articles. In fact, these articles as well as others prompted the federal government to bring an indictment against *The Masses* for sedition. Reed failed to appear at the first trial; however, he returned to the United States in time for the second, which, like the first, resulted in a split decision by the jury. Reed spoke of revolution to groups of workers in several cities and consequently was arrested several times.

In 1919 *Red Russia* and *Ten Days that Shook the World,* the latter an extraordinary book based on the articles he had written in Russia, were published. Indeed, through documentation and careful analysis, Reed presented one of the most important dramatic events of his day. His descriptions, which were based on personal observation, were almost poetic.

In *Ten Days that Shook the World,* Reed presented the intricacies of the revolution through scene-by-scene construction. He also employed other elements found in fiction, such as realistic dialogue, in this work. *Ten Days that Shook the World,* like his other work, was an example of literary journalism.

The book was probably Reed's greatest achievement because it accurately informed readers about a major event. Reed, who was not recognized at the National Socialist Convention in 1919, spearheaded the Communist Labor Party, which was formed when disharmony occurred between factions within the Socialist Party. Reed was responsible for the organization's manifesto, platform, and publication. Before 1920, he returned to Russia, where he was accepted by the communists, especially Lenin. Reed spent some time in a Finnish prison because of his involvement with the Russian communists, then was released to the Russians in a prisoner exchange program. Reed worked for the communists and was even made a member of the Executive Committee of the Communist International. He died from typhus on October 17, 1920, at age 32. He was honored by the communists, who buried him in Red Square.

WORKS: *Insurgent Mexico* (1914); *The War on the Eastern Front* (1916); *Ten Days that Shook the World* (1919).

Rex Reed
(1938–   )

Born to Jewell and J. M. Reed on October 2, 1938, in Fort Worth, Texas, Rex Reed became perhaps the most perceptive interviewer of celebrities in the U.S. He wrote in 1968:

I was born . . . at a time when the big stars were Brenda Frazier and Hitler, and for the first ten years of my life I moved around from one Texas oil town to the next (with time out at the age of two to appear on a radio show in Pampa saying my ABC's, which made me something of a smarty-pants before I ever heard of a typewriter).[1]

His father was an oil company field supervisor, a position that required extensive travel. By the time Reed graduated from high school in Louisiana, he had attended 13 public schools. He went to Louisiana State University, where he edited the literary magazine and worked in various capacities for the campus newspaper. One of his editorials, "The Price of Prejudice," which attacked segregation and almost got him expelled after the Ku Klux Klan stoned the journalism school, was reprinted in the *New York Times*. Despite the incident, Reed received his bachelor's degree in 1960 and moved to New York City, where he was offered a job as a copy boy by the *New York Times*. He turned it down.

For the next five years, while he tried freelance writing, he held a number of jobs—from jazz singer to cook, from record salesman to actor. However, his career as a professional writer refused to blossom. Finally, in 1965, he attended the Venice Biennale Film Festival and interviewed Buster Keaton and Jean-Paul Belmondo. The *New York Times* purchased the Keaton interview, and *New York* magazine, which was published by the old *New York Herald Tribune*, purchased the Belmondo interview. When Reed returned to New York City, he was immediately hired as a film critic by *Women's Wear Daily, Cosmopolitan, Status*, and *Holiday*. In addition, he contributed incisive interviews with such celebrities as Marlene Dietrich, Natalie Wood, Sandy Dennis, Warren Beatty, Michelangelo Antonioni, Governor Lester Maddox, Lucille Ball, Angela Lansbury, and Barbra Streisand to *Esquire*, the *New York Times, Cosmopolitan, Ladies Home Journal, Playboy*, and *Harper's Bazaar*. As his popularity increased, so did the demand for his reviews and interviews. For instance, in 1968 he became a music critic for *Stereo Review*, a position he held until 1975. The same year his first collection of interviews, or stories, as he termed them, was published. Provocatively titled *Do You Sleep in the Nude?*, the book became a best-seller, even though some critics claimed that he had sacrificed objectivity in order to create a story. Tom Wolfe, on the other hand, believed that Reed had "raised the celebrity interview to a new level through his frankness and his eye for social detail."[2]

In 1970 a second collection of articles and interviews with such celebrities as Simone Signore, Leslie Caron, Ingrid Bergman, and Jean Seberg, to name a few, appeared. Another popular book, it, too, had a provocative title, *Conversations in the Raw.*

Reed eventually became a film critic for the *New York Daily News* and *Vogue,* and later for the *New York Post* and *Gentleman's Quarterly.* In addition, he contributed a column to the Chicago Tribune Syndicate. He praised and criticized actors and actresses, including Paul Newman, George C. Scott, Jack Nicholson, Patty Duke, Barbra Streisand, and Glenda Jackson, and criticized award ceremonies and the power of certain New York City critics.

Reed, who was a jury member at several film festivals, compiled his articles and interviews in *Big Screen, Little Screen* (1971), *People Are Crazy Here* (1974), *Valentines and Vitriol* (1977), and *Travolta to Keaton* (1979).

In 1986 he wrote *Personal Effects,* a glitzy novel about Hollywood and the murder of a 1940s film star. The novel was controversial, to say the least, because of its subject matter. Later in the 1980s Reed became a co-host of the syndicated television series "At the Movies." His reviews for the series contained the same biting wit as his published reviews. His interviews, however, exhibited his powers of observation and insight more than his reviews.

Although Reed claimed he did not have any particular philosophy about interviewing celebrities, his ability to capture through the use of his senses the true personage enlightened readers from coast to coast and subsequently made him as much of a celebrity as those he interviewed. The popularity of his articles and books stemmed from his approach. As he put it: "I don't really do interviews at all. . . . I just kind of follow people around and they tell me about their lives and I tell them about my life and suddenly a story forms in my head. I write what I see, sense, touch, smell, and taste."[3]

His articles illustrated his ability to describe expertly the person he was interviewing. For instance, in "Patricia Neal," his use of description was rampant. He described the furniture, then Patricia Neal's smile—indeed, the reader could visualize the movements of her mouth. Then he recorded the words spoken by that mouth, which was only fitting, and allowed the actress to converse freely, openly, without any interruptions.

WORKS: *Do You Sleep in the Nude?* (1968); *Conversations in the Raw* (1970); *Big Screen, Little Screen* (1971); *People Are Crazy Here* (1974); *Valentines and Vitriol* (1977); *Travolta to Keaton* (1979).

NOTES

1. Rex Reed, *Do You Sleep in the Nude?* (New York: New American Library, 1968), p. ix.

2. Tom Wolfe, *The New Journalism,* with an anthology edited by Tom Wolfe and E. W. Johnson (New York: Harper and Row, 1973), p. 56.

3. Reed, *Do You Sleep in the Nude?,* p. xi.

Richard Reeves
(1936–)

Born in New York City on November 28, 1936, to Dorothy and Furman Reeves, Richard Reeves attended Stevens Institute of Technology, from which he received his degree in 1960. After a year of working at Ingersoll-Rand Company as an engineer, he abandoned the profession for which he was educated and became an editor of the *Phillipsburg Free Press,* where he worked until 1963. For the next two years he worked as a reporter for the *Newark News.* His writing, which was concise, accurate, and arresting, enabled him to obtain a position with the *New York Herald Tribune,* then the *New York Times,* for which he worked as chief political correspondent. His experience in political reporting eventually led him to write articles and several books that exposed as well as analyzed politicians and the political process. In 1971 he became an editor of *New York* magazine, a position he held until 1977. In addition, he contributed a column to *Harper's* in the early 1970s. He served as national editor at *Esquire* from 1977 to 1979, then became a syndicated columnist. He also joined the editorial advisory board of the *Washington Monthly.*

Reeves, a political columnist of national magnitude, wrote the investigative analytical study *A Ford, Not a Lincoln* (1975), which explored the first 100 days of the Ford presidency. Reeves failed to hide his biases in his study, but the book was nonetheless a well-written and informative document of immense importance. In 1977 his book *Convention* was published. Concerned with the shenanigans of presidential conventions, Reeves stripped away the gloss and glitter from the 1976 Democratic Convention in New York City and revealed in vignettes the carnival atmosphere that was typical of any political convention. The writing was representative of literary journalism in that Reeves used descriptive vignettes of scenes and characters, and incorporated actual dialogue spoken by the numerous participants.

American Journey: Traveling with Tocqueville in Search of Democracy in America, in which Reeves traced Alexis de Tocqueville's steps to learn what American democracy had become, was published in 1982. Reeves compared Tocqueville's journals with his own to determine whether American democracy was still the same, and whether it was still working. Reeves' findings were basically the same as Tocqueville's: "It does work. . . . The glory and the frustration of American democracy is that greatness is defined by each American— and that's the way we meant it to be."[1]

In 1985 he examined quite critically the conservative philosophy of Ronald Reagan in *The Reagan Detour: Conservative Revolutionary.* Reeves deplored Reagan's conservative belief that the best way to increase investment was to let the wealthy keep more of their money. He believed that this would reduce the bargaining power of the poor. Reeves also discussed three areas of opportunity for the Democrats: (1) the weaknesses of Reaganism; (2) the decline of America's industrial competitiveness; and (3) problems with the nation's foreign policy. Unfortunately, Reeves failed to offer solutions to the problems he discussed; he did, however, offer suggestions. The same year he published the insightful *A Passage to Peshawar: Pakistan Between the Hindu Kush and the Arabian Sea*, based on his journey through the Asian country. Reeves recorded his reactions to the country and its people. As a Westener with certain biases, he found the culture difficult to comprehend and accept. Nonetheless, through a series of interwoven essays, Reeves provided the reader with a glimpse of the country's problems as it attempted to retain some seemingly antiquated customs in the midst of progress.

Reeves returned to a familiar subject in *President Kennedy: Profile of Power* (1993). Although the biography fell short of capturing the human dimensions of Kennedy, the man, it was an engaging and even elegant recounting of the Kennedy era. In short, Reeves succeeded in presenting the president as he actually was—strong and courageous, with certain flaws in his character.

WORKS: *A Ford, Not a Lincoln* (1975); *Convention* (1977); *American Journey: Traveling with Tocqueville in Search of Democracy in America* (1982); *The Reagan Detour: Conservative Revolutionary* (1985); *A Passage to Peshawar: Pakistan Between the Hindu Kush and the Arabian Sea* (1985); *President Kennedy: Profile of Power* (1993).
NOTE
1. Richard Reeves, *American Journey: Traveling with Tocqueville in Search of Democracy in America* (New York: Simon and Schuster, 1982), p. 357.

Richard Rhodes
(1937–)

Born on July 4, 1937, Richard Rhodes grew up in Kansas City, Kansas, and Independence, Missouri. His mother committed suicide when he was an infant, and his father, who drifted for several years, finally married a sadistic woman who abused Rhodes and his brother until a court placed them in the Andrew Drumm Institute, a working farm outside Independence. Rhodes remained at the farm for six years, until he was 18.

In 1955 he received a scholarship from Yale University. Rhodes, who wrote for the *Yale Daily News*, earned his bachelor's degree in 1959, and found employment as a writer for *Newsweek*. A year later he married Linda Hampton, with whom he had two children, and worked for Radio Free Europe in New York City.

He taught English at Westminster College in Missouri, then in 1962 accepted an editor's position at Hallmark Cards in Kansas City. The urge to write full time led him to leave Hallmark in 1970.

His first book, *The Inland Ground: An Evocation of the American Middle West* (1970), was a compilation of 15 articles, 5 of which had appeared in national magazines. It focused on Midwest America, including several prominent midwesterners such as Harry S. Truman and Dwight D. Eisenhower. Several reviewers pointed out that the book lacked direction and was as a result uneven. Most also found the writing flat and prosaic at times. Rhodes even admitted that some of his writing suffered from his fear of expressing himself.

Rhodes worked as a contributing editor for *Harper's* until 1974, when he and his wife divorced. Then he worked for *Playboy,* and contributed articles to other publications, including *Redbook, American Heritage, Reader's Digest, Esquire,* and *Audience.* Rhodes eventually became a contributing editor to *Rolling Stone.*

Rhodes' next book was *The Ungodly: A Novel of the Donner Pass,* which was based on the wagon-train expedition in which many people died of cold and hunger; it was published in 1973. The novel was dismissed by critics.

The Ozarks, a work of nonfiction, was published in 1974, two years before he married Mary Evans. *Holy Secrets,* a novel, followed in 1978. Neither book was found interesting by critics. *Looking for America: A Writer's Odyssey,* a compilation of 20 magazine articles from the 1970s, was published a year later. The subjects ranged from skywriting to various personalities. The writing was characteristic of literary journalism.

His next several books were novels. Then, in 1986, Rhodes published *The Making of the Atomic Bomb,* a careful historical analysis of nuclear physics. Rhodes traced the development of atomic theory as well as the explosions at the end of World War II. The book, which was critically acclaimed, described the individuals and the technological innovations that produced the first atomic bombs. It received the National Book Award and the Pulitzer Prize in 1987 and 1988, respectively.

Rhodes' second marriage ended in divorce before his next book, *Farm: A Year in the Life of an American Farmer,* was published in 1989. In it Rhodes chronicled one year in the life of a large farm in Missouri. He admitted that in writing *Farm* he felt as though he were going home—to the Andrew Drumm Institute, which had been his salvation.[1]

Rhodes used a prose style that incorporated dialect. Images of nature gave the reader some insight into the natural world of farming. Rhodes also used abundant description; indeed, he even described in detail tractors, planters, mowers, cultivators, and combines.

For the most part, the book was favorably reviewed. Maxine Kumin wrote: "Mr. Rhodes brings empathy and intelligence to his subject, and he projects for the reader that continuing identification with the day-to-day complexities, disappointments and gratifications encountered by his pseudonymous family, the Bauers."[2]

Rhodes used authentic dialogue as well as accurate description—two elements found in literary journalism—to depict the individuals with whom he lived and worked. Thus, the reader learned about these individuals through Rhodes' eyes and ears.

Rhodes, the recipient of numerous grants and fellowships, wrote *A Hole in the World: An American Boyhood* in 1990, which described his early life. In

1992 he published the controversial *Making Love: An Erotic Odyssey,* an exhaustive and unabashed chronicle of his sex life. Rhodes revealed that the size of his penis was average, that he enjoyed masturbating, that he had several homosexual encounters when he was an adolescent, and that he had numerous lovers, including Ginger Untrif, with whom he lived. Most critics disliked the book's candor and subject matter.

In 1993 he investigated the numerous problems of the nuclear energy industry in the United States in *Nuclear Renewal: Common Sense About Energy.* Rhodes interviewed officials in the United States, France, and Japan, and concluded that manufacturers, some utilities, and government regulators in the United States had been responsible for the nuclear energy impasse through poor design, neglect of safety issues, gross mismanagement, and employing inexperienced labor.

In 1995 he wrote the helpful guide *How to Write: Advice and Reflections,* and *Dark Sun: The Making of the Hydrogen Bomb,* which was similar to his book about the atomic bomb.

WORKS: *The Inland Ground: An Evocation of the American Middle West* (1970); *Looking for America: A Writer's Odyssey* (1979); *The Making of the Atomic Bomb* (1986); *Farm: A Year in the Life of an American Farmer* (1989); *Nuclear Renewal: Common Sense About Energy* (1993); *Dark Sun: The Making of the Hydrogen Bomb* (1995).

NOTES

1. Molly McQuade, "PW Interviews: Richard Rhodes," *Publishers Weekly,* October 20, 1989, p. 39.

2. Maxine Kumin, "A Covenant with the Soil," *New York Times Book Review,* September 24, 1989, p. 30.

Steven Roberts
(1943–)

Steven Roberts was born in 1943 in New Jersey and received his education at Harvard University, from which he earned his bachelor's degree in 1964. He joined the *New York Times* in 1965 and for four years worked as a metropolitan reporter. From 1969 to 1974 he served as the *Times'* Los Angeles bureau chief, where he gathered information on the California scene and subsequently wrote numerous impressionistic articles for the *Times, Commonweal, Playboy, Esquire,* and *Saturday Review.* In 1974, the year he became bureau chief in Athens, he published his collection of essays on California, *Eureka! Earthquakes, Chicanos, Celebrities, Smog, Fads, Outdoor Living, Charles Manson's Legacy, Berkeley Rebels, San Francisco Scenes, Southern California Style, Ronald Reagan, and Other Discoveries in the Golden State of California.* The work captured the inner feelings and motivations of people ranging from Charles Manson and Cesar Chavez to Mae West and Joseph Wambaugh.

WORK: *Eureka! Earthquakes, Chicanos, Celebrities, Smog, Fads, Outdoor*

Living, Charles Manson's Legacy, Berkeley Rebels, San Francisco Scenes, Southern California Style, Ronald Reagan, and Other Discoveries in the Golden State of California (1974).

Ron Rosenbaum
(1946–   )

Ron Rosenbaum was born on November 27, 1946, in New York City and lived with his parents in Bay Shore, Long Island. He left Bay Shore to enroll at Yale University, where he majored in English literature and composed a popular, obscene football cheer. He received his bachelor's degree in 1968.

During the summer of the same year, he covered the Democratic Convention in Chicago for the *Suffolk Sun.* Rosenbaum received a Carnegie Fellowship from Yale; he taught English but abandoned the position almost in mid-term. Reporting called him again, so he returned to the *Suffolk Sun.*

In the summer of 1969, he worked as the assistant editor, then editor, of the *Fire Island News,* a summer weekly that focused on the wealthy. By September, he had applied for a staff position at the *Village Voice.* Dan Wolf, one of the newspaper's founders, was impressed with Rosenbaum and consequently hired him.

Rosenbaum worked odd hours; often he wrote at night, usually producing a story for the newspaper about every three weeks. Concurrently, he produced articles for *Esquire.* He covered antiwar demonstrations and later presidential politics. Indeed, as the newspaper's White House correspondent, he covered Congress, particularly the proceedings leading to the possible impeachment of President Nixon. Rosenbaum also covered underground media stars such as Ray Mungo, one of the founders of the Liberation News Service. He exposed the Washington public relations firm that had employed E. Howard Hunt, one of the Watergate conspirators. He investigated construction trade unions in New York City and revealed that minority employees were juggled between construction sites primarily to fool inspectors. For *Esquire,* he wrote about "Tommy the Traveler," a shadowy undercover agent, and about "Phone Phreaks" who cheated the telephone company whenever they made long distance calls. Rosenbaum also wrote about unusual deaths of certain individuals.

Shortly after Clay Felker purchased the *Village Voice,* Rosenbaum left; it was 1975. He felt that the paper had become too conventional under Felker. Also, several of his friends had been dismissed.

Rosenbaum wrote about the mysterious firing of John Bartels, Jr., a Federal Drug Enforcement Agency administrator, for *New Times.* He subsequently became editor of *MORE,* a journalism review.

In 1979 several of his articles that had appeared in *Esquire, MORE,* the *Village Voice, New Times,* and *New York* were collected and published under the title *Rebirth of the Salesman: Tales of the Song & Dance 70's.* They illustrated his use of certain literary devices, particularly accurate description, scene-by-scene construction, and realistic or authentic dialogue, and thus were examples of literary journalism.

Rosenbaum wrote several novels, as well as articles for *Harper's* and *Rolling Stone*. For *Manhattan, inc.,* he wrote articles about famous people; they were collected and published as *Manhattan Passions: True Tales of Power, Wealth, and Excess* in 1987. In a review of the book, Bruce Nussbaum wrote, "Listening to these millionaires through Rosenbaum's fine ear gives us a wonderful glimpse at the easy-money attitude of the Eighties, where wealth is the measure of the man—or woman."[1] One article depicted Rosenbaum and Robin Leach having lunch; more important, it illustrated Rosenbaum remaining somewhat silent. Rosenbaum realized that the reader could learn more about someone by simply allowing him to speak; thus Rosenbaum merely recorded what the individual said. As a result, the reader had a more detailed image of the individual. Rosenbaum's use of description throughout the article also benefitted the reader.

In 1991 another compilation of his articles and essays appeared under the title *Travels with Dr. Death: And Other Unusual Investigations.* The book contained several gems, including "Oswald's Ghost" and "Tales of the Cancer Cure Underground," and dealt with various subjects, including public scandals, private investigations, and clandestine subcultures. The articles were examples of literary journalism primarily because of Rosenbaum's use of literary devices such as dialogue and personal points of view.

WORKS: *Rebirth of the Salesman: Tales of the Song & Dance 70's* (1979); *Manhattan Passions: True Tales of Power, Wealth, and Excess* (1987); *Travels with Dr. Death: And Other Unusual Investigations* (1991).
NOTE
   1. Bruce Nussbaum, "When Too Much Isn't Enough," *Business Week,* April 6, 1987, p. 18.

Lillian Ross
(1927–)

Lillian Ross was born in Syracuse, New York, in 1927. She began her career at 21 as a staff writer of the *New Yorker*. Her articles, which included a mixture of fiction and fact, appeared in several sections of the magazine, including "The Talk of the Town," "Profiles," and "Reporter at Large." Her 1950 dramatic profile of Ernest Hemingway, a minute-by-minute account of several hours in the author's life, was severely criticized because of her unusual style of reporting. However, the profile was not only approved by Hemingway before its publication but received his support when the critics denounced it for its inclusion of elements usually found in fiction, that is, thorough descriptions of characters, including dress, speech, and action. The profile was expanded and published as *Portrait of Hemingway* in 1962.

Ross helped initiate a new form of reportage at the *New Yorker*. In a series of articles about the filming of *The Red Badge of Courage,* she captured realistically the intricacies of movie making. The articles were ultimately collected and published as *Picture* in 1952. The book was indicative of her artistic style. Though she provided candid descriptions of characters, her ear for dialogue was perhaps her greatest attribute as a writer.

Ross revealed the person she interviewed. For instance, in her interview with John Huston, she informed the reader about Huston's mood, how he was seated, what he was doing, what he thought, and how he responded to others, nonverbally as well as verbally. From the description and dialogue, the reader learned how Huston acted off-camera. Though Rex Reed perfected this kind of profile in the 1960s, Ross was writing a few before that decade.

Her book *Reporting* appeared in 1964 and included narratives similar to her Hemingway profile and her articles about movie making. Most critics approved of her arresting stories.

WORKS: "The Talk of the Town" (column, *New Yorker*); "Profiles" (column, *New Yorker*); "Reporter at Large" (column, *New Yorker*); *Picture* (1952); *Portrait of Hemingway* (1962); *Reporting* (1964).

Mike Royko
(1932–   )

Journalist Mike Royko was born in Chicago on September 19, 1932. He attended Wright Junior College in the early 1950s and enlisted in the U.S. Air Force in 1952. Royko was a street-wise adolescent who grew up on the northwest side of the city. His writing, influenced less by his education than by an Air Force base newspaper, enabled him to obtain a position as a reporter with the Chicago North Side Newspapers upon his release in 1956. Within a few months he had transferred to the Chicago City News bureau, for which he served not only as a reporter but as an assistant city editor.

The experience he obtained was enormously beneficial three years later, when he moved to the *Chicago Daily News* as a reporter and columnist. His columns for the *News* contained information about the Chicago political structure to which few rival columnists had access. According to Barbara A. Welch, "Columnist Royko, it has been said, 'owns' the city of Chicago. His intimate knowledge of how the city runs and its people has made his column required reading for Chicagoans; he is attracting a national following as well."[1] Indeed, William Brashler said, "He wields enough power and influence to alter the course of major elections: the mayoralty of the city of Chicago, seats in the United States Senate, and some insist, the presidency."[2]

Royko also wrote about other people, especially those who were downtrodden or who had seen the American Dream fade before their eyes. In addition, he did in Chicago what Jimmy Breslin did in New York City; he returned to where he had lived as a child and drew characters from that area, including his alter egos Slats Grobnik and Dr. I. M. Kookie. Through these characters Royko presented the numerous issues Chicagoans faced; he seldomed editorialized, however.

Several collections of his columns appeared in the late 1960s and early 1970s, under the titles *Up Against It* (1967), *I May Be Wrong, but I Doubt It* (1968), and *Slats Grobnik and Some Other Friends* (1973). His best known book, *Boss: Richard J. Daley of Chicago,* was published in 1971. A witty but candid portrait of a man and his city, the book explicitly showed how Daley used as well as abused his power. It sold well throughout the country.

Royko joined the *Chicago Sun-Times* when the *News* ceased publication in 1978. However, when Australian-born Fleet Street newspaper magnate Rupert Murdoch purchased the paper in 1984, Royko moved to the *Chicago Tribune.*

His fourth collection of columns, *Sez Who? Sez Me,* was published in 1982. Royko examined such topics as drinking in bars, disabled Vietnam veterans who were mistreated by the Veterans Administration, Jane Fonda, and, of course, various characters in and around Chicago. Two years later another collection, entitled *Like I Was Sayin',* was published. It included columns about Tiny Tim, the bureaucratic gobbledygook in Chicago school system memos, and the history of knavery. Of course, he discussed politics, organized crime, and modern trends.

In the late 1980s he satirized religious fanaticism by creating his own religion, the Church of Asylumism, which was founded by Dr. I. M. Kookie. According to the Book of Kook, man was not native to Earth. Indeed, a society of peaceful, loving beings on another planet apparently developed a social problem. Several hundred of these beings became mentally deranged and subsequently were shipped to Earth, because Earth was uninhabited and the word "Earth" meant "booby hatch." These columns became the basis for the collection *Dr. Kookie, You're Right!,* which was published in 1990. Royko, through Dr. Kookie, discussed various issues, including dieting, technological progress, art, baseball, the film *The Last Temptation of Christ,* and upscale restaurants.

Royko's biting wit was evident in the early 1990s when he spoofed Sergeant Joe Friday and his partner by having them use racist and sexist language that had been taken verbatim from transmissions of the Los Angeles Police Department.

WORKS: *Up Against It* (1967); *I May Be Wrong, but I Doubt It* (1968); *Slats Grobnik and Some Other Friends* (1973); *Sez Who? Sez Me* (1982); *Like I Was Sayin'* (1984); *Dr. Kookie, You're Right!* (1990).

NOTES

1. Barbara A. Welch, "Royko, Mike," *Contemporary Authors: Volumes 89–92,* edited by Frances C. Locker (Detroit: Gale Research, 1980), p. 443.

2. Ibid.

Damon Runyon
(1880–1946)

Damon Runyon was born in 1880 in Manhattan, Kansas. His early life was filled with rejection and rebellion. When his mother became ill with tuberculosis, his family moved to Pueblo, Colorado, where his father worked as a printer on the *Pueblo Chieftain*. Runyon, dismissed from school in the sixth grade for being mischievous, was similar to his father in that he cared little about responsibility and a great deal about enjoying life. Ironically, he was rescued by his father, who secured a job for him on the *Pueblo Evening Press*. Runyon became a reporter at 15; he wrote features for the *Press* and the *Evening Post*.

In 1898 he joined the Thirteenth Minnesota Volunteers and went to the Philippines. His taste for drink grew, as did his ability to write. When he was released a year later he worked for the *Pueblo Chieftain;* experience on several other Colorado newspapers followed. His reputation for writing news stories and features spread. In 1905 he became a sports reporter for the *Denver Post,* then, a year later, a political reporter for the *Rocky Mountain News*. As his writing experience broadened, he began to write short stories for various magazines. His perceptive use of descriptive detail soon made his name known to readers of national magazines. By 1911 he was in New York City, occasionally selling stories to magazines like *Harper's* and *Everybody's;* however, he failed to earn enough to support himself. He obtained a position as a sports writer with Hearst's *New York American;* Harry Cashman, the sports editor, sent him to San Antonio in 1911 to cover spring training for the New York Giants. According to Thomas Grant, Runyon enjoyed hobnobbing with baseball players and writing about their antics for the paper:

Readers soon preferred these stories to conventional summaries of game strategy and recitations of statistics concluding with box scores. Hence, he was encouraged to write about the players, and by the time he returned to New York, . . . he was a recognized baseball writer and key reporter.[1]

His sports writing was unusual, mixing fact with fantasy. It was also humorous, and in time he was writing about other sports. In 1914 he wrote a column titled "The Mornin's Mornin' " in which he commented on whatever he wished. In addition, he served as a correspondent in Mexico, where he reported on Pancho Villa, and in France, where he reported on World War I. When he returned he wrote a series of boxing articles on Jack Dempsey and continued his column.

In the 1920s he contributed character sketches to the Sunday *American* and reported on several murder trials. In 1929 his first Broadway story was published in *Cosmopolitan*. Usually mixing fact with fantasy in these stories, Runyon wrote about gangsters, actors, and actresses. These stories were collected in several volumes in the next decade, and several were adapted for the screen.

In 1937, when Hearst's *American* suspended publication, Runyon moved to the *New York Daily Mirror,* where he wrote a new column and a new humorous series. However, his writing was less popular than it had been, for his brand of humor was somewhat dated.

Lured away from New York City by the motion picture industry, he lived in Hollywood from 1941 to 1943. When he had a throat operation a year later, doctors discovered that he had cancer. Within two years he was dead.

Runyon's sports writing contained the elements of literary journalism; his eye for portraying his subjects realistically was unequalled by his contemporaries.
NOTE

1. Thomas Grant, "Damon Runyon," *American Humorists 1800–1950: Part 2: M–Z,* edited by Stanley Trachtenberg (Detroit: Gale Research, 1982), p. 421.

Cornelius Ryan
(1920–1974)

Cornelius Ryan was an unequalled historian of World War II. Born in 1920, in Dublin, Ireland, he began his writing career in 1940 as a reporter for Reuters News Agency in London. In 1943 he worked for the London *Daily Telegraph,* first as a war correspondent (he covered D-Day and General Patton's race across France and Germany), then as a reporter in the paper's Tokyo bureau, then as the paper's Middle East bureau chief in Jerusalem. While in Jerusalem, he also worked as a stringer for *Time* magazine and the *St. Louis Post-Dispatch.* Four years later, he moved to the United States and worked as a contributing editor for *Time.* He then moved to *Collier's* magazine, where he eventually became an associate editor before the magazine folded in 1956. His collection of short stories, *One Minute to Ditch!,* appeared a year later. In 1959 his first World War II historical account, *The Longest Day: June 6, 1944,* was published. The book took 10 years to research and write. He conducted more than 1,000 interviews with enlisted men as well as generals, and the information from these interviews was woven into the chronologically depicted events.

The Longest Day used actual conversation, interior monologue, and actual incidents to engage the reader's imagination and to illuminate the historical event. In short, the historical event became more than a mere occurrence in time; it became an incident the reader could easily understand. The book was a critical and commercial success, for it told of an actual event in humanistic terms.

In 1962 Ryan worked as a staff reporter for *Reader's Digest,* a position he held until 1965, when the magazine offered him the post of roving editor. In 1965 he published a second historical account, *The Last Battle.* Researched and written in the same manner as *The Longest Day, The Last Battle* was well received by critics and the reading public alike. His last book on World War II, *A Bridge Too Far,* was researched and written as he suffered from cancer.

Published in 1974, the book had not reached its zenith with the critics or the reading public when the disease killed him.

WORKS: *The Longest Day: June 6, 1944* (1959); *The Last Battle* (1966); *A Bridge Too Far* (1974).

S

John Sack
(1930–   )

John Sack, a former United Press correspondent and CBS Television documentary writer and producer, was born on March 24, 1930, in New York City and graduated from Harvard University in 1951. He served in the U.S. Army for two years after receiving his degree.

Upon his release from the service he worked for the United Press until 1955, the year his book *From Here to Shimbashi* was published. Sack, who had served in Korea, uproariously recounted his numerous misadventures and escapades while serving his country—from the day he entered boot camp to the day he returned to civilian life. For the next several years he traveled throughout Europe and contributed articles to such periodicals as *Playboy, Town and Country, Harper's, Holiday,* and the *Atlantic;* they were eventually collected under the title *Report from Practically Nowhere,* which was published in 1959.

From the early to mid-1960s he worked for the Columbia Broadcasting System, where he wrote and produced documentaries. In 1966 he moved to *Esquire* and for the first year served as the magazine's correspondent in Vietnam. His perceptive accounts of M Company were first published in *Esquire,* then in *M,* which appeared in 1967. Sack had interviewed soldiers of M Company about what they thought. These thoughts became part of the action he described.

Instead of the uproarious personal misadventures he once reported, Sack now wrote of other soldiers' adventures. He realistically captured the language used by the soldiers of M Company; he reported in impressionistic prose the varied aspects of war; and he compassionately revealed the penetrating effects of war on soldiers' lives. The book was both critically and commercially successful; it opened readers' eyes and minds, providing sufficient evidence that the war in Vietnam was not just another war. Leonard Kriegel wrote:

M is one of the finest examples of what has come to be called the "documentary novel." Sack manages to make M Company both vivid and human, deeply human, to the extent that even when M Company makes its first "kill," a 7-year-old Vietnamese girl whose head is blown open, our sympathy is with these soldiers caught in a world they neither made nor understand nor want.[1]

Sack employed incisive description, scene-by-scene construction, realistic dialogue, and interior monologue to candidly portray incidents experienced by men of M Company. Indeed, he captured the sounds, the mood, and the soldiers who lived and died in Vietnam. Through repeated letters of the alphabet, he provided the sounds of machine guns. Through words, he dramatically captured the language used by military personnel. Little was left to the reader's imagination. He even included incidents that were out of the ordinary or unusual primarily to demonstrate that perhaps war, itself, was out of the ordinary. Only by using such literary devices and incidents could Sack have presented the realities of Vietnam. Conventional reporting would not have been enough to convey such lunacy.

Sack remained at *Esquire* until 1978, the year he became a contributing editor at *Playboy*. During the 1970s he wrote the disturbing *Lieutenant Calley,* about the My Lai massacre in Vietnam. While writing this book, Sack was arrested and indicted by the federal government; however, he was never prosecuted.

From 1982 to 1984 he worked as a newswriter and producer at KCBS-TV in Los Angeles. In 1983 he published the insightful polemic book *Fingerprint,* which some reviewers compared to Laurence Sterne's *Tristam Shandy*. It began with the events that led up to Sack's conception and birth. The book, which was full of dialogue and in-depth description, concerned not only the author's precarious life, but society's numerous problems.

Ten years later he wrote *An Eye for an Eye,* which recounted disturbing events that happened in the aftermath of World War II. During the Russian occupation of Poland and part of Germany, some 10 million Germans were placed under Russian jurisdiction. As part of the de-Nazification program, the Russians recruited Holocaust survivors, including numerous Jews, to capture Germans and place them in concentration camps. According to Sack, some of the Germans were tortured, and about 80,000 died. This atrocity occurred in 1945, when Jews killed German civilians, including men, women, children, and babies. Although Sack acknowledged that the Holocaust occurred, he claimed that another atrocity also happened, even though the Jews who had been responsible for it attempted to cover it up. Although the Jews had been provoked by what had happened in the Nazi death camps, they committed a similar atrocity. Sack, a Jew, recounted the event with somber remorse.

In 1995 he wrote *Company C: The Real War in Iraq.* Sack followed a company from stateside to overseas deployment and combat. Like *M,* the book offered insight into the war from the perspective of soldiers engaged in combat.

WORKS: *From Here to Shimbashi* (1955); *Report from Practically Nowhere* (1959); *M* (1967); *Lieutenant Calley* (1971); *Fingerprint* (1983); *An Eye for an Eye* (1993).

NOTE

1. Leonard Kriegel, "Why Are We in Vietnam?" *Nation,* October 23, 1967, pp. 407–408.

Harrison E. Salisbury
(1908–1993)

Harrison E. Salisbury was born in Minneapolis in 1908 and attended public schools. After graduating from high school in 1925, he entered the University of Minnesota, where he eventually became editor of the campus newspaper and, in his off hours, worked part time as a reporter for the Minneapolis *Journal.* In 1930, after he had received his bachelor's degree, he became a reporter and rewrite man for the United Press in St. Paul. Salisbury, an excellent journalist, worked for the United Press in Chicago, Washington, D.C., New York City, and London, where he first served as manager in 1943, then as foreign news editor a year later, a position he held in London and in New York City until 1948.

Before he left the United Press he had reported in 1944 on conditions in Russia during the final days of World War II. His eight-month stay in that country enabled him to witness not only the battlefields on which the Red Army had tasted victory, but the Soviet arsenals that had been kept secret. His first book, *Russia on the Way,* was based on his candid observations for the United Press and for *Collier's* magazine.

Salisbury was hired by the *New York Times* in 1949 to man its Moscow bureau. For five years he tried to observe Russia again, but to little avail. The Cold War put new restrictions on what journalists could and could not report. Consequently, Salisbury's efforts were censored. Joseph Stalin was more militant in his philosophy than his predecessor, Lenin. As a result, scrutiny was imposed on every facet of Russian life.

When Salisbury returned to the United States in 1954, however, he wrote a series of articles that graphically described the horror of Stalin's Russia; he even speculated that Stalin may have been murdered in 1953 by his comrades. The 14-part series, "Russia Re-viewed," received the Pulitzer Prize for international reporting and was published in book form in 1955.

Although he was barred from Russia for a few years after his series appeared, he gained admission to its satellite countries in 1957. Visiting Albania, Bulgaria, Poland, and Rumania, Salisbury filed reports that depicted the ruinous effects of communism in those countries.

Before he was finally readmitted to Russia in 1959, Salisbury wrote extensively about the problems of New York City. In addition to investigating the chaotic state of rubbish disposal in New York, he covered the street gangs in Brooklyn. His shocking but sympathetic account was later expanded and published as *The Shook-Up Generation* in 1958.

He journeyed through the Soviet Union and Central Asia before the decade ended and again in 1961 and 1962. His books *To Moscow—and Beyond: A Reporter's Narrative* and *A New Russia?* reported progress. Salisbury believed that Russia had changed since Stalin's death. He considered Nikita Khrushchev an improvement, indeed, a man of peace.

In the 1960s Salisbury not only became the *Times'* director of national correspondence and later assistant managing editor, but toured the People's Republic of China and North Vietnam. What he witnessed in Hanoi contradicted what President Johnson was telling the American people. Bombing missions meant for concrete and steel actually had inflicted countless fatalities. Such missions had hardened Hanoi's heart, not weakened it. His observations appeared in the *Times,* much to the dismay of President Johnson, his administrative officials, and certain journalists. The accounts eventually were expanded and published in *Behind the Lines—Hanoi, December 23, 1966–January 7, 1967.*

In 1970 Salisbury became the first editor of the *Times'* new op-ed page, which was devoted to opinion and commentary. In addition to publishing regular *Times* columnists such as Russell Baker, Tom Wicker, and James Reston, he published contributions from such writers as William F. Buckley, Jr., and Richard Moore. In 1972 he was promoted to associate editor.

On the last day of 1973, at the age of 65, he retired from the *Times.* Salisbury died in 1993.

Salisbury's writing may be considered literary journalism in the sense that he used the techniques or devices Tom Wolfe and other practicing literary journalists identified. For example, his *Shook-Up Generation* was not only an investigative account, but a realistic account. The reader learned from the candid descriptions and the faithful dialogue what the characters were like. The story was revealed to the reader through scenes not unlike those found in novels.

WORKS: *Russia on the Way* (1946); *The Shook-Up Generation* (1958); *To Moscow—and Beyond: A Reporter's Narrative* (1960); *A New Russia?* (1962); *Behind the Lines—Hanoi, December 23, 1966–January 7, 1967* (1967); *The 900 Days: The Siege of Leningrad* (1969).

Dick Schaap
(1934–)

Dick Schaap was born in New York City in 1934 and received degrees from Cornell University and Columbia University in 1955 and 1956, respectively. Schaap, who eventually turned to broadcasting, first as a sportscaster for WNBC-TV in 1971, then as a broadcaster for NBC News in 1978, and finally as a broadcaster for ABC News in 1980, began his career in print journalism in 1956 as a sports editor for *Newsweek*. After advancing to general editor and later senior editor, he moved to the *New York Herald Tribune* in 1964, where he held the position of city editor, and later columnist, until the paper ceased publication in 1967.

Schaap, primarily a sports writer in his early years, wrote several biographies of sports personalities, including Mickey Mantle, Paul Hornung, and Jerry Kramer. In addition, he wrote books about the Olympics, the New York Mets, professional golf tournaments, and professional football. He collaborated with Jimmy Breslin on the novel *.44*, which was published in 1978. He contributed numerous articles to such publications as *Look, Playboy,* and *Sport,* which he edited from 1973 to 1978.

In 1966 he wrote the investigative account *Turned On: The Friede-Crenshaw Case,* which depicted the unforgettable, tragic story of Celeste Crenshaw and Robert Friede, two lives that were affected by drugs. As Schaap wrote:

The reporting led deep into the drug world, an unmistakably expanding world that is being populated increasingly by people like Celeste Crenshaw and Robert Friede, people who come not out of slums, not out of minority ghettoes, but out of fine homes and fine schools, looking to drugs for excitement and knowledge and escape.[1]

Schaap was so intrigued by the Friede-Crenshaw case that he devoted six months to his investigation. He employed a different form of reporting, painting scenes appropriate to the macabre incidents.

In 1984 he wrote *The 1984 Olympic Games: Sarajevo/Los Angeles,* which was filled with colorful photographs of the events, the various winners, and the award ceremonies. Unfortunately, Schaap's accompanying essays, although lighthearted and occasionally sarcastic, provided few new insights. The book presented a day-by-day account of both the Winter and Summer Olympics.

In 1992 Schaap, with Mort Gerberg, edited *Joy in Mudville: The Big Book of Baseball Humor.* Most of the humor had been told by others.

WORK: *Turned On: The Friede-Crenshaw Case* (1966).
NOTE
1. Dick Schaap, *Turned On: The Friede-Crenshaw Case* (New York: New American Library, 1966), p. 1.

Jonathan Schell
(1943–   )

Jonathan Schell was born on August 21, 1943, in New York City, and was educated at Harvard University. In 1968 he became a contributing editor at the *New Yorker.* Schell wrote about the Vietnam War, the Nixon presidency, nuclear war, and politics in the United States.

His first book, which was serialized in the *New Yorker,* was *The Village of Ben Suc.* Published in 1967, it depicted in graphic detail the destruction of selected villages in South Vietnam that supposedly had become hiding places for Viet Cong weaponry. Ben Suc, a small farming community, was one of these hiding places. In January 1967, American forces evacuated the inhabitants, then destroyed the town. Schell observed the process and reported on it with incredible accuracy. However, it was *how* Schell reported the events that needs discussion. Through the use of scene-by-scene construction and careful description, he depicted the events and individuals involved. Through the use of realistic dialogue, he caused the individuals to become actual characters who had thoughts as well as feelings. The book was praised for its mature style of persuasion. Several reviewers thought the book should have been required reading by officers working in the Pentagon, because it showed that American officers in Vietnam failed to understand guerrilla warfare.

Schell's second book was about the destruction of two villages, along with the inhabitants, from the air. Titled *The Military Half: An Account of Destruction in Quang Ngai and Quang Tin* (1968), it first appeared in the *New Yorker.* Schell pointed out that air strikes often destroyed villages where innocent people lived. Some reviewers criticized the author for selecting isolated incidents, then generalizing that many mountainous provinces as well as villages were filled with friendly people, not the enemy.

In 1976 he published *The Time of Illusion,* an account of the Nixon presidency. A work of literary journalism, the book presented through the use of scene-by-scene construction, accurate description, realistic dialogue, and Schell's point of view a careful analysis of Nixon in the White House. Schell saw Nixon, like Kennedy and Johnson before him, as a manufacturer of images, not of anything substantive.

The Fate of the Earth, published in 1982, concerned nuclear war. Two years later, Schell produced *The Abolition,* another philosophical cry for peace. Neither was a work of literary journalism; however, both were important because of the subjects discussed and the ideas presented.

His next book of literary journalism was *History in Sherman Park: An American Family and the Reagan-Mondale Election,* which appeared in 1987. To write this informal piece of political sociology, Schell tried to learn as much as he could about a married couple who lived in Sherman Park, Wisconsin. Specifically, he attempted to learn about their political leanings in the Reagan-Mondale presidential election. However, the author was not without his critics. James Wolcott wrote:

He wishes to change the course of mighty rivers without getting his hands dirty. He seems content to stare at a potential sea of "sober, opaque, impassive" citizens. His approach to politics, like his attempts at prose, bears a noble slump of futility. His shoulders are hunched with the weight of nuclear dread.[1]

Schell observed, inquired, and reported on what he saw and heard, and the book depicted—perhaps with incredible accuracy—just how apathetic Americans had become about learning about presidential candidates.

In one section of the book, Schell and the couple watched the coverage of a Reagan rally on television. Schell used realistic dialogue to capture and characterize Bill and Gina. This is merely one of the elements that Schell employed in his writing.

The same year *The Real War: The Classic Reporting on the Vietnam War* was published. It included two earlier publications—*The Village of Ben Suc* and *The Military Half*—as well as a new piece, "The Real War." This book illustrated Schell's use of careful description and authentic dialogue, essential elements in literary journalism.

Schell published a book of editorial comment, *Observing the Nixon Years: "Notes and Comment" from the New Yorker on the Vietnam War and the Watergate Crisis, 1969–1975,* in 1989, two years after he had left the staff of the *New Yorker.* Schell criticized the conduct of the United States in Vietnam as well as the misdeeds of the Nixon administration.

He became a current affairs columnist at *Newsday* in 1990.

WORKS: *The Village of Ben Suc* (1967); *The Military Half* (1968); *The Time of Illusion* (1976); *History in Sherman Park: An American Family and the Reagan-Mondale Election* (1987); *The Real War: The Classic Reporting on the Vietnam War* (1987).

NOTE

1. James Wolcott, "The Fate of the Hearth," *New Republic,* November 2, 1987, p. 42.

William Shawn
(1907–1992)

William Shawn, editor of the *New Yorker,* was born in Chicago in 1907. Although he attended the University of Michigan from 1925 to 1927, he never graduated. Instead he turned to reporting and editing newspapers in Las Vegas, New Mexico, and in Chicago until he moved to the *New Yorker* in 1933 as a reporter. The *New Yorker*'s editor, Harold Ross, had founded the magazine in 1925 to reflect metropolitan life in word and picture. As Ross said:

As compared to the newspaper, the *New Yorker* will be interpretive rather than stenographic. It will print facts that it will have to go behind the scenes to get, but it will not deal in scandal for the sake of scandal nor sensation for the sake of sensation. Its integrity will be above suspicion.[1]

The magazine reflected not only metropolitan life, but its editor's prospectus practically verbatim. It eventually increased its circulation by publishing writers and humorists such as James Thurber, E. B. White, Wolcott Gibbs, S. J. Perelman, Ogden Nash, Robert Benchley, Edmund Wilson, Dorothy Parker, Lewis Mumford, Clarence Day, H. L. Mencken, Rebecca West, Clifton Fadiman, John O'Hara, Lillian Ross, A. J. Liebling, and St. Clair McKelway. Cartoonists, too, contributed and enlivened the pages for thousands of readers. The *New Yorker* became somewhat of a who's who, publishing humor, critical essays, short stories, profiles, and cartoons by writers and cartoonists of great merit.

When Shawn joined the staff, the magazine was eight years old and financially sound. For two years he contributed to the column "Talk of the Town." Then, in 1935, he became an associate editor, a position he held for four years. In addition to his duties as an associate editor, he contributed to the magazine. One of his pieces, perhaps the only one with his by-line, appeared in 1936. Titled "The Catastrophe," the story told how New York City was obliterated by a meteorite and eventually forgotten, as if it had never existed. In 1939 Shawn was advanced to managing editor. In this position he persuaded Ross to publish John Hersey's controversial account of the annihilation of Hiroshima. The article later appeared in book form, like many other articles, cartoons, and stories that had first appeared in the magazine.

When Ross died in 1952, Shawn became editor, and the magazine changed slightly. James Playsted Wood wrote: "The *New Yorker* is quieter. It is more serious. It is wordier. Its long stories have grown interminable. The *New Yorker* has kept its imperturbability, but it has lost its ferocity and most of its humor.[2]

The magazine published articles that conceivably could be termed investigative or advocative, including Charles Reich's "The Greening of America," a comprehensive indictment of America's synthetic, artificial, counterproductive consumer-oriented society; Daniel Lang's "Casualties of War," which exposed the rape and murder of a Vietnamese girl by four soldiers; James Baldwin's "The Fire Next Time"; and Hannah Arendt's "Eichmann in Jerusalem."

Shawn's contributions both as a staff writer and as an editor considerably increased the magazine's appeal. He died in 1992.

WORKS: "Talk of the Town," *New Yorker* (1933–1935); *New Yorker*.
NOTES
1. John Tebbel, *The American Magazine: A Compact History* (New York: Hawthorn Books, 1969), p. 234.
2. James Playsted Wood, *Magazines in the United States* (New York: Ronald Press, 1971), pp. 270–271.

Vincent Sheean
(1899–1975)

Vincent Sheean was born in Pana, Illinois, in 1899. Sheean, who attended the University of Chicago, entered journalism with the *Chicago Daily News*. Within a month he was dismissed. Determined to make journalism a career, he immediately traveled to New York City, where eventually he was hired by the *New York Daily News*. For two years he practiced the traditional techniques of journalism until they came easy to him. In 1922 he worked as a correspondent for the *Chicago Tribune,* and traveled to Paris, Lausanne, Geneva, the Rhineland, Rome, Madrid, London, and Morocco, where he reported on the Rif rebellion. Three years later he became a freelance political journalist and correspondent, and worked for the North American Newspaper Alliance and the *New York Herald Tribune* syndicate. In 1926 his first literary journalistic work, *An American Among the Riffi,* was published.

Sheean reported on many important events that ultimately changed the course of history. His assignments included the communist revolution in China, the Arab-Jewish confrontations of 1929, the effects of Bolshevism in Russia, the growth of Nazi Germany, the civil war in Spain, the power of Nazi Germany in Czechoslovakia and France, the bombing of London, the war in Africa, and the war in the Pacific. Wherever a major political, social, national, or international disturbance occurred, he was there reporting it for millions of readers. More important, his books detailed the events from personal perspectives. Such volumes as *The New Persia, Personal History, Not Peace but a Sword, Between the Thunder and the Sun,* and *This House Against This House* informed and entertained thousands of readers.

Personal History used a style that was quite personal, not unlike Norman Mailer's style in *Armies of the Night.*

Sheean wrote several novels and biographies, but none equalled his personal accounts. He died in 1975.

WORKS: *An American Among the Riffi* (1926); *The New Persia* (1927); *Personal History* (1935); *Not Peace but a Sword* (1939); *Between the Thunder and the Sun* (1943); *This House Against This House* (1946).

Wilfrid Sheed
(1930-)

Wilfrid Sheed, a novelist as well as an essayist, was born on December 27, 1930, in London, England. His parents, Frank Sheed and Maisie Ward, were Roman Catholic writers and publishers; indeed, they had founded Sheed and Ward, one of the most prestigious publishing houses of religious literature in the world, four years before their son was born. They opened a branch office in New York City in 1933.

When World War II began in Europe, Sheed moved with his parents and his sister, Rosemary, to the United States. They settled in Torresdale, Pennsylvania, a small town in which Sheed spent part of his youth. As a child he was interested in sports; he did not acquire a taste for literature until he was stricken with poliomyelitis at age 14.

Sheed returned to England after his recuperation to attend the famous Benedictine preparatory school Downside Abbey, where he read works by Ernest Hemingway, Ring Lardner, E. M. Forster, P. G. Wodehouse, and James Thurber.

Upon graduation, Sheed matriculated at Lincoln College, Oxford University, where he majored in history. He received his bachelor's degree in 1954. Within three years, he had earned a master's degree at Oxford. Part of his master's work, however, was completed at Columbia University in New York City.

Sheed then moved to Australia, where he lived with relatives. His desire to become a journalist was realized when he was hired by the Australian Broadcasting Company to report about sharks. This job did not last, and Sheed returned to the United States, where he supported himself by writing book and movie reviews as well as essays for various periodicals. He served as the film critic for the Catholic publication *Jubilee* from 1959 to 1961 and as its associate editor from 1959 to 1966. He served as drama critic as well as book review editor at *Commonweal,* another Catholic publication, from 1964 to 1967. In 1967 he became a film critic at *Esquire,* a position that lasted two years. Although he contributed to the *New York Times Book Review* in 1971, his column, "The Good Word," did not appear until later. Sheed also contributed numerous articles and essays to various other publications, including the *New York Review of Books, Saturday Evening Post, Life, Sports Illustrated, Commonweal,* and *Esquire.*

His first novel, *A Middle Class Education,* published in 1960, was partly autobiographical. It was a satirical work about John Chote, who skipped classes at Oxford University. Despite this habit, he received a scholarship to conduct graduate work at a university in the United States. Chote became involved with a woman and learned about life, but not through books. Finally, he returned to England, where he straightened out his life.

Sheed wrote other novels, some of which were about journalism and writers; like his first, some were based on incidents in his life. *Office Politics* (1966), *Max Jamison* (1970), and *People Will Always Be Kind* (1973) received considerable favorable criticism.

His nonfiction, some of it written in a literary journalistic style, brought him additional recognition. His book and film reviews as well as essays about sports, politics, politicians, and writers were published under the title *The Morning After: Selected Essays and Reviews,* which appeared in 1971. Another volume of reviews and essays appeared under the title *The Good Word and Other Words* in 1978. These collections were widely reviewed; many considered Sheed one of the best essayists writing for popular periodicals. Morris Freedman said in his review of *The Morning After:*

Mr. Sheed writes to order, mostly pithy essays on movies, plays or books, in the pages of *Life, Esquire, Book World, Sports Illustrated.* The formal demands of this occasional writing, like those of the heroic couplet itself, force a concentration on the epigram, the compact summation, the striking generalization. . . . To this highly professional skill Sheed fortunately brings the restraint of common sense, balance and, most importantly, a sense of responsibility.[1]

Unlike some essayists, Sheed did not assert any particular ideology in his writing. Rather he parodied and even revised conventional notions about his subjects. As John Leonard pointed out, "What's most characteristic about Sheed . . . is the care with which he chooses his subjects. He probes instead of devouring and understands without destroying."[2]

In *The Morning After* Sheed recounted an incident that occurred while he was involved in the presidential campaign of Eugene McCarthy. Sheed recorded his own movements as well as his own thoughts as Robert Kennedy was shot and killed. Like some literary journalists, Sheed became a participant in what he reported. He described in depth what he and others felt. He reported what individuals said. Accurate description, thoughts or interior monologue, and realistic dialogue made up the article, and the reader gained an insight into one terrible moment in man's uneven history as a result.

Sheed wrote other forms of nonfiction, including biographies of Muhammad Ali and Clare Booth Luce. He wrote an intimate account of his parents in *Frank & Maisie: A Memoir with Parents,* which appeared in 1985.

In 1987 he wrote *The Boys of Winter,* a novel about a burned-out editor at a prestigious publishing house in New York City. Three years later he published *Essays in Disguise,* another collection of informative essays that revealed Sheed's eye for detail and ear for language. He employed an exciting prose style to present enlightening information about Frank Sinatra, Ernest Hemingway, John Updike, J. D. Salinger, the Mafia, and the Catholic Church, among other subjects.

Sheed had grown fond of cricket when he lived in England. However, when he moved to the United States, this fondness was replaced by an affection for baseball. In *Baseball and Lesser Sports* (1991) Sheed shared his affection with the reader, as he displayed his knowledge about baseball legends Connie Mack, Joe DiMaggio, and Ted Williams, among others. He also discussed certain sportswriters and broadcasters, as well as the "lesser sports" boxing and football.

Two years later he wrote the witty, acerbic personal baseball memoir, *My Life as a Fan,* in which he affectionately recalled the Brooklyn Dodgers of the 1940s and 1950s. In 1955 he wrote *In Love with Daylight: A Memoir of Recovery,* a beautifully written book about his battle with cancer, alcohol, and prescription drugs.

WORKS: *The Morning After: Selected Essays and Reviews* (1971); *The Good Word and Other Words* (1978); *Essays in Disguise* (1990).

NOTES

1. Morris Freedman, "Mr. Sheed's Dryden," *New Republic,* October 2, 1971, p. 20.

2. Wilfrid Sheed, *The Morning After: Selected Essays and Reviews,* with a foreword by John Leonard (New York: Farrar, Straus and Giroux, 1971), p. xx.

Neil Sheehan
(1936–)

Neil Sheehan, a former bureau chief in Saigon for the United Press International (UPI), was born on October 27, 1936, in Holyoke, Massachusetts. Sheehan graduated from Harvard University in 1958, then entered the U.S. Army a year later.

When he was released he worked for UPI, then joined the news staff of the *New York Times* in 1964. Primarily an investigative reporter, Sheehan worked in New York City, Indonesia, and Vietnam. When he returned from the horrors of war, he was assigned first to the Pentagon, then to the White House. He was on special assignment when he released the Pentagon Papers to the *Times,* which not only published the controversial political reports, but issued the series as a book, which Sheehan edited, in 1971. The series exposed America's poorly designed Vietnam policy and made Sheehan's reputation as an investigative journalist.

His reputation was secured in 1971 with the publication of *The Arnheiter Affair,* an exposé of the questionable circumstances surrounding the removal of Commander Marcus Arnheiter from the *Vance,* a warship assigned to patrol off South Vietnam. Sheehan's book was an in-depth report, similar in some ways to Herman Wouk's novel, *The Caine Mutiny.*

In 1972 he left the *Times* primarily to devote all of his time to writing. For the next 15 years he researched and wrote the award-winning book *A Bright Shining Lie: John Paul Vann and America in Vietnam,* which was published in 1988. Sheehan blended biography with history and, of course, his own experiences in Vietnam. He examined the role of the United States in the Vietnam War. Sheehan had gone to Vietnam as a foreign correspondent for UPI in 1962, when the United States had approximately 3,000 military advisors whose role was to instruct the forces of South Vietnam. Sheehan admitted that he, like other reporters, had supported the United States in this effort. However, as the war developed, his perceptions changed, especially when he discovered that American commanders in Saigon were not necessarily honest in their dealings with members of the press.

Sheehan eventually met John Paul Vann, a lieutenant colonel and an advisor to the South Vietnamese. Vann disclosed that the South Vietnamese government as well as its forces fought reluctantly and as a result had suffered major defeats. Vann also criticized American policy regarding indiscriminate bombing. Of course, Vann was rebuked by his superiors. In 1963 he left Vietnam and retired from the army. However, he had gained the trust of numerous reporters who had grown disillusioned with the American military leadership.

Sheehan returned to the United States in the mid-1960s, while Vann had gone back to Vietnam as a civilian pacification advisor. As the war mushroomed, Vann's influence increased, until he died in a helicopter crash in 1972.

Sheehan, who had idolized Vann, learned that he had not left Vietnam and the army in protest; he had retired because charges of statutory rape had made it impossible for him to advance to the rank of general. Vann's opinion of the war had changed, too. Indeed, before his death, he had grown to enjoy the stench of battle. Although Sheehan admitted that Vann was a brave soldier, he was also a hypocrite. In short, he represented the United States in Vietnam.

In his review of the book for the *New York Times Book Review,* Ronald Steel wrote, ''The truth he learned about Vann was that in his personal life he would twist reality to suit his purposes. For him the admired Vann became, like the war itself, another 'bright shining lie.' ''[1]

The book, as Steel pointed out, was not so much a biography as a montage. Indeed, it presented a graphic history of the war as well as the story of Vann and his role in it:

But a dazzling montage it is: vividly written and deeply felt, with a power that comes from long reflection and strong emotions. The dramatic scenes of lonely men locked in combat, the striking portraits of those who made and reported the conflict, the clash of wills and egos, the palpable touch and feel of the war, the sensitivity to the politics and psychology behind the battles, the creation of a memorable, though still mysterious, man—all these combine in a work that captures the Vietnam War like no other.[2]

The book was an example of literary journalism in the sense that Sheehan, in addition to being a participant, used dialogue, scene-by-scene construction, and other literary devices usually found in fiction to depict what occurred in Vietnam.

In 1992, after returning to Vietnam and seeing the immense poverty, he asked, ''Why did we bomb a country as poor as this?'' His book *After the War Was Over: Hanoi and Saigon* was filled with incredible, vivid description, and the people he described were forgiving. The book served as an afterword to *A Bright Shining Lie.*

WORKS: *The Pentagon Papers* (1971); *The Arnheiter Affair* (1971); *A Bright Shining Lie: John Paul Vann and America in Vietnam* (1988); *After the War Was Over: Hanoi and Saigon* (1992).
NOTES
1. Ronald Steel, ''The Man Who Was the War,'' *New York Times Book Review,* September 25, 1988, p. 53.
2. Ibid.

Gail Sheehy
(1937–)

Born on November 27, 1937, in Mamaroneck, New York, Gail Sheehy received her bachelor's degree from the University of Vermont in 1958. For the next two years, she worked as a home economist for the J. C. Penney Company. In 1961 she was hired as the fashion editor by the Rochester, New York, *Democrat and Chronicle;* this position lasted two years, until she moved to the *New York Herald-Tribune.* For three years, until 1966, Sheehy wrote features on various subjects. This experience enabled her to move to *New York* magazine as a contributing editor in 1968. She remained at *New York* until 1977, when she left to write full time.

Sheehy married in 1960 and divorced eight years later. In 1970 her first book, *Lovesounds,* was published. A novel, it concerned a husband and wife, their child, and a marriage that had grown stale; divorce was inevitable. Although the novel received some positive reviews, Sheehy turned to nonfiction, which she found easier to write. In 1971 *New York* published ''Redpants,'' an article for which Sheehy interviewed numerous prostitutes. Redpants was a composite character based on a number of prostitutes. However, the reader was not made aware of this, and as a result Sheehy was criticized by several journalists. The article and her subsequent book, *Hustling: Prostitution in Our Wide Open Society* (1973), were examples of literary journalism because both included literary devices such as careful description, scene-by-scene construction, and authentic dialogue.

Sheehy also wrote two best-selling books that explored psychological as well as sociological issues. *Passages: Predictable Crises of Adult Life,* published in 1976, concerned the four major passages that people experience. *Pathfinders,* which followed in 1981, explored other areas or ''paths'' that would help people learn about themselves.

In 1986 Sheehy wrote *Spirit of Survival,* about her adopted daughter, Mohm, whose family was annihilated by the Pol Dot regime in Cambodia, and her years of witnessing countless murders. The book was insightful and passionate. Two years later she wrote *Character: America's Search for Leadership,* in which she focused on individuals who wanted to enter politics primarily to become president: Gary Hart, Albert Gore, Michael Dukakis, Jesse Jackson, Robert Dole, George Bush, and Ronald Reagan. In 1990 she wrote *The Man Who Changed the World: The Lives of Mikhail S. Gorbachev,* a perceptive biography that conveyed Gorbachev's ambition and self-assurance. Two years later she examined the medical, psychological, and social aspects of menopause in *The Silent Passage: Menopause.* Sheehy claimed that the process spanned five to seven years and that it had three stages: perimenopause, menopause, and coalescence.

Her book *New Passages: Mapping Your Life Across Time* was published in 1995 and explained how people could customize their life cycles. Sheehy also wrote numerous articles for *Cosmopolitan, McCall's, Paris Match, Good Housekeeping,* and the *New York Times Magazine,* as well as for several newspapers.

WORK: *Hustling: Prostitution in Our Wide Open Society* (1973).

Upton Sinclair
(1878–1968)

Upton Sinclair was born in 1878 in Baltimore and learned about privation at an early age. His father was from an aristocratic southern family that had been ruined by the Civil War. A traveling salesman who turned to alcohol to forget his problems, he seldom earned enough to support his family. Sinclair's mother came from a wealthy Baltimore family. Though she could have used financial help from her parents to raise Upton, she refused to ask them. The contrast between wealth and poverty not only molded Sinclair's philosophy and writing, but affected him so much that he eventually joined the socialist movement.

When he was 14 he attended City College of the City University of New York, where he started writing for magazines. He advanced to writing novels, mostly pulp fiction, by the time he graduated in 1897. From 1897 to 1901 he attended graduate school at Columbia University, where he learned that serious fiction could have an impact on society. He soon realized that readers were not appreciative of or receptive to novels advocating reform. After three efforts he produced a romantic Civil War novel, *Manassas,* in which his socialistic ideas were disguised. Published in 1904, it was perhaps the best of his early novels.

In 1904 Fred D. Warren, editor of the magazine *Appeal to Reason,* asked Sinclair to write about the slaves of industry. Warren had apparently read *Manassas,* which concerned the slave problem in the South and the abolitionist movement, and had been intrigued by Sinclair's radical ideas. Sinclair immediately responded to Warren's offer and went to Chicago, where for seven weeks he investigated the meat-packing industry. *The Jungle,* a novel which was more fact than fiction, was the result. The book was first serialized in Warren's magazine, then, after several rejections because of its controversial subject matter, it was finally accepted by Doubleday, Page and Company in 1906 when the company learned that what Sinclair had written was basically true. The book, published when muckraking journalism was popular, became an instant bestseller.

When *The Jungle* was published, *Manassas* was forgotten, and justifiably so. *The Jungle* presented the story of a Lithuanian family who had moved to Chicago to find the American dream, only to have that dream turn into a nightmare of death, brutality, and exploitation. Sinclair declared that improvements in working and living conditions could only be achieved under a new economic structure: socialism. *The Jungle,* although it had flaws, was a powerful story. It ultimately led to investigations of the meat-packing industry by the federal government, which eventually applied pressure and instituted regulations.

The Jungle contained elements of literary journalism. For instance, Sinclair used scene-by-scene construction, the third-person point of view, abundant description, and realistic, if not actual, dialogue. Though Sinclair was writing literary journalism, he was exposing the corruption within the meat-packing industry; consequently, he was considered a muckraker who used the elements of fiction to expose crime and other ills of society.

So graphic was *The Jungle*'s depiction of the unsanitary conditions in meat-packing plants and the unequal treatment of immigrants that readers became outraged. The federal government enacted the Pure Food and Drug Act and the Meat Inspection Act, to name two, which attempted to counter the grim picture Sinclair had painted.

Sinclair wrote several other muckraking novels, including *The Metropolis* (1908), *The Moneychangers* (1908), *King Coal* (1917), *Oil* (1927), and *The Flivver King* (1937), the Lanny Budd series, and nonfiction. He died in 1968.

WORK: *The Jungle* (1906).

Mark Singer
(1950–   )

Born on October 19, 1950, in Tulsa, Oklahoma, Mark Singer attended Yale University, from which he received his bachelor's degree with honors in 1972. Upon graduation, Singer worked as a staff member at the university's alumni magazine, which was edited by William Zinsser, whose nonfiction writing course Singer had taken.

Within two years Singer was introduced to William Shawn, the editor of the *New Yorker*, and was hired to write for the magazine's "Talk of the Town" column. Singer admitted in an interview that he had no idea why he was hired; however, Shawn's instinct paid off. Indeed, Singer wrote one profile after another about interesting or unusual individuals—from Ben Shine, who attended murder trials, to Robin Levine, who played a violin on the streets of New York City.

Singer had written more than 200 profiles for the magazine when he returned to Oklahoma in 1983 to write a book about the banking and oil businesses. *Funny Money*, his insightful account of the rise and collapse of the Penn Square Bank in Oklahoma City, was published in 1985. During the late 1970s and early 1980s, Penn Square grew extremely large as a result of its loan officers making liberal oil and gas loans, which were then sold to larger banks such as Chase Manhattan. Singer chronicled not only the rise and collapse of Penn Square Bank, but the Oklahoma oil-boom years. Even though the subject was serious, he presented it in a humorous fashion. For instance, the reader learned that one of Penn Square's loan officers, Bill "Monkeybrains" Patterson, enjoyed wearing Mickey Mouse ears or a duck cap to work. One reviewer commented, "Singer . . . accomplishes what few other writers on banking have done: his first-person observations of the players and their shenanigans are readable, memorable, and downright funny."[1]

The book illustrated Singer's ability to observe, then report using scene-by-scene construction, authentic dialogue, and abundant description. Through humor the reader could relish to a certain extent what would normally be considered sad occasions.

In 1989 Singer collected and published 31 profiles that originally appeared in the *New Yorker* under the title *Mr. Personality: Profiles and Talk Pieces.* A zipper repairman, superintendents of apartment buildings, a knife sharpener, a dealer in rare prints, two television news producers, and a radio humorist were among those profiled. To say the least, Singer had captured some of the more interesting if not unusual characters who lived in New York City, and most, if not all, of the articles were examples of literary journalism.

WORKS: *Funny Money* (1985); *Mr. Personality: Profiles and Talk Pieces* (1989).

NOTE

1. Joseph P. Kahn, "Required Reading," *INC.,* July 1987, p. 16.

Susan Sontag
(1933-)

Born in New York City in 1933 and reared in Tucson, Arizona, and Los Angeles, critic, essayist, novelist, and filmmaker Susan Sontag graduated from North Hollywood High School, the University of Chicago, and Harvard University. She received a bachelor's degree and two master's degrees, and completed the course work for a doctorate, but failed to write the dissertation. Nonetheless, she continued to study at St. Anne's College, Oxford, in 1957, and at the University of Paris a year later.

When she returned to the United States she worked as an editor for *Commentary.* Within months she returned to academia, but as a teacher instead of a student. She taught at the City College of New York, then at Sarah Lawrence, and later at Columbia University. She was writer-in-residence at Rutgers University in the early 1960s.

Although her first novel, *The Benefactor,* appeared in 1963, her credibility as a writer did not come from fiction. The articles she wrote for various periodicals, including the *Partisan Review,* the *Evergreen Review,* and the *Nation,* were praised by some critics and criticized by others. Her essays were collected and published under the title *Against Interpretation, and Other Essays* in 1966. The title essay as well as the other articles received mixed reviews. Sontag, who believed that experiencing art—whether literature, photography, or film—was more important than analyzing it, wrote a second novel, *Death Kit,* a year later. Her second volume of essays was published in 1969. Entitled *Styles of Radical Will,* the philosophical pieces ranged in subject from the emptiness of communication by certain artists to the value of pornography. One piece, "Trip to Hanoi," which was expanded into a book, was based on her visit to North Vietnam, and presented her impressions of the North Vietnamese people and their relentless fight. Similar to Wolfe in one sense and to Mailer in another, she not only understood the North Vietnamese, but also presented their culture, their rebellion, their revolution openly and without prejudice. As Michael L. Johnson wrote, "It is interesting to note that her account of being open, intentionally or not, to a new experience as a means of journalistically tuning-in to it is similar to Mailer's in 'A Fire on the Moon.' "[1] Sontag asked the reader to think of the American Revolution and of the Founding Fathers. Did they not fight for a revolutionary cause?

In the early 1970s she wrote several screenplays. The critics did not like the films made from the screenplays and felt that Sontag had little dramatic sense.

In 1976 another collection of her essays was published. The six essays in *On Photography* focused on individual photographers and the philosophical differences between professional and amateur and between the subject photographed and its photographic image.

Sontag, who contributed articles, short stories, and essays to the *Atlantic Monthly, Playboy,* and *Harper's,* among others, wrote a third novel, *I, etcetera,* in 1978. The same year *Illness as Metaphor* appeared. The articles in this collection were written after she had been hospitalized for breast cancer and concerned the kinds of language used to describe cancer as well as other diseases. *Under the Sign of Saturn,* a fifth collection of essays, appeared in 1980. Sontag explored the work of philosopher Walter Benjamin as well as Nazi documentary film-maker Leni Riefenstahl. *A Susan Sontag Reader,* a collection of her work from the 1960s and 1970s, was published in 1982. *AIDS and Its Metaphors,* a sequel to *Illness as Metaphor,* appeared in 1988. Sontag questioned the medical profession's pursuit, or lack thereof, of a cure and the right-wingers who associated the illness with homosexuals.

WORKS: *Trip to Hanoi* (1968); *Styles of Radical Will* (1969).
NOTE
1. Michael L. Johnson, *The New Journalism: The Underground Press, the Artists of Nonfiction, and Changes in the Established Media* (Lawrence: University Press of Kansas, 1971), p. 91.

Terry Southern
(1926–1995)

Terry Southern was born May 1, 1926, in Alvarado, Texas. His father, a pharmacist, made certain that his son attended college. However, Southern's education was interrupted by World War II; he served in the U.S. Army from 1943 to 1945. Upon his release, he attended Southern Methodist University in Dallas, the University of Chicago, and Northwestern University, from which he received his bachelor's degree in 1948. For the next two years, he studied at the Sorbonne in France.

Southern co-wrote his first screenplay in 1955, but devoted very little time to screenplays for the next several years. Instead, he wrote the first of several satirical novels. *Flash and Filigree,* published in 1958, concerned Dr. Frederick Eichner, a dermatologist, and Babs Mintner, a nurse. Both lost their innocence, but in different ways. Southern, the satirist, made fun of American society—from medicine to sexual relations. His second novel, *Candy,* co-written with Mason Hoffenberg, was published the same year in Paris. Another satire, it featured Candy Christian, who found herself in precarious situations. Because of its sexual content, the book was almost banned in several countries. *The Magic Christian,* about man's attraction to material goods, was published in 1959. It received mixed reviews.

During the 1960s, Southern was prolific as a screenwriter as well as a contributor to various periodicals, including *Esquire, Argosy, Paris Review,* the *Nation,* and *Playboy.* At least four movies based on his screenplays were international hits: *Dr. Strangelove: Or How I Learned to Stop Worrying and Love the Bomb* (1964), *The Cincinnati Kid* (1965), *Barbarella* (1968), and *Easy Rider* (1969). Some of his articles, particularly "Twirling at Ole Miss," which appeared in *Esquire,* focused on a baton twirling contest in the South. Southern's form of reporting, which was faintly autobiographical, preceded by several years Hunter S. Thompson's gonzo journalism.

In his *Red-Dirt Marijuana and Other Tastes* (1967), which contained short stories as well as several articles, Southern examined the drug culture, music, and, not surprisingly, young women. The book was criticized for its unevenness, although certain reviewers found some of the stories and articles clever. Several articles, because of the literary devices employed, bordered on literary journalism.

In 1970 he returned to the satirical novel with *Blue Movie.* Southern described a Hollywood director who wanted to produce an explicit sex film because he believed that sex in films could be depicted artistically. Perhaps one of Southern's best-written novels, the book was dismissed by most critics because of its concentration on sexual relations.

Southern eventually became an advisory editor to the *Paris Review,* and continued to write books, most of them fiction. And his efforts at literary journalism were minimal at best. For instance, in 1992 *Texas Summer* appeared, but it was merely a rehash of two works that had appeared in *Red-Dirt Marijuana and Other Tastes.* A year later, he wrote the essay for the photographic book *The Early Stones: Legendary Photographs of a Band in the Making 1963–1973.* The book was filled with grainy photographs of the Rolling Stones, first decade by Michael Cooper, who killed himself in 1973. The book also contained reminiscences by Keith Richards, Anita Pallenberg, and Marianne Faithful. The essay by Southern was appropriate and reflected what the photographs depicted.

Southern died in 1995.

WORKS: "Twirling at Ole Miss," *Esquire*; *Red-Dirt Marijuana and Other Tastes* (1967).

Freya Madeline Stark
(1893–1993)

Dame Freya Stark was born on January 31, 1893, in Paris, France, to parents who enjoyed traveling. Her father, Robert Stark, was a sculptor; her mother, Flora, was a painter and pianist. They owned several homes in England and Italy, and Freya and her sister, Vera, learned to speak a number of languages, including German, by age five.

A gypsy-like lifestyle prevented Stark from becoming close to any particular group of children; like her father, she preferred being alone, as well as walking in the woods and riding her pony on the moors. From him she learned to respect nature.

Stark learned to read before she attended school, even though her parents thought she should wait several years. In fact, she learned to read and speak Arabic while living in northern Italy in the early 1900s. She also read various books on history and philosophy.

When she was 19 she moved to England and enrolled in the School of Oriental and African Studies at the University of London, where she remained for at least two years, until World War I erupted. Then she learned nursing, which, she believed, would allow her to play a major role in the war effort; after all, nurses would be needed, not women with bachelor's degrees in Arabic.

During World War I she worked as a nurse in Italy; as a result of her responsibilities she overcame any shyness that may have developed as a result of her solitary lifestyle. When the war ended she did not return to the University of London to finish her degree. She considered painting, even though her parents, especially her mother, had discouraged her from becoming an artist. Eventually, she attended classes and realized that she had a certain skill. Concurrently, she acknowledged that she enjoyed writing. Stark decided to stop taking classes in art so that she could devote most of her time to traveling and writing.

In the 1920s, after reading *Travels in Arabia Deserta* by Charles Montagu Doughty, she began her first journey through the Middle East. Over the next five or six decades, she visited countless countries in the Middle East, Asia, and the Eastern Mediterranean. She particularly enjoyed visiting the Arab countries. Then she wrote about the places and people she saw and met. In 1929, for instance, she was in Baghdad, where she observed men and women dressed in unusual but colorful attire. The men, she noticed, were dark and exceedingly attractive. The women had most of their beauty covered. Stark photographed captivating landscapes, rare artifacts, exotic animals, and native men, women, and children, and included these photographs in most of her books. Her early experiences in Baghdad were faithfully described in *Baghdad Sketches,* which was published in 1933. Other early exploits in this part of the world were accurately recorded in four autobiographical travel books: *Traveller's Prelude* (1950), *Beyond Euphrates: Autobiography, 1928–1933* (1951), *The Coast of*

Incense: Autobiography, 1933–1939 (1953), and *Dust in the Lion's Paw: Autobiography, 1939–1946* (1961). Stark, like other writers who recounted their travels, captured the sights as well as the sounds of the country and its people; yet, at the same time, she intermixed the past with the present. Thus, she informed as well as entertained the reader. Her books had a strong poetic flavor. As Alexander Maitland wrote, "It is not merely their descriptive or imaginative quality that marks them, but the way in which she evokes experience and, by treating it as a product of time, a moving thing, heightens and confers upon it the essence of poetry."[1]

Indeed, Stark was not just a traveler who described what she observed; she was a historian, a philosopher, and a poet who also described a country's culture and heritage to present a balanced, representative portrait of what she had experienced.

Three of her earliest books—*The Valleys of the Assassins and Other Persian Travels* (1934), *The Southern Gates of Arabia: A Journey in the Hadhramaut* (1936), and *Seen in the Hadhramaut* (1938)—not only described her travels but entertained readers with a certain amount of danger, intrigue, and romance, elements usually reserved for novels.

In *A Winter in Arabia,* published in 1940, Stark wrote about a female archaeologist who, as a result of her eccentric behavior and constant inquiries, annoyed Stark and the Arab women. On occasion she used humor to illustrate a point.

During World War II Stark worked for the British Information Ministry, and, according to Peter B. Flint, earned "prominence and honors for enhancing British influence and countering Axis propaganda in Aden, Yemen, Egypt, Iraq, and India."[2] In Iraq, for instance, she served as attaché to the British Embassy. Then she was sent to the United States, an experience she later described in *Dust in the Lion's Paw* and in *Letters: New Worlds for Old, 1943–46* (1978). Before the war ended, she worked for Lady Wavell, who was the Vicereine in India.

In 1947, at the age of 54, she married Stewart Perowne, a diplomat. However, they separated five years later, before she was awarded a Cross of the British Empire. Stark continued to travel and write. Indeed, she wrote a book on her journeys or a volume about her life every two or three years, until the late 1970s. She traveled to practically every country in Europe, Asia, and Africa, and described her numerous experiences in graphic detail. For instance, after traveling by vehicle and animal through Turkey, she wrote about Alexander the Great and his relationship with the Queen of Caria in *Alexander's Path: From Caria to Cilicia,* (1958). Again, she mixed the past with the present to make the story more fascinating than it would have been otherwise. Other books about Turkey, including *Gateways and Caravans: A Portrait of Turkey* (1971), and other places of interest followed.

In the early 1970s she was named a Dame of the British Empire. In the late 1970s and early 1980s, television film crews followed her as she explored the Euphrates River by raft and the Himalayas by donkey.

Stark made her home in Asolo, Italy, when she was not traveling. She died in May 1993; she was 100.

Her books of travel, primarily because of the various literary devices employed, were examples of literary journalism. In short, Stark was not just an observer who reported what she saw; she was a participant. She revealed each scene, examined the people involved, and captured the milieu. Thus, the reader learned to understand the country and its culture and consequently gained a much greater appreciation for the inhabitants and their customs, even if they seemed extremely different from the reader's own.

WORKS: *Baghdad Sketches* (1933); *The Valleys of the Assassins and Other Persian Travels* (1934); *The Southern Gates of Arabia: A Journey in the Hadhramaut* (1936); *Seen in the Hadhramaut* (1938); *A Winter in Arabia* (1940); *Traveller's Prelude* (1950); *Alexander's Path: From Caria to Cilicia* (1958).

NOTES

1. Alexander Maitland, "Dame Freya Stark: Journeys Through Space and Time," *Blackwood's Magazine* 328, no. 1982 (1980): 535.

2. Peter B. Flint, "Dame Freya Stark, Travel Writer, Is Dead at 100," *New York Times,* May 11, 1993, p. B7.

Richard Steele
(1672–1729)

Richard Steele and Joseph Addison met at the Charterhouse School and became lifelong friends. They attended Oxford. Addison, who studied Greek and Roman writers and published Latin compositions before graduation, was a more accomplished writer than Steele. Unlike Addison, Steele never graduated; he enlisted in the Guards. When he composed a poem on Queen Mary's death, which he dedicated to Lord Cutts, he was commissioned an ensign. He wrote several plays which were moderately successful, but he failed to make a comfortable living. He received a salary when he was appointed Gazetteer in 1709. His expenses, however, exceeded his income.

In the years following he frequently saw Addison and Jonathan Swift, both of whom contributed to the *Tatler,* which Steele published under the pseudonym Isaac Bickerstaff, a name he borrowed with permission from Swift's "Predictions for the year 1708, wherein the month and day of the month are set down, the persons named, and the great actions and events of next year particularly related, as they will come to pass. Written to prevent the people of England from being further imposed on by vulgar almanack-makers. By Isaac Bickerstaff, Esq."[1] The first issue appeared April 12, 1709. According to George Aitken, "the aim was to instruct the public what to think, after their reading, and there was to be something for the entertainment of the fair sex."[2]

The *Tatler,* a single folio sheet, appeared three times a week and cost a penny. Although initiated for the purpose of providing news (in his position as Gazetteer Steele knew what political activities were occurring), the need for these items died after the first 80 issues; rarely did Steele believe that some issue needed reporting.³ As Aitken explained:

The subject of each article was to be indicated by the name of the coffee-house or other place from which it was supposed to come: "All accounts of gallantry, pleasure, and entertainment shall be under the article of White's chocolate-house; Poetry, under that of Will's coffee-house; Learning, under the title of Grecian; Foreign and Domestic News you will have from Saint James's coffee-house; and what else I have to offer on any other subject shall be dated from my own apartment."⁴

The *Tatler* belonged to Steele; it was his idea, and most of the material was written by him. When the publication began, Addison was living in Ireland; in fact, he was unaware that Steele published the paper until a statement he had made to Steele appeared in one of the issues. Only then did he occasionally submit contributions. According to Aitken, Steele wrote approximately 188 of the 271 papers, while Addison wrote 42; together they were responsible for 36.⁵

The first four issues were characteristic of the paper. The reader found an account of a gentleman at White's chocolate-house who was saddened by a passing young lady; a notice of a benefit performance for Thomas Betterton; an account of the war with France; a declaration against John Partridge; a discussion on the morality of the stage; the benefit for Mrs. Bignell, which included a discourse on manners since a young man had attended the benefit intoxicated; a comparison of Chloe and Clarissa or Mrs. Chetwine and Mrs. Hales respectively; a satiric critique of the Italian opera, "Pyrrhus and Demetrius"; and an allegorical article on Felicia or Britain.⁶

According to Aitken, in addition to the disappearance of the news, the *Tatler*'s principal change "was the development of the sustained essay on morals or manners, and the less frequent indulgence in satire upon individual offenders, and in personal allusions in general."⁷ Addison's interests probably were taken into consideration, since he and Steele occasionally worked together and were close friends.

Although the *Tatler* was read for its genial treatment of human follies and weaknesses such as pride, vanity, and impudence, Steele incorporated sharp attacks on gambling, dueling, brutality, and drinking. His various characters were alive: they brought the reader from the clubs to the coffee-houses; the reader saw the poets, the politicians, the Templars, the merchants at the various coffee-houses; the reader saw Betterton, the plays, the audience; the reader saw Powell's puppetshow, the bear-baiting and prize-fights at Hockley-in-the-Hole; the reader experienced the Mall at St. James's or the Ring in Hyde Park; the reader visualized the fine ladies who shopped in Charles Lillie's, the perfumer, or in Mather's toy-shop, or in Motteux's china warehouse; the reader saw the men who shopped in the stores in the New Exchange and their expressions; the reader saw the prominent clergymen in their respective churches, and heard their messages on High and Low Church, Whig and Tory; the reader learned about the war with France, about the military leaders and their soldiers; the reader experienced the battles, including the glorious victories and the battered defeats.[8]

Steele lost his post as Gazetteer in October 1710 when the Whigs fell from power. The *Tatler* ceased publication on January 2, 1711. Steele died in 1729.

WORK: *Tatler* (1709–1711).

NOTES

1. George A. Aitken, ed., *The Tatler* (New York: Hadley and Mathews, 1899), pp. vii–x.

2. Ibid., p. xi.

3. Ibid.

4. Ibid., p. xii.

5. Ibid., p. xiv.

6. Ibid., pp. 11–45.

7. Ibid., p. xix.

8. Ibid., pp. xxiii–xxiv.

Lincoln Steffens
(1866–1936)

Born in San Francisco in 1866, Lincoln Steffens attended a military academy in San Mateo and the University of California, from which he graduated in 1889. Immediately following, he traveled abroad and attended the universities of Berlin, Heidelberg, and Liepzig, and the Sorbonne in Paris. When he returned to the United States in 1892 he settled in New York City, where he obtained a reporting position on the *New York Evening Post.* For five years he worked at the *Post,* advancing from reporting general news to covering Wall Street and later the police when Theodore Roosevelt was the commissioner. Steffens' reporting for the *Post,* which included Reverend Charles H. Parkhurst's accusations and revelations of a corrupt police force, helped earn him an excellent reputation. When he was offered the position of city editor of the *Commercial Advertiser* in 1897, he immediately accepted. Under Steffens, the paper published literary journalism by such writers as Abraham Cahan, who wrote about the Jewish ghetto, and Hutchins Hapgood, who wrote about the Bowery. Steffens encouraged this form of writing primarily because it allowed reporters to capture the unfortunate and their dismal environment.

Four years later, at the invitation of John S. Phillips, he became part of the staff of *McClure's* magazine, which included such revolutionary figures as Ida Tarbell and Ray Stannard Baker. Steffens, although he had accepted the managing editor's position, believed that he could better serve *McClure's* by traveling and reporting; S. S. McClure, the publisher, agreed.

Steffens traveled to St. Paul to write an article about Frederick Weyerhaeuser, who had become a millionnaire from the lumber business. He then traveled to St. Louis to investigate political corruption, which Joseph Folk, the circuit attorney, was fighting. With Claude H. Wetmore, a local journalist, Steffens wrote

"Tweed Days in St. Louis."[1] "The Shame of Minneapolis" followed. This article concerned Mayor Albert Alonzo Ames, who had been elected to the office four times, twice by the Republicans and twice by the Democrats. During his fourth term in office, he appointed his brother chief of police and appointed an ex-gambler chief of detectives. Approximately one-half of the police force was dismissed primarily because they were honest. Ames surrounded himself with criminals. In fact, prisoners from jails collected revenues. Steffens also informed readers how Minneapolis had been saved from Ames and his gang of criminals.[2]

Steffens revisited St. Louis and claimed that conditions there were worse than those he had witnessed in Minneapolis. Next, he visited Pittsburgh and found similar conditions there. Steffens then visited Philadelphia, Chicago, Cleveland, and Cincinnati. It seemed that every major city had problems—from police corruption to city bosses who hired common criminals.

As each article appeared, Steffens' popularity increased. In 1904 *The Shame of the Cities*, a collection of his city articles, was published. The same year he turned his attention to state governments and wrote several articles about Tom L. Johnson of Ohio and Robert M. La Follette of Wisconsin, who were fighting corruption in their states.

Two years later he and several other *McClure's* journalists purchased *Frank Leslie's Popular Monthly* and changed its name to the *American Magazine*. The same year his second book, *The Struggle for Self-Government*, appeared.

In 1907 he resigned from the *American* and worked as an editor at *Everybody's*, contributing background articles on the new reformers, who included Theodore Roosevelt and Eugene Debs. Two years later he published *Upbuilders*, which contained positive portraits of various reformers throughout the country.

For the next several years he traveled to Boston and to Los Angeles to report on conditions there and on the trial of two labor leaders, the McNamara brothers, who had been accused of exploding dynamite in the offices of the *Times*. The dynamite devastated the building and killed 21 persons. But instead of merely reporting the trial, Steffens tried to intervene; indeed, he attempted to negotiate a settlement between the newspaper's proprietor and the McNamaras. When his negotiations failed, Steffens was severely criticized and ostracized by the anti-reformist press and by his friends.

Before World War I, he traveled to Europe to gather information on municipal conditions; he found conditions there similar to those he had observed in American cities.

He traveled to Mexico to observe the Mexican Revolution. He admired Venustiano Carranza's courage and leadership.

Three years later he returned to Europe with Charles R. Crane to observe the war and study the February Revolution in Russia. He covered the Armistice negotiations, and in 1919 interviewed Lenin, whom he greatly respected. For the next eight years he spent most of his time in Europe. Reform was occurring there, and he was determined to witness the progress.

In 1927 he made his home in Carmel, California. His *Autobiography*, which was published in 1931, became a best-seller. Because of the book's popularity, he was asked to lecture throughout the country and to write for newspapers, which he did until suffering a heart attack in 1933. He died three years later.

WORKS: *The Shame of the Cities* (1904); *The Struggle for Self-Government* (1906); *Upbuilders* (1909); *Autobiography* (1931).

NOTES

1. Louis Filler, "Steffens, Lincoln," *Dictionary of American Biography,* edited by Robert Livingston Schuyler (New York: Charles Scribner's Sons, 1958), Vol. 22, pp. 625–626.

2. C. C. Regier, *The Era of the Muckrakers* (Chapel Hill: University of North Carolina Press, 1932), pp. 60–61.

Gloria Steinem
(1934–   )

Feminist, activist, columnist, writer, and editor Gloria Steinem was born on March 25, 1934, in Toledo, Ohio. Her father and mother divorced before she reached adolescence, but her mother, who had worked as a reporter before she married, obtained a similar position in Toledo and was able to support herself and her daughter somewhat modestly.

Steinem moved to Washington, D.C., to live with her older sister. When she completed her secondary education, her mother made financial arrangements for her to attend Smith College. Steinem proved to be an excellent student and soon received scholarships. When she graduated in 1956 she received a fellowship to travel and study at the universities of Delhi and Calcutta. Upon her return to the United States she first worked as the director of the Independent Research Service in Cambridge, Massachusetts, then as a writer for *Esquire* in New York City, to which she contributed "The Moral Disarmament of Betty Coed" and "Student Prince." Although she remained with *Esquire* for several years, she moved to *Show* in 1963. Perhaps her most important contribution to *Show* was "A Bunny Tale," which was based on her experience as a Bunny in a Playboy Club and was an example of literary journalism. Articles about her humorous exposé on Hugh Hefner's dream turned reality appeared in news magazines, and Steinem's career as a journalist was secure. Her by-line was seen in *Life, Vogue, McCall's, Cosmopolitan,* and *Glamour,* and she wrote for the NBC series "That Was the Week That Was."

Steinem, who became a celebrity not only for what she wrote but for what she advocated for women, wrote features on celebrities like James Baldwin, Julie Andrews, Jackie Kennedy, Barbra Streisand, Truman Capote, Michael Caine, Dame Margot Fonteyn, and Lee Bouvier, and on "Women and Power," Englishmen and their opinions of American women, fashion, "Pop Culture," Lefrak City, "*What* Culture," and women's liberation, to mention a few topics.

In each interview she conducted, Steinem intelligently captured the scene and her subject's personality, mannerisms, and moods. Some of her profiles included colorful descriptive passages that allowed the personalities to present themselves in their own words. For most interviews she included background information useful to the reader. Her advocacy articles logically explored issues that concerned her as a woman. Usually, she presented the facts, then what she believed should be done to correct the problems. If she believed that a problem could be better illustrated with description or anecdotes, she would use either or both.

In 1968 she was hired by Clay Felker to write for his newly resurrected *New York* magazine. Steinem wrote numerous advocacy articles about women, marriage, and politics. She attacked Eugene McCarthy and Richard Nixon; she supported Norman Mailer's and Jimmy Breslin's political aspirations; and she wrote and spoke with vehemence for numerous minority groups. Her *New York* column, "The City Politic," was never subtle as long as there was a cause of some kind to be espoused.

In the late 1960s she became involved in the feminist movement, and in 1972 became editor of *Ms.,* a magazine founded for the liberated woman. Its articles and columns promoted the ideas of Steinem and other feminists. The magazine had attracted 500,000 readers by the mid-1970s.

Steinem was one of the commissioners appointed by President Jimmy Carter to the National Committee on the Observance of International Women's Year in 1977. She was awarded a Woodrow Wilson Scholarship to study feminism at the Woodrow Wilson International Center for Scholars the same year.

During the 1980s she continued editing *Ms.* as well as supporting various women's organizations. A collection of her essays, articles, and diary entries was published in 1983 under the title *Outrageous Acts and Everyday Rebellions.* Included were "I Was a Playboy Bunny," "Ruth's Song," about her mother, and articles on several famous women. The collection was representative of literary journalism as well as advocacy journalism.

In 1986 her insightful biography of Marilyn Monroe was published. *Marilyn: Norma Jeane* was more realistic than earlier biographies of Monroe in the sense that it focused on her personality and her entire life, not just the years in Hollywood. Indeed, Steinem revealed a warm human being who had childlike qualities. Unfortunately, the child was trapped in a woman's body.

One year later *Ms.* was sold to a large Australian communications conglomerate. Steinem was retained as a consultant to the publication. Even when *Ms.* was sold again, Steinem remained at the publication. In 1988 she became an editorial consultant to Random House, a publishing firm.

In 1992 she published *Revolution from Within: A Book of Self-Esteem,* a self-help book aimed at helping readers boost their self-esteem. Steinem used numerous sources, including Margaret Mead and Chief Seattle, as well as her own life for inspiration. She offered literature, nature, art, meditation, and connectedness as means of finding and exploring the self.

In her review of the book for *Newsweek,* Laura Shapiro wrote:

Self-help books sell like crazy, especially among women, and Steinem's has everything: goddesses, guided meditation, directions on how to find the child within, dream diaries and droplets of wisdom from a range of sources including the Gnostic Gospels and Koko, the talking gorilla.[1]

Moving Beyond Words, a book of six essays (three previously published in magazines) appeared in 1994. Included were "What if *Freud* Were *Phyllis?*," in which she claimed that Freud's theories were based on the assumption of male superiority; "Sex, Lies and Advertising," in which she examined the advertising business as it applied to magazines; "The Strongest Woman in the World," about the female bodybuilder Bev Francis; "The Masculinization of Wealth," about wealthy women who had lost control of their trust funds; "Revolving Economics," in which she detailed how worldwide census and accounting practices undervalued women's labor; and "Doing Sixty," in which she explored her life at age 60.

WORKS: *Ms.* (co-founder and editor); *Outrageous Acts and Everyday Rebellions* (1983); *Revolution from Within: A Book of Self-Esteem* (1992); *Moving Beyond Words* (1994).

NOTE

1. Laura Shapiro, "Little Gloria, Happy at Last: Dear Ms. Steinem: All is forgiven. Please come home. We miss you," *Newsweek,* January 13, 1992, p. 64.

Harvey Swados
(1920–1972)

Better known as a novelist than as a journalist and essayist who promoted socialism for the working man, especially the blue-collar worker, Harvey Swados was born in Buffalo and received his bachelor's degree from the University of Michigan in 1940. Ironically, he was from the middle class. Upon graduation he worked for a few years in several factories while he tried to establish himself as a writer. From 1942 to 1945 he served as a radio officer in the U.S. Merchant Marine.

Swados wrote short stories and essays for various periodicals, including *Esquire, Partisan Review, Saturday Evening Post,* and the *Nation.* In 1955 his first novel, *Out Went the Candle,* was published, followed a year later by a collection of short stories, *On the Line,* about the problems of factory employees. Charles Shapiro wrote:

Swados has chosen to dramatize a steady tension between the dehumanizing effect of the line and the dreams of the workers who try, at first, to preserve their private enthusiasms—one man plans to be a professional singer, another worker wishes for a new car, a third wants his son's love—as the assembly belt rolls on. The factory must destroy the individuality of each man, and as this cruel process is exposed, we come to accept the line as well as despair of it. The little tragedies, placed together, become a damning indictment.[1]

Swados taught at several universities, including the University of Iowa, Sarah Lawrence College, San Francisco State University, and the University of Massachusetts at Amherst. He continued to write novels, among them *False Coin, The Will, Standing Fast,* and *Celebration* (published posthumously in 1975), as well as short stories, essays, and a biography of Estes Kefauver. His essays and short stories were collected and published as separate volumes. Swados died in 1972.

His essay "The Jungle Revisited" showed that although times had changed since Upton Sinclair wrote *The Jungle,* the basic problem was the same—a job in a meat-packing plant was not attractive to most workers. Indeed, it was not challenging, glamorous, or lucrative. An employee performed basically the same job as in Sinclair's day.

WORKS: *On the Line* (1956); *A Radical's America* (1962).

NOTE

1. Charles Shapiro, "Harvey Swados: Private Stories and Public Fiction," *Contemporary American Novelists,* edited by Harry T. Moore (Carbondale: Southern Illinois University Press, 1964), pp. 188–189.

T

Gay Talese
(1932-)

Gay Talese, the literary journalist whose *Esquire* article "Joe Lewis: The King as a Middle-Aged Man" influenced Tom Wolfe, was born in Ocean City, New Jersey, on February 7, 1932. A graduate of Ocean City High School, Talese attended the University of Alabama. Majoring in journalism, he wrote sports columns for the campus newspaper and contributed sports stories to the *Birmingham Post Herald*. His writing was greatly influenced by Red Smith of the *New York Herald Tribune*.

Upon graduation in 1953, Talese tried to get a job with the *Herald Tribune* as well as several other New York newspapers. Eventually, he obtained a position with the *New York Times*, for which he wrote—at least for the first two years—traditional news stories. In 1955, however, one of his vignettes of New York City life appeared in the *New York Times Magazine*. After that, his slices of city life appeared often in this publication.

Talese's talents were recognized by the *Times'* editors, and they promoted him to chief human interest writer when Meyer Berger, the *Times'* popular colorful feature writer (and literary journalist), died in 1959. A year later he contributed his first article to *Esquire*. According to Talese, it was "an essay on obscurity in New York City, a series of vignettes on the unnoticed people, the odd facts and bizarre events that had caught my fancy during my travels around town as a newspaperman."[1]

His contributions were collected and published under the title *New York—A Serendipiter's Journey* in 1961. Talese, who had tried to use the techniques of fiction in this collection, confessed that he had failed to do so. As he put it, "I did not get very far, . . . finally relying more on the selection of my material than on style to reflect the glamour and gloom that I have always felt so strongly in New York."[2]

His first literary journalistic articles were profiles of celebrities and were written for *Esquire.* His candid features on Joshua Logan, Frank Sinatra, Joe DiMaggio, and Peter O'Toole contained the ingredients necessary to be literary journalism. Indeed, Talese's ability to capture scenes and conversations, and even what the characters were thinking through interior monologues enabled the reader to learn more about them.

Talese spent several months researching his first book-length piece of nonfiction, *The Bridge,* about the building of the Verrazano-Narrows Bridge linking Brooklyn to Staten Island. Although the book was well received by reviewers, Talese believed he had not investigated the subject long enough. This was characteristic of Talese the reporter; he felt that he had to remain with a subject long enough to see life change in some way.

A second collection of articles entitled *The Overreachers* appeared in 1965, the year he resigned from the *Times* to devote his energy to writing articles and books. In 1966 he became a contributing editor at *Esquire,* for which he wrote articles about various subjects.

His next book was, ironically, a human interest history of that newspaper. Published in 1969, *The Kingdom and the Power* began with the purchase of the newspaper by Adolph Ochs and covered some 60 years. Talese, who had perfected the technique of interior monologue, used it frequently in his colorful, descriptive mammoth account; and he left nothing unsaid. Unlike most historical narratives, *The Kingdom and the Power* candidly presented the anguish, the tension, the petty squabbles, and the ill feelings among management, editors, and reporters. Critics praised the book for its intimate detail and dramatization, and it became a best-seller. However, a few of those portrayed did not particularly care for Talese's work, nor did they particularly enjoy his use of interior monologue. Some questioned whether he or any other reporter could actually know what a person was thinking. They failed to realize that Talese had spent several years researching the book and that he had worked at the newspaper for years.

A third book of articles, *Fame and Obscurity,* appeared in 1970. One year later, *Honor Thy Father,* Talese's revealing portrayal of the Mafia family headed by Joe Bonanno, was published. Talese, who had received the cooperation of Bonanno's son, Bill, researched the machinations of the underworld for six years and presented not only an accurate historical account of organized crime, but a tender portrait of Bill's life as well as his wife's and children's. Talese, who emphasized the differences in thinking between generations, removed the tarnished stereotypes and painted reality.

Talese did not have another book appear in bookstores until *Thy Neighbor's Wife* was published in 1980. A study of American sexuality, especially men's, the book was severely criticized by reviewers for its shallowness. However, psychologists and sociologists praised its honest portrayal of Americans after the sexual revolution. Talese was not pretending to be a psychologist or sociologist; rather, he reported on what he saw and heard.

Unto the Sons, the story of the great wave of Italian immigration that began about 1900, was published in 1992. Talese, through one family's experience, primarily his grandfather's and father's, detailed the difficult world the immigrants had left behind as well as the world that seemed to offer hope. The book was Talese's first about people he had known and loved.

WORKS: *New York—A Serendipiter's Journey* (1961); *The Bridge* (1964); *The Overreachers* (1965); *The Kingdom and the Power* (1969); *Fame and Obscurity* (1970); *Honor Thy Father* (1971); *Thy Neighbor's Wife* (1980); *Unto the Sons* (1992).

NOTES

1. Gay Talese, *Fame and Obscurity* (New York: World Publishing, 1970), p. viii.
2. Ibid., p. ix.

Ida Tarbell
(1857–1944)

Samuel Sidney McClure founded *McClure's* magazine in 1893. McClure had a stable of writers who contributed dozens of articles. One was Ida Tarbell, who was born in 1857 in Pennsylvania. Her father was a carpenter who later built wooden oil tanks, and her mother was a teacher. In high school, Tarbell developed an interest in science, particularly biology. After she graduated she attended Allegheny College. Upon graduation she accepted a teaching position at Poland Union Seminary in Poland, Ohio. Within two years she had had enough of teaching and returned to Allegheny College, where she received a master's degree. She was hired by the editor of the *Chautauguan,* a monthly magazine that was conservative in its editorial policy. After a year she became the managing editor.

After eight years of writing and editing, she traveled to Paris, where she remained for two years. She lived with friends, wrote articles about Paris and France for American newspapers, wrote a short story for *Scribner's* magazine, attended lectures at the Sorbonne, and did research on the French Revolution, especially on Madame Roland.

In 1892 S. S. McClure met her and persuaded her to write a biography of Louis Pasteur. This was published a year later. When she returned to the United States in 1894, McClure hired her to write more biographies, including a series on Napoleon Bonaparte and a series on Abraham Lincoln.

Her biographies were so successful that Tarbell was made an associate editor of the magazine. McClure realized her potential and valued her past work; it was no surprise when he gave her what eventually became the most ambitious assignment of her career, *The History of the Standard Oil Company.* For five years she researched and investigated the company. The 19 articles she wrote for *McClure's* were published in a two-volume set in 1904. According to James Playsted Wood:

The articles showed that Standard Oil was magnificently organized, that it functioned superbly, but that the methods by which the corporation had been built included bribery, fraud, violence, the corruption of public officials and railroads, and the wrecking of competitors by fair means and foul. What had started out to be a study of a great business became, by virtue of the facts uncovered, an expose of big business as sometimes practiced.[1]

The articles glorified her name in the public's eye, but some businessmen and politicians had little respect for her. They believed she had unjustly given the Standard Oil Company a bad name. However, for fear of being exposed, they tolerated her.

In 1905 she traveled through Kansas and Oklahoma and reported on the oil strikes and the controversies that resulted. Two years later the federal government filed antitrust suits against the Standard Oil Company.

Tarbell, together with other frustrated editors and writers at *McClure's*, including John S. Phillips, Ray Stannard Baker, Lincoln Steffens, and Albert Boyden, purchased *Frank Leslie's Popular Monthly* in 1906. They immediately changed the periodical's name to the *American Magazine* and recruited Finley Peter Dunne and William Allen White.

Tarbell wrote articles for the new magazine about the tariff and about women. An independent woman herself, Tarbell did not sympathize with the suffrage movement. Through observation and investigation she had grown to distrust politicians and other leaders who claimed they could achieve human progress through politics and group activity.

When Henry Ford implemented his assembly line system, Tarbell traveled extensively from one factory to another and reported on her observations. Perhaps progress was on the way. She resigned from the *American Magazine* in 1915 but continued to write and lecture for the next 20 years. For instance, in 1919 she traveled abroad to report on the Paris Peace Conference. In 1926 she went to Italy to report on Mussolini's industrial ideas, which she respected.

In addition to articles and short stories, she wrote several biographies. She died in 1944.

WORK: *The History of the Standard Oil Company* (1904).
NOTE
1. James Playsted Wood, *Magazines in the United States* (New York: Ronald Press, 1971), p. 132.

Studs Terkel
(1912–)

Studs Terkel, who practiced what he called "guerrilla journalism" when he wrote *Division Street: America* (1967), *Hard Times: An Oral History of the*

Great Depression (1970), *Working: People Talk About What They Do All Day and How They Feel About What They Do* (1974), and *American Dreams: Lost and Found* (1980), was born in the Bronx on May 16, 1912. When he was 11 he moved with his family to Chicago, where his father, Samuel, worked as a tailor until he developed heart disease; his mother, Anna, operated the Wells-Grand Hotel, which catered to blue-collar employees. Terkel attended public schools, Crane Junior College, the University of Chicago, from which he graduated in 1932, and the University of Chicago Law School.

After he received his law degree, he accepted a position with the government that required him to move first to Omaha, Nebraska, then to Washington, D.C. Before he returned to Chicago in 1935 he had performed in a theatrical production of *It Can't Happen Here*. In Chicago he wrote radio shows and acted in radio soap operas and in theatrical productions. According to *Current Biography:*

In 1945 he established *Wax Museum,* the first of the diversified radio programs he has since conducted on station WFMT, Chicago. In that, as in *Studs Terkel Almanac,* launched in 1958, he exhibited an uncanny flair for engaging people in spontaneous interviews, thanks to his warmth, curiosity, and empathy.[1]

"Studs' Place," a television program that lasted from 1949 to 1953, shared the same traits as his radio program.

In the 1950s and 1960s he wrote a jazz column for the *Chicago Sun-Times,* wrote a book about jazz artists, acted in several theatrical productions, lectured, narrated documentary films, hosted several music festivals, and wrote a play that was eventually produced. However, it was his books that gained him national and international recognition. Especially popular was *"The Good War": An Oral History of World War II* (1984), which portrayed the national experience through the words of the men and women who lived it.

In 1987 he wrote a realistic memoir that captured the contradictions, ethnic diversities, colorful personalities, and moods of a large midwestern city in *Chicago.* Terkel discussed controversial politicians as well as other questionable characters.

A year later he portrayed the America of the 1980s in *The Great Divide: Second Thoughts on the American Dream.* For this book, Terkel interviewed many interesting characters, including Pastor Douglas Roth, a defrocked steel-town minister; Tom Grissom, a nuclear physicist who grew disillusioned with producing nuclear weapons and subsequently quit his position; and Jean Gump, a mother of 12 who was sentenced to prison for destroying federal property in connection with a 1986 peace demonstration at a Missouri missile site. This book contained the same ingredients as his other notable books in that he allowed others, particularly average citizens, to share their beliefs and concerns about life as well as their country.

Terkel explored race relations in *Race: How Blacks and Whites Think and*

Feel About the American Obsession, which was published in 1992. Terkel interviewed almost 80 men and women, both black and white, who lived in or near Chicago. Most of the whites had lived or worked alongside blacks for most of their adult lives, and most came across as being tolerant and sensitive to signs of prejudice. In essence, overt racism seldom surfaced in any of the interviews, which was a positive sign that society, at least in and around Chicago, had made great strides toward racial harmony.

In *Coming of Age,* published in 1995, he examined the elderly's hopes and fears. From his interviews with people over 70, he found them to be stubborn, skeptical of politicians, and even despairing of the young. He also learned that they were in touch with themselves.

Unlike most writers, Terkel used a tape recorder to record his numerous conversations with people. For example, his *Division Street: America* contained almost 100 conversations with as many people. These conversations with rich, poor, young, and old Americans showed their attitudes toward a number of issues. He used the same formula for his other books. For instance, *American Dreams: Lost and Found* exemplified Terkel's unique form of reportage; in most cases, he included descriptions of the interviewees' offices or the rooms where the interviews took place. Like *Division Street, Coming of Age* and *American Dreams* were critically and commercially successful.

WORKS: *Division Street: America* (1967); *Hard Times: An Oral History of the Great Depression* (1970); *Working: People Talk About What They Do All Day and How They Feel About What They Do* (1974); *American Dreams: Lost and Found* (1980); *"The Good War": An Oral History of World War II* (1984); *Chicago* (1987); *The Great Divide: Second Thoughts on the American Dream* (1988); *Race: How Blacks and Whites Think and Feel About the American Obsession* (1992).

NOTE

1. Charles Moritz, ed., *Current Biography 1974* (New York: H. W. Wilson, 1974), p. 405.

Hunter S. Thompson
(1939–)

Gonzo (participatory) journalist Hunter S. Thompson was born to Virginia and Jack Thompson on July 18, 1939, in Louisville, Kentucky. His career as a reporter began when he wrote sports stories for an air force base newspaper in Florida. Thompson, who would later exhibit his disagreeable temperament, was honorably discharged two years before his enlistment was up because of his nonconformist attitude toward the military.

On his release from the air force, he accepted a position as a reporter with the *Middletown Record,* where his attitude toward a story differed from that of the editors. Thompson was immediately dismissed. He landed a job with *Time,* but the same thing happened.

Such misfortune would have forced some journalists to reflect and reconsider their attitudes or beliefs on editorial policy, but not Thompson. He rebelled. (And this may be the key to his popularity, especially in the late 1960s and early 1970s.) Thompson moved to the Caribbean, where he worked for a bowling magazine and contributed to the *New York Herald Tribune.* When the magazine ceased publication he returned to California, where he tried writing a novel. It was never published.

For the next two years he traveled through South America and wrote stories for the old *National Observer.* According to *Current Biography,* he continued to write for the newspaper when he returned to the United States, but quit "when it refused to let him cover the 'Free Speech' movement at the University of California at Berkeley."[1]

Thompson remained in California and wrote articles for such publications as the *Nation* and the *Realist.* One article for the *Nation,* suggested by the magazine's editor, Carey McWilliams, concerned the Hell's Angels, the infamous motorcycle gang. According to Leonard Downie, Jr., Thompson began riding with them in California:

Their drinking and brawling was wild, although Thompson's research, including the searching out of original police records, disproved many of the reports of gang rapes and terrorizing of entire towns that had been reported as fact in the California attorney general's report and other articles.[2]

The article brought offers from publishing companies, and Thompson quickly signed a contract with Random House. He rode with the gang for a few additional months, until he was physically harmed by several members:

The first blow was launched with no hint of warning and I thought for a moment that it was just one of those drunken accidents that a man has to live with in this league. But within seconds I was clubbed from behind by the Angel I'd been talking to just a moment earlier. Then I was swarmed in a general flail.[3]

When *Hell's Angels* was published critics praised Thompson's personal, realistic, appropriate style and his use of factual description. Many considered the book the most accurate depiction of the motorcycle gang ever written.

Two years later Thompson covered the 1968 Democratic convention in Chicago and witnessed confrontations between antiwar demonstrators and police officers. What he experienced influenced his attitudes toward the Establishment, attitudes that later shaped his reporting.

In 1970 he produced perhaps the first piece of what was later described as gonzo journalism. "The Kentucky Derby Is Decadent and Depraved," an emotionally charged first-person account of his experiences at the Derby, appeared in *Scanlan's Monthly.* Thompson depicted himself as an out-of-focus character on the border of lunacy. The story was indicative of Thompson's style and of literary journalism. Though he used the first-person point of view in this story, he used personae in other stories.

In 1970 Thompson joined the staff of Jann Wenner's *Rolling Stone,* which had been founded in 1967 primarily for readers who enjoyed popular music. By 1970 the magazine's coverage had expanded. Other publications, most of which were considered underground or alternative rags, began to compete. Thompson's ability to entertain as well as inform readers what was happening nationally gave *Rolling Stone* an edge over its competitors. Article followed article, from "The Battle of Aspen: Freak Power in the Rockies" to "Fear and Loathing in Las Vegas," and Thompson's reputation as *the* gonzo journalist grew. Crawford Woods said of the book *Fear and Loathing in Las Vegas: A Savage Journey to the Heart of the American Dream* (1971): "The form that reached apotheosis in *Armies of the Night* reaches the end of its rope in Fear and Loathing, a chronicle of addiction and dismemberment so vicious that it requires a lot of resilience to sense that the author's purpose is more moralizing than sadistic."[4]

Thompson's persona in the book was called "Raoul Duke," a name referred to by still another persona, "Dr. Thompson," in his 1973 book *Fear and Loathing on the Campaign Trail '72.* Although the latter book was for the most part true to gonzo journalism, Thompson mixed fantasy with fact to depict the 1972 presidential campaign and as a result received some criticism. However, his knowledge of political shenanigans was unequalled, as was his ability to forecast George McGovern's rise in the Democratic party.

Thompson's output for *Rolling Stone* began to decline after 1973. Although he wrote a comparative gonzo article on Vince Lombardi and Richard Nixon, several articles on the Vietnam War, and a political piece on Jimmy Carter, disagreements with Wenner and physical fatigue forced Thompson to leave the magazine in the mid-1970s. A collection of his writing, *The Great Shark Hunt: Strange Tales from a Strange Time,* was published in 1979. A year later he worked on the film *Where the Buffalo Roam,* which portrayed several of his characters.

His high-energy personal reporting was evident in *The Curse of Lono,* published in 1983. This book chronicled his various misadventures in Hawaii. Thompson's longtime illustrator, Ralph Steadman, had traveled with him. The book was vintage Thompson, to say the least, as he ranted and raved in a number of passages. Indeed, it seemed to have been written not in the conservative 1980s, but during the liberal 1960s, when Thompson was frequently using drugs and alcohol and then writing about incidents from his dazed perspective.

Generation of Swine: Tales of Shame and Degradation in the Eighties, Gonzo Papers, Vol. 2 (1988) collected articles previously published in the *San Francisco Chronicle* and other publications. *Songs of the Doomed: More Notes from the Death of the American Dream,* another collection of previously published articles, appeared three years later.

Thompson, who contributed articles to *Esquire,* the *Nation,* and *Harper's,* was listed on the masthead of *Rolling Stone* in 1994. The same year *Better than*

Sex: Confessions of a Political Junkie: Gonzo Papers Volume 4 was published. In this book, Thompson examined the Clinton presidential campaign to the point that he became a part of it.

WORKS: *Hell's Angels: A Strange and Terrible Saga* (1966); *Fear and Loathing in Las Vegas: A Savage Journey to the Heart of the American Dream* (1971); *Fear and Loathing on the Campaign Trail '72* (1973); *The Great Shark Hunt: Strange Tales from a Strange Time* (1979); *The Curse of Lono* (1983); *Generation of Swine: Tales of Shame and Degradation in the Eighties, Gonzo Papers, Vol. 2* (1988); *Songs of the Doomed: More Notes from the Death of the American Dream* (1991); *Better than Sex: Confessions of a Political Junkie: Gonzo Papers Volume 4* (1994).

NOTES

1. Charles Moritz, ed., *Current Biography Yearbook 1981* (New York: H. W. Wilson, 1981), p. 417.

2. Leonard Downie, Jr., *The New Muckrakers* (Washington, D.C.: New Republic Book Co., 1976), p. 216.

3. Hunter S. Thompson, *Hell's Angels: A Strange and Terrible Saga* (New York: Random House, 1966), p. 277.

4. Crawford Woods, "Fear and Loathing in Las Vegas by Hunter S. Thompson," *New York Times Book Review*, Sunday, July 23, 1972, p. 17.

Thomas Thompson
(1933–1982)

Reporter and editor Thomas Thompson, who was born in Texas in 1933, graduated from the University of Texas in 1955. For the next six years he worked as a reporter and later city editor at the *Houston Press*. He spent the next eleven years working in various capacities—from staff writer to Paris bureau chief—at *Life*. In 1972 he resigned to devote his time to writing book-length pieces of literary nonfiction. In 1973 his dramatic account of a Long Island father killing his drug addict son appeared. Titled *Richie: The Ultimate Tragedy Between One Decent Man and the Son He Loved*, the book contained the intensity and the emotion usually reserved for novels.

Thompson, who contributed articles and features to such periodicals as *New West, New Times, New York, McCall's,* and *Cosmopolitan,* wrote the disturbing *Blood and Money* in 1976, which was made into a mini-series for television. The book concerned the tragic death of a Texas socialite and the odd events that followed it. Thompson's narrative raised more questions than it answered about how the socialite died. Had she been murdered by her husband? Had her husband been murdered by a burglar?

Thompson died in 1982.

WORKS: *Richie: The Ultimate Tragedy Between One Decent Man and the Son He Loved* (1973); *Blood and Money* (1976).

Calvin Trillin
(1935–)

Calvin Trillin, a practitioner of personal journalism or literary journalism primarily for the *New Yorker,* was born on December 5, 1935, to Jewish immigrants from Eastern Europe who had settled in Kansas City, Missouri. His father, Abe Trillin, owned several grocery stores in addition to a restaurant. However, Calvin was a regular at Arthur Bryant's Barbecue, which he later made famous.

Trillin attended Southwest High School in Kansas City, but he did not display any talent in writing. Upon his graduation, his father urged him to attend Yale University. Trillin accepted his father's advice. At Yale, he majored in English and edited the *Yale Daily News.* Trillin received his bachelor's degree in 1957.

For the next two years, he served in the U.S. Army. Upon his release, he was hired as a correspondent for *Time* magazine. He worked out of Atlanta, Georgia, before he became a staff writer at *Time*'s offices in New York City. Trillin stayed at *Time* three years, until 1963, when he moved to the *New Yorker,* where William Shawn allowed him the freedom to cover practically any topic he desired. Indeed, Trillin's first article, which appeared in three parts in the magazine, was an example of personal journalism in the sense that he was a participant as well as an observer in what he reported. The article covered racial integration on the campus of the University of Georgia, specifically the experience of Charlayne Hunter (Gault) and Hamilton Holmes, who were the first black students admitted to the university. Trillin expanded the article for the book *An Education in Georgia: The Integration of Charlayne Hunter and Hamilton Holmes,* which was published in 1964.

Trillin's next book, *Barnett Frummer Is an Unbloomed Flower, and Other Adventures of Barnett Frummer, Rosalie Mondle, Roland Magruder, and Their Friends* (1969), was a collection of humorous short stories that had appeared in the *New Yorker* from 1963 to 1967.

In 1971 his *New Yorker* "U.S. Journal" articles, contributed to the magazine from 1967 to 1970, were published as *U.S. Journal.* The collection was arranged in seven sections—"Killings," "Traveling People," "The South," "Middle-Sized Events," "Home Front," "Buying and Selling," and "Black and White"—and the articles in each section focused on ordinary individuals who murdered, fought with, or kidnapped others. Of course, as he traveled across the United States, he met others who were not necessarily criminals in the strictest sense of the term but who suffered from anger or hostility and consequently caused pain in others nonetheless. Trillin's writing was personal; yet his style was such that it often caused the reader to become emotional, even upset. His style sparkled with humor, too, primarily for balance.

Trillin's next subject was food. Beginning in 1970, he contributed articles about restaurants and food to several publications, including *Life,* the *Atlantic, Playboy,* and the *New Yorker.* However, he did not write about so-called highly rated places; instead, he examined restaurants that catered to the masses, even to the lower classes—establishments that served hamburgers, hot dogs, pizzas, and spaghetti, for instance. These articles were collected and published under the title *American Fried: Adventures of a Happy Eater* in 1974. A second collection of articles about food and eateries, *Alice, Let's Eat: Further Adventures of a Happy Eater,* appeared in 1978. This collection was nominated for a National Book Award in 1980. A third collection appeared in 1983. *Third Helpings* featured restaurants that served turkey, roast pigeon, fried seaweed, sausage sandwiches, fried chicken, fried catfish, and oysters, among other foods.

In 1978, when Victor Navasky became editor of the *Nation,* he asked Trillin to contribute a column. Trillin agreed; it began as "Variations" and soon became "Uncivil Liberties" and appeared every three weeks. Eight years later, the column became a weekly for the King Features Syndicate, which distributed it to newspapers. The *Nation* continued to publish Trillin's column every three weeks, as before. It was about 1,000 words in length and covered any topic Trillin desired to explore. Through humor and fabrication, Trillin's columns presented unusual insights into what was ailing the nation, and every politician was fair game. They were collected in the books *Uncivil Liberties* (1982) and *With All Disrespect: More Uncivil Liberties* (1985).

In 1984, 16 of his "U.S. Journal" stories about suicide, murder, and manslaughter were collected and published under the title *Killings.* These stories concerned the deaths of ordinary citizens. Empathy as well as intelligence were present in each story, as several reviewers noted. William E. Geist wrote:

Mr. Trillin lays out his thorough reporting in simple, straightforward fashion, allowing himself only a few jabs and one-liners. For the most part this unornamental style is all to the good, the material being engrossing, even riveting in such cases as "Melisha Morganna Gibson," about child abuse in Cleveland, Tenn., and "It's Just Too Late," about a Knoxville girl who foretells her death in a poem.[1]

In the same review, Geist referred to Trillin's reportage as art.

Trillin explored individuals and their behavior almost from a sociological perspective. Indeed, he observed individuals and questioned their motives; he seemed to penetrate their minds, until he understood the causes for their animalistic behavior. He described individuals about whom he wrote in depth, and he allowed readers to hear them speak, as long as the words helped define their character.

These articles were examples of literary journalism. Trillin also wrote fiction. *Runestruck,* his first novel, was published in 1977; *Floater,* his second, was published in 1980. However, his nonfiction columns and magazine articles attracted the most attention.

If You Can't Say Something Nice (1987), a collection of essays, dealt in somewhat humorous terms with people and places, including bellhops in the Southwest, Trillin's children, public figures, George Gipp ("the Gipper"), yuppies, a 25th wedding anniversary, and a neon beer sign. Two years later another collection, *Travels with Alice,* appeared. It was based on his tours to Europe and elsewhere with his wife and two daughters. The collection was similar to his earlier books about restaurants and food.

Enough's Enough (And Other Rules of Life), another collection of columns about the lighter sides of life, was published in 1990. Trillin wrote in smartly tailored prose about visiting Italy with his family, where he ultimately learned that every member of his family was smarter than he. A year later 12 articles that had appeared in the *New Yorker* were published in *American Stories.* They examined people who were not necessarily representative of average citizens. Indeed, Trillin looked at camp celebrities as well as certain criminals from a fresh, insightful perspective.

Remembering Denny, about his friend Denny Hansen, was published in 1993. Hansen, who in 1957 seemed to have everything—a dazzling smile, a degree from Yale, an appointment as a Rhodes Scholar, a seemingly prosperous future, and friends who regarded him practically as an icon—committed suicide in 1991. Trillin attempted to learn why he had taken his life. He explored various problems that had plagued Hansen, particularly during his last few years. Trillin emphasized that Hansen, who had been expected to succeed, who had been expected to be something great, had failed—at least to his own mind. He was bothered by failure so much that it caused him to end his life. By concentrating on the last few years of his life, Trillin failed to depict the psychological changes that apparently had occurred in Hansen from 1957 until his death. Nonetheless, the book was an interesting study of how social pressure can influence one's perception of oneself.

Trillin published a collection of satirical poems and essays entitled *Deadline Poet: Or, My Life as a Doggerelist* in 1994. His essays deflated the images of Ross Perot, Dan Quayle, David Duke, and Margaret Thatcher. He satirized the Supreme Court, Madonna, Father's Day, Germany's reunification, and Princess Di, among others, in witty verse. He examined the Bush-Clinton presidential campaigns and concluded that both seemed to blend together, somewhere in the middle. The collection was vintage Trillin.

In 1995 the collection *Too Soon to Tell* was published. Funny and acerbic, the book contained some 90 columns about topics like monkfish and ghost-written books.

WORKS: *An Education in Georgia: The Integration of Charlayne Hunter and Hamilton Holmes* (1964); *U.S. Journal* (1971); *Killings* (1984); *If You Can't Say Something Nice* (1987); *American Stories* (1991); *Remembering Denny* (1993).

NOTE

1. William E. Geist, "Death in These United States," *New York Times Book Review,* February 19, 1984, p. 15.

Mark Twain
(1835–1910)

Mark Twain (born Samuel Langhorn Clemens) was the author of perhaps the greatest novel ever to appear in the United States, *The Adventures of Huckleberry Finn,* which was published in 1885. Like *The Adventures of Tom Sawyer,* which had been published nine years earlier, it was based on experiences Twain had as a child. Twain had written an even earlier book, *The Innocents Abroad, or The New Pilgrims' Progress; Being Some Account of the Steamship Quaker City's Pleasure Excursion to Europe and the Holy Land, with Descriptions of Countries, Nations, Incidents and Adventures, as They Appeared to the Author,* which was entertaining and informative. This book of foreign travel was based partly on the notebook he had used to record his observations and partly on the letters he had contributed to the *New York Herald,* the *New York Tribune,* and the San Francisco *Daily Alta California. The Innocents Abroad* was an early example of literary journalism.

Twain, who had been born in Florida, Missouri, on November 30, 1835, apprenticed to a printer at 12 and piloted boats on the Mississippi at 17, before he worked for the *Territorial Enterprise* of Virginia City, Nevada, and later the *Morning Call* of San Francisco. He contributed articles to the *Golden Era,* the *Californian,* the *Union,* and *Harper's Magazine.* He wrote letters and short stories for various newspapers and magazines, including the *Sunday Mercury* and the *Saturday Press.*

When Twain made the trip abroad he was traveling correspondent for the San Francisco *Daily Alta California.* Consequently, the paper received 50 of the 58 letters in which he described his journey.[1] Twain visited Gibraltar, Tangier, Marseilles, Paris, Versailles, Genoa, Milan, Venice, Florence, Pisa, Rome, Naples, Athens, Constantinople, Odessa, Yalta, Syria, Palestine, Egypt, and Spain, among other cities and countries.[2]

When *The Innocents Abroad* was published in 1869, Twain was no longer writing for the *Daily Alta California.* He had moved east and was seeing Olivia Langdon, whom he married a year later.

Throughout the rest of his life, Twain enjoyed what seemed unparalleled popularity both in the United States and abroad from writing and lecturing. Stories he had heard, together with people he had met, filled novel after novel. Yet during the 1890s his life shattered like glass. Having very little business sense, he was unexpectedly bankrupt; the daughter whom he favored suddenly died; and the thought of having to sell himself through novels and lectures irritated him to the extent that he grew insecure. For 11 years—from about 1878 to 1900—he lived abroad; during 1895 and 1896 he lectured throughout the world.

Trying desperately to earn enough to pay his debts, this self-imposed exile caused his health to deteriorate; he defied death, however, and lived an additional 10 years, until 1910.

WORKS: *The Innocents Abroad, or The New Pilgrims' Progress; Being Some Account of the Steamship Quaker City's Pleasure Excursion to Europe and the Holy Land, with Descriptions of Countries, Nations, Incidents and Adventures, as They Appeared to the Author* (1869).

NOTES

1. Daniel McKeithan, ed., *(Traveling with the) The Innocents Abroad—Mark Twain* (Norman: University of Oklahoma Press, 1958), p. ix.

2. Ibid.

V

Gore Vidal
(1925–   )

Eugene Luther Vidal, known as Gore Vidal, was born on October 3, 1925, at the United States Military Academy at West Point, New York. His father was an instructor in aeronautics. Vidal favored his father over his mother, although he enjoyed being with his grandfather, Thomas Pryor Gore, who was Oklahoma's first senator. Vidal stayed with his grandfather in Washington, D.C., until his parents divorced in 1935. He learned about history and politics from reading books on the subjects to his grandfather, who was blind, as well as from leading his grandfather around the nation's capital. He attended St. Alban's School, then the Los Alamos School in New Mexico for a year. He completed his high school education at the prestigious Phillips Exeter Academy where, in addition to writing for the academy's *Review,* he organized a student group that opposed America's involvement in World War II. His political philosophy had been molded by his grandfather's isolationist beliefs.

When he graduated in 1943, he had intended to enroll at Harvard. However, he enlisted in the U.S. Army Reserve Corps and served on a transport ship in the Aleutians. Vidal read in his off-duty hours and wrote a novel, *Williwaw,* about the conflicts between crew members on board a military craft. It was published in 1946.

Vidal was released from service in 1946, and obtained a position editing books at E. P. Dutton in New York City. Within six months he left Dutton and moved to Antigua, Guatemala; Vidal believed he could earn his living by writing novels. *In a Yellow Wood,* which he had completed before he left New York City, appeared in 1947, to mostly favorable reviews. The novel concerned a veteran of World War II who had to adjust to civilian life. *The City and the Pillar* dealt with one character's realization that he was a homosexual. Some reviewers attacked it for its subject matter, when it was published in 1948.

Vidal, who had hepatitis in 1947, returned to the United States before he toured Europe. He traveled through North Africa as well as Italy. After about two years, he returned to the United States. In 1950 he purchased "Edgewater," a mansion at Tarrytown, New York. Over the next several years he wrote *The Season of Comfort* (1949), a slightly disguised autobiography of his early years; *A Search for the King* (1950), which described the search of Blondel de Neel for Richard the Lion-Hearted; *Dark Green, Bright Red* (1950), on the various exploits of an American mercenary soldier; *The Judgment of Paris* (1952), about an American who wandered through Europe; and *Messiah* (1954), which focused on a new religion. These novels were dismissed by most critics, and Vidal's financial resources dwindled. His estate required maintenance, and it was evident that his novels were not going to sell.

Vidal wrote teleplays for several television programs. Later, he moved to Hollywood and wrote screenplays for Metro-Goldwyn-Mayer. Vidal's intention was to earn enough money in a relatively brief period to enable him to return to writing novels. Toward the end of the 1950s, however, he wrote for the stage. His first success was an adaptation of his *Visit to a Small Planet,* which had appeared on television in 1955. *The Best Man,* a satire about American politics, followed in 1960. He wrote other plays, but they were less successful.

By the early 1960s he had returned to the novel. *Julian,* published in 1964, concerned Flavius Claudius Julianus, the Roman emperor who attempted to restore paganism. *Washington, D.C.,* the first novel in his series about American history and politics, was published in 1967. *Burr* followed in 1973, and was enjoyed by critics. The last book in the series, *1876,* was published in 1976; some reviewers criticized it for not having a major character to carry the plot.

Vidal also wrote the controversial satire *Myra Breckinridge* (1968), which focused on transsexuality and American culture. It was followed in 1974 by *Myron,* about the further exploits of Myra. The critics panned the latter because its situations were too repetitive.

Although Vidal penned other historical and political novels, including *Creation* (1981), *Lincoln* (1984), *Empire* (1987), *Hollywood* (1990), and *Live from Golgotha* (1992), he also wrote numerous advocacy essays for periodicals throughout the 1950s, 1960s, 1970s, and 1980s. These essays, on politics, Broadway, literature, public television, writers, pornography, sex, flying, and himself, were collected in numerous books, including *Rocking the Boat, Sex, Death, and Money, Reflections Upon a Sinking Ship, Matters of Fact and Fiction (Essays 1973–1976), The Second American Revolution and Other Essays (1976–1982), At Home: Essays 1982–1988, A View from the Diner's Club: Essays 1987–1991, The Decline and Fall of the American Empire,* and *United States: Essays, 1952–1992.* Robert Graalman wrote of his essays:

Vidal argues just as emphatically for his beliefs as he does to reject a political tag. He can be an articulate and vigorous commentator against, for example, such a topic as the horrors of television advertising, for something as grand as governmental responsibility, and most forcibly for a more humane, realistic, and finally liberating attitude on the subject of sexuality in Western civilization.[1]

His essays contained personal references to others as well as allusions to historical events and figures. Many contained clips from his past. However, in several essays about politics, one theme was ever present—that the United States was controlled by a few power brokers and corporations such as the Chase Manhattan Bank and CBS. Robert E. Kiernan called Vidal "a vocal critic of the American establishment."[2] In summarizing his assessment of Vidal's essays, Kiernan wrote: "The essays, like the novels, are a banquet of canapes. They may leave one hungry for logical fair play, as the novels leave one hungry for plot, but the canapes are so tasty withal that more conventional fare seems unflavored."[3]

In his review of *Reflections Upon a Sinking Ship*, Edgar Z. Friedenberg wrote that

Americans who are devoted to freedom remain by and large committed to the belief that freedom should be enjoyed by all the people; that democracy is the proper source of liberty and dignity, which all would come to share and prize if democracy were functioning properly. Vidal's book is both haunted and held together by the implication that this belief is false. But he himself never concludes that it is.[4]

The book revealed Vidal's ability to capture certain moments in time. For instance, he painted an accurate portrait of Richard Nixon as he was about to speak at the 1968 Republican convention. The essay was an example of literary journalism primarily because Vidal incorporated realistic, if not authentic, dialogue, accurate description, and scene-by-scene construction to depict a historical event.

In 1992 he wrote *The Screening of History*, in which he mixed reminiscences of his childhood and early manhood with films he saw when he was young. An unusual autobiography because of this technique, it nonetheless showed another side of Vidal.

His *Palimpsest: A Memoir* was published in 1995. Vidal discussed various people, including many celebrities, he had met or known in this unkindly memoir.

WORKS: *Rocking the Boat* (1962); *Sex, Death, and Money* (1968); *Reflections Upon a Sinking Ship* (1968); *Homage to Daniel Shays: Collected Essays, 1952–1972* (1972); *Matters of Fact and Fiction (Essays 1973–1976)* (1977); *The Second American Revolution and Other Essays (1976–1982)* (1982); *Armageddon? Essays, 1983–1987* (1987); *At Home: Essays 1982–1988* (1988); *A*

View from the Diner's Club: Essays 1987–1991 (1991); *The Decline and Fall of the American Empire* (1992); *United States: Essays, 1952–1992* (1993).
NOTES

1. Robert Graalman, "Gore Vidal (3 October 1925–   )," *American Novelists Since World War II: Second Series,* edited by James E. Kibler, Jr. (Detroit: Gale Research, 1980), p. 346.
2. Robert F. Kiernan, *Gore Vidal* (New York: Frederick Ungar, 1982), p. 111.
3. Kiernan, *Gore Vidal,* p. 117.
4. Edgar Z. Friedenberg, "Patriotic Gore," *New York Review of Books,* June 19, 1969, p. 35.

Nicholas von Hoffman
(1929–   )

Advocacy and literary journalist Nicholas von Hoffman, who was born in New York City on October 16, 1929, and educated at the Fordham Prep School, "can't write a news story to save his prematurely gray head," according to Benjamin Bradlee, former editor of the *Washington Post.* "But von Hoffman's dispatches as written were landmarks in the early, timid years of the new journalism: personal, pertinent, articulate, vital glimpses of man trying to make it in a more and more complicated world."[1]

Nicholas von Hoffman entered journalism in the 1960s, after he had served as an associate director of the Industrial Areas Foundation and as Saul Alinsky's chief organizer of the Woodlawn Organization, which was founded to serve the needs of Chicago's southside black community.

In 1963 he became a staff member of the *Chicago Daily News,* for which he covered the civil rights movement, including the movement called "Freedom Summer" in Mississippi. His revelations were ultimately collected in the diarylike *Mississippi Notebook,* which appeared in 1964. In addition, he wrote interpretive stories on American universities and students who attended various campuses. His book *The Multiversity: A Personal Report on What Happens to Today's Students at American Universities,* which was published in 1966, explored the same issues.

In 1966 he joined the staff of the *Washington Post* where, in addition to writing a column several times a week, he wrote stories on student riots, hippies, the Chicago Democratic convention, and Watergate. His book *We Are the People Our Parents Warned Us Against,* which told through the characters' own words what life in San Francisco's Haight-Ashbury district was like, was published in 1968.

A collection of his columns for the *Washington Post* appeared under the title *Left at the Post* in 1970. Von Hoffman's columns were powerful, to say the least. Indeed, what he wrote "produced more angry letters to the editor than the work of any other single reporter" in the newspaper's history, according to Chalmers M. Roberts.[2]

Von Hoffman broadened his interests in the 1970s when he debated James J. Kirkpatrick on CBS's "Sixty Minutes" and contributed numerous articles to such periodicals as the *Progressive, Harper's Bazaar, New Times,* and *Esquire.* Although he left the *Post* in 1976, he became the Washington correspondent for the London-based *Spectator* magazine the same year. In addition, he continued to write articles as well as books. For instance, his critical examination of politics in America, *Make-Believe Presidents: Illusions of Power from McKinley to Carter,* appeared in 1978.

In 1984 he wrote the critically acclaimed novel *Organized Crimes,* which concerned the Chicago underworld of the 1930s. He had not written a novel since the 1960s.

Four years later he returned to nonfiction with *Citizen Cohn,* a biography that penetrated the social environment of controversial lawyer Roy Cohn. Von Hoffman began with Cohn's death from AIDS, then presented in chronological order almost every villainous deed that he committed. Von Hoffman examined his possessive mother, who had despised her husband and had a commanding effect on her son. Cohn, according to von Hoffman, was a closet homosexual until his mother died, then his affairs became well known. Von Hoffman also discussed Cohn's ongoing battles with the IRS and the New York State Bar Association. The book contained numerous quotes from Cohn's friends and enemies, and revealed that he was merely interested in law because it had provided the means to an end. It was praised by critics for its coverage but not necessarily for its depth.

In 1992 von Hoffman produced *Capitalist Fools: Tales of American Business, from Carnegie to Forbes to the Milken Gang,* which was part biography and part history. He critically examined Malcolm Forbes and the men he profiled in his magazine, claiming that the executives had profited from buyouts and stock-option plans while their businesses declined. Although sarcasm appeared throughout the narrative, von Hoffman honored certain heroes such as B. C. Forbes, Malcolm's father, who had founded *Forbes* magazine; Daniel Mc-Callum, who had operated railroads during the Civil War; and John Patterson, the maverick tyrant who had been responsible for building the National Cash Register company. According to von Hoffman, the number of executives who could be classified as heroes has decreased:

These sorts of people are far more infrequent now. There are some marvelous people who have done wonderful things—I mention a few in the book—but the culture has changed enormously. One of the themes of this book is that in the process of creating itself, business changed the culture that made it—it ate its young. The commercial parts of our society use pleasure ubiquitously to sell merchandise and teach people to become obsessive pleasure lovers: "I won't do it unless it's fun; I don't like that teacher because he or she is not entertaining." Well, some things are arduous and they do hurt.[3]

WORKS: *Mississippi Notebook* (1964); *We Are the People Our Parents Warned Us Against* (1968); *Left at the Post* (1970); *Make-Believe Presidents:*

Illusions of Power from McKinley to Carter (1978); *Citizen Cohn* (1988); *Capitalist Fools: Tales of American Business, from Carnegie to Forbes to the Milken Gang* (1992).

NOTES

1. Nicholas von Hoffman, *Left at the Post* (Chicago: Quadrangle Books, 1970), p. 8.

2. Chalmers M. Roberts, "Hoffman, Nicholas von," *Contemporary Authors: Volumes 81–84,* edited by Francis Carol Locher (Detroit: Gale Research, 1979), p. 586.

3. Wendy Smith, "PW Interviews: Nicholas von Hoffman," *Publishers Weekly,* September 21, 1992, p. 72.

Dan Wakefield
(1932–)

Personal journalist Dan Wakefield, who was born in 1932 and reared in Indianapolis, attended Indiana University before he transferred to Columbia University in 1951. However, the idea of writing professionally did not germinate while he was in college, though he had written for student newspapers in both his elementary and high schools. Wakefield had aspired to be an athlete, but noted, "My inability to break the seven-minute mile marked the end of my dreams of glory on the athletic field; I turned forever from running to writing."[1] Wakefield, who confessed that he could not break away from the sports world, wrote about other runners for the Shortridge *Daily Echo,* his high school newspaper, and the *Indianapolis Star.*

When he attended Columbia he covered sports for the *Daily Spectator* and, during the summer before his senior year, worked for the Grand Rapids *Press.* Upon graduation in 1955, he became a news editor with the *Princeton Packet* of Princeton, New Jersey, a position he held for a year.

Wakefield longed for New York City. When he was offered a position with the *Nation* in 1956, he immediately returned to New York to accept the task of writing for a magazine that did not always reflect his views. Nonetheless, he apparently enjoyed the camaraderie he had with editors and staff members, for he stayed with the magazine for three years, until he resigned to become a full-time freelancer.

His first book, *Island in the City: The World of Spanish Harlem,* which depicted with warmth, understanding, and compassion the story of one of the world's worst slums, was published in 1959. Two years later *Revolt in the South* appeared. Wakefield, who contributed numerous articles to such publications as the *Atlantic, Playboy,* and *Esquire,* published some of them, together with informative personal pieces that described what was happening to him at the time he was writing the articles, in *Between the Lines* (1966). Wakefield wrote his informative personal pieces for readers who had "grown increasingly mistrustful of and bored with anonymous reports about the world."[2] By incorporating personal information, Wakefield presented more accurate pictures of the subjects discussed. The reader learned not only from the articles, but from the author's personal impressions.

Supernation at Peace and War, which grew out of an assignment for the *Atlantic,* appeared in 1968. Wakefield, who had traveled for several months across the country, witnessed the nation's separation over the war at home and the war abroad. He divided society into three attitudinal categories: Protest, Patriotism, and Pacification. Although his study was not scientific in the sense that he did not use a representative sample from each societal group or class, his observations showed that what was being reported by the conventional press was incorrect, that the established press had indeed supported the status quo by relying on "official" reports about the war that were provided by government leaders.

Although Wakefield wrote numerous short stories and two popular novels, he returned to nonfiction in 1976 with *All Her Children,* part autobiography and part documentary on how he became attuned to the soap opera "All My Children" and its varied cast.

He returned to the novel in 1985 with *Selling Out,* about a writer and college professor in New England who was lured to Hollywood to write scripts for television. The novel was well written.

In 1988 Wakefield explored himself in *Returning: A Spiritual Journey.* As the title suggests, the book was a therapeutic act of reinterpreting the past in a spirit of forgiveness and gratitude, and concerned his years as a child, an adolescent, a student at Columbia University, and a journalist. Wakefield acknowledged that he had learned the meaning of life during a very late stage in his.

He capitalized on the same theme in 1991 in the how-to manual *The Story of Your Life: Writing a Spiritual Autobiography.* The book was based in part on his experiences teaching workshops on the subject.

In 1992 he reminisced about New York City during the 1950s in the appropriately titled *New York in the Fifties.* A recollection of sorts, the book recounted his experiences at Columbia University, where he met Mark Van Doren, a poet; Lionel Trilling, the liberal intellectual; C. Wright Mills, a sociologist; and Murray Kempton, a journalist who helped him get an assignment from the *Nation.* Wakefield also recalled such notables as Dorothy Day, who spearheaded the Catholic Worker movement, as well as other young journalists and writers like himself, including William F. Buckley, Jr., Joan Didion, John Gregory Dunne, Michael Harrington, Seymour Krim, and James Baldwin, among others. The book was favorably reviewed for its fond insight.

In *Expect a Miracle: The Miraculous Things that Happen to Ordinary People,* published in 1995, Wakefield explored various miracles, including those of healing and recovery, as well as love and re-creation. He recounted numerous stories about ordinary people who had experienced what could be termed miracles.

WORKS: *Between the Lines* (1966); *Supernation at Peace and War* (1968); *Returning: A Spiritual Journey* (1988); *New York in the Fifties* (1992).
NOTES
1. Dan Wakefield, *Between the Lines* (New York: New American Library, 1966), p. 13.
2. Ibid., p. 1.

Joseph Wambaugh
(1937–)

Best-selling novelist Joseph Wambaugh was born on January 22, 1937, in East Pittsburgh, Pennsylvania. When he was 14 he moved with his mother and father to California, where he attended high school until he entered the Marine Corps in 1954. For three years he served as a recruit during the day and attended college classes at night. After his discharge he worked in a steel mill and attended Chaffey College, from which he received an associate of arts degree in 1958; two years later he received a bachelor's degree from California State College (University) in Los Angeles.

Wambaugh, who joined the Los Angeles Police Department before his graduation, had majored in English. His first novel was published in 1970. Based on his experiences as a police officer, *The New Centurions* candidly revealed the complexities of police work and police officers' lives.

Although Wambaugh became somewhat of a celebrity because of the book's popularity, he remained with the police department. His second novel, *The Blue Knight,* appeared in 1972 and was also successful.

His next book was different in the sense that it was based on fact. According to David K. Jeffrey, "Wambaugh set to work on the story that had driven him to become a writer, the kidnapping of two of his fellow Los Angeles policemen, Ian Campbell and Karl Hettinger, who were driven to an onion field where Campbell was murdered while Hettinger managed to escape."[1] The book was divided into two parts. The first part graphically described the evening when Gregory Powell and Jimmy Smith were stopped for a minor violation by Officers Karl Hettinger and Ian Campbell, and the surprise attack by Smith and Powell, who, at point-blank range, forced the officers to drive to an onion field outside Bakersfield and there murdered Officer Campbell. Hettinger, shocked by the killing, escaped. The second part depicted justice at its worst. The accused received two lengthy trials because of changes in the law by the U.S. Supreme Court, and Hettinger experienced guilt as well as other psychological trauma.

The Onion Field exemplified Wambaugh's explosive power of graphic description. The book was successful both critically and commercially. A year after its publication, Wambaugh, primarily because of his popularity as a writer, resigned from the Los Angeles Police Department even though he had become a detective sergeant.

Additional novels about police officers followed, including *The Choirboys* in 1975, *The Black Marble* in 1978, *The Glitter Dome* in 1981, *The Delta Star* in 1983, *The Secrets of Harry Bright* in 1985, *The Golden Orange* in 1990, *Fugitive Nights* in 1992, and *Finnegan's Week* in 1993; the same energy that had produced the previous best-sellers was present on every page of these novels.

In 1984 he wrote *Lines and Shadows,* another piece of nonfiction that explored the chaotic relationship between police officers of the Border Alien Robbery Force (Barf Squad) of the San Diego Police Department and illegal aliens along the California-Mexico border. Wambaugh was praised for his ability to create suspense and drama based on actual events.

Echoes in the Darkness, a mystery about three murders in an upper-middle-class high school in suburban Philadelphia, appeared in 1987. Wambaugh recounted how Susan Reinert, an English teacher, and her two children were the victims of a bizarre conspiracy methodically plotted by William Bradfield, a colleague, and Jay Smith, a former principal. The men were eventually apprehended and convicted.

In 1989 he wrote *The Blooding,* which Walter Walker described as "a well-written, meticulously researched, nontechnical tour de force."[2] The book chronicled the efforts of an English murder squad that searched for a rapist and killer of two 15-year-old girls. Dr. Alec Jeffreys, a young geneticist who had developed a process that enabled him to obtain X-ray patterns of DNA molecules found in blood and semen, was asked to test various samples of blood from suspects to determine who had been the perpetrator. Wambaugh, in a no-nonsense fashion, reported the various events and procedures in chronological order, including the arrest of the killer.

WORKS: *The New Centurions* (1970); *The Onion Field* (1973); *Lines and Shadows* (1984); *Echoes in the Darkness* (1987); *The Blooding* (1989).
NOTES
1. David L. Jeffrey, "Joseph Wambaugh," *American Novelists Since World War II: Second Series, Dictionary of Literary Biography,* edited by James E. Kibler, Jr. (Detroit: Gale Research, 1980), p. 359.
2. Walter Walker, "In Cold DNA," *New York Times Book Review,* February 19, 1989, p. 11.

Edward "Ned" Ward
(1667–1731)

Edward "Ned" Ward, who lived from 1667 to 1731, wrote *A Trip to Jamaica* and *A Trip to New-England, with a Character of the Country and People, Both English and Indians,* which presented an informal glimpse of the colonists, and also published the *London Spy.*

The periodical, first published in November 1698, was instantly successful. Readers familiar with *A Trip to Jamaica* were attracted to Ward's satiric accounts of London. In December the second issue appeared. Howard William Troyer said of the *London Spy:*

For the first nine numbers . . . the trip about town remains the basic pattern. Even here, however, Ward does not confine himself to the narration of a trip or a formal account of the sights of the city. From the very beginning the progress of the journey is interrupted by numerous characterizations of taverns and coffee-houses, tobacco shops, and bagnios along the way. Even more significant of the periodical nature of *The London Spy* are the occasional verses and songs, presented under the pretext of having been scribbled en route, and the characters of personages presumably encountered with which Ward padded his sixteen folio pages.[1]

To attract readers, Ward used none of the devices later perfected by Defoe and others—flashy titles, shocking prefaces, and answered letters. He used the technique he had perfected in his other work: continuous narration, with interruptions at strategic points, so that readers had to purchase the next issue to learn what happened.

Although readers of the *London Spy* were interested in London, the main attraction was the narrator's experience. According to Troyer:

The uniqueness of Ward's method lay in turning the ordinary world, already familiar to his readers, into the extraordinary and the unusual. Readers . . . toured their city in the company of a facile and loquacious pedestrian, concerned equally with the trivial or imposing, one whose sharp eyes were always set for the amusing or idiosyncratic. What they had not seen before, and were now intrigued with, were the comic possibilities in subjecting their every day world to the caricature and burlesque of Ward's impudent and racy prose.[2]

Ward wrote of London's low-life—pimps, thieves, panderers, chimney-sweeps, brothelkeepers, and informers. He wrote of customers who frequented taverns, one of which he owned. His reporting was insightful as well as critical.

The *London Spy* preceded by several years Daniel Defoe's *Review,* Richard Steele's *Tatler,* and Joseph Addison's *Spectator,* which were more literary in spirit, particularly the latter.

WORKS: *A Trip to Jamaica* (1698); *A Trip to New-England, with a Character of the Country and People, Both English and Indians* (1699).
NOTES
1. Howard William Troyer, *Ned Ward of Grubstreet: A Study of Sub-Literary London in the Eighteenth Century* (Cambridge, Mass.: Harvard University Press, 1946), pp. 30–31.
2. Ibid., p. 35.

Jann Wenner
(1946–)

Born on January 7, 1946, in New York City, Jann Wenner was reared in California, where he attended the University of California at Berkeley. He left the university after his junior year. Wenner gained some early experience in journalism by contributing a music column to the *Daily Californian*. Like others his age, he experienced the alternative lifestyles, the radical politics, the attitudinal changes brought about by differences in opinion toward the Vietnam War during the 1960s.

After dropping out of college Wenner moved to London. He tried unsuccessfully to write a novel, then accepted an offer from Ralph Gleason, a music columnist, who asked him to return to San Francisco to edit the entertainment page of the *Sunday Ramparts*. Within months the venture died. According to Robert Sam Anson, "The experience was valuable, if only because it gave Gleason and Wenner time to plan a far more ambitious undertaking: a publication that would take the new music and what went by the vague appellation 'youth culture' seriously."[1]

Wenner persuaded relatives and friends to loan him $7,500 to launch the new publication. Among the journalists who devoted their work free of charge were Michael Lydon, a *Newsweek* correspondent; his wife, Susan; John Williams, an art director; Baron Wolman, a photographer; and Jane Schindelheim, who later married Wenner.

Before the first issue appeared on November 9, 1967, Wenner had been inclined to name it the *Electric Newspaper* because of the popularity of drugs among the intended readership. However, Gleason persuaded him to use the name *Rolling Stone*. The first issue contained an in-depth interview with Donovan, brief columns about various groups, including one on the formation of the band Blood, Sweat & Tears, an investigative account of the profits from the Monterey Pop Festival, and, of course, record reviews. Wenner contributed an editorial statement of purpose that the magazine followed in its early years.

The magazine's editorial stance, which allowed four-letter words and nudity, kept away some prospective advertisers. In the first few months tensions mounted among certain members of the staff. By January, Michael Lydon was gone. His wife, Susan, left the magazine six months later.

Undeniably, *Rolling Stone* reflected its publisher's beliefs. Wenner gave his attention to every aspect of the magazine. Indeed, it had to meet his requirements—from the cover to the last page. Wenner communicated a different world. According to Anson, this world was "a fantasy universe where people never got old, dope was always good and cops were always bad, a land where rock stars sang."[2] Since the magazine eventually grew, it could be said that Wenner's tastes were for the most part correct.

Within two years the number of subscribers increased to 75,000, and more advertisers, especially recording companies, began to purchase space. The staff, on the other hand, was composed predominantly of the same energetic, young talented writers and editors that had helped the magazine survive while similar publications died. Writers such as Joe Eszterhas and Grover Lewis contributed articles. Regular columnists added another flavor to the periodical's pages.

Wenner expanded the magazine's operations in the late 1960s and early 1970s, beginning with other offices in Los Angeles and New York. With Mick Jagger of the Rolling Stones, he launched a short-lived British version of *Rolling Stone*. Wenner then purchased *New York Scenes,* a magazine similar to *New York,* which lasted only a few months.

When interest in the environment and ecology grew, he launched the short-lived *Earth Times* in 1970. Unfortunately, Wenner hired an inexperienced editor and gave her three staff members. Only a few issues appeared before costs forced him to stop publication.

Straight Arrow Books was another Wenner venture. Under its imprint books like *Lennon Remembers* and *Garcia* were published. The company eventually ceased operation, although most of its titles were sold to other publishers. For example, *Lennon Remembers* was sold to Popular Library.

Wenner, who made friends with prominent and wealthy Americans, including William Randolph Hearst III and Max Palevsky, remained in control of *Rolling Stone* even though several editors, especially John Burks and Marianne Partridge, contributed expertise that helped the magazine prosper during the late 1960s. Indeed, by the early 1970s *Rolling Stone* had more than a million readers, and justifiably so. Greil Marcus presented the tragic account of how four persons were killed and others injured at the Rolling Stones concert at Altamont in 1971, and several reporters, including David Dalton, explored the Manson family and its messianic mystique. These stories earned the magazine the National Magazine Award for Specialized Journalism in 1971.

Jon Landau's reviews of rock music were perhaps the most arresting found in any publication. However, when Hunter S. Thompson arrived at the magazine in the early 1970s coverage of rock music was losing its appeal. Thompson, who had written a book about the Hell's Angels, helped change *Rolling Stone*'s direction. Wenner realized that the magazine had to change to survive, and Thompson, with his "gonzo" style of reporting, was the right person to initiate the process. He covered the Super Bowl like no other sports writer; he wrote of running for office in Aspen, Colorado; he wrote indiscriminately about Las Vegas; and he reported on the 1972 presidential campaign.

His campaign coverage helped establish Thompson as a major writer, and, concurrently, changed public opinion toward the magazine. Thompson's coverage was filled with insight—so much so that other reporters who had been assigned to the campaign wondered where they were at the time. Timothy Crouse, who had been assigned to help Thompson cover the campaign, also enjoyed success when his book *The Boys on the Bus* was published.

The recognition that Thompson and Crouse brought to the magazine influenced Wenner to turn to politics. He interviewed Daniel Ellsberg about the Pentagon Papers; more important, he attempted to launch another magazine about politics. Opening an office in Washington, D.C., he persuaded former speechwriter Dick Goodwin to head the venture. Goodwin, who had been involved in American politics for years, contributed essays and commissioned other writers, most notably Joe Klein; however, Wenner realized that the venture was too expensive when he had paid thousands of dollars to Goodwin and contributors before the first issue had been planned. Goodwin, on the other hand, suffered from fatigue, and the magazine was never published.

Wenner received additional attention from the press, nonetheless. For example, Klein wrote a very disturbing piece on an employee at a chemical company who had contracted cancer from the misuse of PCBs; Tim Ferris introduced readers to Carl Sagan; Jonathan Cott explored another form of music when he introduced readers to pianist Glenn Gould; and Eszterhas, in a compelling and thought-provoking story, explained how an innocent youth was murdered by a narcotics officer.

Wenner, of course, made it possible for writers to investigate what they believed to be important and relevant to the magazine's readers. Indeed, certain writers received recognition for stories they would not have been allowed to write elsewhere.

In the mid-1970s the magazine changed again. When Joe Armstrong, a former assistant to the publisher of *Family Weekly*, was hired as president and publisher in 1975 the editorial stance of the magazine underwent a change. Four-letter words and nude photographs were reduced. The number of advertisements increased as well as the number of subscribers. Advertising revenue, for instance, increased from $1.5 million in 1972 to $5.5 million in 1976.[3] Wenner remained in control of the magazine.

Ralph Gleason died in 1975. The magazine paid a tribute to him by devoting an entire issue to comments made by those he had inspired or helped; Wenner wrote perhaps the most moving memorial.

Rolling Stone's most popular writer, Hunter S. Thompson, left after several disagreements with Wenner. (He returned later, however, providing the magazine with additional material in the "gonzo" style.) Political writers such as Crouse and Klein remained, but their copy lacked the commercial appeal of Thompson's. Wenner recruited other celebrities to capture readers' attention, such as Andy Warhol, John Dean, and Lillian Hellman. Unfortunately, their contributions prompted criticism from members of the press. *Rolling Stone,* which Wenner eventually moved to New York City, had begun as a music magazine; but music seemed to be less important to the staff. Consequently, some readers and members of the press criticized the magazine's direction.

Eventually, other writers, including Eszterhas and Crouse, left the magazine. Wenner secured capable writers to replace them, but the magazine failed to produce the kind of "firsts" it once had.

In New York City, Wenner launched a glossy, expensive monthly for backpackers entitled *Outside.* The magazine was sold after a few issues. Two years later, in 1979, he served as editor and publisher of *Look,* which had been resurrected by Daniel Filipacchi. However, after just three issues Filipacchi halted the magazine. Wenner produced *Rolling Stone College Papers,* a magazine for college students.

Rolling Stone continued to grow in circulation in the early 1980s, with some 4 million readers reading approximately 700,000 copies. Publishing articles about various film personalities as well as fiction primarily to maintain reader interest, the magazine changed again. Indeed, few musicians graced the covers. By the mid-1980s, apparently dissatisfied with the magazine's coverage, Wenner dismissed the managing editor. The magazine's emphasis shifted to music again, including concerts, recordings, and rock musicians. In 1985 a major advertising campaign called ''Perception-Reality'' informed potential advertisers about the magazine's readers (predominantly male, about 26 years of age, with an average annual income of $35,000–$40,000). Soon advertisements for cars, clothes, shoes, liquor, soft drinks, tobacco, and other products appeared in *Rolling Stone*'s pages. The campaign angered some readers, and critics complained that the magazine had grown contented, that it had become less adversarial. Of course, the critics were writing about the magazine as it had been during the 1960s, not the 1980s.

Also in 1985, Wenner appeared in the film *Perfect,* which starred John Travolta and Jamie Lee Curtis. Wenner played a character based on himself. The same year, with Lorimar Telepictures, he purchased *US* magazine from the New York Times Company.

In 1987 he wrote *Twenty Years of Rolling Stone: What a Long, Strange Trip It's Been,* which described the ups and downs of both the publication and the generation it served. Two years later he became sole owner of *US* and repositioned it as *US The Entertainment Magazine,* which covered television, film, and music. In 1991, in an effort to compete with *People* and *Entertainment Weekly,* he transformed it from a twice-monthly to a monthly and increased the number of pages. The transformation seemed successful; by the mid-1990s the publication's circulation exceeded 1 million.

Men's Journal, which was similar to *Outside* in the sense that it catered to the adventurous male, was launched in 1992. The magazine covered participatory sports, adventure, and travel. Wenner was determined to reach the active male with a new, slick publication that contained plenty of photographs and articles. Meanwhile, *Rolling Stone*'s circulation passed 1 million.

WORK: *Rolling Stone* (co-founder and publisher).
NOTES
1. Robert Sam Anson, ''Citizen Wenner,'' *New Times,* November 26, 1976, p. 18.
2. Ibid., p. 33.
3. Robert Sam Anson, ''The *Rolling Stone* Saga: Part Two,'' *New Times,* December 10, 1976, p. 34.

Richard West
(1941–)

Richard West was born in Dallas, Texas, in 1941, and was reared in an upper-middle-class suburb outside Dallas. His father, a prominent journalist, encouraged his son to get a solid education. West majored in journalism and political science at the University of Texas in Austin. Upon graduation, he accepted a position as a reporter for the *Longview Daily News* in Longview, Texas.

In 1973, along with Michael Levy, he helped found the *Texas Monthly*, a muckraking magazine that published investigative pieces about sex among Texas politicians, racial prejudice, police officers in Dallas, drug smugglers, college football, the Miss Texas Pageant, the banking business, and show business. West contributed the column "Texas Monthly Reporter," in which he wrote about various subjects from throughout the state, including nuclear waste, politics, the oil business, game laws, and medical controversies; he also contributed profiles.

His three-part article "In Search of Rural America" helped the magazine win a National Magazine Award for reporting in 1979. Although West was the magazine's senior editor, he traveled throughout Texas to research articles. In 1977, for instance, he moved to one region of the state and remained there for several months while he gathered information; then he moved to another region. He did this until he had covered the state. In 1981 the book *Richard West's Texas*, a work of literary journalism based on his experiences, was published.

In the early 1980s West moved to New York City and wrote several articles for *New York* magazine, including an in-depth analysis of the restaurant "21." "The Power of '21,' " a piece of literary journalism, revealed how the restaurant catered to the wealthy. Indeed, West followed as well as interviewed the employees; he learned from observing just how the restaurant operated.

West then worked as a national correspondent for *Newsweek*, a position he eventually gave up to become a freelance writer. In the *Diamonds and the Necklace: A South African Journey* (1991), he explored that nation's cities and how they connected the past to the present. He claimed that urban middle-class intellectuals from the Cape rather than Afrikaners had been responsible for implementing apartheid. The same year his book *Thailand: The Last Domino* was published. West explored Thailand and presented the good as well as the bad. He traveled throughout the countryside and reported that Americanization had been responsible for the evils that had infested the culture and government. Tradition, identity, and community had made the country great. He felt that feminism, homosexuality, and socialism had caused considerable harm. The book was a colorful portrait of a country and its people.

In 1995 he wrote *Tito and the Rise and Fall of Yugoslavia*, which was a combined history and biography that emphasized World War II, not Tito's crucial last decade. The book was filled with personal anecdotes.

WORKS: *Richard West's Texas* (1981); *Diamonds and the Necklace: A South African Journey* (1991); *Thailand: The Last Domino* (1991).

Theodore H. White
(1915–1986)

Journalist and political historian Theodore H. White, who was born in Boston in 1915, attended the Boston Latin School and Harvard, where he studied the history of China and its languages. After he graduated in 1938, he traveled to England, which was the beginning of a round-the-world journey. By 1939 he was in China, where he remained for several years, first as a freelancer for the *Manchester Guardian* and the *Boston Globe,* then as a correspondent for *Time* magazine. He witnessed the bombing of Peking, the battles between Chinese and Japanese soldiers, the worsening Honan famine, the Chinese political battlings, and the defeat of Japan. Although he had become chief of the China bureau, he resigned and returned to the United States in 1946.

He collaborated with Annalee Jacoby on the book *Thunder Out of China,* which examined and criticized the American-supported Kuomintang regime.

Over the next several years he devoted his time to several projects. For example, he served as senior editor of the *New Republic* for six months; he wrote for the *Saturday Review of Literature, Harper's,* and the *New York Times Magazine;* he edited *The Stilwell Papers;* he reported from Paris for the Overseas News Agency and the *Reporter;* and he wrote *Fire in the Ashes: Europe in Mid-Century,* a positive account of Europe's rebirth.

In 1953 he returned to the United States and wrote about politics for the *Reporter* and later *Collier's* magazine. This experience, together with the experience he gained from writing the novels *The Mountain Road* and *The View from the Fortieth Floor,* served him well when he explored quite candidly the mechanics of political campaigns.

The Making of the President 1960, which appeared in 1961, was hailed by critics as a new form of political reporting, and justifiably so. White traveled the campaign trail extensively and evolved a new form of political coverage. He presented the tidbits, the anecdotes, the little stories, as well as the issues, the trials, the wins, the losses, employing techniques usually associated with the novel to report about actual events.

The book was successful; consequently, he wrote a series of similar books about presidential campaigns. The final one, *Breach of Faith: The Fall of Richard Nixon,* which traced Nixon's political career, was published in 1975.

White died in 1986.

WORK: *The Making of the President 1960* (1961).

Tom Wicker
(1926–   )

Born in North Carolina in 1926, Tom Wicker was destined to become an author as well as a journalist of considerable foresight. Although he tried writing fiction while attending the University of North Carolina, fame did not come until years later.

After graduating he worked in various positions, including editor, correspondent, reporter, and editorial writer, at the Aberdeen, North Carolina, *Sandhill Citizen;* the Lumberton Democratic daily, the *Robesonian;* and the Winston-Salem *Journal.* In addition, he wrote the novels *Get Out of Town, Tears Are for Angels,* and *So Fair, So Evil,* published under the pseudonym Paul Connally. Although not best-sellers, they widened his experience and influenced his later work.

In 1959 he became associate editor of the Nashville *Tennessean.* He resigned after six months when he was offered a position with the Washington bureau of the *New York Times.* Until 1964, Wicker worked as a Capitol Hill reporter and as a White House and national political correspondent. He was with the presidential party in Dallas when President Kennedy was assassinated:

Relying on . . . instinct, . . . Wicker sifted through rumors, second-hand reports, tips from other reporters, lists of official information, and his own notes scribbled on the mimeographed Presidential itinerary to piece together a detailed account of the assassination of President John F. Kennedy.[1]

A year later, when the chief of the Washington bureau, James B. Reston, asked to be replaced, Wicker was appointed to the position. The same year his book *Kennedy Without Tears: The Man Behind the Myth* was published. In addition to fulfilling his obligations as chief, Wicker continued to write news stories, articles, and analyses for the *New York Times,* its Sunday magazine, and other publications. Such activity created unwarranted criticism among editors in the New York offices. In 1966 managing editor Turner Catledge promised Wicker that Arthur Krock's column would be his when Krock retired. Wicker resigned his Washington post to write "In the Nation," the column that Catledge had promised him. In addition, he became an associate editor of the newspaper. Wicker's *JFK and LBJ: The Influence of Personality upon Politics,* which examined each president's flaws, appeared the same year.

Wicker, who had time to write whatever interested him, returned to the novel, a form he had not touched for several years. After three years of frustration, he produced a novel about politics in the South. *Facing the Lions,* which was published in 1973, was instantly successful.

In 1975 he published a literary journalistic account of the Attica prison riots, which had occurred several months earlier in 1974. Since inmates had appointed him a member of the Citizens' Mediating Committee, he had access to the prison and the prisoners, and subsequently to the ensuing disturbance. *A Time to Die,* which read like a novel, depicted unforeseen incidents through description, dialogue, and interior monologue.

Wicker received the Edgar Allan Poe Award in 1976. Two years later he described his experiences as a journalist in *On Press.* He criticized the press for being too timid in its relationship with the federal government, and cited other problems. However, he failed to suggest any measures to correct the problems he noted.

In 1984 he returned to fiction with *Unto This Hour,* about American life during the Civil War. Specifically, the novel focused on the battle of August 1862, which became known as the Second Battle of Bull Run in the North and the Second Manassas in the South.

He wrote *One of Us: Richard Nixon and the American Dream* in 1991. The book received considerable criticism from reviewers because of its open support of the Nixon presidency. Wicker, who had covered the Nixon administration, wrote candidly about Nixon and politics as well as what Americans expected of the man who occupied the Oval office. Wicker reminded the reader that the presidency was a political position, not a ministerial position for morally upright people.

In 1992, after 30 years with the *New York Times,* he retired as a result of his age. The same year he wrote *Donovan's Wife,* a novel about a candidate for the Senate.

WORK: *A Time to Die* (1975).

NOTE

1. Charles Moritz, ed., *Current Biography 1973* (New York: H. W. Wilson, 1973), p. 435.

Josiah Flynt Willard
(1869–1907)

Josiah Flynt Willard, better known as Josiah Flynt, was born on January 23, 1869, to Mary Bannister and Oliver Willard, in Appleton, Wisconsin. He was reared in Evanston, Illinois. His father, a retired minister and former editor of the *Chicago Post,* taught at the Biblical Institute; he died when Flynt was eight.

Flynt wandered away from home numerous times. He also wandered away from the boarding school he attended. His mother and his two sisters traveled to Germany when he was 15. Flynt, who eventually finished school, lived with a friend of the family and attended a small college in Illinois. However, formal education was not to his liking. He preferred tramping throughout the country-side to sitting in a classroom listening to someone lecture. He left college and worked briefly on a farm in Pennsylvania, then worked briefly for a railroad in Buffalo, New York. Flynt stole a horse and buggy, sold it, then stole another and was apprehended. He was sent to a reform school, from which he eventually escaped, and tramped throughout the countryside for several months. Finally, he was arrested and subsequently incarcerated for a month.

After his release he worked briefly on a farm in New York, then sailed to Germany to join his family. His mother, who operated a school for girls in Berlin, enrolled Flynt in the University of Berlin. Flynt tried to study and even majored in economics, but the desire to be somewhere else instead of sitting in a classroom was overwhelming, and he left the university without earning a degree.

As he had in the United States, Flynt tramped throughout Europe. He became known as "Cigarette," primarily because of his slight stature. He met Oscar Wilde, Arthur Symons, and Aubrey Beardsley, among other notable literary and artistic figures, in England in 1890.

Although he had much to write about, including literature and art, one of his first articles concerned his experiences as a hobo. "The American Tramp" was published in the *Contemporary Review* in August 1891. Flynt returned to Berlin, where he continued his studies and found employment. However, the urge to wander struck him again, and he tramped to Russia. He met Ibsen and Tolstoy, and worked briefly on the latter's farm. He continued to write about his numerous exploits for various magazines. These articles depicted with incredible accuracy the dismal life of a hobo. For instance, in 1897 he wrote "The Criminal in the Open," which recounted the act of stealing that resulted in his incarceration.

Flynt returned to America in 1898, primarily to work as a writer. He was immediately asked by a manager of the Pennsylvania Railroad to inspect the company's policies concerning tramps, who frequently jumped freight trains to travel to other cities. Flynt accepted the assignment, which lasted several months.

In 1899 his first book was published. *Tramping with Tramps,* based on his personal experience, made him famous almost immediately. Indeed, no writer before Flynt had depicted with such authority and uncanny realism an existence that most readers had never known.

The following year Flynt met Alfred Hodder, who had been an academician, and together they wrote a series of articles for *McClure's* magazine. "True Stories from the Under-World," which concerned criminal behavior, especially that of those who comprised the community called the underworld, began in the August 1900 issue and was one of the first muckraking series. Because of the literary devices employed, it was an example of literary journalism. Part of the editor's introduction read:

These stories are not fiction in the ordinary sense; they are entertaining stories, but more than this they are philosophical studies, about a class concerning which the great mass of people knows nothing, except that they are law-breakers. All the names in these stories are fictitious, but the characters are real and the incidents have all occurred at various times and places. The stories are intended to point a moral as well as adorn a tale.[1]

The series revealed that the police and certain criminals were not necessarily enemies. It was extremely popular among readers and was published in book form under the title *The Powers that Prey* the same year.

Flynt continued with his exploration of this topic in *Notes of an Itinerant Policeman,* also published in 1900. According to Flynt, the police had to have ties with some criminals in order to serve society. After all, certain criminals knew the streets, the shady characters, and the identity of those who had committed crimes.

His series "In the World of Graft" was an excellent example of muckraking journalism and brought him additional acclaim because of its popularity. The editor's introduction in the February 1901 issue of *McClure's* stated:

For fifteen years Mr. Flynt has spent much of his time among the vagrant and criminal classes of this country and Europe, living with them under their own conditions. It is a mere coincidence that these articles are published just as Chicago and New York are arousing to the need of reform. It should be remembered that Mr. Flynt writes of what he saw in the spring of 1900, but practically the same conditions exist today.[2]

Flynt had interviewed certain criminals and reported their opinions about criminal activity. He included explanations of terms and phrases so that readers could easily understand the criminals' language. For instance, he introduced the terms "joint" (an illegal liquor store), "fix" (bribe), "mob" (organized crime), "pinch" (arrest), "pull" (influence), and "one who had squared it" (becoming honest), among others.

According to the criminals, police departments were corrupt, and consequently police officers were responsible for as much, if not more, criminal activity than criminals. Harold S. Wilson wrote, "The magazine had published many articles on criminals and their apprehension, but nothing had equaled Flynt's conversation with 'guns,' the full-time thieves, who seem to have been better informed about the 'system' than many in public office."[3]

Flynt's interviews had taken place in New York, Chicago, Boston, Philadelphia, Pittsburgh, and other cities, and he reported that Chicago was the only honest city (frankly corrupt), while New York was a dishonest city. The series was published in book form under the title *The World of Graft* the same year.

Flynt then turned to fiction, completing a novel that was published in 1902. He was drinking alcohol almost every day. In order to stop drinking, he accepted a position with a railroad in the Indian Territory, where alcohol was prohibited. However, within a few weeks, he missed the taste of alcohol so badly that he returned east.

By 1905 his health was poor; alcohol had taken its toll. Nonetheless, he accepted an assignment from a magazine to visit Russia and report about what he observed. Flynt contributed several articles, then became seriously ill in Germany. Eventually, after spending several weeks in bed, he returned to the United States.

In 1906 he accepted an assignment from a magazine to investigate poolroom racketeering in Chicago. Unable to do all the research himself because of poor health, Flynt sought help from friends. The articles that resulted discussed various gambling activities and the unusual criminals who were responsible. They used the same fluid style but lacked the punch of the moralistic muckraking journalist.

In 1907, soon after these articles were published, Flynt died of pneumonia.

His autobiography, *My Life,* which was filled with sketches, was published a year later.

Although Flynt abused his body by living like a tramp and drinking heavily, he wrote two insightful series on topics that other muckraking journalists subsequently investigated. In essence, he laid the groundwork and, to a certain extent, established the tone for other muckraking journalists. He also used literary devices found in fiction to describe scenes and characters. Thus his articles were examples of literary journalism.

WORKS: *Tramping with Tramps* (1899); "True Stories from the Under-World" (1900); *The Powers that Prey* (1900); *Notes of an Itinerant Policeman* (1900); "In the World of Graft" (1901); *The World of Graft* (1901); *My Life* (1908).

NOTES

1. Josiah Flynt and Francis Walton, "True Stories from the Under-World," *McClure's Magazine,* August 1900, p. 356.

2. Josiah Flynt, "In the World of Graft," *McClure's Magazine,* February 1901, p. 327.

3. Harold S. Wilson, *McClure's Magazine and the Muckrakers* (Princeton, N.J.: Princeton University Press, 1970), pp. 123–124.

Garry Wills
(1934–   )

Essayist and political journalist Garry Wills was born in Atlanta on May 22, 1934, and reared in Wisconsin and Michigan. Wills, a Catholic, attended St. Louis University, from which he received his bachelor's degree in 1957. Wills then entered Xavier University in Cincinnati. When he submitted a parody to the *National Review,* William F. Buckley, Jr., was so impressed that he asked Wills to come to New York to work for the magazine. Although Wills respectfully declined to work for the weekly full time, he nonetheless went to New York to write reviews for it before the beginning of Xavier's fall term. Wills reminisced about the incident in his autobiography, *Confessions of a Conservative,* which was published in 1979.

Wills received his first master's degree in 1958. Then he entered Yale University, from which he earned a second master's degree and a doctorate in 1959 and 1961, respectively. During the latter year he worked as the associate editor of the *Richmond News Leader.* Wills, who had majored in philosophy and classics, was determined to teach, and was not necessarily interested in working as a journalist. His first book, *Chesterton: Man and Mask* (1961), was an intellectual, philosophical biography of a controversial Catholic as well as a historical record of the period.

In 1962 Wills became a member of the faculty at Johns Hopkins University. Two years later he wrote *Politics and Catholic Freedom,* which argued that "Catholic encyclical letters on social problems did not impose, by papal authority, a specifically Catholic politics on all Catholics around the world."[1] Although it was discussed and reviewed by people like William F. Buckley, Jr., the book failed to sell; it did, however, persuade Bob Hoyt, who published the *National Catholic Reporter,* to ask Wills to become a conservative columnist. Wills accepted. He later noted, "The strange thing about my time as an NCR columnist is that I earned my conservative reputation mainly by taking a liberal position on civil disobedience in the antiwar and civil-rights movements."[2]

Wills was denied tenure as a result of his column. His department chairman believed that he could have spent his time on scholarly writing instead. (Wills had written as much as his peers. The department chairman believed that a Johns Hopkins professor should not have contributed to mainstream periodicals.)

Wills taught another year, then became a contributing editor at *Esquire,* which was edited by Harold Hayes. For *Esquire,* Wills wrote an article on Jack Ruby's motive for killing Lee Harvey Oswald, articles on Ruby's trial, an article on Joseph Stalin's daughter, Svetlana Alilluyena, and an article on the preparations made by police before riots, among others. These articles were written in the literary journalistic style. Each relied on realistic description, dramatic dialogue, and personal insight to portray characters—their thoughts, their behavior, and their flaws—and intense but accurate scenes. With Ovid Demaris, an investigative reporter, Wills expanded his articles on Ruby and published them under the title *Jack Ruby* in 1968. His lengthy article on police preparations for urban war was published the same year under the title *The Second Civil War: Arming for Armageddon.* Although Wills discussed the eventual battle between races and mentioned prejudice as the cause, the book failed to receive the attention it deserved.

Wills covered the 1968 Democratic National Convention in Chicago for the *National Review.* The article he submitted was severely critical of Mayor Richard J. Daley's handling of the antiwar demonstrators, and was reluctantly published by Buckley. His next article was not, however. Criticizing the Vietnam War, Wills "argued from Stephen Decatur's famous maxim, from the example of Robert E. Lee and George Washington, that self-defense is the only justification for war."[3]

In 1970 he began his column "Outrider" for the Universal Press Syndicate and wrote the controversial analytical, political book, *Nixon Agonistes: The Crisis of the Self-Made Man,* which, according to Wills, "attacked the splintered legacy of nineteenth century liberalism as it had been enunciated by men like William Graham Sumner, who believed in the free market of ideas *and* dollars."[4]

The book was praised by some reviewers and condemned by others for its portrayal of Nixon as a liberal. However, after Watergate, Wills gained new support for his accurate depiction.

A collection of his controversial essays on Catholicism, *Bare Ruined Choirs: Doubt, Prophecy, and Radical Religion,* appeared in 1972, but his next major work did not appear until six years later. In *Inventing America: Jefferson's*

Declaration of Independence, Wills analyzed Jefferson's often misunderstood political philosophy. In *Explaining America: The Federalist,* which was published in 1980, the year he became a professor of American culture and public policy at Northwestern University, Wills explored the philosophical background of Alexander Hamilton and James Madison by analyzing their political paper, *The Federalist.* In 1982, in *The Kennedy Imprisonment: A Meditation on Power,* he critically analyzed the Kennedy brothers and their political achievements.

Wills examined the myth of George Washington in 1984 in *Cincinnatus: George Washington and the Enlightenment.* The book's major contribution was the original evolution of the iconography of Washington from the Moses figure to that of Cincinnatus, who was a citizen turned soldier as well as a hero of Rome. In 1987 he analyzed Ronald Reagan's behavior at different stages in his life in *Reagan's America: Innocents at Home.* The book focused on three questions: Who was Reagan? How had he become what he was? What American beliefs and myths had he embodied?

Wills turned to religion and its role in American politics in *Under God: Religion and American Politics* (1991). He claimed that religion had always been a force in America and would remain so and that the founding fathers had desired religious freedom primarily because they wanted religion to operate freely, even as a political influence. The Scopes trial, biblical prophecy, Roger Williams, abortion, and feminism were among the topics discussed.

A year later he examined the words of perhaps the most famous address ever delivered by an American president in *Lincoln at Gettysburg: The Words that Remade America.* Wills demonstrated how Lincoln changed the bearing of Jefferson's "all men are created equal" clause. He claimed that Lincoln brilliantly redirected the "equal" clause homeward, taking it to mean that no man had any right to own another.

In 1994 he examined, through various personalities and their opposites, different types of leaders and leadership in *Certain Trumpets: The Call of Leaders.* His leaders were not necessarily democratic by belief or temperament, but they knew how to be ingratiating. Wills included Franklin and Eleanor Roosevelt, Napoleon, King David, Pope John XXIII, Washington, Martin Luther King, Ross Perot, Harriet Tubman, Socrates, Mary Baker Eddy, Carl Stotz, Martha Graham, Cesare Borgia, Dorothy Day, and Andrew Young. Their opposites were meant to help the reader understand the positive qualities of the primary figures.

WORKS: *Politics and Catholic Freedom* (1964); *Jack Ruby* (1968); *The Second Civil War: Arming for Armageddon* (1968); *Nixon Agonistes: The Crisis of the Self-Made Man* (1970); *Confessions of a Conservative* (1979); *Reagan's America: Innocents at Home* (1987); *Certain Trumpets: The Call of Leaders* (1994).

NOTES

1. Garry Wills, *Confessions of a Conservative* (New York: Doubleday, 1979), p. 62.

2. Ibid., pp. 67–68.

3. Ibid., p. 79.
4. Ibid., p. 122.

Edmund Wilson
(1895–1972)

Edmund Wilson was born on May 8, 1895, in Red Bank, New Jersey, and attended Hill School in Pottstown, Pennsylvania, and Princeton University, from which he graduated in 1916. Rebellious in the sense that he openly criticized the American bourgeoisie, of which he was a member, he began his career as a critic of literature and society early; he had been a member of Princeton's *Nassau Lits'* editorial staff.

Wilson moved to New York City and worked as a reporter for the *New York Evening Sun* until the United States entered World War I. Despite his family's social standing and his education, he enlisted as a private and served in France. When the war ended he became managing editor of *Vanity Fair* and, from 1926 to 1931, wrote book reviews for the *New Republic*. In 1931 his literary criticism reigned in *Axel's Castle*. A year later, in *The American Jitters—A Year of the Slump* (nonfiction), his attention turned to the weakening of the American spirit, caused primarily by the Great Depression and class structure.

In 1935 he toured Russia, then wrote *Travels in Two Democracies*, in which he compared Russia to the United States. Wilson favored Russia because of its revolutionary philosophy and people; the United States was suffering from the Great Depression. To Wilson, Russia was a land of hope; America was a land of despair.

Two years later Wilson returned to literary criticism in *The Triple Thinkers*, a book of essays on Pushkin, Henry James, George Bernard Shaw, Karl Marx, and others. Although he praised Shaw, he criticized Stalin and what he had done to Russia in his essay on Karl Marx.

Throughout the 1940s and 1950s Wilson contributed critical essays to numerous magazines, including the *Nation, New Republic,* and the *New Yorker.* From 1944 to 1948 he was the latter magazine's book reviewer and, in 1947, correspondent in Europe. His observations were recorded in *Europe Without Baedeker: Sketches Among the Ruins of Italy, Greece, and England,* which was published in 1947.

The Scrolls from the Dead Sea, an enlargement of a *New Yorker* article, was published in 1955. This was followed by numerous volumes of collected articles, in-depth studies, and memoirs, including *A Piece of My Mind: Reflections at Sixty* (1956), *Apologies to the Iroquois* (1960), *Patriotic Gore: Studies in the Literature of the American Civil War* (1962), *The Cold War and the Income Tax* (1963), and *The Bit Between My Teeth: A Literary Chronicle of 1950–1965* (1965). Wilson died in 1972.

Many of his articles and essays, especially his critical essays, contained elements of literary journalism. The article "Frank Keeney's Coal Diggers," which was collected in *The American Earthquake,* was an example of literary journalism.

WORK: *The American Earthquake* (1958).

Jules Witcover
(1927–   )

Political investigative reporter and columnist Jules Witcover was born in 1927. He graduated from Columbia University in 1949 and began his career as a newspaperman in Hackensack, New Jersey, the same year. He moved from one newspaper to another during the next several years, and worked as a Washington correspondent for the *Syracuse Herald-Journal* from 1954 to 1962. He was attracted to Washington's political climate. From 1962 to 1968 he was a senior correspondent and chief political writer for the Newhouse National News Service. His reporting, which was expertly written and candid, enabled him to become a Washington columnist, a position he held until 1972, when he accepted a correspondent's position with the Washington bureau of the *Los Angeles Times.*

Witcover learned the political ins and outs of Washington. His first book, *85 Days: The Last Campaign of Robert Kennedy* (1969), written in the form of a documentary and filled with dialogue and interior monologue, accurately depicted Kennedy's presidential campaign and death. It revealed Witcover's talents as a political reporter who desired to present the facts from various sources. His mixture of dialogue and description was both effective and informative. The book was an example of literary journalism and was respected by reviewers for its honesty.

He wrote *The Resurrection of Richard Nixon,* another well-constructed book of political reporting, in 1970. However, unlike his first book, which contained very little political analysis, his second contained more than enough to satisfy any reader. Witcover's power of observation and analysis appeared on practically every page.

Witcover, who also wrote *White Knight: The Rise of Spiro Agnew* in 1972 and, with Jack W. Germond, *Blue Smoke and Mirrors: How Reagan Won and Why Carter Lost the Election of 1980* in 1981, contributed articles to such periodicals as *Saturday Review, Esquire, Columbia Journalism Review,* the *Nation,* and the *New Republic.* He joined the *Washington Post* in 1973, then teamed up with Germond to write a syndicated newspaper column on national politics. The column, based at the *Baltimore Sun,* became popular. Witcover and Germond also contributed a column on politics to the *National Journal,* a weekly magazine in Washington, D.C.

In 1989 he wrote *Sabotage at Black Tom: Imperial Germany's Secret War in America, 1914–1917.* Witcover recounted how the German embassy in Washington orchestrated the bombing of the munitions depot known as Black Tom, which was located on a promontory in New York harbor near the Statue of Liberty. The explosion occurred in the early hours of July 30, 1916.

Three years later he dissected the vice presidency—from the earliest times to the present—in *Crapshoot: Rolling the Dice on the Vice Presidency.* Witcover attempted to persuade readers that the vice presidency was a very important position and that when deciding on a presidential candidate they should examine the candidate's running mate more seriously.

Mad as Hell: Revolt at the Ballot Box, 1992, written with Jack Germond, analyzed the 1992 presidential election. The book contained numerous clichés, but the authors presented an intriguing behind-the-scenes glance at what occurred.

WORKS: *85 Days: The Last Campaign of Robert Kennedy* (1969); *Sabotage at Black Tom: Imperial Germany's Secret War in America, 1914–1917.*

Tom Wolfe
(1931–   )

Tom Wolfe—no relation to the novelist Thomas Wolfe—was born in Richmond, Virginia, on March 2, 1931. His father, a former professor of agronomy, edited *Southern Planter.* Wolfe, perhaps the most visible of the literary journalists because of his fad-making dress and his numerous articles about new journalism, attended St. Christopher's School in Richmond, Washington and Lee University, from which he graduated in 1951, and, after a couple of seasons of semi-professional baseball, Yale University, where he received his Ph.D. degree in 1957.

Wolfe, who had enough of academic life, tried to get a job with the *New York Daily News;* unfortunately, the only position available was copy boy. Wolfe wrote to other newspapers. Finally, after four months, the *Springfield Union* of Springfield, Massachusetts, hired him as a reporter. He told Elaine Dundy, "It was the first time I realized that a city could be made up of more than one ethnic group that was politically powerful, that had its own way of life and its own restaurants."[1]

Wolfe joined the staff of the *Washington Post* in 1959. Although he reported on Latin America, for which he won a Washington Newspaper Guild award in 1960, his primary interests were features and humor. The editors at the *Post,* however, considered almost every subject worthy to be a feature, much to Wolfe's dismay. In 1962, as a result of his dissatisfaction, he left the *Post* to become a reporter, writer, and artist for the *New York Herald Tribune* and its Sunday magazine, *New York.* He fondly wrote:

I looked out across the city room of the *Herald Tribune . . .* with a feeling of amazed bohemian bliss. . . . Either this is the real world, Tom, or there is no real world. . . . The place looked like the receiving bin at the Good Will . . . a promiscuous heap of junk. . . . Wreckage and exhaustion everywhere.[2]

In 1963, when a four-month newspaper strike hit, Wolfe, having read Gay Talese's literary journalistic profile entitled "Joe Lewis: The King as a Middle-Aged Man" a year earlier, went to California to write an article on customized cars for *Esquire.* When he returned to New York, however, he found that he could not write the story using the traditional journalistic techniques. When he informed Byron Dobell, the managing editor at *Esquire,* that he could not write the article, Dobell told him to type his notes so that another writer could do it. Wolfe explained:

I started typing away, starting right with the first time I saw any custom cars in California. I just started recording it all, and inside of a couple of hours, typing along like a madman, I could tell that something was beginning to happen. . . . I wrapped up the memorandum about 6:15 a.m., and by this time it was 49 pages long. I took it over to *Esquire* as soon as they opened up, about 9:30 a.m. About 4 p.m. I got a call from Byron Dobell. He told me they were striking out the "Dear Byron" at the top of the memorandum and running the rest of it in the magazine.[3]

Wolfe explained the art of customizing cars in the artists' language. He used punctuation to reinforce the message. The title, "There Goes (Varoom! Varoom!) That Kandy-Kolored (Thphhhhhh!) Tangerine-Flake Streamline Baby (Rahghhh!) Around the Bend (Brummmmmmmmmmmmmmmmm) . . . ," was the first from his typewriter to literally characterize his articles.

Wolfe worked two days a week as a general assignments reporter and three days a week as a writer for the Sunday supplement, and wrote additional articles for *Esquire* and other magazines. Over the next year and a half he produced some 40 articles covering such topics as stock car racing, Las Vegas, the Peppermint Lounge, and Baby Jane Holzer. More than 20 of his impressionistic articles were collected and published in 1965 under the title *The Kandy-Kolored Tangerine-Flake Streamline Baby,* which was not only well received by the critics, but remained on best-seller lists for months. The same year, however, Wolfe wrote the controversial, critical, satirical articles "Tiny Mummies! The True Story of the Ruler of 43rd Street's Land of the Walking Dead!" and "Lost in the Whichy Thicket," which attacked William Shawn and the *New Yorker.* Wolfe, who claimed the articles were mere anti-parodies or attacks and not literary journalism, was severely criticized by Dwight MacDonald and Leonard Levin, among other journalists, for the articles' errors and demeaning tone. Wolfe responded:

My article on the *New Yorker* had not even been an example of the new genre; it used neither the reporting techniques nor the literary technique; underneath a bit of red-flock *Police Gazette* rhetoric, it was a traditional critique, a needle, an attack, an "essay" of the old school. It had little or nothing to do with anything I had written before.[4]

Wolfe, of course, presented his side of the whole affair in another article entitled "The New Journalism: A la Recherche des Whichy Thickets."

When the *New York Herald Tribune* merged with the *New York World Journal* in 1966, Wolfe remained until the paper collapsed a year later. Clay Felker, who had edited *New York,* produced the magazine in 1968, and Wolfe worked as a contributing editor. The same year another collection of Wolfe's articles appeared to a receptive audience. *The Pump House Gang* contained articles on Hugh Hefner, the Mac Meda Destruction Company, Carol Doda, a go-go dancer with silicone breasts, and others. His first book-length piece of literary journalism, *The Electric Kool-Aid Acid Test,* also appeared in 1968. Wolfe, who traveled around the country with novelist Ken Kesey and his Merry Pranksters, had recorded on paper the experiences of hippies and their drug-related culture. The book was praised by reviewers for its objective revelations of psychedelic life.

In 1970 Wolfe received criticism of another kind from his peers when he first attended a party given by Leonard Bernstein to raise money for the Black Panthers, then wrote a critical article about how the "cultivated parvenue Jews" enjoyed mixing with the social misfits of primitivism. It was paired with a humorous article on African Americans who terrorized a bureaucrat in *Radical Chic and Mau-Mauing the Flak Catchers* the same year.

Wolfe, the sociologist of pop, turned to modern art in 1975 with *The Painted Word,* an expanded *Harper's* article. The book, which was critical of the art world—more precisely of how the value of certain artists and their respective paintings was manipulated by critics and others in the art world—was for the most part dismissed by reviewers. Some, such as Robert Hughes and John Russell, questioned whether Wolfe knew anything about art or how the art world functioned.

Although another collection of articles, *Mauve Gloves & Madmen, Clutter & Vine,* appeared in 1976, it was three years before he received the recognition he deserved. With the publication of *The Right Stuff,* an inside, tidbit filled, award-winning sociological study of the original seven astronauts and America's space program, numerous critics acknowledged Wolfe as the supreme literary journalist.

The Right Stuff illustrated his ability to capture the actual dialects of his subjects. By using scene-by-scene construction, dramatic but realistic dialogue, extensive description, and the third-person point of view, Wolfe allowed the reader to experience what certain pioneers experienced. In short, by using these elements, he made a body of facts come to life. Wolfe, who had left *New York* magazine to become a contributing editor to *Esquire,* was back on top.

Within a year he brought out another collection of articles, *In Our Time,* followed by a much discussed book on modern architecture, *From Bauhaus to Our House* (1981), which critics compared to his book on modern art. Another collection, *The Purple Decades: A Reader* (1982), gathered material that had appeared in earlier books.

In the mid-1980s, Wolfe, who had criticized novelists for not representing reality, labored on a novel about the greed and hate in modern New York City. *The Bonfire of the Vanities,* which was published in 1987, concerned a Wall Streeter named Sherman McCoy who was implicated in the hit-and-run death of a young African American, even though his girlfriend had actually driven the car. The novel became an instant best-seller. The film version starred Tom Hanks.

Wolfe became a contributing editor to *Harper's,* and a member of the editorial board of the *American Spectator.*

WORKS: *The Kandy-Kolored Tangerine-Flake Streamline Baby* (1965); *The Pump House Gang* (1968); *The Electric Kool-Aid Acid Test* (1968); *Radical Chic and Mau-Mauing the Flak Catchers* (1970); *The Painted Word* (1975); *Mauve Gloves & Madmen, Clutter & Vine* (1976); *The Right Stuff* (1979); *In Our Time* (1980); *From Bauhaus to Our House* (1981); *The Purple Decades: A Reader* (1982).

NOTES

1. Elaine Dundy, "Tom Wolfe . . . But Exactly, Yes!," *Vogue,* April 15, 1966, p. 155.

2. Tom Wolfe, *The New Journalism,* with an anthology edited by Tom Wolfe and E. W. Johnson (New York: Harper and Row, 1973), p. 4.

3. Tom Wolfe, *The Kandy-Kolored Tangerine-Flake Streamline Baby* (New York: Pocket Books, 1966), pp. xiii–xiv.

4. Wolfe, *The New Journalism,* p. 24.

Bob Woodward
(1943–)

Bob Woodward and Carl Bernstein uncovered a series of events that first angered then indirectly forced President Richard Nixon from office. Woodward, who did not enter journalism until he was 27, was born in Geneva, Illinois, on March 26, 1943. Upon his graduation from high school in 1961, he entered Yale University on a naval ROTC scholarship. When he received his degree in 1965, he fulfilled his obligation to the navy by serving as a communications officer aboard two ships and as a communications liaison officer in Washington, D.C.

After he completed five years of duty, he applied to Harvard Law School. Although he was accepted, he decided to become a reporter instead. First he tried the *Washington Post,* where for two weeks he wrote stories that were not published. The editors of the *Post* advised him to return when he had some journalistic experience and helped him get a job with the *Montgomery County Sentinel.* There he was assigned civic association meetings and press releases. Woodward emphatically hated the work. Within weeks he was covering stories in his off hours; if the topics were interesting the *Sentinel* used them.

Woodward returned to the *Post* in 1971 and became an investigative reporter. Although he was not considered the *Post*'s best writer, he was energetic and persistent, and his stories on drugs, police corruption, restaurants, business corruption, Blue Cross–Blue Shield, and Medicaid abuses made the front pages. In short, he would follow a tip or lead until the end.

In 1972 Barry Sussman, the *Post*'s city editor, called Woodward and informed him that five well-dressed men had been arrested for burglarizing the Democratic National Committee's headquarters in the Watergate complex. Woodward attended the arraignment and subsequently helped write a front-page story on the break-in. Story after story appeared, each disclosing another link between the burglars and the White House.

Woodward had been assigned to cover the burglary and had written several other stories concerning Watergate, but Carl Bernstein, another *Post* reporter, realized that Woodward could not cover all the tips and leads, and persuaded the editors to make him a member of the team. Within four months "Woodstein" had traced the money to Attorney General John Mitchell, the campaign director of CREEP (Committee to Re-Elect the President) at the time of the break-in. According to *Current Biography:*

By mid-1973 the team's list of scoops was staggering: the participation of the FBI and the CIA in the Watergate coverup; laundered, illegal corporate campaign contributions; the planned character assassination of Senator Edward M. Kennedy; and the harassment of Nixon's "enemies" by the Internal Revenue Service.[1]

In 1974 the reporters' first book, *All the President's Men,* which was meant to be the culmination of their tedious, meticulous work until other major reporters began investigating Watergate, was published. The book, which disclosed how the team investigated the various leads, including successes as well as failures in obtaining information for stories, was written from the third-person point of view for the sake of objectivity. It was praised by critics for its realistic depiction of the newspaper business and its authentic record of history.

Without question, the work performed by Woodward and Bernstein was of the utmost importance. After all, an American president was involved in a coverup. If Nixon had been allowed to commit an illegal act without having to pay any consequences whatsoever, future presidents might have been inclined to commit similar acts. Being chosen to serve as president did not entitle one to break the law or put one above the law. Woodward and Bernstein indirectly made that point.

Two years later the reporters' second book, *The Final Days,* appeared. They had intended to write of the impeachment and subsequent trial of the president from the perspective of six senators involved in the case; however, when they learned that Nixon would resign the idea was dismissed. Woodward and Bernstein received a year's leave of absence and began investigating the last 15 months of the Nixon White House. After interviewing almost 400 persons, they wrote an in-depth account of the last days. The book sold well, but several critics, including James J. Kilpatrick and William Safire, lambasted the book for its disregard of historical reporting. The scenes of the president with Henry Kissinger were considered by some critics to be "brutal, needless, tasteless, and profitable," according to *Current Biography.*[2] Other critics termed the book a nonfiction novel because of its style and anonymous sources. Most reviewers, however, considered it an extraordinary piece of contemporary history.

The authors used dialogue, interior monologue, and candid description to depict characters, scenes, and emotions. The book was an example of literary journalism.

Woodward returned to the *Post,* while Bernstein resigned to devote his time to freelance writing. In 1979 Woodward, with Scott Armstrong, wrote *The Brethren: Inside the Supreme Court,* which examined the Supreme Court justices during the years 1969 to 1976 and specific cases such as *Moore v. Illinois.* Although the authors claimed they had access to several justices and at least 170 law clerks, some critics complained that no source was mentioned by name and that so-called facts were incorrect. Nonetheless, the book was an example of literary journalism in the sense that it contained scene-by-scene construction, dialogue, and other literary techniques commonly found in short stories and novels.

Woodward was asked by John Belushi's widow, Judy Jacklin Belushi, to write about her husband's death in 1982. Woodward interviewed numerous individuals and wrote a stark account of Belushi's death from drugs, *Wired: The Short Life and Fast Times of John Belushi* (1984). Woodward was criticized for focusing on the comedian's dark side, particularly on the drugs and alcohol that ultimately destroyed his life. Even Belushi's widow complained about the book's negative perspective.

In 1987 Woodward wrote *Veil: The Secret Wars of the CIA, 1981–1987,* which concerned the late William Casey, the former director of the Central Intelligence Agency, and the agency's covert operations during the Reagan administration. Indeed, the book chronicled Casey's six-year tenure as the nation's chief intelligence officer, which ended with his resignation and death in 1987. Woodward disclosed the agency's attempted assassination of Sheikh Mohammed Hussein Fadlallah, who led the militant Lebanese Shi'ite faction known as Hizbollah. The car bombing killed 80 people; Fadlallah was unharmed. The book was an example of literary journalism, but Woodward was criticized for not identifying sources. He claimed that he had interviewed Casey numerous times before his death; however, Casey's family, including his widow, refuted this claim.

Woodward examined the Bush administration, especially the policies pertaining to the invasion of Panama and the war in the Persian Gulf, in *The Commanders,* which was published in 1991. Woodward claimed that he interviewed more than 400 individuals for the book; however, not one of them was cited. Woodward confirmed that Bush was responsible for the policy in the Gulf. He also revealed that Colin Powell was a leader who respected those who used restraint.

In 1994 Woodward examined the White House under the Clinton administration in *The Agenda: Inside the Clinton White House.* The book focused on

Clinton's first year as president, providing a behind-the-scenes glance at his presidency, including the pluses and the minuses.

WORKS: *All the President's Men* (with Carl Bernstein, 1974); *The Final Days* (with Carl Bernstein, 1976); *The Brethren: Inside the Supreme Court* (with Scott Armstrong, 1979); *Wired: The Short Life and Fast Times of John Belushi* (1984); *Veil: The Secret Wars of the CIA, 1981–1987* (1987); *The Commanders* (1991); *The Agenda: Inside the Clinton White House* (1994).

NOTES

1. Charles Moritz, ed., *Current Biography Yearbook 1976* (New York: H. W. Wilson, 1976), p. 454.

2. Ibid., p. 35.

Bibliography

BOOKS

Ade, George. *Chicago Stories*. Selected/edited with an introduction by Franklin J. Meine. Chicago: Henry Regnery, 1963.

Aitken, George A., ed. *The Tatler*. New York: Hadley and Mathews, 1899.

Anderson, Chris, ed. *Literary Nonfiction: Theory, Criticism, Pedagogy*. Carbondale: Southern Illinois University Press, 1989.

Arlen, Michael J. *Living-Room War*. New York: Viking Press, 1969.

Barich, Bill. *Traveling Light*. New York: Viking Press, 1984.

Bishop, Jim. *The Day Kennedy Was Shot*. New York: Funk and Wagnalls, 1968.

Bloom, Edward A., and Lillian D. Bloom. *Joseph Addison's Sociable Animal*. Providence, R.I.: Brown University Press, 1971.

Bly, Carol. *Letters from the Country*. New York: Harper and Row, 1981.

Brown, Claude. *Manchild in the Promised Land*. New York: Macmillan, 1965.

Brownstone, David M., and Irene M. Franck. *The Dictionary of Publishing*. New York: Van Nostrand Reinhold, 1982.

Bruccoli, Matthew J. *The O'Hara Concern: A Biography of John O'Hara*. New York: Random House, 1975.

Capote, Truman. *Music for Chameleons*. New York: Random House, 1980.

Christgau, Robert. *Christgau's Record Guide: Rock Albums of the Seventies*. New York: Ticknor and Fields, 1981.

Connery, Thomas B., ed. *A Sourcebook of American Literary Journalism: Representative Writers in an Emerging Genre*. Westport, Conn.: Greenwood Press, 1992.

Curtis, Laura Ann, ed. *The Versatile Defoe*. Totowa, N.J.: Rowman and Littlefield, 1979.

Dennis, Everette, ed. *The Magic Writing Machine: Student Probes of the New Journalism*. Eugene: University of Oregon School of Journalism, 1971.

Dennis, Everette E., and William L. Rivers. *Other Voices: The New Journalism in America*. San Francisco: Canfield Press, 1974.

Dickens, Charles. *Sketches by Boz.* With an introduction by Thea Holme. London: Oxford University Press, 1957.

Didion, Joan. *Slouching Towards Bethlehem.* New York: Simon and Schuster, 1968.

Downie, Leonard. *The New Muckrakers.* Washington, D.C.: New Republic Books, 1976.

Dreiser, Theodore. *Sister Carrie.* Philadelphia: University of Pennsylvania Press, 1981.

Drewry, John E., ed. *Post Biographies of Famous Journalists.* Athens: University of Georgia Press, 1942.

Dunne, Finley Peter. *Mr. Dooley at His Best.* Edited by Elmer Ellis, with a foreword by Franklin P. Adams. New York: Charles Scribner's Sons, 1938.

Edwards, Julia. *Women of the World: The Great Foreign Correspondents.* Boston: Houghton Mifflin, 1988.

Emerson, Gloria. *Gaza: A Year in the Intifada. A Personal Account from an Occupied Land.* New York: Atlantic Monthly Press, 1991.

Evory, Ann, ed. *Contemporary Authors: New Revision Series.* Vols. 3, 4. Detroit: Gale Research, 1981.

Fishkin, Shelly Fisher. *From Fact to Fiction: Journalism and Imaginative Writing in America.* Baltimore: Johns Hopkins University Press, 1985.

Flippin, Charles C., ed. *Liberating the Media: The New Journalism.* Washington, D.C.: Acropolis Books, 1974.

Frady, Marshall. *Southerners: A Journalist's Odyssey.* New York: New American Library, 1980.

Frank, Gerold. *The Boston Strangler.* New York: New American Library, 1966.

Gallico, Paul. *Further Confessions of a Story Writer.* New York: Doubleday, 1961.

Garraty, John A., ed. *Dictionary of American Biography: Supplement Six 1956–1960.* New York: Charles Scribner's Sons, 1980.

Greer, Germaine. *The Female Eunuch.* New York: McGraw-Hill, 1971.

Gullason, Thomas A., ed. *Maggie: A Girl of the Streets,* by Stephen Crane. New York: W. W. Norton, 1979.

Hamill, Pete. *Irrational Ravings.* New York: G. P. Putnam's Sons, 1971.

Hapgood, Hutchins. *The Spirit of the Ghetto.* Edited by Moses Rischin. Cambridge, Mass.: Belknap Press of Harvard University Press, 1967.

Hayes, Harold, ed. *Smiling Through the Apocalypse.* New York: McCall Publishing, 1969.

Hecht, Ben. *A Child of the Century.* New York: Simon and Schuster, 1954.

Hellman, John. *Fables of Fact: The New Journalism as New Fiction.* Urbana: University of Illinois Press, 1981.

Helterman, Jeffrey, and Richard Layman. *Dictionary of Literary Biography: American Novelists Since World War II.* Detroit: Gale Research, 1978.

Hollowell, John. *Fact and Fiction: The New Journalism and the Nonfiction Novel.* Chapel Hill: University of North Carolina Press, 1977.

Howarth, William L., ed. *The John McPhee Reader.* New York: Farrar, Straus and Giroux, 1976.

Hynds, Ernest C. *American Newspapers in the 1980s.* New York: Hastings House, 1980.

Jackson, Joseph Henry, ed. *Tales of Soldiers and Civilians—Ambrose Bierce.* New York: Heritage Press, 1943.

James, Edward T., ed. *Dictionary of American Biography: Supplement Three, 1941–1945.* New York: Charles Scribner's Sons, 1973.

Johnson, Michael L. *The New Journalism: The Underground Press, the Artists of Non-*

fiction, and Changes in the Established Media. Lawrence: University Press of Kansas, 1971.

Keynes, Geoffrey, ed. *Selected Essays of William Hazlitt.* London: Nonesuch Press, 1934.

Kibler, James E., Jr., ed. *Dictionary of Literary Biography: American Novelists Since World War II: Second Series.* Detroit: Gale Research, 1980.

Kiernan, Robert F. *Gore Vidal.* New York: Frederick Ungar, 1982.

King, Larry L. *Of Outlaws, Con Men, Whores, Politicians, and Other Artists.* New York: Viking Press, 1980.

Kramer, Jane. *The Last Cowboy.* New York: Harper and Row, 1977.

Kunitz, Stanley J., and Howard Haycraft, eds. *Twentieth Century Authors: A Biographical Dictionary of Modern Literature.* New York: H. W. Wilson, 1942.

Landsberg, Melvin. *Dos Passos' Path to U.S.A.: A Political Biography 1912–1936.* Boulder: Colorado Associated University Press, 1972.

Lefkowitz, Bernard, and Kenneth Gross. *The Victims: The Wylie-Hoffert Murder Case—and Its Strange Aftermath.* New York: G. P. Putnam's Sons, 1969.

Locher, Frances Carol, ed. *Contemporary Authors: Volumes 81–96.* Detroit: Gale Research, 1979–1980.

London, Jack. *Jack London Reports.* Edited by King Hendricks and Irving Shepard. New York: Doubleday, 1970.

Lounsberry, Barbara. *The Art of Fact: Contemporary Artists of Nonfiction.* Westport, Conn.: Greenwood Press, 1990.

Lukas, J. Anthony. *Don't Shoot: We Are Your Children!* New York: Random House, 1971.

MacDougall, Curtis D. *Interpretative Reporting.* New York: Macmillan, 1977.

Mailer, Norman. *Advertisements for Myself.* New York: G. P. Putnam's Sons, 1959.

Malone, Dumas, ed. *Dictionary of American Biography.* New York: Charles Scribner's Sons, 1935.

Marsh, Dave. *Fortunate Son: Criticism and Journalism by America's Best-Known Rock Writer.* New York: Random House, 1985.

Marsh, Irving T., and Edward Ehre, eds. *Best of the Best Sports Stories.* New York: E. P. Dutton, 1964.

Martine, James J., ed. *Dictionary of Literary Biography: American Novelists, 1910–1945.* Vol. 9. Detroit: Gale Research, 1981.

May, Hal, ed. *Contemporary Authors.* Detroit: Gale Research, 1983.

McKeithan, Daniel, ed. *(Traveling with the) The Innocents Abroad—Mark Twain.* Norman: University of Oklahoma Press, 1958.

McNeill, Don. *Moving Through Here.* New York: Alfred A. Knopf, 1970.

McNulty, John. *The World of John McNulty.* Garden City, N.Y.: Doubleday, 1957.

McQuade, Donald, and Robert Atwan. *Popular Writing in America: The Interaction of Style and Audience.* New York: Oxford University Press, 1993.

Mills, Nicolaus, ed. *The New Journalism: A Historical Anthology.* New York: McGraw-Hill, 1974.

Moore, Harry T., ed. *Contemporary American Novelists.* Carbondale: Southern Illinois University Press, 1964.

Morgan, Thomas B. *Self-Creations: Thirteen Impersonalities.* New York: Holt, Rinehart and Winston, 1965.

Moritz, Charles, ed. *Current Biography.* New York: H. W. Wilson, June 1983.

———. *Current Biography 1973.* New York: H. W. Wilson, 1973.

———. *Current Biography 1974.* New York: H. W. Wilson, 1974.

———. *Current Biography Yearbook 1976.* New York: H. W. Wilson, 1976.

———. *Current Biography Yearbook 1981.* New York: H. W. Wilson, 1981.

Morris, Willie. *North Toward Home.* Boston: Houghton Mifflin, 1967.

Newfield, Jack, and Jeff Greenfield. *A Populist Manifesto: The Making of a New Majority.* New York: Praeger, 1972.

Newquist, Roy. *A Special Kind of Magic.* Chicago: Rand McNally, 1968.

Nicholson, Watson. *The Historical Sources of Defoe's Journal of the Plague Year.* Boston: Stratford Co., 1919.

Olsen, Tillie. *Silences.* New York: Delacorte Press/Seymour Lawrence, 1978.

Orwell, George. *The Orwell Reader.* With an introduction by Richard H. Rovere. New York: Harcourt, Brace and World, 1956.

Reed, Rex. *Do You Sleep in the Nude?* New York: New American Library, 1968.

Reeves, Richard. *American Journey: Traveling with Tocqueville in Search of Democracy in America.* New York: Simon and Schuster, 1982.

Regier, C. C. *The Era of the Muckrakers.* Chapel Hill: University of North Carolina Press, 1932.

Rischin, Moses, ed. *Grandma Never Lived in America: The New Journalism of Abraham Cahan.* With an introduction by Moses Rischin. Bloomington: Indiana University Press, 1985.

Rood, Karen L., Jean W. Ross, and Richard Ziegfeld, eds. *Dictionary of Literary Biography Yearbook: 1980.* Detroit: Gale Research, 1981.

Ross, Ishbell. *Ladies of the Press: The Story of Women in Journalism by an Insider.* New York: Harper and Brothers, 1936.

Schaap, Dick. *Turned On: The Friede-Crenshaw Case.* New York: New American Library, 1966.

Schudson, Michael. *Discovering the News.* New York: Basic Books, 1978.

Schuyler, Robert Livingston, ed. *Dictionary of American Biography.* New York: Charles Scribner's Sons, 1958.

Sheed, Wilfrid. *The Morning After: Selected Essays and Reviews.* With a foreword by John Leonard. New York: Farrar, Straus and Giroux, 1971.

Showalter, Elaine, ed. *Modern American Women Writers.* New York: Charles Scribner's Sons, 1991.

Sims, Norman, ed. *Literary Journalism in the Twentieth Century.* New York: Oxford University Press, 1990.

———. *The Literary Journalists.* New York: Ballantine Books, 1984.

Smith, G. Gregory, ed. *The Spectator, with Introduction by Austin Dobson.* New York: Charles Scribner's Sons, 1987.

Synder, Louis L., and Richard B. Morris. *A Treasury of Great Reporting.* New York: Simon and Schuster, 1949.

Stallman, R. W., and E. R. Hagemann, eds. *The New York City Sketches of Stephen Crane (and Related Pieces).* New York: New York University Press, 1966.

Stott, William. *Documentary Expression and Thirties America.* New York: Oxford University Press, 1973.

Talese, Gay. *Fame and Obscurity.* New York: World Publishing, 1970.

———. *The Kingdom and the Power.* New York: World Publishing, 1969.

Tebbel, John. *The American Magazine: A Compact History.* New York: Hawthorn Books, 1969.

Thompson, Hunter S. *Hell's Angels: A Strange and Terrible Saga.* New York: Random House, 1966.

Trachtenberg, Stanley, ed. *The Dictionary of Literary Biography: American Humorists, 1800–1950.* 2 parts. Detroit: Gale Research, 1982.

Troyer, Howard William. *Ned Ward of Grubstreet: A Study of Sub-literary London in the Eighteenth Century.* Cambridge, Mass.: Harvard University Press, 1946.

von Hoffman, Nicholas. *Left at the Post.* Chicago: Quadrangle Books, 1970.

Wakefield, Dan. *Between the Lines.* New York: New American Library, 1966.

Weber, Ronald. *The Literature of Fact: Literary Nonfiction in American Writing.* Athens: Ohio University Press, 1980.

Weber, Ronald, ed. *The Reporter as Artist: A Look at the New Journalism Controversy.* New York: Hastings House, 1974.

White, William, ed. *By-line: Ernest Hemingway.* New York: Charles Scribner's Sons, 1967.

Wills, Garry. *Confessions of a Conservative.* New York: Doubleday, 1979.

Wilson, Harold S. *McClure's Magazine and the Muckrakers.* Princeton, N.J.: Princeton University Press, 1970.

Witcover, Jules. *85 Days: The Last Campaign of Robert Kennedy.* New York: G. P. Putnam's Sons, 1969.

Wolfe, Tom. *The Kandy-Kolored Tangerine-Flake Streamline Baby.* New York: Pocket Books, 1966.

———. *The New Journalism.* With an anthology edited by Tom Wolfe and E. W. Johnson. New York: Harper and Row, 1973.

Wood, James Playsted. *Magazines in the United States.* New York: Ronald Press, 1971.

MONOGRAPHS

Berner, R. Thomas. *Literary Newswriting: The Death of an Oxymoron.* Journalism Monographs 99. Columbia, S.C.: Association for Education in Journalism and Mass Communication, October 1986.

Murphy, James E. *The New Journalism: A Critical Perspective.* Journalism Monographs 34. Lexington, Ky.: Association for Education in Journalism, May 1974.

ARTICLES

Adams, Robert M. "Blue Sheep Zen." *New York Review of Books,* September 28, 1978.

Ahearn, Marie L. "*The People of the Abyss:* Jack London as New Journalist." *Modern Fiction Studies* 22, no. 1 (Spring 1976).

"Alva Johnston, 62, Noted Writer, Dies." *New York Times,* November 24, 1950.

Anson, Robert Sam. "Citizen Wenner." *New Times,* November 26, 1976.

———. "The *Rolling Stone* Saga: Part Two." *New Times,* December 10, 1976.

Bernstein, Jeremy. "Modern Times." *New York Review,* October 8, 1987.

Blount, Roy, Jr. "Fresh Homebaked Goods." *New York Times Book Review,* August 12, 1979.

Bonn, Maria S. "The Lust of the Eye: Michael Herr, Gloria Emerson and the Art of Observation." *Papers on Language and Literature: A Journal for Scholars and Critics of Language and Literature,* Winter 1993.

Braudy, Susan. "The Johnston Papers." *Ms.,* October 1974.

Brisick, William C. "PW Interviews: Greil Marcus." *Publishers Weekly,* November 15, 1991.

Brown, Edward M. "Addicts' Odyssey." *New York Times Book Review,* May 22, 1966.

Brown, Rosellen. "*Letters from the Country* by Carol Bly." *New Republic,* June 20, 1981.

Clemons, Walter. "Lest We Forget." *Newsweek,* January 10, 1977.

Cook, Joan. "Carlton Beals Dies; Correspondent, 85." *New York Times,* June 28, 1979.

Cooper, Arthur. "Man Bites Ball." *Newsweek,* October 29, 1973.

DeMott, Benjamin. "Alone in Cover-Up Country." *Atlantic,* October 1973.

Dong, Stella. "PW Interviews: Jane O'Reilly." *Publishers Weekly,* October 31, 1980.

Dundy, Elaine. "Tom Wolfe . . . But Exactly, Yes!" *Vogue,* April 15, 1966.

Eason, David L. "New Journalism, Metaphor and Culture." *Journal of Popular Culture,* Spring 1982.

"Felker: 'Bully . . . Boor . . . Genius.' " *Time,* January 17, 1977.

Finke, Nikki. "Shake it up, Baby!" *Los Angeles,* January 1993.

Flaherty, Joe. "Saving Your Soul at the Track." *New York Times Book Review,* June 15, 1980.

Flint, Peter B. "Dame Freya Stark, Travel Writer, Is Dead at 100." *New York Times,* May 11, 1993.

Flynt, Josiah. "In the World of Graft." *McClure's Magazine,* February 1901.

Flynt, Josiah, and Francis Walton. "True Stories from the Underworld." *McClure's Magazine,* August 1900.

Forman, Jack. "Franks, Zwinda." *Library Journal,* May 15, 1974.

Freedman, Morris. "Mr. Sheed's Dryden." *New Republic,* October 2, 1971.

Friedenberg, Edgar Z. "Patriotic Gore." *New York Review of Books,* June 19, 1969.

Geist, William E. "Death in These United States." *New York Times Book Review,* February 19, 1984.

Gottlieb, Annie. "Charlie Simpson's Apocalypse." *New York Times Book Review,* January 27, 1974.

Hendrickson, Paul. "The Shriek of a Woman from the War Zones: Gloria Emerson's Piercing Views of Vietnam and Gaza." *Washington Post,* June 5, 1991.

Howe, Irving. "The Subculture of Yiddishkeit." *New York Times Book Review,* March 19, 1967.

Johnson, Diane. "Playtime." *New York Review of Books,* January 29, 1987.

Kahn, Joseph P. "Required Reading." *INC.,* July 1987.

Kazin, Alfred. "Vietnam: It Was Us vs. Us: Michael Herr's *Dispatches:* More than Just the Best Vietnam Book." *Esquire,* March 1, 1978.

Kempton, Murray. "Jock-Sniffing." *New York Review of Books,* February 11, 1971.

Kriegel, Leonard. "Why Are We in Vietnam?" *Nation,* October 23, 1967.

Kumin, Maxine. "A Covenant with the Soil." *New York Times Book Review,* September 24, 1989.

Lardner, Rex. "And They Did It Without a Superstar." *New York Times Book Review,* November 29, 1970.

Little, Craig. "PW Interviews: Roger Kahn." *Publishers Weekly,* October 4, 1993.

Maddocks, Melvin. "George Ade's Chicago." *Christian Science Monitor,* February 27, 1964.

Maitland, Alexander. "Dame Freya Stark: Journeys Through Space and Time." *Blackwood's Magazine* 328, no. 1982 (1980).

McGee, Celia. "Novel Harvest." *New York,* August 26, 1991.

McGinniss, Joe. "Doctors, Operating." *New York Times Book Review,* September 18, 1983.

McQuade, Molly. "PW Interviews: Richard Rhodes." *Publishers Weekly,* October 20, 1989.

Menn, Thorpe. "To Be Alive Is All." *Saturday Review,* February 24, 1968.

Miller, Alan L. "True Accounts." *National Review,* March 20, 1981.

Miller, Mark Crispin. "Where All the Flowers Went." *New York Review of Books,* February 3, 1977.

Mirsky, Jonathan. "The War in Vietnam." *New York Times Book Review,* November 26, 1967.

Nussbaum, Bruce. "When Too Much Isn't Enough." *Business Week,* April 6, 1987.

Parshall, Gerald. "The Yarn Spinner from Yazoo: At Home in the Land of Cotton, Willie Morris Plays Pranks, Haunts Cemeteries and Pens an Evocative Memoir of New York." *U.S. News & World Report,* September 13, 1993.

Perrin, Noel. "Paragon of Reporters Joseph Mitchell." *Sewanee Review,* Spring 1983.

Pizer, Donald. "Documentary Narrative as Art: William Manchester and Truman Capote." *Journal of Modern Literature,* September 1971.

Plummer, William. "Ecstasy and Death: Dispatches by Michael Herr." *Saturday Review,* January 7, 1978.

Roberts, Steven V. "I Ain't Marchin' Anymore." *New York Times Book Review,* May 25, 1969.

Sale, Roger. "Golden Gaits." *New York Review of Books,* March 5, 1981.

Sander, Ellen. "The Journalists of Rock." *Saturday Review,* July 31, 1971.

Shapiro, Laura. "Little Gloria, Happy at Last: Dear Ms. Steinem: All is forgiven. Please come home. We miss you." *Newsweek,* January 13, 1992.

Sherrill, Robert. "People from Georgia and Nearby Places." *New York Times Book Review,* September 28, 1980.

Skow, John. "Voyager." *Time,* February 6, 1984.

Smith, Wendy. "PW Interviews: Dave Marsh." *Publishers Weekly,* October 21, 1983.

———. "PW Interviews: Nicholas von Hoffman." *Publishers Weekly,* September 21, 1992.

Steel, Ronald. "The Man Who Was the War." *New York Times Book Review,* September 25, 1988.

"Street Scene." *Time,* November 4, 1957.

Walker, Walter. "In Cold DNA." *New York Times Book Review,* February 19, 1989.

Weber, Ronald. "Art-Journalism Revisited." *South Atlantic Quarterly,* Summer 1979.

Wenner, Jann. "Ralph J. Gleason in Perspective." *Rolling Stone,* July 17, 1975.

Wolcott, James. "The Fate of the Hearth." *New Republic,* November 2, 1987.

Wolfe, Tom. "The Birth of ''The New Journalism''; Eyewitness Report by Tom Wolfe." *New York,* February 14, 1972.

Woods, Crawford. "Fear and Loathing in Las Vegas by Hunter S. Thompson." *New York Times Book Review,* July 23, 1972.

Woods, William Crawford. "Demon in the Counterculture." *New Republic,* January 4, 1975.

Yoder, Edwin M., Jr. "Voices from Burning Slums." *Saturday Review,* August 26, 1967.

Index

About the Author

EDD APPLEGATE is an Associate Professor of Journalism at Middle Tennessee State University. His articles and reviews have been published in several academic journals, including *Journalism and Mass Communication Quarterly*, *Journalism and Mass Communication Educator*, and *American Journalism*. He is the editor of *The Ad Men and Women: A Biographical Dictionary of Advertising* (Greenwood, 1994).

ISBN 0-313-29949-8

90000>

EAN

9 780313 299490

HARDCOVER BAR CODE